D0847726

THE ESTRANGEMENT OF
GREAT BRITAIN AND JAPAN
1917–35

General Araki Sadao
Japanese War Minister, 1931–4

The Estrangement of Great Britain and Japan
1917–35

by

CAPTAIN MALCOLM D. KENNEDY, O.B.E.

'The annulment [of the Anglo-Japanese Alliance]
caused a profound impression in Japan, and was viewed
as the spurning of an Asiatic Power by the Western World.'
WINSTON S. CHURCHILL
in *The Second World War*, Vol. I.

UNIVERSITY OF CALIFORNIA PRESS
Berkeley and Los Angeles · 1969

University of California Press
Berkeley and Los Angeles, California
© 1969 Malcolm D. Kennedy

Library of Congress Catalog Card Number: 71–77517

Printed in Great Britain

Contents

Illustrations

Note and Acknowledgement

Throughout these pages, the normal Japanese practice of giving a person's surname before his or her personal name has been adopted. The only exceptions to this rule, so far as persons mentioned in this book are concerned, are Toyotomi Hideyoshi and Baron Dan. The former has always been known as Hideyoshi and the latter as Takuma Dan, not Dan Takuma as would be the normal rendering.

The list of works consulted is given in the bibliographical notes at the end of this volume. To their authors and publishers I readily acknowledge my thanks for the information derived from their studies.

MALCOLM D. KENNEDY

Inverurr
Kippford, by Dalbeattie
Kirkcudbrightshire

CHAPTER I

Introduction

It is one of the tragic ironies of history that Japan, our valued friend and ally for twenty years, became our mortal enemy in the Pacific War twenty years later. The reasons for this were many and complex—the influence of geographical, economic, strategic and ideological considerations, the impact of historical and psychological factors, the ever-changing interplay of international relations. Singly or in combination, they served to stir up a devil's brew of frustrations and grievances, driving Japan little by little into the arms of the Axis partners, Germany and Italy, and finally into the desperate gamble which was to plunge her from early victory into disastrous defeat. The real start to this unhappy drama, however, can be traced to the abrogation of the twenty-year-old Anglo-Japanese Alliance in February 1922, which severed Japan's old close ties with Britain and left her with a feeling of isolation and resentment.

While the ending of the Alliance was an all-important factor in stirring up a sense of grievance, Japanese pride had already been hurt by successive pieces of anti-Japanese legislation in the United States, prior to the First World War, and by failure to obtain the demand for racial equality put forward by the Japanese Government at the Versailles Conference after it. Further blows to her pride were to follow. In considering these and other causes of resentment, which later turned to wrath, one is tempted to speculate on how different the world situation might have been today if the Alliance had been retained in some modified form, with the United States, for instance, as a consultant partner as proposed by Mr Balfour, and if Theodore Roosevelt's warning of the dangers of humiliating Japan had been heeded. 'With so proud and sensitive a people', he had cautioned in a letter to Philander Knox early in 1909, 'neither lack of money nor possible future complications will prevent a war if once they get sufficiently hurt and angry'.[1]

So far as lack of money was concerned, it was a warning echoed in part by Sir Charles Eliot twelve years later on the eve of the

[1] Quoted by Raymond A. Esthus in *Theodore Roosevelt and Japan*, p. 297.

Washington Conference, when he was the British Ambassador in Tokyo. In a despatch to Mr Balfour he said, 'They [the Japanese people] believe Japan has a mission on the mainland of Asia, and if they were made to feel they were abandoning that mission by any policy of retrenchment, patriotic sentiment would probably get the better of prudence and financial considerations'.[1]

In the pages which follow, something of the nature of the frustrations and grievances, which finally led to Japan becoming 'sufficiently hurt and angry' to throw prudence to the wind, should become apparent. But before going on to describe them, it may be apposite to indicate why it was that Japan valued the Alliance so highly. Only by doing so will it be possible to understand her sense of grievance and dismay when it was terminated.

For both partners, the Alliance, at its inception,[2] had been welcome, as it ensured a united front against the growing threat to each from Russia. For Japan it was doubly welcome, as it served also as a warning to Russia's German and French friends not to line up against her again as they had done in 1895. The bitter memory of the Triple Intervention, which had robbed her of the foothold she had obtained in Manchuria by her victory over China and had led soon after to its shameless acquisition by the Russians, had seared into her very soul and was to have serious psychological repercussions in the years ahead.

To the British public as a whole, the Alliance had been regarded with satisfaction, but the average phlegmatic Englishman betrayed no particular elation. He was content merely to admire his country's new ally for the way in which she had risen so rapidly from a position of mediaeval obscurity and unimportance to the status of a modern Power, strong enough and game enough to take on, and defeat, her giant Chinese neighbour only a few years previously. If anyone had reason to feel elated, it was the British taxpayer, since the Alliance enabled Great Britain to dispense with the retention of a large and costly naval establishment in the Pacific.

Very different was the reaction of the Japanese to the Alliance. Whereas the British looked on it primarily from the practical point of view, rather as a hard-headed businessman would regard

---

[1] Quoted in Griswold, *The Far Eastern Policy of the United States*, p. 307.

[2] For a detailed study of the negotiations leading up to its conclusion in 1902 and to its first revision in 1905, see Ian Nish, *The Anglo-Japanese Alliance*.

a good piece of business—of benefit to both parties concerned—
the Japanese, while fully alive to this aspect of the transaction,
viewed it also with a strong sense of pride and deep-felt emotion.
To them it marked the attainment of a prolonged effort to win
recognition as an equal among the great Powers of the West.
Until as recently as three years previously, she had suffered the
humiliation of the 'unequal treaties', which placed her in a position of inferiority to these countries by compelling her to accord
extraterritorial rights and privileges to their nationals. She had
still to wait a few more years before recovering the sovereign
rights of tariff autonomy; but Britain's action in entering into
alliance with her in 1902 was of vastly more importance to her
sense of pride and self-respect than anything that had occurred
since her enforced re-opening to intercourse with the outside
world half-a-century earlier.

By 1904, the threat to Japanese security, posed by Russia's
increasing grip on Manchuria and by Russian actions in Korea,
had become too great to be ignored; Japan, assured now of an
ally who could be trusted to hold the ring against the entry of
Germany, France, or any other country onto Russia's side, struck
out at the Czarists. The Russo-Japanese War was launched. From
it, Japan emerged victorious and both she and Britain were thereby relieved from further anxiety about Russia. Ten years later, by
aligning herself with Britain, Japan played her part in helping to
bring about the defeat of Germany and eliminate the German
threat to her British ally.

The Alliance, which had twice been renewed in revised form in
the meantime, had clearly proved of great value to both of its
signatories. As it had formed the basis of her foreign policy ever
since its original conclusion in 1902, Japan, for reasons both of
security and prestige, had been anxious to retain it in some form
or other; but it was not to be. The consequences of her reaction
to its abrogation were to prove calamitous to both the former
partners. These consequences, which included her link-up with
Nazi Germany, will be discussed in the pages that follow; but
before doing so, some words of explanation are necessary.

The account of the developments given in them, and of the
leading actors concerned, is, to a large extent, a personal one,
based on detailed diaries and notes kept at the time. In them are
recorded observations on the main occurrences and on the personalities involved. These jottings were made possible by virtue of

the fact that, throughout the period in question, I had the good fortune to hold a succession of posts, either in Japan or in close touch with Japanese affairs, affording valuable opportunities for seeing and hearing much of what went on behind the scenes. As a British officer seconded to Japan for language study and attachment to the Japanese Army in the closing years of the Alliance, an excellent opportunity was provided for observing Japanese military life, methods, and outlook, noting the strong and weak points of the Army as a whole, studying the characteristics and fighting qualities of officers and men alike, and getting to know many of those who, twenty odd years later, were to figure prominently in the Pacific War. As a member of the Far Eastern Section at the War Office in London at the time when the question of terminating or retaining the Alliance was under discussion, the pros and cons of ending it were among the many questions brought up for study. Two subsequent years in the oil business in Japan and Korea (after being invalided out of the Army on account of war wounds), followed by close on ten years as an accredited foreign correspondent in Tokyo, allowed for firsthand observation of much that went on in the background during the crucial 1920s and 1930s. They also provided opportunities for viewing Japan from two other important angles. Employment in the oil business gave one an insight into Japan's dependence on foreign sources for its vital supplies of oil, a dependence which was to be largely responsible for Japan's eventual plunge into war when these supplies were cut off; as an accredited foreign correspondent, there was the invaluable advantage of being given access to leading personalities in Japan and to sources of information not available to the general public. Finally, after return to England in the summer of 1934, work as a free-lance writer and lecturer on Far Eastern affairs, coupled with employment on Far Eastern research work for the Foreign Office, gave plenty of scope for keeping in touch with what was going on during the years that followed.

    Although much of the information recorded in the diaries and notes was strictly confidential at the time it was obtained, most of my informants of those days are now dead. After the passage of thirty or forty years, the restrictions imposed on information originally received in confidence can no longer, therefore, be regarded as holding good, except in special instances. On the other hand, it is hardly necessary to add that neither in the diaries nor in the notes is there any information of a nature involving a possible breach of the Official Secrets Act.

My original intention had been to continue the story down to the outbreak of the Pacific War, but this would have made the book too unwieldy. In any case, the final years of this period have now been covered very fully by recent specialist histories. Apart, therefore, from an epilogue giving some sidelights and observations on the main developments from shortly after my return to England down to the attack on Pearl Harbour, no attempt will be made to recount in detail the events later than the close of 1934. That was the point at which the preliminary talks in London on the naval conference projected for the following year reached a deadlock, and Japan gave the necessary two years' notice of her intention to terminate the Washington Naval Treaty if no satisfactory compromise had been reached in the meantime.

It is, then, on the notes made, and on the diaries kept, during the period under review, that the pages which follow are largely based. Interlaced, as the narrative is, with more recent reflections on the matters recorded and with information from other stated sources, it is in the nature of observations on history in the context of personal experience rather than straight-forward history. If some of the incidents described bear only indirectly on the main subject matter, they may serve nevertheless to recapture something of the changing atmosphere, and to throw light on happenings behind the scenes, during a period of outstanding importance, not only in the history of the Far East but in world history as well.

CHAPTER II

War-time Ally

Along with Christianity, the Portuguese had introduced fire-arms into Japan in the sixteenth century. The Japanese had shown themselves to be apt pupils in mastering their use and were soon producing similar weapons of their own; but they failed to keep abreast of the great technological advances made in the West from the latter part of the eighteenth century onwards. As a result, they had fallen steadily behind in the matter of modern armaments and methods by the time that Commodore Perry arrived from the United States in 1853 to demand the opening of Japan to foreign trade and intercourse. It took them half a century to make up this leeway. History, in this respect, was to repeat itself to some extent, as a result of the First World War, in so far as the Army was concerned.

From 1905, when they defeated the Russians, until the outbreak of war in Europe in 1914, Japan and her armed forces were regarded with respect by the naval and military leaders of the world. The lessons of the Russo-Japanese War, and the tactics and methods employed by the Japanese in gaining their victories, were carefully studied. Japan ranked high in their estimation. True, the Balkan wars, fought in those intervening years, received some attention, and the fact that the Italians had employed one or two aircraft for reconnaissance purposes in their Tripoli campaign in 1911 was a portent of things to come; but, generally speaking, the Japanese Army and Navy were regarded as the foremost exemplars of methods and skill in modern warfare. It was with considerable surprise, therefore, that when, late in 1917, I arrived in Japan for the first time and saw Japanese troops on parade and in training, I noted that they were still armed with much the same weapons, and employed much the same tactics, as had been in use in the British and other Western armies in what seemed those far-off days of August 1914. This impression was reinforced when, a year later, I attended the annual Grand Manœuvres of the Japanese Army and, soon after, was attached to a Japanese infantry regiment. At the autumn manœuvres, the few aircraft

6

employed were of almost obsolete design and played but a minor role; motor transport was conspicuous by its virtually complete absence; and guns were still horse-drawn. Tanks, armoured vehicles, trench mortars, gas masks, smoke screens, shrapnel helmets and the like were non-existent; and although the Japanese themselves, in their war with Russia, had showed the defensive power of entrenched machine-guns, these invaluable weapons were still on the same small scale as in the pre-1914 British Army, and there were no Lewis guns or other automatic weapons of any kind to supplement them. Infantry units advanced with regimental colours unfurled and officers waving swords, while cavalry charged in mass formation—a stirring sight, but sheer suicide if carried out against an enemy as heavily armed as were the opposing forces in Europe in 1918.

It brought home to one how greatly the Japanese Army, from being rated so highly up to 1914, had fallen behind the armies of the Western nations in arms, equipment, and training in so brief a space of time. It was like 1853 all over again. By being out of touch with the tremendous advances made in the West during the two hundred odd years of her seclusion from the outside world, Japan had fallen far behind in the science of war by the time of Perry's arrival; by having had no practical experience of the fighting which had raged on the various fronts since the outbreak of war in 1914—except for its own brief campaign against the Germans in Kiaochow in the opening months of the war—the Japanese Army had once more failed to keep abreast of the developments that had been taking place in the Western armies.

Japan's subsequent attempts to make up this leeway were to have serious consequences. On the one hand, the Army's demands for the necessary funds to arm and equip the land forces, on a scale which would bring them up to Western standards, were to lead to growing friction and dissatisfaction with the politicians for their refusal to sanction the heavy expenditure entailed; this, in turn, was to lead the Army into increasing its hold on national policy and finally playing the leading role in determining policy. On the other hand, the obvious inferiority of the Japanese Army in the matter of arms, equipment, and modern methods as judged by Western standards, was to lead, in the 1930s, to the fatal mistake, made by all too many Western observers, of under-rating its fighting abilities. The fact that highly mechanized armies, such as those evolved in the West for military operations in Europe, might not be so well suited for conditions in South-East Asia, was overlooked. The opening rounds of the Pacific War were to show how mistaken these observers had been.

It should be added, however, that already by 1920, when I was attached to the Japanese Infantry School at Chiba, it was noticeable that the lessons of the recently concluded World War were being closely studied, and changes in training and equipment based on these lessons were beginning to be carried out. That these changes were regarded with strong disapproval by some of the more conservative elements was indicated, nonetheless, by the action of a retired cavalry commander, Major-General Yoshibashi, in the summer of that year. Horrified by the newly issued cavalry training manual, which did away with massed cavalry charges and decreed that something in the nature of mounted infantry tactics would be more appropriate under modern conditions, the old gentleman protested to the General Staff and urged reconsideration. His recommendations went unheeded, so he disembowelled himself in the traditional warrior manner, by way of stressing his conviction that the contemplated changes would be disastrous for Japan.

I happened to be visiting a Japanese infantry regiment in the Hokkaido at the time and was struck by the reaction of the officers to this incident. Most of them agreed that General Yoshibashi's views on the use of cavalry were out-of-date, but one and all considered that, as he felt so strongly about it, he was quite right to stress his belief in what was best for his country by committing *harakiri*. It was but one of many examples of the difference between Japanese and Western mentality that I came across during my three years with the Japanese Army. Where a retired British officer might blow off a little steam by writing to *The Times*, his Japanese opposite number considered it more honourable to act as Yoshibashi did.

It was one of the advantages of being seconded for attachment to the Japanese Army that it enabled the attached officer to appreciate the 'imponderables', which did so much to compensate for the more obvious deficiencies in arms and equipment. Weapons and equipment might be out-of-date and sadly deficient both in quantity and quality; training methods and tactics might seem almost archaic; but against all this were the fine fighting spirit inculcated by the intense *seishin kyōiku* ('training in morale'), the utter contempt for death, the great powers of endurance, and all

those other military virtues which Napoleon had in mind when he
declared that the moral force is to the physical as three is to one.
These were the qualities which Western observers, with little or
no first-hand experience of Japanese Army morale, were all too
apt to overlook. The tragedy was that, for twenty years prior to
the outbreak of the Pacific War in December 1941, successive
British Military Attachés in Tokyo, and British and Indian Army
officers seconded for attachment to Japanese military units, had
been sending in detailed reports on the Japanese Army and its
remarkable efficiency, but their warnings against under-rating its
ability were either ignored or discounted as being the unbalanced
assessments of biased enthusiasts. The pigeon-holing of these
reports, and the failure to heed the warnings and information they
contained, have been strongly, and rightly, criticised in the official
British history, *The War Against Japan*.

Apart, however, from the opportunities for first-hand study of
Japanese military methods and abilities provided by attachment
to the Japanese Army, opportunity was also afforded for close
and friendly intercourse with one's temporary 'brother officers',
many of whom were to rise to high command and prominence
later, and for gaining an insight into their mentality and general
outlook, not only on purely military matters but on international
and other affairs as well.

At the time of my arrival in Japan in November 1917, the War
had been in progress for over three years and had still another
year to go; yet the Japanese Army was still, in effect, of pre-War
vintage, seemingly oblivious of the tremendous transformations
that had already taken place in military methods and material.
When one expressed surprise at this to Japanese officers, the
almost invariable reply was, either that Japan was too poor to
afford the luxury of modernizing its army, or that the Japanese
fighting spirit was sufficient in itself to compensate for any inferiority in the matter of arms and equipment. It was, in effect, a
reassertion of what the eighteenth-century Japanese poet and
commentator, Rai Sanyo, had declared in his dictum, 'The secret
of victory or defeat lies in the spirit of the men and not in their
weapons'. It overlooked Foch's warning that morale alone could
not conquer.

This confidence in the superiority of their own fighting qualities
over those of other nations, valuable though it might be, had the
logical sequel, a mild contempt for the armies of the West. Even

B

their own highly extolled German model did not escape this somewhat scornful attitude where the question of surrender was concerned. One thing the Japanese could never understand was the
huge numbers of prisoners taken by Allies and Central Powers
alike. To the Japanese mind, especially to the naval and military
mind, nothing was more shameful than for a soldier or a sailor to
surrender to the enemy. Individual surrender was considered
dishonourable; large-scale surrender seemed incredible. One could
respect this point of view without necessarily sharing it in its
entirety; but, at that time, one doubted if even Japanese troops
would have been any less prone than others to lay down their
arms in the circumstances that dictated many of the large-scale
surrenders. The fact nevertheless remained that, in the eyes of the
Japanese as a whole, the great hauls of prisoners made by both
sides in the fighting proved the nations of the West to be vastly
inferior to Japan in the matter of fighting spirit and physical
courage. Twenty years later, the fanatical contempt for death displayed by the Japanese in Burma and elsewhere was to show that
their attitude towards surrender had undergone no change and
was perfectly genuine.

Reflecting, however, on the condition and outlook of the Japanese Army when first I saw it on manœuvres in 1918, one is struck
by certain similarities with French, and other similarities with
German, military opinion during the years immediately prior to
the outbreak of war in 1914. Japanese Army outlook was, of
course, influenced to a large extent by the old traditional *samurai*
code, akin in some respects to the stern, harsh code of the
Prussian Junker class; it was affected also by former close connection with the German Army. But during the initial stages of
creating an army on modern lines, before coming under German
tuition, Japan had accepted the French Army as its model, and
this may have accounted not a little for the way in which Japanese
and French military opinion had so much in common until 1914.
Although, by 1918, four years of first-hand experience in the
harsh realities of modern war had served to bring drastic changes
in the French outlook, Japanese Army doctrine and methods, as
we have seen, remained unaltered. Some of the former similarities
may therefore be worth noting. There was, for example, the same
firm belief in *l'attaque à outrance*, coupled with the same semi-
mystical idea of imprudence being the best form of assurance in
the offensive. Alistair Horne, in *The Price of Glory*, quotes Colonel

de Grandmaison, Chief of the Operations Bureau of the French General Staff, as laying down that, 'For the attack, only two things are necessary: to know where the enemy is and to decide what to do. What the enemy intends to do is of no consequence.' This pre-1914 French doctrine was very much in evidence in the Japanese Army in 1918; so, too, was the teaching that assault by bayonet was the supreme means of imposing one's will upon an enemy and gaining victory. Similarly, the lack of up-to-date weapons in the Japanese Army at that time seemed to reflect the pre-1914 views of the French General Staff, which openly expressed contempt for heavy artillery, aircraft and machine-guns. There was, too, the same love of martial display, which led the French to enter the War in 1914 with their troops clad in conspicuous red *képis* and pantaloons, contemptuous of the Germans for their more sober and sensible field grey. In the case of the Japanese, this fondness for martial glamour was seen in their practice of carrying out attacks with officers waving swords and with regimental colours flying.

Perhaps the most striking similarity between the French of the pre-War years, and the Japanese in 1918 and for many years later, was the patriotic fervour and contempt for death shown by both. The fire-eating League of Patriots, formed in France by Paul Déroulède, was spiritually akin to the Japanese super-patriotic bodies, which already existed and were to proliferate to such an extent later. A poem of the League's founder was an exact expression of Japanese military sentiment:

> En avant! Tant pis pour qui tombe
> La Mort n'est rien. Vive la tombe
> Quand le pays en sort vivant
> En avant.

Déroulède's *La Mort n'est rien*, and the Japanese military aphorism 'Death is lighter than a feather', were expressions of the same dauntless philosophy.

Although the German Army in 1914 showed far greater appreciation of the requirements of modern warfare than either the French or the Japanese, their outlook in other respects had a striking resemblance to that of the Japanese Army. The Spartan habits of the Prussians in particular were akin to those of the Japanese; so, too, was the German genius for organization. There was also the Japanese regard for *harakiri* as the natural means for paying a debt of honour, which, in essence, was not unlike the way in which many Prussian officers considered duelling as essential to the 'honour of the army'. A further similarity in outlook was, that Japanese and German officers alike regarded themselves as a privileged class and were wont to show utter contempt for politicians. Finally, bearing in mind the ruthless behaviour to which Japanese troops were so prone at times in the Pacific War, it is perhaps significant that, during the First World War, von Falkenhayn was held in the highest esteem by Japanese officers. This was mainly due, of course, to the military ability he showed in the opening stages and in his brilliantly conceived lightning campaign against Roumania, but his ruthlessness left them unmoved. He, it will be recalled, was the first to sanction the use of gas; he was also amongst the strongest advocates of unrestricted submarine warfare and promiscuous bombing.

While, however, the Japanese Army had so much in common with both the French and the Germans in certain aspects of their outlook, the Japanese, as already noted, could never understand the large-scale surrenders by these and other Western armies. They found it equally hard to understand how officers from any arm of the Service other than the infantry could be appointed to the highest commands. In Japanese eyes, the infantry was preeminent, and on a number of occasions Japanese officer friends of mine expressed surprise that the two successive British Commanders-in-Chief in France, French and Haig, were both cavalrymen. Even more incomprehensible to them was that a former sapper officer, Joffre, had been the French Commander-in-Chief at the start of the War. To the Japanese infantryman of those days, the sapper was barely classifiable as a soldier; he could not therefore be expected to rise to supreme command.

If, however, the Japanese continued to cling to ideas which had been discarded, or at least modified by other armies since 1914, and if their whole outlook on the War differed greatly from that of belligerents more directly concerned with its prosecution, it must be remembered that life in Japan during the years of the First World War was very different from what it was in Europe. The War was a long way off, and for the great mass of the Japanese people there was little direct interest in it. True, Japan had, at the very outset, thrown in her lot with her British ally and had rendered invaluable services to the Allied cause in the naval operations in the Pacific. Her land forces had likewise played their part in the opening phase of the War by forcing the German garrison in Tsingtao to capitulate; her destroyers were, at the time of my arrival in Japan late in 1917, doing yeoman work in the Mediterranean. Other units of her Navy were engaged elsewhere in the work of patrolling and protecting trade routes.

Important as were all these contributions to the Allied cause, they had very little direct bearing on the life of the Japanese people as a whole. In England, as in France and Germany and in all the other principal belligerent nations, there was probably hardly a family that had not sent a father, sons, brothers, or other close relations to fight. Most families had sad personal losses to mourn. I myself had lost a brother, an uncle, several cousins and a host of friends; my other two brothers—one of whom was to die later—and I had all been wounded. Even those who remained at home—old men, women and even children—were made to suffer by food shortages and other restrictions and by the ever-present threat of aerial bombardment. In Japan, on the other hand, there were comparatively few families with any such direct interests in the War, and life went on much as in peace-time. Moreover, the vast distance separating that country from the main theatres of active operations made it difficult for its people to appreciate the magnitude and horrors of the fighting.

While, therefore, Japan was technically just as much a belligerent as were Britain and France and the other active participants, her people were able to adopt a far more impersonal and detached attitude towards the War as a whole. On two separate occasions, while the War was still in progress, I actually came across Japanese peasant folk who had not even heard that there was a war. They were frankly incredulous when I assured them, that not only was there a war, but that Japan was taking part in it. Their incredulity was based on the fact that the young men of the village had not been called up for service. If Japan was really at war, they argued, surely all the male youth of the country would be summoned to the colours.

Partly because of the impersonal bearing of the War on the bulk of the nation, and partly because Japan's participation was due to her alliance with ourselves rather than to any particular quarrel with Germany, enthusiasm for the Allied cause was, in some quarters, conspicuous by its absence. The Government itself proved loyal to the Alliance with Great Britain by ranging the country alongside its British ally. It even went further than the strict interpretation of its treaty obligations demanded; but in this it did not have the whole-hearted support of the country at large. There were large sections of the nation that openly admitted their sympathy and admiration for Germany. From the Allied standpoint this may have seemed very reprehensible, but it was intelligible; not only had Japan no personal quarrel with the Central Powers, she had much for which to be grateful to the Germans. True, Germany had given her cause for deep resentment in 1895, by ranging herself alongside Russia and France in depriving Japan of the full fruits of her victory over China; but against this was to be set the great help given her by German military advisers in the creation of a first-class modern army, and by German scientists, doctors and others in various important matters connected with her rapid rise to World Power status. It was, in fact, in the higher ranks of the Japanese Army that sympathy for Germany was most pronounced. Senior Army officers had good reason to know how much they owed to German tuition for the high state of efficiency that had enabled Japan to defeat, first the Chinese, and then the Russians. Regrettable, therefore, though it may have been, it spoke well for their high sense of gratitude that, in the hour when Germany had most of the civilized world against her, they should still feel admiration and sympathy for their former tutor, even though circumstances dictated their taking opposite sides in the great struggle.

There was also another reason for their lack of whole-heartedness in wishing for Germany's defeat. The German Army had been specially selected as a model, which Japanese officers and men were always taught to regard as the best in Europe. Japanese Army organization and training alike had been based on those of the German Army. It was perhaps but natural, therefore, that Japanese military leaders should hesitate to wish for the downfall of the model that they had, for so long, considered superior to all others. The defeat of this exemplar, they felt, might reflect seriously on their own powers of judgment.

As illustrating this point, the remarks made to me some years later by a Japanese friend of mine are illuminating. He himself had been called up for service with the colours towards the end of the War; he could therefore speak from personal experience. Whenever the Germans gained a success over the British, he said, the officers of his regiment made a point of impressing on their men that this was due to superior training and organization and, more particularly, to the superiority of conscripts over volunteers. The conscript, they contended, was ruled by no mercenary considerations but purely by love of country; a voluntary army, on the other hand, could only be recruited by the offer of monetary inducements and could not therefore be imbued with such high military qualities. Being anxious to emphasize the superiority of conscription over the voluntary system, British successes were generally minimized, therefore, or ignored altogether; and when finally victory came to the Allied arms in November 1918, no mention was made of it. Most of the men knew nothing about it until their return to barracks several days later, as they had been on manœuvres at the time.

To some extent, this failure to accord proper praise to the British arms must be attributed to the poorness of our own propaganda in Japan. Instead of emphasizing the fine fighting qualities of our own troops and stressing the extraordinary difficulties that they had to overcome, the main emphasis was generally laid on the iniquities of German 'frightfulness'. No doubt, by continual harping on this, it was hoped to gain sympathy for the Allied cause and embitter the feelings of neutral and friendly belligerents alike against the Germans; but its effect on a large section of the Japanese people, especially on the military element, was unfortunate. They considered that this slander of the Germans was merely an attempt on the part of the British and their other allies to excuse their own faults and shortcomings in the field—a case of the bad workman blaming his tools. The fact that we resorted to such 'unsporting' methods was regarded by some, in fact, as proof positive that, man for man, the Germans were the better fighters. If they could be defeated by such means only, it was felt that they were deserving of more sympathy than their detractors.

British propaganda in Japan left much to be desired. It was not, indeed, until half way through the War that any really organized attempt was made to stir up enthusiasm for the Allied cause; and the methods adopted, though improved later, were only effective to a limited extent. Large sums of money were wasted in sending out propaganda of a useless kind. In at least one instance, heavy cable tolls were spent on the despatch of a magazine article of several thousand words that could well have waited to come by mail. As it was, it did not appear in print until a month or two after its receipt.[1] This was Lichnowsky's famous *exposé*, which was cabled *in extenso*.

Instead of concentrating so much attention on showing up the misdeeds of the enemy, better results might have been achieved by striving to bring home to the Japanese the immense difficulties to be overcome and the superhuman efforts that were being made to overcome them. Far removed as they were from the scene of conflict, the bulk of the people had no conception of the vast nature of the undertaking; nor could they understand why, with so many nations on their side, the Allies could not overthrow the four Central Powers. The months and months of virtual stalemate on the Western Front was almost incomprehensible to them. To their minds it could only be explained by poor leadership and lack of the necessary fighting qualities on the part of the armies engaged. When a news despatch came telling of British troops engaging in rat hunts in the trenches, and an illustrated paper depicted a scene in which British 'Tommies' were shown trying to transfix rats with their bayonets, some of the Japanese papers came out with derisive comments. These were to the effect that, if they would devote as much attention to defeating the Germans as they devoted to killing rats, the Allies might make more progress. Similarly, the impression made on most Japanese by the story of a Scottish battalion advancing to the attack at Loos, kicking a football before them, was not that the British troops showed extraordinary coolness under fire. To their minds it seemed to indicate that they were not paying proper attention to their duties.

How great are the pitfalls confronting the would-be propagandist may be illustrated by an experience of my own while attached to a Japanese infantry regiment. I had invited some of the officers to my house one evening. Thinking they might be interested, I showed them some photographs taken at the Front by a brother officer of mine during the opening stages of the War. One of these depicted the C.O. of the 1st Battalion of my regiment, squatting in an open field and shaving himself during a halt on the retreat from Mons. I thought it would impress my Japanese guests as indicating the imperturbability of a British officer under even the most trying conditions. But not a bit of it! Each of my guests looked at it in turn without saying a word; then one of them, more forthright than the others, remarked in a tone of ill-concealed scorn, 'We Japanese would never think of our per-

[1] *The New East*, vol. II, no. 5 (May 1918), pp. 422–36.

sonal appearance in the face of an enemy.' I decided there and then that never again would I try my hand at propaganda!

Had the Japanese been sufficiently close to the main theatres of active operations, they might have been able to visualize the whole scene better, and to appreciate the true significance of incidents such as these. As it was, they had no conception of what it all meant. Time and again the Japanese papers came out with the most scathing and sarcastic criticisms of their allies in the field, simply because they were too far removed to realize either the immensity of the difficulties to be overcome or the paralysing effect of a modern bombardment on those subjected to it. They could only conceive of war as fought by themselves in the sparsely populated regions of Manchuria, regions which, moreover, belonged to neither of the combatants engaged in them in 1904. They could not visualize the vast difference between their war with Russia, in which the armies engaged were numbered in a few hundreds of thousands and were armed only with the weapons of that period, and war as fought in densely populated Europe and on other fronts between armies numbering millions, armed with all the latest and most scientific death-dealing devices—aircraft, tanks, poison gas, heavy artillery and vast numbers of machine-guns. Artillery, of course, had been used in the Russo-Japanese War; but in some of the great battles of the Western Front, a single day's bombardment often meant the expenditure of more artillery ammunition than was fired during the whole period of the Manchurian campaign of 1904–5. Machine-guns, which wrought such havoc in France, Gallipoli, Mesopotamia and elsewhere, were only used on a very small scale in the war between Japan and Russia.

All these things combined, together with the fact that, on account of there being no flanks to turn, manœuvre on the Western Front was virtually out of the question for most of the time, rendered true appreciation of the War impossible for those who could use only the Russo-Japanese War as a standard of comparison.

While, however, the general attitude towards the War, both of the Japanese themselves and of other people living in Japan, seemed so different from the attitude of people in England and elsewhere, there was one outcome of the War that attracted special attention in Japan. This was the development of the Revolution in Russia. The main theatres of war might be sufficiently remote to allow Japan to adopt a somewhat detached air towards the operations as a whole. Russia, on the other hand, was a neighbour. The spread of the revolutionary movement at such close quarters, therefore, aroused a more direct interest. Of this, more will be said in the next chapter.

Partly with a view to stimulating Japanese interest in the important part played by their British ally in the fighting on the Western Front and in other theatres of war, and partly in the hope that Japan might be encouraged to play an active part in the land fighting, the year 1918 opened with the news that the rank of field-marshal in the British Army was to be conferred on the Japanese Emperor. Of the celebrations that followed there is no need to say anything here, except to record, as one who took part in them, that they were marked by a strong emphasis on the Anglo-Japanese Alliance as the key factor in Japan's foreign policy and enthusiastic toasts at official banquets to the continuance of this Treaty. The friendly feelings towards Britain and the great value placed on the Alliance by the Japanese were equally noticeable in June, when Prince Arthur of Connaught arrived in Tokyo at the head of a mission to present the Emperor with the field-marshal's batôn. During the months that had elapsed since the announcement that the Japanese Sovereign was to be made a British field-marshal, however, the situation on the Western Front had undergone a serious change.

While the happenings in Russia were attracting increasing interest in Japan, the War itself had continued to absorb the main attention of the other countries engaged in its prosecution. With the coming of the great German offensive in the Spring of 1918, the cabled accounts showed clearly the seriousness of the situation. Garbled descriptions of the fighting came through, and day by day came reports of towns and villages, intimately connected with my own battalion's doings during the winter of 1914-15, falling into the hands of the Germans. The news of their fall was bitter. With the coming of July, however, the German advance was stemmed; and on the 18th of the month was launched the great counter-stroke, that sent the Germans reeling back, with the British, French and Belgians, now greatly strengthened by the arrival of the Americans, at their heels. All through the summer and on into the autumn the good news continued. With the opening of October came the first real signs that the end was near. First Bulgaria surrendered; a month later came the capitulation of

PLATE I. Prince Arthur of Connaught and his suite, with members of the Japanese reception committee and of the British Embassy in Tokyo, June 1918

Front Row (left to right): Mr Norman, Marquis Inouye, Lt. General Pulteney, Marshal Kawamura, Prince Arthur of Connaught, Sir Conyngham Greene, Admiral Ijuin, Major the Earl of Pembroke and Montgomery, Viscount Inaba
Back Row (left to right): Capt. Bennett, Mr Hobart-Hampden, Commander Imamura, Capt. The Hon. A. St. Clair, Capt. Acton, Lt. Col. Somerville, Capt. Kennedy, Mr Bentinck, Lt. Col. Ninomiya, Mr Crowe, Mr Furuya, Mr Wingfield, Viscount Matsudaira

PLATE II.   Lt. Col. (later Marshal Count) Terauchi and foreign military attachés and observers at the Grand Manœuvres, November 1918

Front Row (left to right): Major Baldwin (U.S.A.), Lt. Col. Aivasoglou (Russia), Major-Gen. Yo Kai-Shen (China), Lt. Col. Terauchi (Japan), Lt. Col. Somerville (Great Britain), Colonel Herrera de la Rosa (Spain), Lt. Col. Gonzalez (Bolivia)

Second Row (left to right): Capt. Komatsubara (Japan), Capt. Kennedy (Great Britain), Capt. Bennett (Great Britain), Capt. Grenier (France), Capt. Rozendaal (Holland), Major Mauere (Italy), Major de Lapomarede (France), Capt. Veloz (Chile), Lt. Tait (U.S.A.), Lt. Ugaki (Japan)

Turkey. From all the theatres of active operations came news of Allied victories and the collapse of the enemy forces. Finally came the news of the Armistice.

To say that the news of Germany suing for terms was recognized immediately by us out in Japan as the end of the long-drawn struggle would be incorrect. In my diary for 14 October 1918, I find the following brief entry: 'Captain Kato [a Japanese officer friend] came in to see me. Tells me the [Japanese] War Office thinks the war will end next month. I rather doubt it.' This is followed, a month later, by an entry under date of 12 November 'News of German surrender received in morning while I was up at the Embassy, the Armistice starting from 11 a.m. yesterday.[1] I wonder if this is really the end of the war? I can't somehow believe it.'

This feeling of incredulity was shared by most of us out in Japan. It was difficult to realize that the long struggle was over at last. How hard it was to appreciate the good news was reflected in the reaction at the Embassy where, on its receipt, there was a certain amount of discussion as to whether or not to run up the flag. If the last shot had been fired, well and good; but suppose the Armistice was merely a temporary truce, a preliminary to further fighting!

In these circumstances, and in view also of what has been said elsewhere about the Japanese attitude toward the War, it is perhaps not surprising that the outburst of enthusiastic rejoicing that greeted the news in London, Paris and the other principal Allied capitals, was almost wholly absent in Tokyo until some days later. Even then, there was but little spontaneous rejoicing; the great lantern processions and other celebrations that were staged by the Japanese themselves were largely of the made-to-order variety. The extraordinary air of detachment, if not of actual indifference, of the people as a whole towards the termination of the greatest conflict of modern times, was well illustrated by the query put to some friends of mine by their Japanese servants. 'Why are the flags out?' they asked. 'Is the Emperor going to pass this way?' When told that it was to celebrate the signing of the Armistice, their only comment was a rather disinterested '*Sō desu ka?*' ('Is that so?').

---

[1] Japanese time was nine hours ahead of G.M.T. This, and the fact that, in the absence of radio and other means of rapid communication, news travelled more slowly in these days, accounts for the lag in time.

As it happened, I had to leave Tokyo on 13 November with the party of foreign military attachés, to attend the annual Japanese Grand Manœuvres. Even then, two days after the last gun had spoken, there was little or nothing in the way of rejoicing to indicate that the War was over at last. On the way to the station, however, I met a Japanese officer friend, who had once been attached to a British regiment in Aldershot and therefore had a rather more personal interest in the war than most of his friends. By him I was warmly congratulated on the fact that, by a strange coincidence, British troops had just occupied Mons when the end came. At the station, too, there was a great deal of mutual exchange of congratulations between the various military attachés assembled there while waiting for the train that was to convey us to the scene of the manœuvres. But apart from this, there was little or nothing in the general attitude of the people at large to indicate that anything out of the ordinary had happened.

Nothing, perhaps, served better to illustrate this curious air of detachment than an incident which occurred on our arrival at the scene of the coming manœuvres. The Chief of the Japanese General Staff came in person to welcome us, but said not a word about the War just ended. Shortly after his departure, however, one of his A.D.C.s galloped up, looking slightly embarrassed as he dismounted. He had been sent by the General, he said, to express his congratulations to the military attachés of Japan's allies on the successful conclusion of the War and his apologies for having forgotten to congratulate them himself. Just a pleasant little afterthought!

It was not until two days later that we came in for the first outward and visible signs of rejoicing on the part of the Japanese. We had had a fairly strenuous day riding around seeing various phases of the mimic warfare, and I had been struck by the difference between these peace-time operations and the real thing in France. It was as though we were back in 1913 once more. There was little change, either in weapons or in tactics, from those employed by our own and other western armies in the days preceding the outbreak of the War. Noting all this, and comparing it with the weapons and equipment, the tactics and general conditions developed during the previous four years of bloodshed, served only to emphasize the strangely detached attitude towards the War that I had noticed amongst the Japanese as a whole ever since my arrival in Japan a year previously.

After returning to our billets on the evening of the 15th, the British, French, American and other officers of the Allied Powers were treated to a lantern procession. It had been specially staged in our honour by local school children, who marched past us shouting *Banzai* for the Allies. Other similar processions were witnessed on our return to Tokyo a few days later; but, prior to this, there had been singularly little to indicate anything in the nature of personal interest in, or general rejoicings at, the return of peace.

So ended the Great War of 1914–18, which was to have such revolutionary social, political and economic effects on the world in general in the years ahead; but the signing of the Armistice and the consequent cessation of hostilities made little perceptible difference in life in Japan. Its immediate effects on my own doings were negligible; it was not until my return to England some two years later, when a medical board decided that I would never again be fit for active soldiering, that I had to face up to the solemn fact that my days were numbered in so far as an Army career was concerned. As a postscript to these observations on Japan during the First World War, however, one final note may be added. The group of foreign military attachés whom I accompanied on the 1918 manoeuvres had, as their principal 'bear-leader', a genial and extremely able young lieutenant-colonel. The eldest son of Marshal Count Terauchi of Russo-Japanese War fame, he himself was to rise to the same high rank as his father and to become Supreme Commander of the Japanese Land Forces in the Southern Region during the Pacific War. Had he survived, he would presumably have had to stand trial as a 'war criminal'; but he died shortly after the surrender of August 1945, and so escaped that humiliating experience. For this I have always been thankful because, following my first meeting with him in 1918, I came to know him well and received much kindness from him; his young brother, a subaltern in the Imperial Guards, had also been a good friend of mine, but he had died while still a junior officer.

Earlier in this chapter, certain similarities in outlook between the Japanese Army of 1918 and the French and German armies up to 1914 were noted. Today, with the benefit of hindsight, similarities between the German military outlook in 1914 and the Japanese outlook twenty-seven years later are equally noticeable. While it is true that Japan, in launching the Pacific War in 1941, was influenced more by economic considerations than by German teachings, some of the parallels are striking. Developments in Europe had led the Chief of the German General Staff in May 1914 to declare that any postponement of the war, for which his country had been preparing for so long, would diminish Germany's chances of success; the failure, in the autumn of 1941, to achieve by negotiation with the United States a settlement which would ease the growing crisis in the matter of Japan's oil requirements, led General Tojo, who was War Minister as well as Premier, to make a similar pronouncement.

Another parallel, and one that reflected the influence of German teaching, was the way in which the Japanese, like the Germans before them, showed their readiness to ignore the odium attaching to the aggressor, and acted on the principle that war is justified, provided you win it. In acting on this principle, they were simply following out Moltke's aphorism of 1914, 'Success alone justifies war'.

One further similarity may be noted. Like the Germans in 1914, their plans were based on the strategy of 'decisive battle'; they would overwhelm their opponents at the outset and ensure that the war would be of short duration. For economic reasons, a short war was essential. By their sweeping victories in the opening stages of the war, they seemed even nearer to winning the decisive battle than the Germans had been in August 1914; but, like the Germans, they miscalculated and their dreams of a short war, on which alone they could hope to emerge victorious, were shattered. The unexpected resistance of the Belgians upset the German calculations; it was the Anglo-American refusal to admit defeat that was Japan's undoing. The Japanese had calculated that, if they themselves could overrun South-East Asia at the very start, the British and Americans would soon tire of the war and be prepared to accept a negotiated peace; but in this they were mistaken.

It was perhaps inevitable that Japanese officers, having been brought up to accept the German Army as their model, should be strongly influenced by German military doctrine. One outstanding example of this was to be seen in their strict adherence to Clausewitz's warning, that military plans which leave no room for the unexpected can lead to disaster. Like other British officers attached to the Japanese Army at different times, this was a point that made a lasting impression on me. Staff officers and regimental officers alike were trained, to a far greater extent than in our own army, to work out plans to meet all conceivable contingencies. In consequence, they were generally able, whether on manœuvres or on regimental training, to produce and apply the necessary plan to cope with whatever situation arose; but this dependence on seemingly fool-proof plans led to a certain lack of flexibility when faced with something entirely unexpected and tended to overlook the very essence of Clausewitz's warning. Had they paid more heed to Foch's stress on the need for constant adaptability and improvisation, rather than on fixed plans to fit all circumstances, they would have been better prepared to cope with the unexpected.

One German doctrine in particular, however, was to stand them in good stead. Schlieffen, architect of the famous plan intended to ensure German victory and a rapidly concluded war in 1914, was never tired of hammering home the need for boldness. 'Be bold, be bold!', was his constant theme. How well the Japanese had taken this precept to heart was to be seen in the opening stages of the Pacific War. It was to be noted ruefully later by the official British historians of *The War Against Japan*. Referring to the Malayan campaign, they commented, 'Where the Japanese acted rapidly, we hesitated; where the Japanese were bold, we were timid.'

CHAPTER III

Intervention in Siberia

Following the conclusion of the Russo-Japanese War, relations between Japan and Russia became markedly friendly. In 1907 the two countries came to an amicable agreement about their respective spheres of interest in Manchuria and Mongolia, and everything went smoothly for the next ten years. With the seizure of power by the Bolsheviks in November 1917, all this was changed.

The rot in Russia had started many months earlier and the spread of the revolutionary movement, especially since March that year, was being watched by the Japanese with a mixture of interest and apprehension. The Kerensky régime was already tottering to its end at the time of my arrival in Japan, and refugees and travellers were coming over from Vladivostok with stories of the terrible happenings they had witnessed. At lunch, on my first day in Tokyo, I met an Indian cavalry colonel, who had just arrived from Russia; from him I heard a first-hand account of the unfortunate plight of Russian Army officers and others. Hundreds of them, he said, were committing suicide out of sheer disgrace; hundreds more were being shot or put to torture by their own men. He spoke highly of the courage of Russian officers generally and told of one instance in which, after vainly endeavouring to urge their men to advance against the Germans, the officers went on by themselves and fought until they fell. Their men stayed behind, laughing and jeering at them and refused to go to their assistance. For Kerensky he had nothing but the most supreme contempt, and characterized him as a useless humbug, whose downfall was a thing to be desired.

An American, whom I met a few days later, had also just arrived from Russia and brought similar tidings. He threw light, too, on an incident of a different kind. Claiming to be a personal friend of Prince Youssoupoff's, he gave a most vivid account of the murder of Rasputin, as described to him by Youssoupoff himself. Whether he had really been on such close terms with the Prince as he professed to have been I never knew, but the details he gave tallied largely with those given some years later in Prince

Youssoupoff's own published account of the incident[1]—the luring of the Russian monk to Youssoupoff's house, the poisoned cakes and wine which took no effect, and the nightmarish episode of Rasputin's final attempt, after apparently being shot dead, to throttle his assailant.

Some months later came Lady Muriel Paget and her party of Red Cross workers from Russia. From them we learned of the ghastly atrocities they had witnessed at Kieff and elsewhere, and of others of which they had heard at first hand—of Russian officers being seized and crushed to death under steam hammers, of wounded men being dragged out of hospitals and bayonetted, of naval officers thrown overboard with weights tied to them, and of numerous other brutalities. Of their own treatment, however, they had little to complain. When during the bombardment of Kieff, where 2,500 Czarist officers were put to death in a single day, they themselves, they said, were allowed to move about freely and were always well treated.

Stories such as these were constantly being brought to Japan by refugees and others arriving from Russia, but it was not wholly one-way traffic. British, American, French and other army officers and civilians were continually passing through Japan on their way to Vladivostok and beyond, to find out for themselves what really was happening and to assess the existing situation and probable future developments. One such transient visitor early in 1918 was a young British subaltern of Finnish origin, who came to lunch with me and seemed extremely intelligent and well-informed. I never saw him again, but years later he was to spring into prominence as the left-wing Labour M.P., Konni Zilliacus, who died in 1967.

In the early stage of the Bolshevik revolution, this to-ing and fro-ing was on a relatively small scale; but as the months went by and the question of Allied intervention in Siberia came increasingly to the fore, the numbers increased considerably and the Japanese Press showed a growing interest in the developments taking place. In Britain, the general public was probably too absorbed in the life and death struggle raging nearer home—in France and Flanders and in the other main theatres of war—to pay more than passing attention to developments in the Far East; but to the Japanese, events on the neighbouring mainland were of far more immediate concern. Finally, after months of bickering

[1] *Rasputin: His Malignant Influence and Assassination* (Jonathan Cape, 1927).

c

and of conflicting views amongst the Allies, the decision was taken, in the summer of 1918, to despatch Japanese and other Allied troops to Siberia. The prime purpose was the rescue of Czecho-Slovak forces, whose attempt to break their way through from European Russia had brought them into conflict with heavy concentrations of Bolshevik troops, aided, in some instances, by former German, Austrian and Hungarian prisoners-of-war. Long after the last gun had been fired on the Western Front and the last Czechs had sailed safely away from Vladivostok, this curious off-shoot of the Great War—the armed intervention in Siberia—continued. It was 1925 before the last Japanese troops had been withdrawn.

Bearing, as it did, on the growing tension between Japan and the United States and on the important consequences of their increasingly strained relations, the Siberian intervention, and the discussions and events leading up to it, call for consideration. Some of the details that follow were public knowledge at the time, or broadly hinted at in the Japanese Press, but others have only been made generally known in the past few years, through such scholarly works as Ullman's *Intervention and the War*.

The story of the Siberian Intervention was a tragic mixture of conflicting aims and policies, of muddled thinking, of dithering and growing friction between all concerned. As originally conceived by the British and French governments early in 1917, the primary object was to strengthen or replace the Russian armies fighting the Germans. Being the only Allied Power with large forces available, Japan seemed the natural country to provide them. An attempt was therefore made to persuade the Japanese Government to send a great army of fresh troops through Siberia to the Eastern Front (a force of two-and-a-half million was optimistically envisaged by Lloyd George) to fill the gaps caused by the growing disintegration of the Russian forces. The Russian break-up was already arousing serious misgivings even before the initial revolution of March that year. Apart, however, from the almost insuperable difficulties of transporting huge masses of troops and material by a totally inadequate railway system for a distance of some 7,000 miles, Japan lacked the economic strength to support such an undertaking and the price demanded by her for assistance on this vast scale was considered too great. Following the Bolshevik revolution of November that year, a modification of the original proposal was put forward by the French, but again the Japanese declined. By then, however, new factors had been introduced into the situation, and the aims of the various parties concerned became increasingly conflicting.

The growing chaos which followed the overthrow of the Kerensky régime, the rapid spread of revolutionary doctrines even as far afield as Eastern Siberia, and exaggerated reports of former German, Hungarian and Austrian prisoners-of-war (released by the Bolsheviks) planning to seize control of Siberia, aroused alarm concerning the vast stores of Allied war material in Vladivostok. Britain and France, however, continued for some time to think mainly of finding new armies to hold the Germans on the Eastern Front in order to prevent their transfer to the West; Japan and the United States, each eyeing the other with suspicion, were far more concerned with the repercussions which the Russian collapse and the establishment of a Soviet régime would have on the situation in the Far East.

From early in 1918, when disturbances in Irkutsk led France to propose Allied intervention in Siberia for the purpose of restoring and maintaining order, until May that year, when Czech troops on their way by rail to Vladivostok clashed at Chelyabinsk with former German and Hungarian prisoners-of-war, heated discussions raged between the Allies as to the right policy to follow in regard to Siberia and the huge dumps of arms and munitions at Vladivostok. As against suggestions for intervention by contingents from all the Allied countries, Britain urged that Japan, being the nearest and most immediately concerned, should be called on to act for the Allies and be given a free hand to deal with the situation as she saw fit. The United States refused to consider any such action, as intervention, it was contended, would play into German hands by driving the Siberian Russians into the arms of the Bolsheviks, in opposition to any interference by Allied forces. In particular, intervention by Japan was the last thing wanted by the Americans, who distrusted Japanese intentions. The Japanese, for their part, were ready enough to intervene, but wished to ensure American assent before they did so and made it clear that, as evidence of Allied trust in her good faith, Japan should be left to handle the situation by herself. It was the clash between the Czechs and Hungarians at Chelyabinsk, just east of the Urals, in May that finally paved the way to Allied intervention in Siberia, with American concurrence and participation, three months later.

The Czechs, like the Germans and Hungarians with whom they had clashed at Chelyabinsk, were former prisoners in Russian hands; but many of them had been released even before the Bolsheviks came into power. Having been forced against their will to fight for the Germans, they had surrendered in large numbers to the Russians. When released, they had readily offered their services to fight against their former masters and had been incorporated into the Czech forces already aligned with the Czarists. Being unable, after the Russian collapse in the summer of 1917, to accomplish much, they had agreed to a French suggestion that they should make their way to Vladivostok; from there they were to be transported to the Western Front to serve under the French. Owing to the tremendous difficulties inherent in arranging for this long and involved journey by land and sea, it was March 1918 before they were able to start the long trek eastward, after fighting their way through the German forces encircling them. Their difficulties were increased when the Bolsheviks, after agreeing to their departure, had second thoughts and began to place impediments in their way. Then came the clash with the Hungarians at Chelyabinsk, which was promptly followed by more serious Soviet attempts to stop their further progress eastwards. The Czechs responded by turning against the Bolsheviks attempting to bar their way, and within two weeks they had made themselves masters of virtually the whole Trans-Siberian Railway, almost as far eastwards as Irkutsk. Having struggled thus far, however, they found themselves faced by strong concentrations of Bolshevik forces, assisted by former German and Hungarian prisoners, in the Baikal area around Irkutsk. The situation was therefore precarious in the extreme and was recognized as such by the 15,000 Czechs who had already reached Vladivostok. These latter accordingly appealed to the Allies for a force of 100,000 men, to help them break their way through to the relief of their 45,000 compatriots cut off west of Lake Baikal.

These were the circumstances that finally led the United States to reverse their original opposition to intervention; but they themselves could not spare more than 7,000 men and they were not prepared to let the Japanese contingent be stronger than their own. The arbitrary figure of 7,000 troops from each of the Allies concerned was, therefore, fixed, although it bore little relation to actual military requirements. This poor compromise was made worse by clumsy handling. Through an extraordinary oversight, the British, French and Italians were not informed of this decision until twenty-four hours after it had been communicated to the Japanese. Their indignation at this omission only increased the friction already existing between the Allies; further friction followed. The Americans wished to confine their intervention to guarding the lines of communication of the Czech forces making their way from Vladivostok to Irkutsk and were openly suspicious of British motives. The British, for their part, urged that Japan be allowed to send a far larger force than the stipulated 7,000, as the Far East was Japan's special sphere of interest and the Japanese had plenty of troops available. The British, moreover, were still thinking in terms of the war against Germany and of re-establishing an Eastern Front, with the aid of the Japanese. There was, however, one point in common between the United States and Japan; both insisted that intervention should be confined to Eastern Siberia and should not be extended west of Lake Baikal.

Of the wrangling between the Allies that followed, no more need be said. The French hopes of using the Czech Army Corps as a badly needed reinforcement on the Western Front were thwarted, as the Czechs remained in Siberia till 1920. The British assumption that the Japanese, in the event of intervention, would be prepared to operate as far west as the Urals, was proved unfounded. The Japanese had, in fact, indicated at an early stage that they were only interested in Eastern Siberia. The American opposition to intervention of any kind was replaced by anxiety to assist in the rescue of the Czechs. The Japanese, despite their dislike of joint intervention, finally agreed to it; but, from the start, they showed a spirit of independence by despatching a force of 70,000 men as against the contingents of 7,000 each employed by the British, Americans and French. Later they obtained the free hand they wanted by remaining in Siberia after all the other contingents had been withdrawn. Being nearer at hand, and therefore more concerned with preventing the establishment of a Bolshevik régime in such close proximity to their possessions in Manchuria and Korea than in rescuing the Czechs, they regarded this as only right and proper.

This understandable anxiety concerning the Bolshevization of Eastern Siberia had, in fact, led them, only a few months previously, to enter into a military agreement with the Chinese. By invoking this agreement when intervention took place, they were able to take control of the Chinese Eastern Railway for the purpose of transporting their troops westward to the Baikal area and eastward to Vladivostok. Although nominally Chinese, this railway had been largely under Czarist administration; but by the end of 1917 the Bolsheviks had obtained part control. Under pressure of the Allied ministers in Peking, Chinese troops had been sent to drive the Bolsheviks out and to restore the authority of General Horvath, the Czarist administrator. That they succeeded in doing so was in strong contrast to what happened twelve years later. In 1917 the Bolsheviks were still too weak and disorganized militarily to stand up to the Chinese; by 1929, when the Chinese again seized control of the railway, Soviet forces had no difficulty in driving them out and regaining control. As will be seen in a later chapter, the unexpected strength and ability of the Soviet Army revealed in the 1929 incident was to play an important part in precipitating Japan's incursion into Manchuria in 1931 and in the serious developments that stemmed from it. But this is looking ahead.

In view of all the circumstances involved in the Siberian venture, friction between Japan and her allies was inevitable. Between the Japanese and the Americans in particular, the friction developed rapidly; it was increased by the support given by the Japanese to Semenov and other Cossack adventurers, whose ruthlessness and unreliability did far more harm than good to the crusade against Bolshevik control.[1] While, however, Japan may have been ill-advised to use such men as allies, it is ironical that, thirty and forty years later, the Western Powers felt similarly constrained to support reactionary autocrats like Syngman Rhee, Chiang Kai-shek and Ngo Dinh Diem, for lack of more democratic leaders, in their attempt to stem the Communist flood in East Asia.

While anti-American sentiment had been endemic in Japan for some years past, it showed a marked increase in intensity from the outset of the Siberian Intervention. Nowhere was it more pronounced than in Army circles. From the start of the Intervention down to the close of 1920, when my first tour of duty in Japan ended, I was in close touch with Japanese officers and was struck by the growing vehemence of their criticism of the United States. Whether attached to an army unit in Japan or attending manoeuvres, on visits to Japanese garrisons in Korea, Manchuria,

[1] Although Semenov came under Japanese control, the British were the first to recognize his apparent potentialities as an anti-Bolshevik leader and to provide him with financial support accordingly.

China or Vladivostok, or when visiting Japanese Army friends in various parts of Japan itself, this strong feeling against the Americans was constantly in evidence. Time and again 'the coming war with America' was discussed as though it were inevitable and even to be welcomed. When, on one occasion, I pointed out the preponderance that the United States would have in men and material resources and asked what would happen if Japan was defeated, the logic of the reply was revealing. If Japan won, she would obtain territorial gains sufficient for her surplus population; if she lost, it would only be after so many of her men had been killed that there would no longer be a surplus population to worry about. It was as simple as that!

Occasionally, but only very seldom, was any criticism of Britain voiced by my Japanese brother officers. When it was, it was generally mild and made more in sorrow than in anger. This may have been due in part to politeness, out of a desire to avoid giving offence; but there was more to it than that. The Japanese might feel critical of Britain on some matters; but the spell of the Anglo-Japanese Alliance and all it implied still held good. Moreover, as an island nation under a stable and respected monarchy like their own, they felt towards her a certain affinity, which was lacking so far as the republican United States and the continental countries of the West were concerned. The army, as a whole, might have pro-German sentiments, but this did not mean that it was actively anti-British. On one occasion only did I experience an outright attack on Britain as well as on America, and it was by an officer who had drunk rather more than was good for him. The gist of his tirade was that Britain, in spite of her alliance with Japan, was in league with America against her, and that Australia, Canada and the United States were at one in trying, by means of their immigration laws, to prevent the Japanese from easing their growing pressure of population. Deep resentment was voiced also against the implications of racial inferiority in the 'White Australia' policy and in the dismissal of Japan's proposal for racial equality at the Versailles Peace Conference. In the context of the 'colour' question and of Japan's surplus population problem, it was a view that was to find increasing expression in the years ahead and to lead Japan later to set herself up as champion of the Pan-Asiatic movement.

Although my main contacts during the first two years or so of the Siberian Intervention were with Japanese officers, I was able from time to time to meet individual British officers passing through Japan on their way back from Vladivostok. From their first-hand accounts of the confused situation, it was possible to obtain a clearer and more accurate picture than was possible from reports appearing in the Japanese and foreign Press, strongly tinged with propaganda and prejudice as many of these reports were. By the spring of 1920, however, the Czechs, whose relief from their sorry plight had been the main object of the Intervention, had been rescued and evacuated. With the exception of a handful of British officers, retained as military observers or for special duties, all the Western Allied contingents had therefore been withdrawn. Only the Japanese remained.

From the early days of the Intervention, the Japanese had been the target of growing criticism. By remaining in Siberia after the other Allies had withdrawn, they brought still more criticism upon themselves. Some of it was merited, but much of it was due to Bolshevik and other propaganda and to allegations which, on investigation, were generally shown to have little or no firm basis. Unpopular, however, as the Japanese undoubtedly were, it was widely admitted by Western observers on the spot that Japanese fears of the chaos and bloodshed that would follow, if they withdrew before a stable government had been established, were well founded. Vitally concerned as she was with ensuring the safety of her own interests in the adjoining territories, Japan could not afford to take as dispassionate a view of the situation in Eastern Siberia as could Britain or America.

From what I myself saw and heard during a visit to Vladivostok and district, and on through Manchuria and Korea, in the early autumn of 1920, it seemed clear that Japan was, to some extent, the victim of a dilemma. Some of her troops were already said to have been infected by revolutionary theories. If Eastern Siberia came under Bolshevik control, these disturbing doctrines seemed likely to find even readier acceptance in Manchuria, China and Korea, with disastrous effects on Japan's vital interests in those areas. Rather than see stability restored to Siberia by the imposition of Soviet rule, the Japanese therefore preferred to support anti-Bolshevik leaders, who set up local forms of government of their own. This had the additional advantage of ensuring a measure of Japanese control, as these leaders were dependent on Japan for the material aid they required. The Russians themselves, however, were also faced with a dilemma. Apart from the large numbers of refugees from European Russia, who were naturally fearful of falling into Bolshevik hands, the great majority of the local inhabitants had no desire to come under Soviet domination. Much as they disliked and criticized the Japanese, they realized that this would be their fate if the Japanese withdrew. Those who denounced the Japanese most volubly were often, therefore, the first to urge the Japanese to stay on to protect them whenever the question of withdrawal was raised. This occurred on more than one occasion. Meantime, between the brutalities perpetrated by the autocratic anti-Bolshevik leaders and those carried out by the Bolsheviks, there was little to choose. Even Japanese officers, with whom I discussed this aspect of the situation, expressed disgust at the excesses of their own hirelings, although they generally sought to exonerate Semenov and other anti-Bolshevik leaders by laying the blame on their ill-disciplined followers.

By the time of my visit to Vladivostok, the Japanese had withdrawn most of their troops from the more outlying areas and had concentrated them in and around Vladivostok itself and in Khabarovsk and Saghalien. Only a few days previously they had evacuated Chita and, in consequence, had aroused cries of dismay from the local Russians and others, who viewed the withdrawal of these protective forces with alarm. A proclamation issued by General Oi, the Japanese Commander-in-Chief, while I was in Vladivostok explained why the evacuation of the Chita area had been carried out. It was because the original purpose of occupying it—to assist the Czechs—had been achieved. The proclamation went on, however, to express regret that it was not yet possible to leave Vladivostok, as, in Bolshevik hands, it would be a menace to Korea and would leave the many Japanese living in the town without protection. Not only that but, so long as there were Japanese troops in Khabharovsk and Saghalien, it was essential to retain Vladivostok for their safety.

If the retention of Vladivostok was required for the safety of the Japanese troops in Khabarovsk and Saghalien, it might be asked why it was necessary to keep armed forces in those two areas. In so far as Saghalien was concerned, the explanation is that the Japanese had occupied it only a few months previously, in retaliation for the massacre of a large number of their nationals at Nikolaevsk by Bolshevik partisans in April. At the time of the massacre, I was attached to the Japanese Infantry School in Chiba, and my diary of that period reflects the intense indignation aroused amongst the Japanese officers there by the incident. One young subaltern, who was particularly distressed, told me that two companies of his own regiment had been stationed there for the protection of the Japanese community; they had been wiped out to a man in the fighting that ensued before the town was finally overwhelmed by the attackers, who had the advantage of greatly superior numbers. The main cause of the indignation, however, was that virtually the whole Japanese community, men, women, and children, had been ruthlessly butchered. As the weeks went by and further horrible details appeared in the Japanese Press, feeling in Japan rose to fever pitch and demands for drastic punishment increased. At the Infantry School itself, talk of declaring war was frequent. Great bitterness was expressed that, whereas the Germans had been given Kiaochow in 1897 as compensation for the murder of two missionaries in China, nothing was done when several hundred Japanese were massacred in Siberia. Retribution, however, was coming; in the course of the summer the Japanese took possession of the northern half of Saghalien Island and the neighbouring mainland.

The occupation of this territory was to add further to American disquiet concerning Japanese intentions and provided Moscow with an excellent opportunity for fishing in troubled waters. By granting oil concessions in Saghalien to an American oil company, the Soviet Government sought to play off the United States against Japan. The Russians hoped that Washington would try to force Japan to recognize the validity of these concessions, and that Japan's refusal to do so would cause an armed clash. Washington wisely declined to play the Russian game.

CHAPTER IV

Mastery of the Far East

The Siberian Intervention was but one of a number of causes of friction between Japan and the United States in recent years. Some of these were minor irritants, others far more serious; the cumulative effect was grave tension. Living, as I was, in close daily contact with Japanese officers and civilians, I came inevitably to learn the Japanese point of view on all these topics of the day and, without necessarily agreeing with it, to understand it. The Shantung question and China, the Californian question and immigration, racial equality and the colour question, Korea, the race in naval armaments—all these were matters arousing strong feelings against the Americans at that time. To understand how they arose, a brief excursion into the historical background may be helpful.

From earliest times, Japan had had close contacts with the neighbouring mainland of Asia. Apart from cultural and economic relations with China and Korea in the past, there had also been less peaceful interludes. Notable examples of these were seen in the thirteenth century, when Kublai Khan, using Korea as his base, twice attempted to invade Japan with his Mongol hordes, and in the late sixteenth century, when the Japanese warrior-statesman Hideyoshi, dreaming of bringing China under his sway, invaded Korea. This was after the Koreans had refused to let his troops use their territory as a passage-way to his goal. During the two hundred odd years of the seclusion policy which started soon after, Japan remained at peace with the world, neither invading nor being invaded; but with the arrival of the western nations in the 1850s demanding her re-opening to foreign trade and intercourse, schools of thought grew up advocating the strengthening of Japan's strategic position by obtaining a foothold on the neighbouring mainland in Korea and Manchuria and taking possession of Formosa and other outlying islands guarding her approaches. At the time that these suggestions were made, Japan, with her antiquated armaments and lack of naval forces, was in no condition to carry them out and her

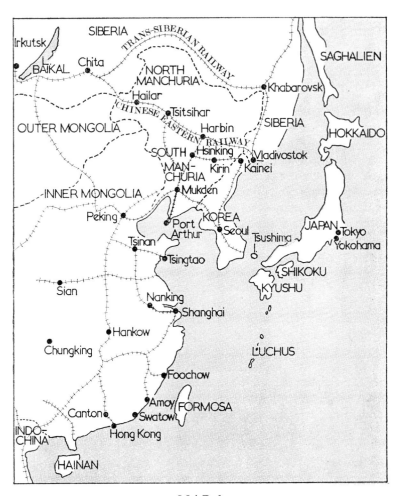

MAP 1

Japan and her mainland neighbours.

rulers wisely insisted on internal consolidation and modernization as an essential preliminary to any thought of overseas expansion. Remembering, however, that Kublai Khan had used Korea as a base for his attempted invasions of Japan, and that Hideyoshi's invasions of that peninsular kingdom had ended in disaster because of his failure to ensure the safety of his sea communications, the importance of a friendly or controlled Korea, and of a powerful navy, was fully recognized.

By 1876 Japan had already established treaty relations with her Korean neighbour. Her subsequent policy towards Korea was to come under severe criticism from time to time, sometimes deservedly; but it has to be remembered that Korean weakness, disorderliness and instability served as an invitation to others to intervene and that Korea was to Japan what the Low Countries have been to Britain from Marlborough's time onwards. Just as Britain was unable to dissociate herself from events in the Low Countries, so, too, was Japan unable to dissociate herself from events in Korea. Her policy was therefore conditioned by her determination to ensure that never again would Korea be allowed to serve as a jumping-off point for an invasion of her shores. With this object in view, she sought to stabilize and strengthen it sufficiently to remove any pretext for intervention by any third party. If at times she herself interfered in its internal affairs, she did so for much the same reason that sometimes impelled the United States to intervene in Mexico or in the so-called 'banana republics', or forced Britain to intervene in Egypt or the Arab States. Finally, of course, she annexed it outright in 1910, but this was not until after she had fought and won two wars, in both of which Korea had figured to a large extent as the bone of contention.

In passing it may be noted that, time and again during my attachment to the Japanese Army, Japanese officers, exasperated at American criticism of Japanese actions in Korea, China or Eastern Siberia, asked me why Americans should demand a higher standard of international behaviour from Japan in protecting her own vital interests in the Far East than they themselves set in the Caribbean and Latin America.

If Japanese rule in Korea was sometimes harsh, it did at least bring great material benefits to a country, whose people seemed quite incapable of producing orderly government and political stability by their own efforts. When, however, the Koreans—in the happy belief that the principle of self-determination enunciated by President Wilson implied immediate independence for all subject peoples—launched an independence movement in 1919, the Japanese clamped down on it with a severity that brought a fresh outburst of criticism against Japan, especially from the United States. Four years previously, a similar outburst had occurred when Japan had sought to strengthen her political and economic hold on China by the presentation of her Twenty-One Demands on the Chinese Government. In both instances, criticism had come from other countries besides the United States, but in both instances it had been from America that the most scathing censure had emanated. By 1919, therefore, Chinese and Koreans alike were looking to the United States for sympathy and support and were finding her a ready listener to their grievances. Some of these were real enough, but others stemmed from their own follies and shortcomings and were employed for mischief-making. To the great majority of Japanese they smacked all too heavily of tendentious propaganda! The fact that they received such ready credence in the United States merely added to Japanese exasperation and indignation with America. But there were other causes of the growing anti-American sentiment in Japan, some of them, even more fundamental, going back to the turn of the century.

Until the Spanish-American War of 1898, the nearest American possession to the Far East had been Pago Pago Harbour, some 4,000 miles out in the Pacific; its use had been granted to her for naval purposes by the Samoan government in 1878. The Philippines and Guam, which were among the main fruits of her victory over Spain, brought the United States appreciably nearer; together with the Hawaian islands, which she annexed the same year, they enabled her to have a greater say in Far Eastern affairs and to exercise a much stronger influence in the Far East. Her determination to do so was shown in the following year, when she enunciated the famous doctrine of the Open Door and Equal Opportunity in China. This was accepted by the other Powers in principle, but was to give rise to much quibbling and to become a source of grievance to the Japanese later. Why, they argued, should they be expected to give strict observance to the Open Door in the Far East if the door was to be closed to them in America? In Japanese eyes, moreover, it was inconsistent with the Monroe Doctrine which, in effect, enabled the United States

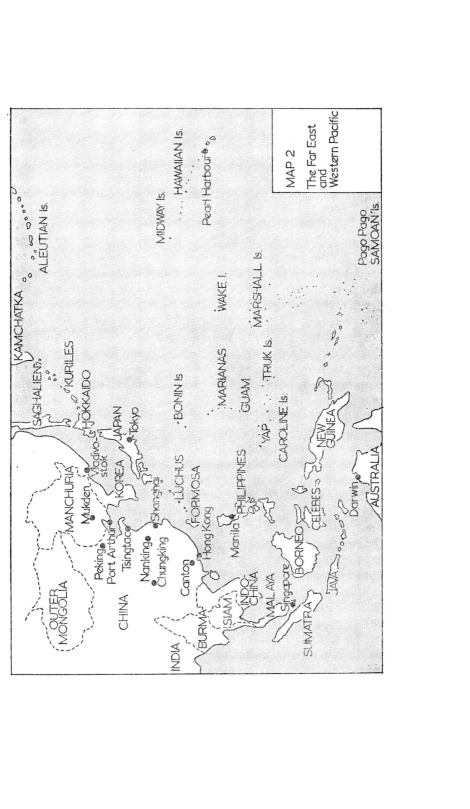

MAP 2

The Far East
and
Western Pacific

to interfere in the political affairs of the other republics of the American continent, but debarred other countries from doing so. The Japanese had no objection to this doctrine as such, but felt that what was sauce for the goose should be sauce for the gander as well. If the United States exercised a monopoly right of this kind in Central and South America, why should not Japan be allowed a Monroe Doctrine for the Far East? There, especially in the regions adjacent to her own shores, her rights and interests were just as vital to her as were those of the United States in the Western Hemisphere, in Mexico and the various Central American states.

These grievances, it is true, were only voiced later; but by the close of the last century, America's newly acquired ability to exert a growing influence in the Far East meant that, sooner or later, her 'manifest destiny' would be brought face to face with Japan's sense of a divine mission. At the turn of the century, however, it was Russian rather than Japanese ascendancy in the Far East that the United States feared; moral and financial support was therefore given to Japan during the period of the Russo-Japanese War. But what the American President had hoped to see was an indecisive war, which would have left both contestants more or less evenly balanced when it ended and strong enough to prevent each other from obtaining a free hand in East Asia. As he frankly admitted later, his readiness to fall in with Japan's request for American mediation, to bring the conflict to an end by means of a peace settlement, was largely due to his desire to preserve the balance of power in the Far East; his aim was, in fact, to ensure that Russia's defeat would not entail her elimination as a counter to Japan. In this he was successful, but the short-term result was unexpected; the restoration of peace was followed soon after by the two former enemies pegging out claims to separate spheres of influence and agreeing, not only to respect each other's spheres but to show a united front against any third party attempting to interfere in them.

The compromise peace that resulted from Theodore Roosevelt's mediation aroused intense indignation in Japan. It had given her the territorial prizes she wanted, but had deprived her of the war indemnity on which she had counted. The main target of the immediate attack was Marquis Komura, who had been Japan's chief delegate at the peace talks; but in the years ahead the blame was shifted to the United States and played its part in the growth of anti-American sentiment.

It was during the years immediately following the defeat of Russia that this sentiment became increasingly prominent. A number of circumstances contributed to building it up. They included the disputes over immigration and anti-Japanese legislation in California, the Knox attempt to internationalize the railways in Manchuria in 1909, American censoriousness in connection with the Twenty-One Demands on China in 1915 and with the Shantung question, and the race in naval armaments. While the Californian question was a blow to Japan's pride rather than to her economic well-being, it had a bearing also on her problem of surplus population and aroused deep resentment on both scores. The questions of the Manchurian railways, the Twenty-One Demands and Shantung, on the other hand, bore directly on matters of vital strategic and economic concern to Japan; so, too, did the race in naval armaments.

Although pledged to respect the territorial integrity of China and to observe the principle of the Open Door and Equal Opportunity, the Japanese, in common with the Russians, drew a sharp distinction between Manchuria and metropolitan China. Their rejection of the Knox proposal to internationalize the railways in that region was therefore inevitable; but it added to the growing apprehension in Washington and to the strain in relations, which was further accentuated during the next few years by a series of war scares revolving around American suspicions of Japan and Japanese indignation over anti-Japanese legislation in California. How serious the strain had become, by the time war broke out in Europe in 1914, was brought home to me some years later by the remark of a Japanese officer who had taken part in the Tsingtao campaign. When his regiment received mobilization orders in August that year, he told me, the general assumption amongst officers and men alike was that it was for war with the United States. Great was their surprise on learning that it was Germans, not Americans, whom they were about to fight.

With America's entry into the War in April 1917 there had come a temporary easing of tension; it was still noticeable at the time of my arrival in Japan seven months later. During the intervening three years, however, American misgivings had been further aroused by Japan's occupation of the former German islands in the Pacific. These, in effect, drove a great wedge between the United States and the Philippines and provided potential bases for submarines, thus threatening the American line of communication with Manila. But it was the presentation of the Twenty-One Demands to China in 1915, coupled with Japan's refusal to restore Tsingtao and the Shantung railway to China after driving out the Germans, that aroused American apprehension even more. By 1916, therefore, the United States had launched her famous naval construction programme. The race in naval armaments, which had already started in a relatively mild way some years earlier, was now begun in earnest and was symptomatic.

The indignation aroused by the presentation of the Twenty-One Demands was due more to the clumsy way in which the presentation was handled than to the actual substance of the demands. The more objectionable of these were, in fact, withdrawn, Japan explaining somewhat naïvely that those particular ones had been intended as suggestions, not as actual demands. It may be recalled, moreover, that Lord Grey in his memoirs.[1] commenting on the way in which the Japanese took advantage of Europe's preoccupation with the War to 'strengthen their position with China in East Asia', observed: 'The opportunity for Japan was immense and unique. What Western nation with a population feeling the need for territorial outlets would have used such an opportunity with more, or even with as much restraint?'

This was probably true, but to understand the circumstances in which the demands were presented, it is necessary to recall the nagging fear which was ever-present in the minds of the Japanese Government after aligning Japan on the side of her British ally. From the very outset of the War, the Japanese had regarded Russia as the weakest link in the Allied chain. The fear, a two-fold one, was that Russia might be forced into making a separate peace with Germany and then enter into alliance with her against Japan. If so, Japan could not expect assistance from any of her allies in meeting the consequent threat to herself in the Far East. The Brest Litovsk Treaty of March 1918 was to show that the first of these two nightmares was justified, though by then the Russians themselves were under a new régime, far too absorbed in fighting for its very existence to think of allying itself with the hated imperialists of Germany. Had Russia's collapse come early in 1916, however (it might well have done so if Falkenhayn, instead of striking at Verdun in an attempt to bleed the French white, had resumed the attack on the Russians while they were still reeling from the blows struck at them the previous year), the whole course

[1] *Twenty-Five Years*, vol. III, p. 34.

of history might have been different. In that event, a Russo-German alliance against Japan might quite possibly have materialized. Be that as it may, the fear of such a development undoubtedly played its part in determining Japan to improve her position on the neighbouring mainland while the other belligerents were preoccupied with the war in Europe and in other theatres of active operations. By the presentation of her twenty-one demands to China in 1915, she hoped, therefore, to strengthen her political, economic and strategic hold on the Far East so as to guard against such a contingency. The United States, however, with her own ideas about manifest destiny, could not be expected to stomach such a move; Japan's clumsy handling of the whole affair merely added to American indignation.

As revealed many years later by Viscount Ishii in his *Diplomatic Commentaries*, the welcome easing of tension, brought about for a brief space of time by America's entry into the War in 1917, was utilized by the Japanese Government in an attempt to clear up misunderstandings with the United States. Ishii's soundings for recognition of some kind of Asiatic Monroe Doctrine failed to bring any definite response from Washington, but formal notes were eventually exchanged, recognizing that 'territorial propinquity creates special relations and, consequently, the Government of the United States recognizes that Japan has special interests in China, particularly in the part to which her possessions are contiguous'. Under strong pressure from the American Senate, this recognition was to be withdrawn six years later—not at the Washington Conference as often supposed, but sixteen months after it had ended; but at the time that this Ishii–Lansing Agreement was signed, the announcement of its conclusion brought a marked improvement in Japanese–American relations.

My arrival in Japan in November 1917 happened to coincide with the jubilation with which the Japanese Press was welcoming the announcement, and a few days later there was a curious little episode bearing closely on the attempts being made to help on the *détente*. While walking through the main shopping centre of Tokyo a day or two after my arrival, I encountered a tall, patriarchal figure with a long white beard, clad incongruously as a sailor and looking for all the world like Coleridge's Ancient Mariner. On enquiry, I was told that it was 'Captain' Hardy, the last survivor of Commodore Perry's expedition to Japan in 1853; because of this, he had been invited to Japan and was to be given the unusual honour of being presented to the Emperor. A week or two later I was able to watch the presentation, as it took place at the annual Imperial Chrysanthemum Garden Party, which I attended as a member of the British Embassy. There had been some apprehension among Japanese officials about this ceremony beforehand, as the old gentleman had a fatherly habit of patting on the shoulder anyone to whom he spoke. They were fearful, therefore, lest he should do so to His Imperial Majesty; but he had been well coached and no such act of *lèse majesté* marred the proceedings. Through the friendly welcome given to this last-surviving link with an event of such historic importance, the clouds overhanging the relations between Japan and the United States seemed to disperse and smiles momentarily replaced frowns. But trouble was in store.

Having been given a royal send-off on his departure from Japan a few days later, Hardy set off back to his homeland. Then came the horrible revelation, splashed in great headlines in the Japanese Press. Instead of being welcomed back like a conquering hero on his return to his native land, 'Captain' Hardy had been met by a posse of police and placed under arrest as a 'wanted' man. The charges against him included sundry instances of defalcation and misrepresentation. Most revealing of all was that his claim to have accompanied the great Commodore Perry to Japan was an entire invention of his own; he had had no connection whatsoever with the expedition and had never before even been to sea. There were red faces in the American Embassy and in the ranks of Japanese officialdom when this news revealed how sadly they had been tricked.

Trivial in itself as this incident was, it was all part and parcel of the attempt to improve relations between Japan and the United States, now that the two countries were aligned together in war against the Central Powers; but, as we have seen, the improvement did not last long. By the time of my return to England three years later, relations were as strained as they had ever been, with Japan staking her claim to supremacy in the Far East, which she regarded as her rightful sphere, and the United States determined to challenge that claim. The inflammatory writings of Japanese Bernhardis such as Sato Kojiro, a retired lieutenant-general, whose *If Japan and America Fight* had become almost a best-seller, were typical of the outlook of the more fiery elements in Japan by then. A further disquietening reflection of anti-American sentiment was the appearance of *Omotokyo*, a neo-Shintō sect, which sprang into prominence in 1920 and was growing rapidly in popularity, especially among retired naval and military officers. Founded on the prophecy of a crazed old woman, who was said to have foretold the wars with China and Russia and also the recently concluded World War, the sect proclaimed that Japan was soon to be at war with the United States and finally with the world. She was to be badly defeated at first, but a huge tidal wave was then to sweep over and submerge a large part of America, whereupon Japan would come into her own and bring the whole world under her sway. The one redeeming feature concerning the rise of this sect was that the Japanese authorities, alarmed at some of its implications, were making strenuous efforts to curb its activities.

One could sympathize with Japan's desire to protect and strengthen her strategic and economic interests in the Far East, and with her resentment at being taken to task by the United States for employing, for similar reasons, methods not unlike America's own 'dollar diplomacy' in Latin and Central America; but, seen in the context of the Open Door and Equal Opportunity, her resort to bribery and corruption for the purpose of ensuring favours from Chinese officials and war lords inevitably laid her open to criticism. Her support of the tyrannical Anfu clique was a case in point. One of its outstanding leaders, known as 'Little' Hsu, I had seen at the 1918 Grand Manœuvres, which he had attended as head of a group of Chinese military observers. A great giant of a man, he was then at the height of his power; but two years later, when visiting Peking, I saw Chinese soldiers with fixed bayonets patrolling the city in search of him and of other Anfu leaders, some of whom had sought refuge in the Legation Quarter. In conspicuous places throughout the city, photographs of these wanted men were posted on walls and hoardings, with notices offering large rewards for information leading to their arrest.

Anti-Japanese agitation had been simmering in China for some years and had come to a head in May the previous year (1919), when Chinese students rioted, in protest against the action of the Powers at the Versailles Peace Conference in agreeing to Japan's retention of the former German rights in Shantung. Although not appreciated at the time, the outburst of national sentiment manifested in these riots marked the start of the Chinese National Revolution, which was to have such fateful consequences, not only for China but for the Far East and the world in general.

From it sprang the unification of China under the leadership of Chiang Kai-shek, the exploitation of the revolution by the Communists and, finally, the transformation of the one-time feeble and effete Chinese Empire into the powerful Communist state that it is today.

The ever-mounting anti-Japanese feeling in the United States, China and Korea, and the increasingly embittered anti-American sentiment in Japan, are well reflected in talks, incidents, and observations recorded in my diary for 1920. An entry on 27th January tells of a Japanese friend expressing his conviction to me, that war with America was inevitable within the next few years and that it would be brought about by America entering into alliance with China. According to him, the Japanese Press, which was becoming increasingly vitriolic, did not in any way exaggerate the intensity of the ill-feeling of the general public towards the United States. Similar sentiments were expressed to me time and again by Japanese officers during my attachment to the Japanese Infantry School at Chiba from January to July that year and, subsequently, in the course of visits I paid to Japanese garrisons in Hokkaido, Vladivostok, Manchuria, Korea and North China. During some of those visits, however, I also heard equally vehement denunciations of Japan by Americans and others, a particularly outspoken attack being made by an American businessman whom I met in Port Arthur in October. Bitterly denouncing the Anglo-Japanese Alliance, which he seemed convinced contained secret clauses aimed at the United States, he talked glibly of 'the coming war between Japan and America' and contended that it would have been a good thing for the Allies if Japan had sided with Germany instead of with Britain, as this would have brought the United States into the War from the start.

While, however, anti-Japanese sentiment was widespread amongst Americans at that time, the more level-headed Americans living in Japan itself adopted a far more objective view, some of them being outspokenly critical of their own government for its pro-Chinese policy and the censorious tones which, it was felt, did more credit to its heart than to its head. Amongst these critics was a much respected member of the American community in Tokyo, whose long residence in Japan as an instructor at one of the Japanese universities had given him a sympathetic understanding of the Japanese point of view. On more than one occasion he stressed to me his conviction that the Chinese had no more love for the United States than they had for Japan, and that Washington should stop being so blatantly partisan. If she did so and adopted a more impartial attitude, the Chinese would soon put an end to deliberate mischief-making and the prospects of peace in the Far East would become far brighter. He was very worried, too, about the way in which the Californian question was being handled, so much so, in fact, that he and other members of the American community in Tokyo sent a petition to the United States Senate in the late summer of 1920 urging tolerance. This was considered essential, since in their view the situation had become so explosive that it only required a minor incident by hot-heads on either side of the Pacific to precipitate war between the two countries.

A similar view was expressed to me by an American Consular friend of mine in Dairen, when I was visiting Manchuria early in October. He considered, however, that the spark which would precipitate the conflagration was more likely to come from China or Eastern Siberia, as a result of American policy, than from the Californian question. By the close of 1920, when I ended my attachment to the Japanese Army and returned to England, the situation was such, therefore, that amongst both Japanese and Americans in Japan the belief was growing that war was virtually inevitable unless some unexpected development occurred to lower the tension. Rather less than a year later, the Washington Conference had been convened and the wished-for development had taken place. Another twenty years were to pass before the peace of the Pacific was finally shattered.

CHAPTER V

The End of an Alliance

I still have in my possession the draft of a letter that I sent to our Military Attaché in Tokyo in December 1919. In it is a detailed account of an informal dinner given to me the previous evening by Colonel Kimura, Commander of the 34th Infantry Regiment, to which I had been attached until a short time previously. Throughout the period of my attachment to his regiment, Colonel Kimura, who was unusually tall for a Japanese, powerfully built, and a noted swordsman, had gone out of his way to make me feel thoroughly at home with himself and his officers; on this occasion he had invited four of them, as well as myself, into the friendly atmosphere of his own house instead of to the more customary local tea-house. From the start, however, it became clear that he had a special purpose in view and that the liberal supply of *sake* was intended to loosen my tongue.

Little by little the conversation turned to the question of the growing tension with the United States and from this to Japan's prospects in the event of war. Then came the cross-examination. What would Britain do if war broke out between the two countries? Would she stand by her Japanese ally, or would blood prove thicker than water and lead her to side with America? Or would she remain neutral and seek to mediate between the two? The inquisition became a bit embarrassing, though I was able to remind the questioners that, as a result of the Japanese Government's voluntary agreement, given subsequent to the revision made when the alliance was renewed in 1911, Britain was relieved from the obligation to go to the help of her ally in the event of a Japanese–American War. This seemed to be news to most of them, though not apparently to a young captain, who had recently joined the regiment after passing through the Staff College. He, I noticed, had done most of the questioning and, unlike the others present, had taken very little *sake*; unlike them too, he had kept remarkably sober in consequence.

The average Japanese has a very poor head for alcohol in any form, and the other officers were already 'well away'. The climax came when one of them, well flushed with rice wine, raised his cup[1] and invited me to join with him in drinking to the downfall of America. It was an awkward moment, as the others, though fuddled with drink, were watching closely to see what my reaction would be. The only way out of the dilemma was to try and laugh it off. All, except the one who had given the toast, seemed satisfied, therefore, when I said I could hardly do that but would gladly propose an alternative, wishing good luck to Japan whatever might happen. The proposer of the original toast, the only one aggressively drunk, showed his disgust by thrusting an orange towards me, pulling it to bits, and chewing it viciously. That, he said, was just what Japan would do to America, tear her to bits and gobble her up.

It was a curious exhibition of individual anger at an otherwise friendly and convivial evening; but the questioning served to indicate the anxiety that Japanese officers were beginning to feel as to what part their British ally would play if Japan and the United States came to blows. A haunting suspicion, that Britain was already leaning towards America and was likely to lean still further in the event of war, was to turn to open resentment when, two years later, the Alliance was abrogated, largely out of deference to American dislike of it.

That Japanese fears on this score were understandable was shown by the British attitude at this time towards plans for the training and reorganization of the Japanese naval and military air services. A French military aviation mission had already arrived in Japan in January 1919 to help bring the Japanese Army Air Service up-to-date; the good work done by it was evidenced by the marked improvement noted in air reconnaissance and aerial combat at the Grand Manœuvres in November that year as compared with the very indifferent showing at the autumn manœuvres in 1918. I had noted, too, in the lectures I attended at the Infantry School in 1920 that, whenever military aviation was discussed, the emphasis was always on French training methods and French tactics; British aviation was seldom mentioned. It seemed clear that, just as German influence had left its mark on the Japanese Army as a result of German training, so now was French influence coming into prominence as a result of French aviation having become the model for Japan's infant Army Air Force. It was only on my last day in Japan as a serving officer that I learned that the

[1] *Sake* is drunk from small cups, not glasses.

Japanese Navy's request to their old British tutor, to send out a British naval air mission, to do for the Navy what the French air mission had done for the Army, had been turned down. The reason? Fear of upsetting the Americans.

This news was broken to me by Wanless O'Gowan, an R.A.F. officer who had been sent to Japan some two years previously for language study and attachment to Japanese units. He had been a bit disgruntled from the time of his arrival, as he had wanted to fly out from England in order to show the Japanese what British airmen could do, but his proposal had been rejected. In view of the lack of facilities for long-distance flights at that time, it was perhaps understandable that the authorities declined to sanction the attempt. If the venture had proved a failure, it might have done more harm than good. On the other hand, if it had succeeded it would certainly have made a good impression on the Japanese and raised British prestige in their eyes. In the event, it was left to two Italian aviators to be the first to complete the journey by air from Europe to Japan. This was in May 1920 and it took them three-and-a-half months.

It was at Shimonoseki, in November 1920, that O'Gowan told me about the rejection of the Japanese request for a British naval air mission. We had just arrived there from Kyūshū, where we had been attending the annual Grand Manœuvres, and I was about to leave for Tsingtao, to study for myself on the spot something of the vexed question of Shantung and its railway. From there I was to go on to visit the Japanese garrisons in Peking and Tientsin before heading south to Hankow and on to Shanghai, where I was to embark for England. Knowing that I would be returning to London, O'Gowan poured out his woes to me and begged me to do what I could to rub in to the powers-that-be the folly of having lost the chance to assist British prestige by taking on the training of the Japanese Army Air Service, and the even greater folly of rejecting the Japanese Navy's request for a British naval air mission. My pleadings on his behalf, however, proved unnecessary. By the time I was appointed to the War Office some four months later, a typically British compromise had been reached. An official British mission to the Japanese Navy might annoy the Americans, but surely no objection could be taken if an unofficial mission was sent and its personnel were given honorary ranks in the Japanese Navy? And so it came about that a mission under the Master of Sempill (later Lord Sempill), composed of a

number of other former flying officers and men, was despatched
to Japan, where they were given Japanese naval ranks and laid the
foundations of a first-class Naval Air Force. How well those
foundations had been laid was to be made painfully clear twenty
years later, when Japanese naval aircraft gained the mastery of the
skies, over Malaya, the Philippines, Burma and Indonesia in rapid
succession, in the opening weeks of the Pacific War.

While fully alive to the desirability of close and friendly relations
with the United States, it surprised and often irritated me, when
working in the Far Eastern section at the War Office after my
return to England, to note how frequently official despatches to
diplomatic representatives abroad contained words to the effect
that 'no action should be taken on this, that, or the other matter
until you have consulted your American opposite number'. It
seemed to indicate that, instead of standing shoulder to shoulder
with the United States as equals, our policy was to stand behind
her like a well-trained dog, eager only to carry out the wishes of
its master. That this attitude was to be found also in unofficial
circles was brought home to me some years later, when I was
serving in Japan as a foreign correspondent. In addition to being
Reuters correspondent in Tokyo, I had been asked by J. L.
Garvin, then editor of *The Observer*, to send him a monthly article
by mail. In one of these articles I had referred to the way in which
the Chinese, at that time, were vilifying and attacking Britain
while, in striking contrast, they were going out of their way to be
friendly to Japan. I added the comment, that this seemed to prove
one of the contentions of those who had opposed the abrogation
of the Anglo-Japanese Alliance; if the Alliance were to be
abrogated, they had said, the absence of this link binding our two
countries together would leave the Chinese free to play us off
against each other and thereby add to the state of unrest in the Far
East. The comment seemed fair enough and quite innocuous, but
back came a personal and most charming letter from Mr Garvin.
Expressing his appreciation of the article, and agreeing that what
I had written was perfectly true, he went on to apologise for not
publishing it. His reason for not doing so was, that the sentiments
expressed in it implied criticism of the United States for persuading Britain to break off the Alliance; they might therefore
upset 'the very lively susceptibilities of the Americans'.[1]

---

[1] Compare Field-Marshal Montgomery's comment on British foreign
policy in recent times: 'We have refrained from taking the right and logical

It seemed amazing and deplorable that a public figure of the calibre and influence of J. L. Garvin should adopt such a stand. 'Lively susceptibilities' though the Americans might have, I found it difficult to believe that such an article could cause offence. In point of fact, when subsequently I showed the letter and the article to an American friend in Tokyo, his prompt reaction was to dub the letter as 'bunk, just bunk'; to this he added that he could not imagine any fair-minded American taking exception to the views expressed in the article, even if he disagreed with them. Slavish attention to American wishes and susceptibilities may, of course, be very satisfying to some Americans and may help to retain their friendship; but it is hardly calculated to gain us their respect, which is just as needful as friendship if mutually helpful co-operation and understanding are to be ensured. It is apt, moreover, to lead us into adopting wrong courses—as undoubtedly it did at times in the Far East during the years between the two wars—and to be positively harmful in the wider field of international affairs.

It was mainly due to American dislike and suspicion of the Anglo-Japanese Alliance that we agreed, at the Washington Conference late in 1921, to abrogate this valuable instrument of policy. Under the terms of the Alliance as revised in 1911, however, the question of renewal or lapse was to be considered in ten years' time. This period of ten years ended some months before the Washington Conference was summoned, and it so happened that my appointment to the Far Eastern section of the War Office started shortly before the opening of the Imperial Conference, in June 1921, to decide what was to be done about it. It was part of my job, therefore, to study the progress of these talks. These showed that the participants held varied views, though the main consensus of opinion was in favour of continuing the Alliance in some form or another, at least for the time being. Contrary, in fact, to a widely held belief, both Australia and New Zealand pressed for continuance of the Alliance on account of its important bearing on national defence; Canada, though opposed to renewal in its existing form, was prepared to support a modified version of the Treaty.

In the meantime, the growing tension in the Far East, together

action for fear of causing offence in Washington' (*The Path to Leadership*, p. 188).

with the costly race in armaments accompanying it, was arousing increasing uneasiness; something had to be done to ease the situation before it exploded into war. As summer drew on, telegrams began to pass between London and Washington. They reflected a kind of psychological probing, carried out in such a way that, if the ideas expressed appealed to the White House, the initiative in proposing a conference would seem to have come from the United States rather than from Britain, 'an invitation for an invitation' as Lord Lee of Fareham so aptly put it some years later. This form of approach proved successful. Washington issued invitations to the countries mainly concerned, and on 11 November the Washington Conference was convened, for the purpose of putting an end to the dangerous race in naval armaments and of considering other ways and means of easing the serious deterioration in the relations between Japan and her American rivals.

Although the Japanese, to the surprise of most observers, were to show a praiseworthy statesmanship at the subsequent talks, it seemed significant that, shortly after the invitations were announced, the Japanese Military Attaché in London, with whom I was in constant touch, remarked to me wryly that, in choosing Armistice Day for the opening of the conference, and marking it with a special ceremony at the graveside of 'An Unknown American Soldier', the Americans clearly had an emotional propaganda purpose in view and would exploit it to the disadvantage of Japan.

Although he had not said so, it was clear that the question of terminating the Anglo-Japanese Alliance would loom large in the subjects under discussion. It fell to my lot, therefore, to draw up a paper beforehand for the guidance of the British military representatives attending the conference, setting forth the principal pros and cons of scrapping the Alliance in so far as military considerations were concerned. The more I studied the question, the less points in favour of ending it could I find. It would, of course, please the Americans, as it would remove the wholly unwarranted fear that the Alliance posed a threat to the United States in the Pacific; to that extent it would assist the cause of Anglo-American friendship, but everything else pointed to the desirability of continuing the Alliance. The Japanese would resent its termination if, as would be clear, it was carried out at their expense in order to ensure American friendship; after twenty years of close and mutually valuable ties, this would certainly be regarded as base ingratitude. It would leave Japan in much the same position as she had been at the time of the Triple Intervention in 1895, isolated and without a firm friend to whom she could look for support in time of need; left friendless, she would almost certainly seek out a new friend in place of Britain and might well turn to either Germany or Russia, which would certainly not be to our advantage. Moreover, so long as the Alliance remained in being, British guidance and counsel could be counted on to exercise a restraining influence on her. Another fact to be borne in mind was that, if the Alliance lapsed, Britain would be put to the expense of taking over defence commitments in the Far East, which had previously been performed for her by her Japanese ally, and it would be necessary to construct a strong naval base at Singapore or some other strategic point in the Pacific. Not only would the heavy cost of such defensive measures affect the pocket of the British taxpayer; it would also be construed in Japan as indicating British mistrust of her intentions. It also seemed likely that, with Britain and Japan no longer bound to assist each other in defending their respective interests and maintaining the peace of the Far East, the Chinese, past-masters in the art of turning one 'foreign barbarian' against another in order to serve their own ends, would be free to play off one against the other, to the detriment of Far Eastern peace and stability.

These were but some of the considerations put forward in favour of retaining the Alliance in some form or another, consistent with the Covenant of the League of Nations; but they proved unavailing in the face of American determination to accept no treaty unless the Alliance was scrapped and to outbuild all others in naval armaments if no treaty was forthcoming. The British Government and the heads of the British delegations at the conference strove hard to find some way round this impenetrable barrier to the maintenance of the Alliance, and Mr Balfour did his utmost to persuade Mr Hughes, the United States Secretary of State, to agree to a modified form of it, with America as a consultant partner in what was termed an 'arrangement' rather than a treaty. The Japanese delegation was consulted on this and submitted a draft of its own; but Mr Hughes firmly rejected all such proposals and substituted what eventually became the innocuous and useless Four-Power Treaty.

On one point only did he yield. He had sought to make it a

Five-Power instrument, with Italy included as the fifth partner; but the British delegation flatly refused to consider the suggestion, as Italy had no possessions in the Far East and the Japanese had made it clear that 'the Treaty would lose much of its sentimental value if it was made the common property of all the Powers, great and small'.[1] Mr Hughes accordingly backed down. While, therefore, the feeling of resentment voiced in Japan over the abrogation of the Alliance was understandable, allegations made later by Viscount Ishii that Britain had cast it aside 'like an old pair of sandals'[2] were based more on emotion than on fact. The unpalatable truth was that, faced by American intransigence, the governments of both countries had been forced reluctantly to agree that their alliance must be ended.

It was at a plenary session on 10 December that the terms of the Four-Power Treaty were read out. It seemed a harmless, somewhat platitudinous document until the concluding words of the text, 'This agreement shall be ratified as soon as possible . . . and thereupon the agreement between Great Britain and Japan . . . shall terminate.'

In his *Broken Thread*, published close on thirty years later, Major-General Piggott, who had been the Japanese expert in the British military delegation at the conference, gives a vivid description of the scene in the Assembly Hall when these terms were read out—the Americans and Chinese (the latter's delegation three times the size of the British Empire delegation) all smiles, the British looking glum and uncomfortable, the Japanese sitting grim and taut, with never a muscle of their faces relaxed. Reading this description, I recalled how 'uncomfortable' I myself had felt when General Itami, the Japanese Military Attaché in London, looked in to see me at the War Office a day or two after the Four-Power Treaty had been announced. I sought to say how sorry I was that our alliance was to end, but that I was sure our two countries would remain as friendly as ever. Noticing my obvious embarrassment, he checked me. 'I understand your feelings and appreciate them,' he said, patting me on my shoulder in a fatherly manner. Then he added, 'But you British will find how mistaken you have been. You think that the Americans will be so pleased that they will cancel your war debts; but they won't, I am sure

[1] Balfour to Sir Charles Eliot, 19 December 1921, quoted by Griswold, p. 310.
[2] Ishii, *Diplomatic Commentaries*, p. 60.

they won't, and you will lose far more than you gain by giving up one friend to win the favour of another.'

The suggestion that we hoped to have our war debts cancelled in return for scrapping the Alliance rather irritated me; but to many Japanese this suspicion seemed confirmed by Lloyd George's attempt, soon after, to persuade the United States to write off the war debts of the Allies in general. The general tenor of Itami's words nevertheless reflected all too well the feeling of resentment, almost amounting to contempt, with which the Japanese reacted to the circumstances in which the Alliance was abrogated. The gloomy forebodings which I had set forth in the paper on the pros and cons of terminating the Alliance were to prove unpleasantly well-founded—Japanese resentment (later turning to anger); a friendless Japan, turning eventually to Germany for friendly support; an impetuous Japan, without a British ally to restrain her, launching into open aggression; heavy expenditure on new defence commitments in the Pacific for Britain; increased bitterness and apprehension in Japan aroused by the building of the Singapore base; the playing off of the former allies against each other by the Chinese. This last result was to be seen in 1927 when, on the despatch of the Shanghai Defence Force to protect British lives and property from Chinese Nationalist excesses, the Japanese declined to co-operate with the British; later, when they themselves became the main target of Chinese attack and vilification, it was the turn of the Japanese to face their troubles alone.

Many years later, no less an authority than Sir Winston Churchill, after stressing that Japan had always 'punctiliously conformed' to the Alliance, was to declare that its annulment had caused 'a profound impression in Japan and was viewed as the spurning of an Asiatic Power by the Western World. Many links were sundered which might afterwards have proved of decisive value to peace.'[1] This was, of course, but one aspect of the situation arising from the abrogation of the Alliance; the fundamental fact was, that a great vacuum had been created in the realm of international relations in the Far East and, in the words of Admiral-of-the-Fleet Lord Chatfield, 'We had turned a proved friend ... into a potential and powerful foe.'[2] Nor was this a purely British view. In his book, *With Japan's Leaders*, Frederick

[1] *The Second World War*, vol. I, p. 11.
[2] *It Might Happen Again*, p. 88.

Moore, an American with many years' experience as an adviser to the Japanese Government, bluntly stated his belief that his country had made a serious blunder in pressing Britain to terminate the Alliance. This, he said, was 'the beginning of the nation's turn toward independent action in preparation for possible war. It opened the way psychologically for co-operation with Germany when that nation recovered military might. It weakened the influence of the Japanese naval men ... and gave the Army men the dominant prestige.'[1]

At the close of 1921 when the decision to end the Alliance was announced, Germany's recovery of her military might was still some way off; but diplomatic relations between Japan and Germany had already been restored. Dr Solf, Germany's first postwar ambassador to Japan, had arrived in Tokyo some months before I left, and a fellow passenger of mine on the ship taking me back to England was Mr Hioki who, as Japanese Minister in Peking in 1915, had presented the Twenty-One Demands to China; he was now on his way to Berlin as Japan's first post-war ambassador to Germany. A few months later, as part of my duties at the War Office, I acted as 'bear-leader' to a party of Japanese officers visiting military establishments in England; amongst them was Lieutenant-Colonel Kashii, the newly-appointed Japanese Military Attaché to Germany.[2] The close links, which were to bind the two countries together in war-time alliance two decades later, were therefore already being forged by the time the Anglo-Japanese Alliance ended.

As bearing on these future developments, and as showing that there were some British as well as Americans opposed to our alliance with Japan, an entry in my diary on 19 November 1920 is perhaps pertinent. Referring to the anti-Japanese sentiments expressed by some local British residents at a dinner party I had attended that evening in Tsingato, I went on to say that, as a result of their dislike of the Japanese,

Most of the British out here are dead against the renewal of our alliance with Japan and are doing their best to prevent it, not realizing that by doing so they are playing into Germany's hands; for if the alliance ends,

---

[1] *With Japan's Leaders*, p. 40.
[2] In 1936 Lieutenant-General Kashii, as he was by then, was to figure as commander of the Martial Law Headquarters set up in Tokyo for the suppression of the Army mutiny.

it is a thousand to one that Germany will step in and form a Japanese-German Alliance, and may eventually get Russia to join in also. If that happens, there is going to be hell for the World within a few years.

Russia, of course, did not join in—except indirectly through her 1939-41 pact with Nazi Germany and her Neutrality Pact with Japan—and it was rather more than 'a few years' before Japan joined forces with Germany; but the fear of a future Japanese-German Alliance coming into being, if our own alliance with Japan ended, was to prove all too well founded.

Serious, however, though the developments stemming from the abrogation of the Alliance were to be, the closing months of the Alliance witnessed an event bearing closely on Anglo-Japanese relations and of considerable significance in itself. In May 1921, the Crown Prince Hirohito of Japan paid a formal visit to Britain, significant as being the first time in Japanese history that an heir to the Japanese throne had left his own country. It was a break with tradition which caused serious misgivings at the time among conservative-minded Japanese, who had already been upset by another recent break with precedent, the choice of a bride for the young prince from a family outside one of those from which, for centuries past, the consorts of heirs to the throne had been chosen. Attempts had been made, in both instances, to prevent these plans from materializing, but without success. The Prince's visit to London, and to some of the European capitals as well, took place, and after his return to Japan he married the Princess chosen for him. The visits were of relatively short duration, but his visit to England in particular left a lasting impression on his mind. His regret at the passing of the Alliance failed to erase the memory of the kindness he had received from the British Royal Family; and when, many years later, the war clouds gathered threateningly over the Pacific, he did his utmost, within the limited scope of a constitutional monarch as he then was, to prevent the outbreak of war with his former British ally and with the United States. Documents published since the close of that war have shown his genuine distress at having been forced to acquiesce in the decision to go to war and how, from the outset of hostilities, he showed his sympathy towards the little group of civilian advisers working surreptitiously for a speedy end to the conflict by means of a negotiated peace.

The friendly atmosphere engendered by the Crown Prince's

visit was to be dispersed a few months later by the abrogation of the Alliance. In his book already mentioned, Frederick Moore, himself an American, emphasized how utterly baseless was the American contention that it was a menace to the United States. The idea that it might lead Britain to join forces with Japan in a war with America he termed 'Preposterous', But, he went on to say, 'the American Navy and the shipbuilders wanted the expansion, begun during the War, to continue, and the Alliance was made to appear inimical to American interests.'

Bearing in mind the fact that, in the words of Lord Vansittart, '[We] abrogated the Anglo-Japanese Alliance to please America—who thereby incurred some responsibility',[1] there is something slightly ironical in the position today—the United States in virtual alliance with Japan and, through the ANZUS Pact, with Australia and New Zealand as well. In neither of these treaties has Britain any part, though Japan is our former ally and Australia and New Zealand stalwart members of our former Empire.

[1] *Roots of the Trouble*, p. 26.

CHAPTER VI

Political and Physical Earthquakes

We are apt to think how greatly Japanese mentality differs from our own; but, of course, the converse is equally true. How difficult it is, at times, for foreigners to appreciate the British line of reasoning was reflected in a remark made to me by General Itami, the Japanese Military Attaché in London, when, on being invalided out of the Army, I was about to leave the War Office and return to Japan in a civilian capacity. In the course of my duties in the Far Eastern Section, I had come to know him well; on the day I was to sail, he came to see me off on the boat train. As he bade farewell, he looked at me quizzically and said, 'Your British Army is very strange. They send you to Japan at great expense to study our language and our military system; they train you up in the Far Eastern Section of your Military Intelligence Directorate; and then they let you go back to Japan as a civilian.' Then, with a chuckle, he added, 'Very funny, I think! Very funny!'

The implication was clear. To him it seemed inconceivable that an officer, who had specialized in this way, should be placed on the retired list and allowed to return to Japan as a civilian, unless there was some hidden motive behind it. His civil employment must surely be 'cover' for more nefarious activities. In fairness to General Itami, however, it should be added that, whatever his suspicions may have been, he remained most friendly, even after his own return to Japan some months later to take up the appointment of Director of Military Intelligence in the Japanese General Staff Office. That friendship continued throughout the remaining twelve years that I spent in Japan, and on at least two occasions proved most useful; once was when my wife was being constantly pestered by an officious little policeman about her own doings and mine, and once, after the destruction of our house in the Great Earthquake of 1923, when we were refugees. On the former occasion, he and his wife were lunching with us, so I referred jokingly to the policeman's visits and to his interest in our welfare. He listened and then, with a twinkle in his eye, said, 'If he comes again, tell him you have already answered all his questions and that he should come to me if he wants any more information about you.' The policeman came once more, my wife repeated what Itami had said, and the little man departed with a slightly worried look. He never came back, and so far as I know he never went to see the General. The very fact of learning that the Director of Military Intelligence was a personal friend of ours had been enough to scare him.

The other occasion was a year or so later, while resting for a few days in Shizuoka after escaping from the area devastated by the earthquake. A *rikisha* passed by and in it, to my surprise, was General Itami. On seeing me, he got out and shook me warmly by the hand. Owing to the complete disruption of communications in the Tokyo area, he said, he had been to Osaka to set up a temporary office there and was now returning to Tokyo. Was there, he asked, anything he could do for me there? Half jokingly I told him that the only thing I wanted was to find out if the mother of our baby *amah* was still alive, as she, the *amah*, was very worried about her. When Itami asked for her address and promised to make enquiries, I imagined that this was merely a polite gesture on his part and that I should hear no more; but I was wrong. A few days later, a smiling *amah* told us she had just had a letter from her mother; the old lady had escaped unhurt and a soldier, who had been round to look for her, had brought a message to say that her daughter was safe and well in Shizuoka.

For a man in General Itami's position, immersed in all the heavy extra duties arising from the destruction wrought by the earthquake, it was a wonderfully kind act to send someone to seek out the mother of a foreigner's servant-maid. Some sixteen or seventeen years later, Itami, like so many other retired officers during the feverish period when Japan was being denounced as an aggressor, was to figure prominently amongst those inveighing against 'perfidious Albion'. By then, the initial resentment caused by the abrogation of the Alliance had turned to anger at what Itami, and so many of his countrymen, regarded as the betrayal of Japan at Geneva by her former ally. Remembering the fundamental friendliness and kindliness of their actions in earlier days it was a sad reversal but, in the existing circumstances, perhaps intelligible.

One further reference to General Itami must be made, as it serves to illustrate a change that had taken place during the year-

and-a-half that I had been away from Japan. At the close of 1920 when I left, Army officers were regarded almost with awe and certainly with respect. By the time I returned there in the Spring of 1922, all this had altered. Partly as a result of the reaction which had set in in all countries after the War, and partly due to the feeling of disillusionment which had followed the Washington Conference, a wave of anti-militarism had swept Japan. No longer was there the deference which had formerly been shown to military officers; on the contrary, instead of the Army officer being regarded as a desirable husband for the daughter of aspiring parents, the marriage market was, for the time being, virtually closed to him. So unpopular had uniform become that officers, when off-duty, had taken to wearing mufti, a practice hardly known before, except when relaxing in their own homes or in the informal atmosphere of convivial high jinks. The truth of this was brought home to me when, some months after my return to Japan, General Itami also returned. Happening to be in Kobe on the day of his arrival there, I went down to the docks to meet him. Perhaps noticing my surprise at seeing him coming ashore in plain clothes, he remarked rather diffidently that he had been advised by friends of his to wear civilian attire, as the wearing of uniform had become so unpopular in Japan.

Along with anti-militarism went social and industrial unrest, the spread of subversive doctrines, a partial break-down in the traditional family life, and changes in moral outlook. Some of these developments had started even before my return to England at the end of 1920 and were largely attributable to the tremendous impetus given to trade and industry by the War, to the slump and general depression that followed, and to the Russian revolution. Though taking little part in the actual fighting, Japan had become an all-important producer and supplier of war material and munitions for her allies and of goods for the markets which normally her allies supplied. The ending of hostilities, however, had put a stop to Japan's war-time prosperity, and retrenchment had taken its place, with drastic cuts in staff and large-scale unemployment. Strikes became less frequent than they had been during the war years, when the workers had the upper hand and could demand higher wages with impunity, but increasing bitterness was a marked feature of the strikes that occurred subsequently; strikers were soon demanding a syndicalist management of the workshops. By 1922, however, Communism was already beginning to take the place of syndicalism, and July that year saw the formal inauguration of the Japanese Communist Party. It was soon suppressed and its leaders placed under lock and key, but from then onwards it was constantly being re-formed and then broken up again. Until legalized by General MacArthur after Japan's defeat in 1945, it never numbered much more than a thousand active members, but its sympathizers amongst students, university professors, and 'unemployed intellectuals' were far more numerous; they were to be a constant thorn in the flesh of the Japanese authorities, who became obsessed with fear of the 'dangerous thoughts' spread by them.

With social and industrial unrest on the increase, and with left-wing socialism regarded as the very antithesis of loyalty to the throne and country, it was perhaps only to be expected that the immediate post-war years were marked also by the appearance of numerous reactionary societies as a counter to these pernicious activities. Unlike the Black Dragon Society and other such super-patriotic bodies, which were mainly concerned with international affairs, however, these reactionary elements were anti-socialist and anti-communist rather than anti-foreign and were more concerned with internal than with external happenings; but strong-arm methods and intimidation were common to both, and by the 1930s the two were to become virtually indistinguishable in their ultra-nationalist outbursts and excesses.

While noting these and other symptoms of the social and political *malaise* spreading over Japan, the change that struck one most, on returning after eighteen months' absence, was the subsidence of anti-American sentiment and a general lowering of tension in the field of foreign affairs. For this, of course, the agreements reached at the Washington Conference were primarily responsible. Against the underlying feeling of resentment over the abrogation of the Anglo-Japanese Alliance was to be set a sense of the increased security given to Japan's position in the Far East by the naval treaties and by the agreement forbidding the construction of new fortifications and bases in specified areas of the Western Pacific. Acceptance of the 5–5–3 ratio in capital ships relegated her to a position of inferiority to both Britain and America in the matter of naval strength—an inferiority which was to cause anxiety and bitterness later—but it brought badly-needed relief to the Japanese exchequer and was more than offset by the non-fortification agreement. This, in effect, left Japan supreme in her own and adjacent waters and removed the threat of new naval and air bases within striking distance of her shores.

Having ensured the removal of this threat, Japan had shown her wisdom at Washington by declaring her readiness to eliminate other causes of friction between herself and the United States and, in effect, to turn from an aggressive to a pacific policy. With this end in view, she had agreed to liquidate the vexed questions of Shantung and Eastern Siberia by withdrawing her forces from both these areas. These pledges were quickly fulfilled, as also was her promise to recall her troops from Northern Manchuria and Saghalien, and her garrison from Hankow. Within a year, too, she had started voluntarily to reduce the size of her army and, in 1925, carried out an even more drastic cut by scrapping four of her twenty-one divisions. These cuts, though helpful at the time in showing her good intentions, bore hardly on the large number of officers deprived of their careers; the resentment of those affected was to be a contributory cause of the outburst which led to the flouting of civilian authority and of world opinion in the 1930s.

A feeling of dissatisfaction at being placed prematurely on the retired list through no fault of their own was understandable, but from it was bred a decline in the high standard of discipline on which the Army had rightly prided itself hitherto. The deterioration, it is true, had started during the Siberian Intervention, when circumstances lent themselves not only to political intrigue, which some of the younger officers quickly mastered, but also to long periods of relative idleness, with inevitable demoralizing effects on officers and men alike. Following this, a month or two before my return to Japan, had come the death of the stern old 'father of the Japanese Army', Marshal Prince Yamagata. Conservative-minded and mentally still living in the feudal times during which he had first made a name for himself, he had nevertheless been a strict disciplinarian and had ensured that the Army lived up to the great Emperor Meiji's injunction to the armed forces, 'Neither be led astray by prevailing opinions nor meddle with politics'. With his firm hand removed, rival factions among the higher ranks began to replace the virtual one-man domination and Chōshū clan monopoly of his days, junior officers recruited from a lower strata of society and lacking the old *samurai* traditions increased in numbers, and the former prohibition against political meddling gradually faded away.

During my attachment to the Japanese Army, I had often been told that the failure to adopt more up-to-date equipment and methods of training was largely due to Yamagata, who had been utterly opposed to what he regarded as new-fangled ideas, out of keeping with *Yamato Damashii*, the warrior spirit of Old Japan. Once he was dead, I had been assured, all would be changed. The assertion proved correct, though some of the changes were in directions hardly anticipated and were to lead Japan into a pile of trouble.

This dissertation on some of the reasons for the subsequent deterioration in Army discipline, however, has led away from the Washington Conference and its outcome. One more result of this meeting calls for mention on account of the situation that sprang from it. The question of China, as has been seen, had loomed large in the deliberations at the American capital. Japan had shown herself unexpectedly conciliatory on this as on other matters. Not only had she agreed to restore most of the interests she had acquired in Shantung and to withdraw her troops from there and from Northern Manchuria; she had also signed the Nine-Power Pact. This was, in effect, a self-denying ordinance, binding its signatories to refrain from any action undermining the independence and territorial integrity of China. The preservation of the integrity of China had been a principle to which lip service had been paid ever since the Triple Intervention of 1895; but, as Lord Grey remarked so astutely in his *Twenty-Five Years*, it was to be 'a principle sacred against Japan, but not against European Powers, who had proclaimed it.'[1] The self-denying clause in the Nine-Power Pact, on the other hand, was applicable to all its signatories, but it involved a far greater sacrifice for Japan than for any of the others; geographical propinquity, combined with consequent strategic and economic considerations, rendered her interests in China far more vital to Japan than the interests of the other signatories were to them. But apart from this, the whole conception of the 'independence and territorial integrity of China' was based on a myth, as China's sovereign rights were still, at that time, considerably curtailed, and parts of her territory were still in foreign hands. The 'inequality of sacrifice' entailed by the Nine-Power Pact, and the legal fiction concerning the independence and territorial integrity of China, were to be the cause of growing dissatisfaction in Japan later; but for the time being she was to abide loyally by the terms

[1] Vol. I, p. 73.

of the agreement and to substitute a policy of friendship towards her Chinese neighbour for her former policy of threats and aggression.

Although friendship towards China as a definite policy did not take shape until after June 1924, when the liberal-minded Baron Shidehara became Foreign Minister for the first time, the improvement in Sino-Japanese relations was already noticeable by the time of my return to Japan in 1922. Taken in conjunction with the other changes noted, this was certainly a turn for the better in so far as Japan's relations with the outside world were concerned, even if the internal situation showed disquieting signs. This internal situation was to be seriously affected by the devastating earthquake of September 1923, but before turning to this disaster and its after-effects, a further event in the realm of Anglo-Japanese relations calls for mention.

Deeply wounded by the abrogation of the Alliance though Japanese feelings had been, the arrival of the Prince of Wales on a visit to Japan in the early Spring of 1922 was welcomed with enthusiasm and helped to soften the blow.[1] It was perhaps unfortunate that he came straight from an exhausting tour of India and that, tired of formality, he tended at times to act in somewhat unorthodox ways. These would have been fully appreciated in a Western democracy, but served to raise eyebrows in a country with set ideas on what constituted princely decorum. The visit was nevertheless timely and helped to smooth the way for Sir Charles Eliot, the greatly respected British Ambassador, who had wished to resign when his urgent pleas for continuing the Alliance had been disregarded. Having been persuaded to continue at his post in order to build up relations anew in the changed circumstances with which he was now faced, Sir Charles had a difficult task, but he accomplished it with signal success. Rightly did *The Times*, in its obituary notice on his death in 1931, describe it as 'a solid if not outwardly brilliant achievement'.[2] To the credit of the Japanese themselves, be it said, it was not until the late 1930s that their resentment over the ending of the Alliance was shown in any way in their personal relations with British friends.

It was, therefore, in an atmosphere of peace and returning

---

[1] By a curious quirk of fortune, his suite included a young naval lieutenant who, twenty years later, was to play a vital part in the operations leading to Japan's defeat. His name was Lord Louis Mountbatten.

[2] *The Times* of 17 March 1931.

prosperity that Japan was struck, on 1 September 1923, by the most disastrous earthquake in her long history of seismic convulsions. In a matter of seconds, the flourishing port city of Yokohama and large parts of Tokyo and of the naval base of Yokosuka had been reduced to ruins; at Kamakura, the mediaeval capital of Japan, a tidal wave had swept in, adding to the damage wrought by the earthquake; numerous lesser towns and villages had also suffered severely and a vast area had been devastated. Minutes later, fires broke out and, whipped by a gale which had blown up suddenly, spread rapidly into roaring furnaces in which tens of thousands of men, women and children, trapped under the ruins, were burned to death. Over 100,000 people perished in Tokyo alone, roughly the same number as those killed in Hiroshima by the atom bomb twenty-two years later.

My own experience on the occasion of the earthquake disaster can best be summed up by saying that, like the winter of 1914–15 in the trenches out in France and Flanders, it was one that I was glad to have had, but have no desire to repeat. Buried with my wife and infant son under the ruins of our house in the Hakone hills, where I had joined them for a long week-end, we bivouacked out in the open for the next two days with other survivors from the lake-side village, in which most of them had been spending the hot summer months. Fresh quakes of varying intensity continued at frequent intervals, making the ground on which we lay at night quiver like a jelly.[1] With all communications severed, we imagined that the quake was purely local and expected that rescue parties would soon arrive to help us. The men in the party took turn about in keeping watch throughout the night, in case fresh disasters were in store for us. As I took my turn with a friend on the first night, we saw a strange glare in the sky over the hills; we wondered what it could be. It was not until the following morning, when a steady flow of refugees began straggling through the village, that we learned the cause. It was the reflection of the fires raging through Yokohama eighty miles or so away. There, to add to the scenes of horror, streams of blazing oil from the nearby storage tanks had poured through the stricken city and spread over the harbour waters. These were soon a vast sheet of flame, setting boats on fire and bringing death to the luckless seamen

[1] Official reports issued later showed that 222 separate shocks had been registered between noon and midnight on 1 September, and 323 the following day. Hundreds more were recorded in the course of the next month or two.

struggling to escape. It was clear that the quake was by no means local, but there was still no news of Tokyo.

After two nights on the hillside, we set off for Mishima, some fourteen miles over the hills, some on foot, some in *kago* (a kind of sedan chair borne by coolies) and some on horse-back—men, women, and children, a motley crowd in all stages of dress and undress. All trace of the road over the pass had been obliterated in places by landslides; but rather surprisingly, on reaching Mishima, drenched to the skin by the rain which had deluged down on us for most of the way, we found the town largely intact. Cars were waiting to take us on to Numazu, the nearest railhead, and there, after being given food, drink, and a change of clothing, we rested until a train was available. Apart from the fact that the line eastward to Yokohama and Tokyo had been severely damaged and was no longer usable, Tokyo, we now learned, had suffered the same fate as Yokohama; but the line westward was still possible, so westward we went.

As indicating the attitude of the Japanese towards foreigners on this occasion, two incidents connected with that journey deserve mention. Refugees were pouring into Numazu in thousands and large numbers of them were crowding around the station, hoping to get on a train. In most countries in similar circumstances, foreigners would have had to take their chance along with the native refugees; but the station master, on learning that there was a party of foreigners, insisted that every one of us be given a seat on the train before any of his fellow Japanese were allowed on. The other incident concerned myself and family. Most of the other members of our party were going on to Kobe, but I decided to go only as far as Shizuoka where, during my army days, I had been attached to the 34th Infantry Regiment and therefore had friends. There we arrived late that evening, clad in the Japanese cotton *kimono* we had received in place of our own soaked clothes earlier in the day. With my wife and small son and our baby *amah*, we must have presented a curious spectacle. As we had neither money nor railway tickets and no identity papers of any kind, the ticket collector was hesitant to let us through the barrier. A crowd of curious spectators began to collect and the argument seemed likely to continue interminably; but suddenly from the back strode a figure, who demanded that we should be let through. A former sergeant in the regiment to which I had been attached, he had recognized me and was able to explain to the ticket collector who I was. Smiles and apologies followed, and everything possible was done to smooth our way during the ten or twelve days we remained in Shizuoka before going on to Kobe. From there I was to take ship to Yokohama, as all road and rail communication with it and Tokyo had been destroyed.

I still have a detailed day-to-day account of the weeks that followed, but as they have little direct bearing on the main subject of these pages, a few brief remarks on the appalling extent of the disaster must suffice. From Kobe I was able to obtain a passage on a Dutch oil tanker to Yokohama and an incredible picture it presented. The recently thriving port city had ceased to exist. In its place was a fantastic expanse of rubble and burnt-up debris, with here and there a blackened wall or the skeleton framework of a building still standing; all else had been levelled to the ground. What remained was a veritable city of the dead, with numberless decaying corpses under the great piles of rubble and fallen masonry, giving off a stench in the hot humid air that was indescribable. The Bluff, the residential quarter on the high ground beyond the business section of the city, was little better off; the houses and hotels, formerly gracing its ridges and hillsides, had been swept away by landslides, leaving bare slopes and destruction in their trail.

With neither shelter nor accommodation of any kind on shore, the next few days were spent salvaging what little could be salvaged and sleeping at night on an oil hulk lying out in the harbour. The hulk had been condemned as unfit for human habitation, but it did at least provide quarters of sorts for the half-dozen or so of us on board. Viewing the scene of desolation with one's own eyes and listening to the accounts of their experiences retailed by others, the magnitude and horror of the disaster, especially in the crowded towns and cities, was vividly brought home to one; and amongst those killed were many old friends and acquaintances. The difference between Yokohama and Tokyo, however, was striking. The former had been virtually wiped off the map; large sections of the latter had suffered much the same fate and presented a terrible scene of ruin and desolation, but other parts of the capital city had escaped relatively lightly. On going to Tokyo a few days later—by the first train to get through from Yokohama since the quake three weeks before—it was surprising to find everyone properly dressed and, amidst all the devastation, carrying out the motto, 'Business as usual'. A veritable city of hastily-constructed wooden shacks had sprung up for sheltering the homeless, and great sections of Tokyo lay desolate and in ruins; but office staffs were working unconcernedly in their accustomed six- and eight-storied ferro-concrete office buildings in the main commercial centre. Many of these structures had gaping holes in their sides where outer walls had collapsed outwards into the streets, leaving, at some levels, little but skeleton steel framework for their support; but work went on. It was this return to work in Tokyo that made the contrast with Yokohama so striking, for there the few people to be seen were engaged almost wholly in salvage work and were dressed accordingly. Office work was out of the question; not one building remained even partly usable.

That Tokyo had not suffered more severely was largely due to the Army. The military authorities had acted promptly in calling out the troops to assist in restoring and maintaining law and order, helping to check the conflagrations which were spreading in all directions and engulfing large sections of the city, and organizing rescue and relief work. In Yokohama, where there had been no troops available, the police and fire brigades, crippled by their own heavy losses, had been unable to cope with the situation. Conditions had been rendered still more chaotic when convicts, released from a nearby prison, had started an orgy of looting and violence. Joined, as they had been, by some of the rougher elements of the city, their activities gave rise to a rumour that Koreans and socialists had taken advantage of the situation to rise in revolt. The rumour proved disastrous. Bands of vigilantes, formed by the local young men's associations to deal with the looters, lost their heads and set to work clubbing to death anyone whom they thought looked like a Korean or a socialist. The number slain in this way has never been known, but is generally believed to have run into hundreds. It was in these circumstances that the well-known Communist, Osugi Sakae, together with his wife and young nephew, were murdered in prison by a gendarme officer, Captain Amakasu,[1] who considered it was his patriotic

---

[1] In his autobiography, *From Emperor to Citizen*, Pu Yi states that, on his arrival at the port of Yingkow in South Manchuria in November 1931, he was met by this same Captain Amakasu, who was then working for some 'undercover' organization of the Kwantung Army. Amakasu escorted him subsequently, in March 1932, to the newly created capital of Manchoukuo, Changchun, re-named Hsinking.

(*a*) Damage in Odawara

(*b*) Around Tokyo Station

PLATE III.   The Great Earthquake disaster, 1 September 1923

PLATE IV. General Baron Tanaka's caricature drawing of his Vice-Minister, General Yamanashi. The signature, in Japanese characters, on the left is that of General Tanaka, and on the right, of General Yamanashi (see chapter IX)

duty to rid his country of these subversive elements while he had the chance to do so.

Perhaps the best tribute to the invaluable work performed by the Army was conveyed in a remark made to me by a British resident in Tokyo, noted previously for his pronounced anti-military views. Retracting everything he had ever said against the Japanese Army, he expressed unbounded admiration for the magnificent work they had done from the outset in bringing the situation under control. Martial Law had been proclaimed four days later and had, he said, been carried out efficiently and unostentatiously, with the minimum of annoyance and interference. From other foreigners and from Japanese friends came similar tributes to the feeling of security and confidence brought by the Army, and everyone was hoping that the military would remain in control until things had righted themselves. It was certainly a change from the unpopularity into which the Army had fallen since the War and brought to mind Kipling's lines on the British Tommy Atkins —slanged all round in peacetime, but 'It's "saviour of 'is country" when the guns begin to shoot'. Except that the change was due to earthquake rather than to war, the parallel was clear.

Martial Law applied not only to Tokyo but to the whole devastated area, troops being brought in from all parts of the country for the purpose of maintaining order and helping in relief and reconstruction work—clearance of wreckage, repairing roads, railways and bridges, and re-establishing telegraphic and telephonic communications. The Mr Hyde element in the Japanese character had been reflected in the hysterical outbursts against the mythical Korean and socialist rebels, but Dr Jekyll was even more prominent in the fine work done by the armed forces, in the ready help and generosity extended by the Japanese in all walks of life to foreign refugees as well as to their own, and by the many acts of heroism by Japanese servants in saving the lives of foreign children in their charge.

One outcome of the disaster wrought by the earthquake, however, was to have a marked effect on Japan's naval and military planners in the years ahead. By the destruction of the oil storage tanks off Yokohama, and of the even greater stores of oil at the Yokosuka naval base, Japan was left for a time with a serious shortage of this fuel, so vital to her navy and merchant marine, to aviation and motor transport, and to industry. The loss was soon made good by fresh supplies rushed in from abroad; but it brought home to the authorities, and to all thinking Japanese, how dependent their country was on foreign sources of supply and on the good will of those in control of such sources. The serious effect that this dependence would have on Japan's national defence and economic welfare if circumstances should ever arise to prevent access to these sources was made startlingly clear. The policy of building up far larger reserves of oil than ever before was therefore introduced soon after, while Mitsui, Mitsubishi and other powerful Japanese concerns entered the oil business on their own account. Instead of relying solely on the great foreign combines to supply their requirements as hitherto, they set up their own refining plants and storage facilities to deal with the crude oil which they themselves imported from abroad.

Bearing in mind that it was the dilemma posed by the imposition of the Anglo-American-Dutch embargo on oil in July 1941 that finally led Japan to launch the Pacific War five months later, the following passage from a book I had published in 1928 is perhaps pertinent:[1]

Japan, if ever she became engaged in a war of long duration, would require very large oil reserves at the start, unless she could be certain of her ability to obtain fresh supplies all the time from abroad. As Britain and America control all sources of supply open to her at the present time, including even the Djambi and other oil fields in the Dutch East Indies, which are closely connected with British commercial interests, Japan would be faced with a very serious problem if she went to war with either of these two Powers. It is to be hoped that no such war will ever take place; but bearing this fact in mind, it is little wonder that the Japanese Government is doing its best to build up large oil reserves and . . . to ensure that adequate supplies will be forthcoming in the event of a war.

It was to ensure herself of these supplies that the oil-fields of the Dutch East Indies became one of her prime targets.

This, however, is looking ahead. Before concluding the present chapter, it may not be out of place, therefore, to refer briefly to Japan's relations with France in the early 1920s and to their bearing on the abrogation of the Anglo-Japanese Alliance. Although it seemed likely that Japan might eventually turn to either Germany or Russia for the friendship and support on which she had previously depended from Britain, there had been indications for a time that she regarded France as a possible alternative. The

[1] *Some Aspects of Japan and Her Defence Forces*, p. 211.

Army, as we have seen, had turned to France for assistance in building up and training its air force, and in 1922 relations with that country had received a boost from the visit paid to Japan by Marshal Joffre, who received a royal welcome. By the spring of 1924, relations between the two countries had become markedly friendly, and stress was being laid on the fact that both of them were anti-Soviet. When, therefore, M. Merlin, Governor-General of French Indo-China, visited Japan in June 1924 for the purpose of concluding a commercial treaty, rumours began to circulate that the main purpose of his visit was to look into the possibilities of a political agreement, which might even take the form of an alliance. Being in Korea at that time, I was not in a position to check up on these rumours; but some years later I learned that the question of a Franco-Japanese alliance had, in fact, been broached to Joffre during his visit to Japan in 1922. His first reaction was said to have been favourable; but apparently, after discussing the suggestion with French diplomats concerned with Far Eastern affairs, he had been dissuaded from pursuing the matter further. The rumours circulating in 1924 were therefore seemingly based on nothing more concrete than wishful thinking on the part of the Japanese Press. There is little doubt, however, that they reflected the continued feeling of isolation engendered by the termination of the Anglo-Japanese Alliance and the anxiety to find a substitute.

F

CHAPTER VII

Shadows of Coming Events

Accustomed as they are to earthquakes, volcanic eruptions, typhoons, tidal waves and other manifestations of Nature in its ugliest moods, the Japanese, throughout the centuries, have developed a philosophic type of fatalism in the face of disaster and an amazing capacity for rapid recuperation. The speed with which they settled down to the tremendous task of reconstruction after the devastation caused by the Great Earthquake of 1923 served to illustrate this national characteristic. Thirty years later, this same temperament and ability was to be reflected even more strikingly in the rapid recovery made by Japan after the still greater disaster wrought by her defeat in the Pacific War.

The main credit for the way in which the work of reconstruction was speeded along after the 1923 earthquake must go to the Japanese themselves, but valuable assistance in relief work had also been given by a number of foreign nations during the weeks immediately following the disaster. Britain and the United States in particular, having sent warships with food and other necessary supplies, earned the gratitude of the Japanese for the prompt and practical sympathy extended in the hour of need. For a time, therefore, a feeling of genuine friendship replaced the underlying feeling of resentment towards Britain and the former hostility towards America. This happy state of affairs, however, was fated to be of but brief duration, the improved atmosphere being dispersed a few months later by the bitter dispute which arose over the introduction of the new Immigration Law in the American Senate.

Under a 'Gentleman's Agreement' concluded in 1908, Japan had recognised the economic implications of an unlimited flow of Japanese workers into the United States and had, ever since, abided by her promise to restrict the numbers going there. The proposed new law, on the other hand, was so worded as to make it clear that all Japanese immigrants were to be debarred and that this was to be enforced on the grounds of non-assimilation and even of inferiority. Following, as it did, the rejection of her demand for racial equality at the Versailles Conference in 1919, the projected legislation was a further blow to Japanese pride. Already smarting under the implications of racial inferiority reflected in such terms as the 'White Australia' policy and the 'Yellow Peril', this latest insult served to stir up once more the old feelings of bitterness and resentment and was to lead later to her espousal of the Pan-Asiatic movement, with its counter-cry of the 'White Peril'. The Americans, for their part, were stirred to anger when, in April 1924, Mr Hanihara, the Japanese Ambassador in Washington, presented a Note of protest against the proposed law and warned the United States of the 'grave consequences' that would follow if it was put into effect. These words were construed in America as a threat to use force; the Japanese denial that they had any such meaning was ignored. Instead of the warning acting as a deterrent, the unfortunate wording of the Note played, therefore, into the hands of those advocating this piece of legislation, and in May it became law.

The indignation aroused in Japan by the passage of the new law found expression in outbursts of anti-Americanism in the Japanese Press and an unofficial boycott of American goods. More spectacular was the action of a group of self-styled patriots. Striding into the ballroom of the Imperial Hotel in Tokyo, where dancing was in progress, they proceeded to denounce not only the Americans but also those Japanese who were dancing at a time when they should have been in mourning for the national disgrace and humiliation to which their country had been subjected. Having delivered themselves of this oration and cleared the floor of the dancers, they then performed an old *samurai* dance with drawn swords. Fortunately no one was injured in this melodramatic demonstration of outraged sentiment, but a day or two earlier a young Japanese had shown his indignation by committing *harakiri* in the grounds of the American Embassy by way of protest. Albeit posthumously, he had become something of a national hero in consequence.

Although other incidents were to follow, the initial outburst of anti-American sentiment was already showing signs of dying down by the early summer. A remark made to me by a senior government official, whom I met while travelling in Korea late in June, seemed reassuring. Commenting on the situation brought about by the passage of the Immigration Law, he expressed his conviction that there was no real cause for worry. The reason for his optimism, he explained, was that the new government, which had come into power in Japan as a result of the recent general elections, was headed by two professional diplomats, Viscount Kato as Premier and Baron Shidehara as Foreign Minister; they could therefore be depended on to smooth matters over. He was right; for although Kato had fallen into strong disfavour with the United States nine years previously when, as Foreign Minister, he had been held responsible for the presentation of the Twenty-One Demands,[1] he now set to work to restore his good name by giving the fullest possible support to Shidehara's policy of friendship with both China and America. This policy was given formal expression some months later, at the opening of the new Diet session in January 1925, when Kato stressed his determination to extend Japan's co-operation with other nations in the Far East and to strengthen her friendship with China. Shidehara, on the same occasion, urged the need for burying the hatchet in the matter of the American Immigration Law and defined his basic policy as being summed up in the phrase, 'Hands Off China'.

Even at the time of the passing of the Immigration Law, many Americans, especially those in Japan, had been bitterly opposed to it on the grounds that it was needlessly discriminating against Japan and provocatively insulting to her. This was the view held by Cyrus Woods, the American Ambassador in Japan, who resigned in protest. What particularly disgusted the American community in Tokyo was that certain United States Senators were believed to have stirred up the immigration question deliberately, in order to divert public attention from the oil scandals which were, at that time, threatening to expose their own part in them.

The conciliatory policy adopted by Viscount Kato and his Foreign Minister, however, did much to soothe the ruffled feelings on both sides of the Pacific; and although the disturbed conditions in China, resulting from the struggle between the numerous Chinese warlords for power, brought demands from the more extreme elements in Japan for intervention for the protection of Japanese lives and property, Baron Shidehara refused to heed

---

[1] Kato was naturally held responsible for the presentation of the demands, but it is perhaps pertinent to recall an assertion made to me on one occasion in strict confidence. This was to the effect that Kato knew nothing of the secret clauses until they were presented, as outside pressure had been brought to bear on Hioki, the Japanese Minister in Peking, to insert them at the last moment without reference to Tokyo.

them and went ahead with his determination to win Chinese friendship. The patent sincerity with which he pursued this aim was not without its effect on Washington. By the autumn of 1924, moreover, there were disturbing signs in China, tending to make some Americans revise their opinions. Hitherto they had been inclined to idealize the Chinese and to regard them as something in the nature of protégés of their own, deserving sympathy and protection from Japan and other rapacious foreign Powers. In consequence, they had assumed that the Chinese, out of gratitude, would always be pro-American. It came as a shock to them, therefore, to find that no small number of American-trained Chinese were turning from their former pro-American tendencies and becoming pro-Russian.

Communism in China was still, at that time, in its initial stages, but Soviet propaganda was proving effective. By constant harping on its readiness to renounce Russia's special rights and interests, Moscow was rapidly replacing the United States as China's best friend. Twenty-odd years later, when the Chinese Communists were fighting their way to power, an even greater shock was to be administered by the revelation that the Chinese were aligning themselves with the Soviet bloc against their former American friends and protectors. The situation in the Far East has been suffering from the effects of this shock ever since.

It was during the civil wars that raged in China in the early 1920s that there occurred an incident which was to play into the hands of Japanese extremists seven years later. In 1924 the so-called Christian General, Feng Yu-hsiang, invaded the Forbidden City and forced Pu Yi, the former Boy Emperor of China, to flee. Accompanied by his British tutor, Sir Reginald Johnston, Pu Yi sought refuge in the British Legation in Peking, but was unable to obtain asylum there. He then went to the Japanese Legation, where the Japanese Minister, Mr Yoshizawa, readily offered him protection and later had him smuggled out to the safety of the Japanese Concession in Tientsin. Had the British Legation given him the asylum he sought, developments in the Far East might well have taken a different turn when, seven years later, the Japanese seized control of Manchuria. As it was, they were able, on that occasion, to make Pu Yi serve their purpose by exploiting his gratitude to them for having saved his life in 1924 and for having acted as his protector ever since.

How the Japanese policy of friendship with China underwent

such a drastic change, between the time of the young Emperor's flight to their legation in Peking in 1924 and the outbreak of the Manchurian trouble in 1931, will be seen later, Here it is enough to say that, during the greater part of the intervening years, Baron Shidehara strove his utmost to obtain a favourable response from the Chinese to his friendly overtures—at first with success, but later with frustrating failure. In Korea, too, a more liberal and conciliatory policy was adopted. Due largely to its handling by the much-respected Governor-General, Admiral Saito, it served greatly to reduce the tension aroused by the stern measures employed in suppressing the independence movement in 1919 and 1920.

I myself had been transferred to Korea some two months after the 1923 earthquake and had plenty of opportunity for noting conditions, not only in and around Seoul where I was stationed, but also in other parts of the country when travelling around on business. The general impression received was one of peace and good order with, outwardly, little sign of the discontent smouldering beneath the surface. A visit to the wild, isolated north-east frontier districts made it clear, however, where the main centre of trouble lay—not so much in Korea itself as along the Manchurian side of the border. There, in the Chientao area bordering the River Tumen, some 300,000 malcontent Koreans had settled, in the hope of ridding themselves of Japanese rule. Most of them desired only to live in peace, but amongst them were bands of extremists, who raided across the border from time to time or, in conjunction with Manchurian bandits, swept down on local towns and villages. Moreover, whereas the general conditions and the military dispositions on the Korean side of the border[1] had much in common with those on the North-West Frontier of India, it was surprising to find that the Chientao area, on the Manchurian side, though nominally Chinese, was mainly populated by Koreans and administered by Japanese. The most conspicuous features in the two local townships of Chientao and Hunchun were, in fact, the strongly fortified Japanese consulates. Each of these had two or three hundred armed police, mostly ex-soldiers, to guard them and had loop-holed walls and turrets. The fact that both buildings had been destroyed in the anti-Japanese disturbances of 1920, and

[1] A detailed account of the conditions and military dispositions along the Korean border at that time will be found in Chapter VI of my *Some Aspects of Japan and her Defence Forces*.

had had to be reconstructed, seemed to indicate that armed protection was necessary.

At the time that these observations were made, the north-east frontier area was difficult of access. Visitors were not encouraged and police permits were necessary; no crossing of the Tumen, which formed the border, was allowed after dusk. The police seemed obsessed with the fear of infiltration by Russian Bolsheviks and American spies, and it was only after satisfying them that I came under neither of these classifications that I was allowed to proceed. They seemed a bit mystified, however, when, in order to assure them further of my respectability, I gave as reference the names of several personal friends among Army officers in Korea. These happened to include the divisional commander, General Sugano, who had been my brigade commander in Japan in 1919 and, in his younger days, had been attached to the Grenadier Guards in Aldershot.

But apart from having no wish to encourage visits by foreigners to the Tumen border area, inadequate transport facilities served as something of a deterrent. Road and rail communications up the east coast were still under construction or wholly non-existent. To travel from Seoul to the north-east border area therefore involved an eight-hour train journey to Gensan and a day and a night voyage by coastal steamer from there northwards to Seishin, followed by another four or five hours by rail to Kainei, a trim little frontier garrison town. From this railhead a heavily overladen Ford car plied its creaking, jolting way once daily some 45 or 50 miles across wild, desolate, mountainous country to Keigen, in the salient formed by a great bend in the Tumen river. The strategic importance of this salient, thrusting northward into Manchuria and sharing a common frontier for a few miles with Siberia, was obvious.[1] Kainei itself, at the base of this salient, was connected with a light railway running along the border, and at one point this railway was linked by a branch line with a similar light railway on the Manchurian side by means of a wooden trestle bridge. The line on the Manchurian side was a joint Sino-Japanese undertaking, the embryo of the Kainei–Kirin railway,

---

[1] This was the region which Lord Curzon described in the 1890s as the point at which three empires met. By 1924, when I visited it, two of the empires, China and Russia, had become republics, and the third, Korea, had been incorporated into the Japanese Empire. Today all three, if we except the southern half of Korea, are Communist States.

which was to play an important part after the outbreak of the Manchurian trouble seven years later. Of this, more will be said later when we come to consider the serious consequences of this outbreak in 1931. Meanwhile it is necessary to turn to developments of far-reaching significance which had been taking place in China.

The Shidehara policy of friendship with that country was not put seriously to the test until mid-1925, when the wars between rival warlords, which had racked the country for the best part of a decade, were replaced by the revolutionary activities of Communists and Nationalists, temporarily allied under the banner of Chinese Nationalism. Without going into any great detail, the main developments leading to this significant change need to be outlined.

Ever since July 1919, when the Soviet Government had sought to win Chinese recognition of the new régime in Russia by offering to renounce all Russia's special rights and privileges in China, Moscow had been sending a steady stream of Communist agents, money, and propaganda into the country and stirring up trouble for the 'imperialist' Powers. Having tried in vain to obtain Peking's recognition, Moscow then turned its attention to Sun Yat-sen who, after setting up a rival Chinese government in Canton in May 1921, had been defeated a year or so later and had fled to Shanghai. There he was approached by the Soviet representative, Adolphe Joffe, and on 26 January 1923 a joint statement was issued, Russia promising to support Sun's plans for the unification and independence of China and to give up all former Czarist claims in Manchuria. Later that year, Sun agreed to adopt the Soviet system of one-party government and army organization, and by August Michael Borodin, representing the Russian Communist Party, had arrived from Moscow, to serve as Sun's adviser. Other developments followed rapidly. By January 1924 the K.M.T., Sun's Nationalist Party, had agreed to work in close alliance with the Chinese communists, who had formed a party of their own in July 1921. Six months later the Whampoa Military College was established for the purpose of building up and training the new revolutionary army, which was to carry out the Nationalist conquest of China. Appointed as Commandant was a young officer, who had just returned from a year's training in Russia. He was destined to achieve world fame, first by fighting and overthrowing his Communist allies, then by helping to defeat the Japanese, and finally, in 1949, by being overthrown by the new Communist rulers of China; his name was Chiang Kai-shek. With him as instructors were several Russians, headed by the future Marshal Blucher, whose identity was hidden at the time under the pseudonym of Galen.

The full significance of these developments was not generally appreciated at the start, but, with the introduction of Communist methods of intensive propaganda, anti-foreign sentiment spread rapidly. This was impressed on me early in 1925 when two young Englishmen, whose business took them frequently into the more remote up-country parts of China, warned me of serious trouble ahead in the near future. People in Shanghai and other port cities, they complained, tended to disregard such warnings as unnecessarily alarmist, but they were in for a big shock, as anti-foreign feeling in country districts was being whipped up and was increasing in intensity. That this warning was fully merited was to be shown three months later.

My two informants were passengers with me on the ship taking me back to Japan for my third tour of duty there. As the 1923 earthquake had put an end to the particular job in the oil business for which I had been brought out eighteen months before, my employers had very generously offered to transfer me to another post in the organization or, if I preferred it, to give me six months' leave on full pay to enable me to look around for something more to my liking. I accepted the alternative, returned to England and, thanks to the kindly recommendations of Colonel Piggott, our Military Attaché in Tokyo, under whom I had previously served at the War Office, I had been appointed Reuter Correspondent in Japan.

My arrival in Shanghai, where I spent a week in the Reuter office learning the tricks of the trade before continuing on to Japan, coincided with the news of Sun Yat-sen's death in March 1925. Already by then there were reports of trouble between the K.M.T. and their Communist allies, and it was thought that, with Sun's removal from the scene, the alliance might break up. But the reports were premature; another year was to pass before the first open split, and two and a half years were to go by before the final dissolution occurred. Instead of Sun's death bringing about the break-up of the alliance, it served to strengthen it for the time being and to broaden support for the Nationalist cause. The reason for this can be explained briefly. The Leninist cult, created by Lenin's death a year previously, had proved of tremendous value to the Soviet in the cause of world Communism; Borodin, therefore, set about exploiting Sun's death in much the same way, by building him up as the god of Chinese nationalism. With Sun thus deified, it only required the creation of a nationalist martyr or two to set nationalism fully ablaze, under the banner of the new Sun cult. A clash between rioters and police in the International Settlement of Shanghai on 30 May, a bare two and a half months after Sun's death, provided the necessary ingredients. In danger of being overrun by an excited mob of strikers led by student demonstrators, a British police post was forced to open fire.

From the Russian point of view, the incident was doubly fortunate; it produced the required 'martyrs' and it ensured that the British would become the main target of inflamed Chinese nationalism. Britain had already been recognized as the principal bulwark against the spread of world revolution. If Britain could be brought to her knees, the whole imperialist structure in Asia would collapse; world revolution would then follow. So, at least, ran the argument. The Shanghai affair therefore seemed a heaven-sent opportunity and was exploited to the full. National indignation was whipped up; a general strike was declared and an anti-British boycott launched; riots in Shanghai were followed by disorders in Hong Kong and other towns and cities; and on 23 June the Shameen affair in Canton produced a further crop of 'martyrs'. The strike and demonstration which had led to the firing in Shanghai on 30 May had been the outcome of labour troubles in a Japanese cotton mill; the main firing from the foreign side in the Shameen Affair came from a French contingent; but in both instances, in accordance with the policy laid down by Moscow, the whole blame was laid on the British, who were accused of 'massacring peaceful, unarmed demonstrators'. The fact that the demonstrators at Shameen included 2,000 soldiers armed with rifles was ignored. Like the Shanghai incident, the Shameen affair was, in fact, a classic example of the Communist technique of deliberately provoking the use of force for the purpose of producing 'martyrs' as a means of stirring up indignation.

Without going into further details, the point to be noted is that, although the Japanese, as well as other foreigners, suffered in these and subsequent anti-foreign outbursts, the Japanese Government of the day was so determined to carry out its policy of winning Chinese friendship that it refused to take retaliatory measures, either on its own or in co-operation with the British and other foreign countries. The Chinese Nationalists, for their part, were equally determined, under Communist instigation, to single out Britain as the sole villain of the piece. By doing so, they confirmed the views of those who, in 1921, had contended that abrogation of the Anglo-Japanese Alliance would make the situation in the Far East more unstable than ever, as it would leave the Chinese free to play off the two former allies against one another. That there were Japanese who held similar views was shown by a remark made to me, in July 1925, by an American friend engaged in teaching at one of the universities in Tokyo. He had, he said, been struck by the number of his students who had given it as their opinion that the troubles in China would never have arisen if the Alliance had remained in force. Had it still been in existence, they said, the British and Japanese would have shown a common front, which the Chinese would have hesitated to provoke.

The question of Anglo-Japanese co-operation in China was very much to the fore at that time in the Japanese Press and there was much conjecture about talks that had been taking place between Sir Charles Eliot and Baron Shidehara. Sir Charles, however, assured me that only the question of general co-operation among the Powers had been discussed; there was, he said, no foundation to the reports that a renewal of the Alliance in any form was contemplated. The denial of these reports was justified; but during a brief visit to Hong Kong and Shanghai a week or two later, I was much struck by the change in attitude of many of the British residents who, only a few years earlier, had been loudest in their demands for ending the Alliance. To their credit, those to whom I spoke were perfectly frank in admitting that they had been mistaken in wishing for the ending of the Alliance. Too late they had come to realize that their present troubles could have been avoided if Britain and Japan, bound together by alliance, had been in a position to present a united front against the excesses of exuberant Chinese nationalism. On the other hand there were some who, though previously denouncing Japan for being too aggressive and too ready to interfere in Chinese affairs, were now blaming her for failing to send armed assistance for the protection of foreign lives and interests and were urging a renewal of the Alliance. They seemed oblivious to the fact that an attempt to renew it would expose the British to the taunt that they were merely using Japan for their own advantage, throwing her over in 1921 to please the United States and picking her up again now because their own interests in the Far East were threatened.

While Moscow was doing its best to aggravate the situation in China and to exploit it for its own purposes, and while Japan was seeking to ensure Chinese friendship for herself, negotiations were in train between the Japanese and Soviet governments for the restoration of diplomatic relations between their two countries. As so often in the past, opinion in Japan was divided, between those who regarded close and friendly relations with Britain and the United States as the best insurance against the machinations of her traditional enemy and those who felt that this could best be achieved by securing an entente with Russia. Britain had already recognized the Soviet régime, in 1924, but Washington continued to hold out against according recognition. If Japan could have been assured of Anglo-American friendship and support in case of trouble, she would probably have followed the American line and withheld recognition. The Moscow creed was anathema to her and she feared that the establishment of a Soviet Embassy and consulates in Japan would be equivalent to the entry of a Trojan horse for the spread and encouragement of subversive doctrines. The assurance she required from the Anglo-Saxon world, however, was not forthcoming, and the Japanese dilemma was aptly reflected in the remark of a Japanese friend. Educated in England and notably pro-British in sentiment, he had been genuinely distressed when the Alliance ended; he was now deeply concerned at the thought of his country recognizing the Soviet régime. Speaking more in sorrow than in anger, he declared, 'It is you and your country who are forcing us into the arms of Russia. We want to be your friends, but you won't let us be.' This was Count Soyeshima, whom I had known well since my army days in Japan and who, in June 1925, told me he was to lose his seat in the Upper House on account of his outspoken criticism of Soviet Russia. By then, Japanese recognition had been given to the new régime in Russia by the ratification of a Convention signed in Peking in January that year, and the restoration of diplomatic relations had been marked by the arrival of the newly appointed Soviet Ambassador in Tokyo in April. This was three weeks after the withdrawal of the last Japanese troops from Northern Saghalien, which had been occupied by Japan ever since 1920, in retaliation for the Nikolaevsk massacre. With their withdrawal, the final trace of the Siberian Intervention had been liquidated.

The restoration of normal relations with her powerful neighbour served to underline the paramount importance that Japan attached to having a friendly Russia on her flank, now that the safeguard of the Anglo-Japanese Alliance had been withdrawn. From talks with Japanese journalists and others, however, it was clear that the move was regarded with mixed feelings, as a necessary evil rather than as a matter for rejoicing. On the other hand, it was noticeable that the Japanese Press, though fully alive to the implications of the anti-British disturbances which followed in China soon after, was careful to avoid any criticism of the Soviet for its part in those troubles. On asking the reason for this, I learned that it was in order to avoid incurring Moscow's disfavour; the leading papers were anxious to send correspondents of their own to the Russian capital, but feared they would be refused permission to do so if they criticized Soviet actions in China.

China and Manchuria, however, were, as always, two very different propositions in Japanese eyes. It was significant, therefore, that, in the treaty restoring Russo-Japanese relations, Moscow had been persuaded to agree that 'the Treaty of 5 September, 1905 shall remain in force'. This was the Treaty of Portsmouth, under which Russia, after her defeat by the Japanese, had restored Port Arthur and the Liaotung Peninsula to Japan. There was no question, therefore, of letting Moscow try to jockey her out of Manchuria. The Japanese could afford to overlook Russian machinations behind the troubles which broke out in China soon after, but they were not prepared to tolerate similar intrigues and disturbances in Manchuria, where their own rights and interests were so vital.

It was a strange, complex, and in some ways unedifying picture that unfolded itself in the Far East from June 1925 onwards. With Britain as the main object of attack in China, and with Russia bent on stirring up the maximum of trouble, Japan held aloof from armed intervention, even though Japanese lives and property were threatened by the disturbances. In part this aloofness was due to fear lest intervention should result in the imposition of another anti-Japanese boycott, China' s most dangerous weapon against Japan in the past; in part, too, it was due to her determination to avoid disturbing the newly-restored relations of friendship with Russia. On the other hand, she was equally determined to show Russia that she would stand no nonsense in Manchuria. That the Soviet authorities clearly understood this subtle distinction was evidenced by the fact that, in spite of occasional differences of opinion, they were careful to avoid giving any provocation to Japan in Manchuria until after the outbreak of the Manchurian trouble in September 1931.

Being no longer bound by alliance to go to the aid of Britain, the stand adopted by Japan was perfectly reasonable, regrettable though it may have been from the British point of view. What was unedifying in the picture that presented itself as the months went by was the way in which certain American and French elements took advantage of Britain's misfortunes to improve their own positions at her expense. Advantage was taken of the anti-British agitation to increase their own trade and there were instances of unscrupulous propaganda, aimed at prejudicing the Chinese against the British, put out by individual Americans and in American Press reports. The Russians, of course, were delighted. Not only did it provide additional grist to their mill for their anti-British campaign; it served also to create friction among the 'imperialist' Powers.

Equally mischievous Press reports were circulated also about alleged Japanese activities in Manchuria when, late in 1925, a rebellion broke out there against the Manchurian warlord, Marshal Chang Tso-lin. Even so reputable a paper as the *New York Times* carried a report that an army of 100,000 Japanese, disguised as Chinese soldiers, was helping Kuo Sung-lin, the rebel leader. It was a report as devoid of foundation as one that had appeared in another American paper a month or so earlier, alleging that Japan was making preparations for war with the United States. Kuo, it is true, had attended the annual Japanese Grand Manoeuvres in October and had caused some comment by leaving before they ended. This, therefore, was probably the basis on which the *New York Times* report had been concocted, the assumption being that he was hand-in-glove with the Japanese and had been to Japan to secure their help. It so happened that I myself had attended these manoeuvres as a foreign correspondent and had noted his sudden departure. At the time, I thought nothing of it and it was not till later that I came to know the reason. Far from giving him any assistance, however, the Japanese had no wish, at that juncture, to see him overthrow Chang, on whose friendly co-operation they counted for maintaining peace and order in Manchuria and for ensuring that Manchuria remained as a buffer between themselves and Soviet Russia. The falsity of the report was shown soon after by the fact that the Japanese disposed their own forces in Manchuria in such a way as to prevent Kuo from delivering the final blow. Thereby they brought about his defeat.

It was on the occasion of this rebellion that the distinction between Manchuria and metropolitan China in Japanese eyes was particularly well illustrated. The Japanese Press had all along supported the Government's policy of non-intervention in China; but, with the rapid deterioration of the situation in Manchuria resulting from Kuo's rebellion, the more excitable elements in the Press began to clamour for the protection of Japanese lives and interests there by means of military action. The threat to Japanese prestige if the situation was allowed to deteriorate further, and the danger of Soviet Russia taking advantage of the situation to seize control of Manchuria, were among the arguments put forward. One right-wing paper, the *Nihon*, went so far as to demand that Baron Shidehara should atone for his failure to act by committing *harakiri*. So outspoken and inflammatory did this paper and another, the *Chūō*, become that both were suppressed. Shidehara, however, remained unperturbed. Eventually troops were sent to reinforce the permanent garrison there, but the widely-held belief that Japan would use this as an excuse for retaining larger forces in Manchuria indefinitely was shown to be unfounded. The rebellion ended and the reinforcements were promptly withdrawn.

The seeds of the outburst that was to occur six years later, however, were already sown. They were indicated in the friction aroused about this time, between the Foreign Office and the Army General Staff, over the question of Manchuria in general and of railway construction in that area in particular. Matsuoka, President of the South Manchurian Railway, who was to figure so prominently in the years ahead, was full of plans for completing a railway network for strategic and economic purposes. He was backed by General Baron Tanaka, who had recently become President of the *Seiyukai* (the Opposition party), and by the General Staff; but for diplomatic reasons the Foreign Office considered that the time was unfavourable, as it was feared that railway construction on the scale proposed by Matsuoka might lead to misunderstandings abroad.

A great advantage of being an accredited foreign correspondent in Japan was, that one was in the privileged position of being able to learn much of the background to these and other controversies from the principal actors concerned, and from other official and unofficial sources. If these sources could not always be quoted, it was generally permissible to wrap up the information obtained in some innocuous phrase without revealing the actual identity of the informant. The fact that I had made a point of maintaining and extending friendly relations with officers, especially those in the General Staff and the War Office, whom I had known when I was attached to the Japanese Army, was also of considerable value. These informants could not, of course, be quoted at the time, any more than could some of the other sources of information; but they provided inside 'dope' and background which was often invaluable, both as a check on what had been learned elsewhere and as a means of understanding the ins and outs of particular happenings.

If the controversies about railway construction in Manchuria sowed the seed of the serious developments that were to take place six years later, an event that had occurred a few months earlier paved the way for the resentment which was to come to a head in Japan in the 1930s. This was the very belated ratification of the Nine-Power Pact, the 'self-denying ordinance' concerning China, by the French in July 1925. All the other signatories had ratified it long before. In the desire to conciliate China as shown at the Washington Conference, not only had this pact been drawn up; it had been agreed also that, within three months of its ratification by all those concerned, consideration would be given to the question of revising the 'unequal treaties', under which China had been deprived of her tariff autonomy and foreigners had been accorded extraterritorial rights. A Tariff Conference was therefore opened in Peking in October, followed three months later, in January 1926, by the opening of a conference on the question of abolishing extraterritoriality. Of the wrangling to which these discussions gave rise, one feature only needs to be noted. This was the vastly different atmosphere in which they took place as compared with that which had prevailed at the time of the Washington talks in late 1921. The upsurge of Chinese nationalism in the intervening years, and more particularly since May 1925, had completely altered the picture. Chinese assertiveness had replaced China's previous relative docility and complaisance. The serious consequences of the increasingly tough, aggressive attitude adopted by Chinese officialdom were to be seen a few years later, when Chinese nationalist exuberance and Japanese national sentiment came into head-on collision. From this clash stemmed the developments leading to Japan's alignment with Nazi Germany and Fascist Italy and to the Pacific War.

CHAPTER VIII

The Turn of an Imperial Era

Today, in the 1960s, the main potential threat to the peace of the Far East may be said to come from Chinese irredentist proclivities, backed by Chinese unity and strength. In the century following the Opium War of 1842, it was China's weakness, incompetence, and lack of unity that presented the principal danger. Paradoxically, therefore, today's threat is from a China capable of aggression against others; previously it came from a China, whose internal stresses and divisions served to stimulate the rivalry of acquisitive foreign Powers and invited their intervention.

Aware that her weakness tended to encourage interference from without, China had, for many years past, followed a policy based on the principle of 'setting one barbarian against another'; by this means, she sought to divert them from lining up against herself. The termination of the Anglo-Japanese Alliance had, as we have seen, been a boon to her in this respect. For the next twenty years she was able to save herself from the worst consequences of her own follies and incompetence by playing off the two former allies against each other and setting everyone else by the ears with impunity.

That the Chinese were able to act in this way without incurring retribution was largely due to the agreements reached at the Washington Conference. The old policy of using force in China had been eschewed by the Powers represented at that meeting. Instead, from then onwards until the Nationalists came into power in 1928—and, indeed, until the inauguration of the Communist régime twenty-one years later—the policies of the foreign Powers towards China were based on a strong element of make-believe.[1] The 'independence and integrity of China', which the signatories of the Nine-Power Pact were pledged to uphold, was as we have seen, largely a figment of the imagination. Apart from

[1] With Chiang Kai-shek's Formosan régime accorded the status of one of the Big Five in the Security Council while recognition of Communist China, with its population nearing 700,000,000 remains withheld, it is clear that the policy of make-believe is by no means dead.

the curtailment of Chinese sovereignty imposed by the existence of foreign settlements and concessions and by extraterritorial jurisdiction and other restrictions, the Government in Peking, though treated by the Powers as the Central Government of China during the greater part of the 1920s, had little influence and was quite incapable of exercising control outside a limited area of the country. Being recognized as the Central Government, it was expected, however, to accept responsibility for the not infrequent attacks on foreign subjects and foreign property, even though these attacks might have been carried out by its political enemies for the express purpose of getting it into trouble with the foreign Powers concerned. At the same time, a largely false and flowery picture of China was created abroad by the able band of silver-tongued Chinese diplomats and politicians who acted as propagandists in the United States and Europe. Amongst these was Wellington Koo, an orator of great charm and skill. His brilliant oratory and ability to play on the emotions of his listeners had served China well at the Washington Conference and in assuring the abrogation of the Anglo-Japanese Alliance. How, by bringing his persuasive powers to bear with equal effect against Japan at Geneva a decade later, he drove Japan into withdrawing from the League of Nations and thereby paved the way for her subsequent alliance with Germany, will be seen when we come to deal with the events stemming from Japan's incursion into Manchuria in 1931.

Closely as the Chinese situation in the 1920s and 1930s bore on Japan's gradual move towards partnership with Nazi Germany, developments in the Pacific during the years immediately following the abrogation of the Anglo-Japanese Alliance also played their part in turning Japan eventually to look to Germany for the support and friendship she craved.

As foreseen when first the question of terminating the Alliance came up for discussion in 1921, the ending of the Alliance faced Britain with the need for a powerful base in the Pacific. This was required for the maintenance and accommodation of a far larger naval force than had been necessary in the days when she had been able to depend on her Japanese ally to assist in guarding her interests. By agreeing at the Washington Conference that Singapore be excluded from the area in which no further fortification was to be permitted, the Japanese Government had recognized that Britain would require to build a base there, or thereabouts, and that it would present no threat to Japan. To the Japanese people as a whole, however, the subsequent announcement that Singapore was to be converted into a strongly fortified naval base came as a disagreeable shock. This was understandable, but mischief-makers made matters worse by stirring up suspicions and distrust of British motives and by denouncing Britain for treating an old and faithful ally as a potential enemy.

It was not until the early summer of 1923 that plans for the proposed naval base began to assume definite shape. The initial criticism was relatively mild; but before long, ill-advised statements in both Britain and America, suggesting that the base would be of value to the United States as well as to Britain, were giving rise to increasing apprehension in Japan. A sigh of relief went up, therefore, when the Labour Party came into power in Britain in 1924 and promptly ordered the cessation of work on the base; but with the return of the Conservatives to power less than a year later, work on its construction was resumed. The former fears were revived in Japan, and to these fears was added a feeling of resentment, when indiscreet speeches by prominent persons in Britain and America were reported in the Japanese Press. One of these urged the need for Anglo-American co-operation against the alleged aggressive designs of Japan; another, made in the House of Commons in March 1925, applauded the construction of the Singapore Base on the grounds that it would be 'a most friendly act towards the United States', whose position in the Philippines was said to be threatened.

That the real purpose of the base was to serve the requirements of British imperial defence was beside the point. In Japanese eyes, statements such as these tended to confirm their fears that its construction was all part and parcel of a deep-laid Anglo-American plot to check Japan's legitimate aspirations and, in conjunction with the 5–5–3 naval ratio, to keep her in a position of permanent inferiority. While it is true that most Japanese with whom I discussed the matter at the time spoke more in sorrow than in anger, the sentiment among the more excitable elements in the country was reflected in two right-wing papers, the *Yorozu* and the *Chūgai Shōgyō*. Deploring the apparent strengthening of the bond between Britain and the United States, both countries were attacked impartially; full credence, moreover, was given to the unfounded rumour that the two great Anglo-Saxon powers had come to an agreement, permitting the use of the Singapore base to the American Fleet in the event of a Japanese-American war.

While jingoist elements were only too ready to adopt this line, and even to urge that Japan should take steps to prevent Britain from building the base if she failed to stop work on it of her own free will, a remark made by a senior Army officer, whom I happened to meet on a railway journey about this time, seemed pertinent. After strongly criticizing the British decision to go ahead with the construction of the base, he turned to me with a disarming smile and said, 'But, of course, we Japanese would have done the same if we had been in your position.'

It was perhaps unfortunate that the resumption of work on the Singapore Base coincided more or less with the large-scale naval manœuvres in the Pacific held by the Americans during the first half of 1925, and that these manœuvres were launched at a time when the Japanese were still nursing the wounds inflicted by the passage of the American Immigration Law. On the other hand, by the time the manœuvres ended, the growing conflict of interests in Manchuria between Japan and Soviet Russia had begun to divert Japanese attention, from the potential Anglo-American naval threat to the seemingly more immediate military menace from Moscow on the neighbouring mainland. Two years later, the fear of collusion between Britain and the United States had been reduced still further. This was due to the open friction between those two countries at the naval conference held in the summer of 1927 at Geneva. Of this, more will be said later; but here it may be noted that, just as Japan's leaders in the past had so often been divided in opinion as to whether Russia should be courted or thwarted, so now, and for the next fifteen or sixteen years, opinion in Japanese naval and military circles was to become increasingly divided on the question of where lay the main potential threat—landward from Russia or seaward from the two great naval Powers of the West. The dilemma was not to be resolved finally until 1941.

Meantime, while the Army, in contrast to the Navy, was more concerned with the potential threat from landward than with the question of Japan's sea defences, both of the fighting services were beginning to feel the effects of financial stringency. The Navy had accepted readily, though hardly with jubilation, the cuts entailed by the naval agreements reached at Washington; now it was the Army's turn to feel the pinch—not on account of any international agreement, but as a result mainly of the drastic economies necessitated by the disquieting financial situation. The resultant discontent among officers, whose military careers had been cut short through no fault of their own, has already been noted. The feeling of resentment engendered was to have a marked effect on Army discipline and on the political situation in the years ahead.

The Army was not alone in feeling discontented. From talks with British and American friends engaged in teaching in Japanese colleges and universities at the time, it was clear that the student class was being strongly influenced by the flood of Communist and other left-wing literature entering the country and was seething with unrest—with *kiken shisō*, 'dangerous thoughts', as it was called. In reaction to this left-wing radicalism, a Japanese form of fascism was growing up and adding to the general social ferment. Filled with alarm, officialdom acted in the characteristically Japanese way of resorting to liberal reforms and promptly curbing them with reactionary legislation. So, at least, it seemed when, in March 1925, the grant of Manhood Suffrage was made, followed a month later by the imposition of the Peace Preservation Law. This forbade anyone to organize, join or induce others to join any society aimed at altering the national Constitution or repudiating the system of private property. Imprisonment up to ten years was the penalty for infringement of this law which, three years later, was revised and made still more drastic; the crime then became punishable by death.

While these actions and counter-actions served to underline the growth of internal unrest and dissatisfaction with the existing social and political order, an event in the summer of 1926, though arousing but mild and passing interest at the time, heralded a development which was to play an important part later—not in the realm of internal politics but in building up anti-Western sentiment. In July that year a Japanese friend had given me details of a Pan-Asiatic Congress, which was to be held shortly in Nagasaki. He professed to make light of it, but hinted that it might be a portent of things to come and would therefore be worth watching.

The Congress, attended by unofficial delegates from various Asian countries, opened on 1 August, but proved somewhat farcical. Instead of proving Asian unity, it showed considerable disunity. This was made particularly evident when Chinese and

Korean delegates proceeded to denounce Japanese imperialism. It required the mediation of some Indian delegates before the consequent uproar was quietened. It did, however, serve to draw the attention of the Japanese Press to the Pan-Asiatic question, which previously had been regarded as a purely academic aberration of a few enthusiastic malcontents. The Government, for its part, had never regarded the matter seriously and had tended to frown on the whole concept of Pan-Asia. Japan was one of the Great Powers and felt it beneath her dignity to set herself up as the leader of Asian nationalism against her Western friends. It was perhaps but natural, therefore, that western observers tended to dismiss the Congress, and the ideals it represented, as chimerical nonsense. Few, if any, could have foreseen that within a few years the Pan-Asian movement would be taking a real hold on Japan and that, by 1941, it would be fully supported as a matter of Government policy.

While it is true that, prior to the 1930s, few Japanese had much interest in Pan-Asianism, and fewer still were imbued with any idea of a crusade to free their fellow-Asiatics from Western bondage, the belief that India was groaning under British oppression was fairly widespread. How strongly this belief was held in the Japanese Army was brought home to me by an Indian friend, who came out to Japan early in 1926 for language study and attachment to the Japanese Army, the first Indian officer, as distinct from British officers of the Indian Army, ever to be sent to Japan for this purpose. This was Captain (later Colonel) Himatsinji of the Dogras, a nephew of the famous cricketer, Duleepsinji. Being an Indian, his Japanese brother officers opened out to him on the subject of India in a way they would never have done if he had been British, and he was amazed to find what false ideas they held about British rule in India. Their first surprise, he said, came when he reported for duty at the Japanese regiment to which he was to be attached, wearing officer's uniform and sword. How was it, he was asked, that he had a sword when it was well known that no Indian, soldier or civilian, was allowed a weapon of any kind? The British, they had been told, ruled by brute force alone and were so fearful of being overthrown by the luckless victims of their oppression that even Indian soldiers were left unarmed and employed solely on non-combatant duties. It took him some time to disillusion them of these beliefs and to assure them that, not only was there an increasing number of fully trained and commissioned Indian officers but that the troops they commanded were fully armed, equipped, and loyal to the British Raj.

There were, of course, plenty of Japanese Staff officers and others well-informed about the Indian Army, but to the general run of unsophisticated regimental officers, who judged only by their own country's experience in Korea, it seemed almost incredible that subject peoples should be sufficiently trusted to be recruited, armed, and trained for combatant duties. Belief in the harshness of British rule in India, however, was in no small part due to the propagandist activities of a handful of Indian political refugees living in Japan. Prominent amongst these was Rash Bihari Bose, a Bengali terrorist, who had fled from India in 1916 to escape the consequences of his crimes. Having made his way to Japan, he had placed himself under the powerful protection of Toyama Mitsuru, the enigmatic leader of the notoriously anti-Western Black Dragon Society. By marrying the daughter of one of Toyama's followers and being adopted into his family, he had become a Japanese citizen. From then onwards, year in and year out, he had engaged in a campaign of vilification, by means of lectures and writings aimed at stirring up anti-British sentiment and persuading his hearers and readers to believe that Japan had a mission to perform, to lead a crusade to free India from British thraldom. The seed he sowed in those preparatory years was to bear fruit after the upsurge of nationalist sentiment aroused by Western condemnation of Japan in the 1930s.

With social unrest causing increasing concern, with the financial situation showing signs of further deterioration, and with Pan-Asianism starting to cast its shadows before, the year 1926 ended on a note of sorrow mixed with hope. On Christmas Day came the news that the Emperor, whose mental faculties had been impaired by illness for some years past and whose condition had been causing anxiety for the last week, had died. The countrywide outburst of grief was intense and clearly genuine. Social grievances might be widespread, but were directed against landlords, capitalists, and politicians; anti-monarchical sentiment, except among a handful of hard-core Communists, was virtually non-existent. But in Japan, as in Great Britain, the death of one monarch is automatically followed by the accession of another. The King is dead! Long live the King! And so it was that sorrow at the Emperor's death, which marked the close of Taishō, the

Era of Great Righteousness, was mixed with high hopes for his successor's reign. The Crown Prince Hirohito, who had been Prince Regent since November 1921, was proclaimed Emperor, and the new era thus ushered in was designated Shōwa, the Era of Radiant Peace. It was to prove a sad misnomer, but at the time it seemed an auspicious choice, reflecting great hopes for the years ahead.

Britain, Japan's former ally, had good reason for welcoming the new occupant of the throne. His visit to the United Kingdom five years previously had, it is true, been of short duration; but he was known to have enjoyed it greatly and to have been particularly touched by the friendly welcome extended to him by the British Royal Family. The lasting impression that this made on his mother as well as on himself was to be strikingly demonstrated when, seven years after his accession to the Throne, the Empress Dowager made a private appeal to the War Minister to take steps to curb the strong anti-British sentiment, so prevalent by then in the Japanese Army. The curiously conspiratorial proceedings that followed, and the part I myself was called upon to play in them as intermediary between General Araki and the British Ambassador, will be found recorded later in these pages.[1]

The marked effect that his visit to England had made on the young man who succeeded to the Japanese throne in December 1926, was to be reflected not only in this episode of 1933; it was reflected also in his subsequent efforts to prevent his country's alliance with Germany and in his genuine distress when, as a constitutional monarch, he was compelled eventually to accept the advice of his ministers to sanction war with Britain and the United States. Today, with the advantage of hindsight, one can see the almost inevitable chain reaction of the events leading up to those last two developments, but at the advent of the Shōwa era, the Era of Radiant Peace, at the close of 1926, only a born pessimist or a sensation-monger could have foreseen them as anything more than a remote possibility.

So far as the Imperial Family was concerned, not only were the new Emperor and his mother very favourably disposed towards their country's former ally; so, too, was his brother and Heir Presumptive, Prince Chichibu, who had left for England in April 1925 to complete his education at Oxford. Although recalled to Japan on the death of his father after little more than a

[1] See pp. 269–72.

year at his Oxford college, he had quickly adapted himself to the British way of life and, like his elder brother, had become a strong advocate of close and friendly relations with Great Britain.

In contrast to his sons, the dead Emperor had never been outside his own country, but in June 1918, as already mentioned, Prince Arthur of Connaught had headed a mission to Japan to present him with the baton of a British field-marshal. When, therefore, his funeral took place on the night of 7 February 1927, this link with the British Army was marked in a simple but striking manner; Colonel Hill, the British Military Attaché, was the sole foreign representative in the solemn procession which wound its way through the silent, darkened streets of the Japanese capital. To those of us privileged to see it, this procession was a strangely moving sight, with its contrasts of ancient and modern —naval and military detachments, priests clad in the age-old Shinto attire, torch-bearers, bannermen and others. The outstanding feature, however, was the catafalque itself, bearing the Emperor's earthly remains—an immense lacquered hearse drawn by oxen and fitted with vast wooden wheels, specially constructed to emit the traditional 'seven mournful sounds'.

While the Japanese were grieving over the death of their Emperor, two developments bearing closely on Anglo-Japanese relations were beginning to attract increasing attention. One resulted from the civil war raging in China; the other, which will be considered in the next chapter, centred around the question of naval armaments.

In China, anti-foreign feeling, stimulated by intensive Communist propaganda, had been rising steadily. This had been particularly marked since the summer of 1926, when Chiang Kai-shek's Nationalist forces, currently termed the Southerners, had set out from Canton on their march northwards, with the avowed intention of overthrowing the central government and provincial warlords and of establishing a nationalist régime throughout China. The first serious clash with a foreign power, in the course of the march northward, had occurred early in September that year, when British naval forces, in an attempt to rescue ships which had been seized by a local Chinese general, had been compelled to bombard the Yangtse city of Wanhsien. Four months later the British were again involved, this time at Hankow, where a Chinese mob invaded and seized the British Concession.

With foreign lives and property increasingly threatened, the Government in London sought the co-operation of Japan and the United States in dealing with the situation; it proposed that each of their three countries should send a brigade to China as a precautionary measure. On the proposal being rejected, Britain decided to act on her own and the Government announced its intention of despatching a defence force of three brigades to Shanghai.

Japan's rejection of this proposal, though regrettable, was understandable, as the Shidehara policy was still in force and the Japanese Press was virtually unanimous in support of its Government's pacific policy. Even so, it was clear from talks I had with naval friends at the time that the Japanese Navy, as a whole, was extremely sympathetic towards Britain in her predicament. Amongst Japanese Army officers, too, there was considerable sympathy, although in both the Army and the Navy there were some who considered that Britain had acted too precipitately. Even those who held this view, however, admitted when pressed that she was in a difficult position. Japan, they conceded, could afford to wait, as she was close at hand and could rush troops over to China in a matter of days if necessary; Britain, on the other hand, required five or six weeks to transport troops there, and much might happen in the intervening period while they were still at sea.

Britain's action in despatching the Shanghai Defence Force was vindicated by developments in the latter part of March. Chinese Nationalist forces had by then reached the outskirts of the International Settlement in Shanghai and heavy fighting occurred between them and the Northerners. The Municipal Council thereupon declared a state of emergency and called out the Volunteers to man the defences and supplement the British forces which had already arrived from England. Although the main fighting was between the Northerners and the Southerners, stray bullets caused a number of casualties in the International Settlement and at some points there were clashes with the British and with the foreign volunteer detachments. Three days later, Nanking was occupied by the Cantonese, and British and American warships were forced to open fire in order to cover the withdrawal of foreign residents; this was after a number of British and other foreigners had been killed or wounded in the anti-foreign outrages which ensued.

Although the Japanese were among those who suffered, the small Japanese naval landing party, which had been sent ashore to assist in rescuing their nationals, was under strict orders to avoid bloodshed. Being forbidden to use force, the luckless young lieutenant in charge had to undergo the humiliation of allowing himself and his men to be disarmed by the Chinese soldiery and of being submitted to other indignities. For a Japanese officer, this was the ultimate disgrace; only self-immolation could atone for it.

The news that he had taken his life caused a momentary stir in Japan, but the Japanese Press remained surprisingly calm. On the other hand, one began to hear murmurs among naval and military friends, who recalled a similarly humiliating experience of just twelve months before. In that instance, three Japanese destroyers, proceeding on their lawful occasions up river to Tientsin, had been fired on by Chinese manning the Taku forts. Instead of returning the fire and continuing on their way, they had been ordered to withdraw. To turn the other cheek was contrary to all the traditions on which their officers and men had been brought up, yet now, once again—this time at Nanking—Japan's armed forces had been called on to submit meekly to insulting behaviour without being allowed to retaliate. In both instances, of course, the underlying reason for the orders to avoid bloodshed was the Government's determination to keep on friendly terms with the Chinese at all costs. The key notes of its policy, as defined by Baron Shidehara shortly before the Nanking incident, were 'Friendship to all nations of the world' and 'Not territory, but markets that we have in view'. Overseas markets were, indeed, essential if the population question was to be solved by providing Japan's surplus millions with remunerative employment through the medium of trade and industry, now that immigration was debarred as a partial solution; to ensure access to these markets, friendly relations with their owners was a *sine qua non*. The one was the corollary of the other. The Chinese market was of particular importance to Japan, and the Government was determined to avoid the use of force lest such action should provide a pretext for a boycott of Japanese goods, China's most effective weapon against Japan.

As well-placed Japanese friends explained to me at the time, there were other reasons, too, why the Government was so reluctant to sanction the use of force. These included the fear of taking any action that might result in uniting the two wings of the

Southerners, just at a time when an open split, between Chiang Kai-shek on the one hand and the Communists and other left-wingers on the other, seemed imminent. Closely linked with this was the fear that forceful measures would play into the hands of Soviet Russia, with whom Japan had no desire for an open clash at that time. Sound and valid though these reasons were, Japanese naval and military circles were nevertheless beginning to feel restive and to resent the idea that the Chinese could go on flouting Japan with apparent impunity.

Although it was the Navy that had been humiliated in the Taku incident and again at Nanking, a talk I had at this time with Colonel Shigeto, head of the Chinese section of the Army General Staff, served to reflect this growing dissatisfaction with the Shidehara policy of peace and conciliation.[1] Though somewhat non-committal about his own personal views, he made it clear that the Army in general was in favour of stronger action and was anxious to show a united front with the British. Barely two weeks later, a serious financial crisis brought about the fall of the Government and its replacement by a new one under General Baron Tanaka. The new Premier had, since Marshal Yamagata's death in 1922, been regarded as the head of what was loosely termed the Military Party. It was not surprising, therefore, that the Shidehara policy was put away into cold storage for the time being; a more forceful policy seemed likely.

[1] Shigeto was to figure later as a trouble-maker in a number of the plots which disfigured the 1930s and did so much to undermine discipline in the Japanese Army.

CHAPTER IX

Developments During the Tanaka Régime

Mention of General Baron Tanaka is apt to conjure up the picture of an overbearing, dyed-in-the-wool militarist, the one-time head of a notoriously corrupt government, and author of the Tanaka Memorial, a document sometimes described as the blue-print of Japanese aggression and likened to Hitler's *Mein Kampf*. It is, however, a misleading caricature. Apart from the fact that the so-called Tanaka Memorial is now generally recognized as having been a forgery, compiled by Chinese propagandists on the basis of views expressed by extremist civilian organizations in Japan, Tanaka himself was neither swashbuckling nor arrogant. On the contrary, he was genial, approachable, and much-liked by his subordinates, for whose interests he was always ready to exert himself. If, while on the active list, he put the needs of the Army first, he did no more than any keen senior officer in any army would do, but he was certainly no swaggering militarist in the Prussian sense of the term; and if his government was riddled with corruption, as undoubtedly it was, he himself was probably more sinned against than sinning in this respect, as he was over-ready to put ability above all else when selecting men for high office and to pay too little heed to the question of their probity.

I myself first came to know General Tanaka during my attachment to the Japanese Army and, like other British officers who knew him personally in those days, was always struck by his friendly, genial manner to those much junior in rank and by his approachability. This attitude underwent no change when, after my return to Japan as a civilian, I met him from time to time at social functions or in the course of my duties as a foreign correspondent. He was always just as friendly as ever and had an engaging way of putting one at one's ease and chatting about old times and mutual friends. I can still hear his jovial chuckle when, shortly after his retirement from the Army in order to become President of the *Seiyukai* in 1925, I saw him clad in mufti for the first time. Smiling broadly, he shook me warmly by the hand as he remarked, 'You see, Kennedy San, I have followed your example.

I have put away my sword and, as a good democrat, have discarded my uniform.' His ideas of what constituted 'a good democrat' may not have been entirely in line with the views of more orthodox upholders of democracy, but he clearly appreciated the humour of his apparent metamorphosis. He may have been a bit of a rogue, as his detractors deemed him to be, but, if so, he was a cheerful rogue—and for that, much may be forgiven him. As to whether he himself was touched by the corruption prevalent among other members of his Administration, I can only say that there was nothing in the outward appearance of his private house in Tokyo to indicate any great wealth. I visited him at it on a number of occasions—a small, unostentatious wooden dwelling, similar to many thousands of other unpretentious Japanese homes in Tokyo.

Seen in retrospect, it seems significant that Tanaka's assumption of the Presidency of the *Seiyukai*, then the main Opposition party in the Lower House of the Japanese Diet, was followed barely two weeks later by Hindenburg's election as President of the German Republic. In both countries at that time, democratic ideals appeared to be making considerable headway and, certainly in Japan, the sentiment against both bureaucracy and militarism was still running strongly; yet Hindenburg remained closely associated in the minds of most people with Prussian militarism, while Tanaka, for some years past, had been regarded as leader of the military party in Japan and was a bureaucrat. That Tanaka should have been chosen at this juncture as head of a political party calls, therefore, for explanation; but before doing so, it is pertinent to recall that, in both instances, the appointment of an outstanding military personality was to pave the way for the fateful developments which later brought Germany and Japan into alliance with one another and finally plunged the world into war once more. From Germany's choice of Hindenburg sprang the circumstances which brought Hitler and the Nazis to power; from Tanaka's entry into politics came, ironically, the developments which led to such serious deterioration in Army discipline and eventually placed power in the hands of the armed forces.

The underlying reason for the curious anomaly of an outstanding military personality being brought into the political field in Japan and Germany alike, at a time when democratic ideals and anti-military sentiment were prevalent, was the same in both countries; social, political and economic unrest was creating a situation which called for a strong leader to hold the forces of disorder in check. Although, in the case of Japan, the *Seiyukai* was out of office at the time, it was hoping to return to power again before long; it therefore felt it advisable to procure, as its head, a man who, besides being a strong party leader, appeared also to have the makings of a great national leader, a kind of Japanese Mussolini. As a soldier and a bureaucrat, Tanaka might be looked on askance, but he was broad-minded and sagacious, possessed of ability, drive, and never-failing optimism, a man of striking personality and wide popularity. Strong personalities have always made more appeal to the Japanese people as a whole than have principles and dogma; the *Seiyukai*'s invitation to Tanaka to become their President was perhaps not such an anomaly, therefore, as some thought it to be at the time; and when, two years later, in April 1927, the *Kenseikai* Government fell and the *Seiyukai* came into power, their choice of Tanaka as their leader appeared vindicated. As Premier, he took a stronger stand against both China and Russia than his predecessor had done, but there was no immediate return to the openly aggressive policy which some had feared would be substituted for the pacific Shidehara policy. Soon he was being hailed as the Mussolini of Japan by a section of the Japanese Press, which was delighted when, shortly after his assumption of the Premiership, he warned Moscow in firm but friendly terms against stirring up troubles in Manchuria and, a year later, gave a similar warning to the warring generals in North China against spreading the fighting into Manchurian territory. In both instances, the warning was taken to heart and Manchuria was left quiet for the time being.

From the outset, however, Tanaka showed that he was prepared, if necessary, to face the possibility of a boycott of Japanese goods in China rather than stand by idly while Japanese lives and property were endangered by the growing disorders. No longer was it a straight-forward fight between Northerners and Southerners; the situation had now become further complicated by the violent clash between the Nationalists and their Communist allies and by an open split between the right wing and the left wing of the *Kuomintang*, the Nationalist Party itself. In view of these circumstances, and of the threat they posed to the Japanese communities in Shantung, the Tokyo government therefore decided, in May 1927, to despatch a force of some 2,000 officers and men to Tsingtao as a precautionary measure. What was feared was a repetition of the disorders and outrages that had occurred in Nanking two months earlier. The fear was probably justified, but the action brought on the anti-Japanese boycott, which Shidehara had always striven to avoid; and early in July, as the situation worsened, the Japanese felt compelled to extend their operations inland from Tsingtao to Tsinan, for the protection of the Japanese communities along the Shantung railway. By the end of August, however, the situation had improved sufficiently to permit the Tokyo Government to order the withdrawal of their troops, though the Chinese were left in no doubt, either on this occasion or in a speech delivered by Tanaka in the Japanese Diet in January the following year, that Japan would not hesitate to take whatever steps might be considered necessary, to protect her rights and interests and safeguard the lives and property of her nationals in China, if similar threats to their security should recur.

That this was no empty threat was shown when, in April 1928, Japanese troops were sent to Tsingtao once more, this time a division at peace strength, about 5,000 all ranks. Again this was done as a precautionary measure, as further fighting was expected in Shantung shortly. On this occasion, however, the situation was worsened by a clash between Japanese and Chinese troops in Tsinan, and reinforcements had to be rushed to Tsingtao. From what I was told privately at the time by a Japanese friend, Tanaka himself had at first been opposed to the despatch of troops on this second occasion, as he had entered into a private agreement with Chiang Kai-shek some months previously and felt confident that Chiang would be able to handle the situation in Shantung if left to his own devices; the presence of Japanese troops, he feared, might only aggravate matters and serve to bring on just such a clash as did, in fact, occur. Outside pressure, however, had been brought to bear on Tanaka and, against his better judgment, he had been persuaded to agree to troops being sent there.

My informant was Iwanaga Yukichi, head of the *Rengo* News Agency; and here a slight digression may not be out of place. As Reuter correspondent in Tokyo, I was entitled to receive all news reports and other information collected by the *Rengo* organization, which was allied to Reuter. Iwanaga, who was extremely well-informed and on the closest terms with many of the leading states-men and politicians in Japan, interpreted this alliance very liber-ally. In addition to the routine reports and news to which I was

H

entitled, he not only gave me a great deal of inside information on a variety of matters invaluable as background, but frequently invited me to his home to meet well-placed friends of his at informal dinners; these were always followed by friendly talks and discussions in the pleasantly informal atmosphere of his study. If at times there may have been an element of propaganda in what was said, it did at least provide an excellent opportunity to understand the Japanese point of view on the principal questions of the day, and to acquire information not available to the general public. In the instance just quoted, it seems probable that Iwanaga was perfectly genuine in what he said about Tanaka. Time and again he gave me information 'off the record' which was proved correct by subsequent events, and I never knew him to give me information intended to mislead. But apart from this, Tanaka, it is now known, was forced to succumb to outside pressure on at least one other occasion; this was when he was persuaded to drop his demands for the punishment of the officers concerned in the assassination of his old friend Marshal Chang Tso-lin, the Manchurian warlord, of which more will be said in the next chapter. There seems no reason, therefore, to doubt that similar pressure was brought to bear on him to sanction the despatch of troops to Shantung in April 1928, the action which led to the fateful clash at Tsinan. So here a passing tribute may be paid to Iwanaga. Kindest and most considerate and hospitable of friends, broad-minded and liberal in outlook, he died before the outbreak of the Pacific War—a great loss, but perhaps a merciful dispensation of Providence, as it would have saddened him greatly.

If Iwanaga's confidences to me may occasionally have had a propagandist slant, they were never deliberately misleading. The Japanese have often in the past been accused, and rightly accused, of blatant propaganda, but it is only fair to recall that not infrequently their utterances have been wrongly dubbed as such and disbelieved accordingly. An instance of this occurred at the time of the Tsinan incident, when it was widely believed that Japan intended to retain her troops in Shantung indefinitely. The Japanese War Office was much perturbed about this, and General Hata Eitaro, who was Vice-Minister of War at the time and had been very friendly to me ever since I had first come to know him in my Army days, asked me to send off a Press telegram, quoting him as declaring that all troops would be withdrawn as soon as the incident had been amicably settled. I did so and was reproved for sending out Japanese propaganda; but a year later, a friendly settlement was reached and the troops were promptly withdrawn as promised. A similar instance was to occur in 1932, when Japanese troops were sent to Shanghai and, contrary to general expectation, were withdrawn as promised as soon as their task was completed, but of this, more will be said in a later chapter.

Tanaka has often been denounced for his 'aggressive policy' towards China, and certain it is that, as a result of the clash at Tsinan in the early summer of 1928, he soured Chiang Kai-shek to such an extent that all proffers of Japanese friendship made to Nationalist China when the peace-loving Shidehara returned as Foreign Minister a year later were rejected. The disastrous results of this rejection are now known; but before condemning Tanaka, the dilemma in which Japan found herself during the troublous period when Chiang was bringing China under Nationalist rule, must be recognised. As a Japanese friend remarked when I was discussing the matter with him at the time, 'It was a case of Hobson's choice. Either we had to risk in Shantung a repetition of the Nanking affair and be put to further humiliation, or we had to send troops there to protect Japanese lives and property and bring on an anti-Japanese boycott in consequence.' Shidehara, of course, favoured the one way, Tanaka the other; both failed in the end. But Tanaka's reasoning was not unlike that which had led the British Government to establish the Shanghai Defence Force, and his action in sending troops to Tsingtao and Tsinan on these two occasions was considered well justified at the time by most foreign residents in China. It did, in fact, give rise to hopes that, as Japan had reversed her former policy of strict non-intervention in China, she would now reconsider the British proposal for Anglo-Japanese co-operation as a means of protecting their mutual interests in that country.

That talks with this end in view were being held both in London and in Tokyo was confided to me by Marquis Komura,[1] only a week or so after the announcement in May 1927 that Japanese troops were being sent to Tsingtao, though he stressed that an actual renewal of the Alliance was out of the question. As recorded in my diary at the time, he also mentioned in confidence that

[1] Marquis Komura, at that time the official spokesman for the Japanese Foreign Office, was a son of the Count (later Marquis) Komura Jutaro who, as Foreign Minister, had negotiated the Anglo-Japanese Alliance in January 1902.

Prince Konoye was acting as a go-between, between Baron Tanaka, who was Foreign Minister as well as Premier, and the *Genro*, Prince Saionji,[1] with a view to obtaining the support of the latter for a contemplated change in foreign policy. Whether the projected change was concerned with this question of co-oper-ation with Britain in China was not made clear, but the reference to Prince Konoye has a certain retrospective interest; thirteen years later, in September 1940, when Konoye himself was Prime Minister, he rejected the pleadings of the aged Saionji to act in concert with Britain and America, and was persuaded against his own better judgment to bring Japan into alliance with Germany and Italy. Of this more will be said later; but here it may be noted that in the early summer of 1927, when I had this talk with Marquis Komura, there was considerable division of opinion in Japan on the matter of foreign policy. It was significant of the vacuum still left by the abrogation of the Anglo-Japanese Alliance nearly six years before, that opinions, as expressed by the leading Japanese newspapers, varied between advocacy of a renewal of the Alliance in some form or another, warnings against any attempt by Britain to undermine Japanese friendship with Russia, and suggestions for alliance with Russia and Ger-many. Reports that a triple alliance of the last-mentioned nature was under consideration were being freely bruited in October that year, but they were flatly denied in official quarters. The fact was, that neither the Washington agreements nor the League of Nations, nor yet the Kellogg Anti-War Pact which was to come into being in 1928, were ever regarded as any real compensation for the security formerly afforded by the Anglo-Japanese Alliance. The consequent feeling of frustration and anxiety was therefore reflected in this periodic heart-searching, this probing for a pos-sible substitute for the former British friend and ally.

What undoubtedly had brought all these conflicting views to the surface in the summer of 1927 was the question of China and of Russian machinations there. The Shidehara policy had been discarded and a more forceful policy towards China, if not towards Moscow as well, had taken its place. In Britain there was a grow-ing feeling that the abrogation of the Alliance had been a mistake and that Britain and Japan had certain common interests in the

---

[1] Saionji, the last surviving *Genro*, or Elder Statesman, continued to wield great influence in the background almost until the time of his death in the autumn of 1940, when in his 91st year.

Far East, which could only be adequately protected if the two former allies acted in close co-operation. In Japan, too, there were those in favour of closer co-operation; but, having once been jilted, the Japanese were too proud to seek an actual alliance once more, and they were not prepared to sever relations with Russia as Britain had done after the Arcos raid in May that year. That, perhaps, was the crux of the whole matter. Tanaka was more out-spoken in his warnings to the Soviet Union than Shidehara had been, but he made it clear that he would continue to foster friendly relations with her so long as she heeded his warnings; and she did.

While the question of co-operation between Britain and Japan in China was attracting no small attention in the Japanese Press and elsewhere, the Japanese were noting with some surprise that Britain and the United States, whom they had previously suspected of planning to 'gang up' against Japan, were becoming increas-ingly at logger-heads with each other over the question of naval limitation. The initial cause of this open friction was a proposal made by Washington in February 1927 to Britain, Japan, France and Italy for a conference to be held at Geneva to discuss plans for the limitation of auxiliary naval craft. The question of capital ships had been settled at Washington in 1921, but nothing had been done about cruisers, destroyers, and submarines. The first reaction in Japan to the new proposal had been favourable, albeit with the proviso that any reduction of armaments should be on fair and reasonable terms and that the 5–5–3 ratio should not be applied to auxiliary vessels. France and Italy, however, rejected the invitation, so it was decided to hold a Three-Power conference instead. This opened at Geneva on 20th June; but even before it did so, it had begun to dawn on a somewhat incredulous Japan that the main clash would be between Britain and America, not between them and herself. Nothing that happened on the opening day, or at any time during the seven weeks that the conference lasted, served to do anything but confirm that impression. In essence, the friction arose over the question of cruiser strength. The British, on account of their world-wide commitments and long lines of sea communications, required a large number of small cruisers and only a very limited number of 10,000 tonners; the United States, being differently placed, had little need for small cruisers and was only interested in those of 10,000 tons. Their strategic requirements could have been amply met by a relatively small force of these large vessels, but the Americans considered it necessary, for purposes of prestige, to have equality with the British in the total number of cruisers, irrespective of the fact that this would give them a very much greater total tonnage. As a senior British naval officer remarked to me at the time, 'The trouble is, that although responsible American naval officers appreciate the British stand, their countrymen at large hate to feel that Britain, or any other nation, should be their equal in armaments or in anything else. Their demands are therefore based on emotion, not on actual requirements.'

Be that as it may, I was surprised when the American Naval Attaché in Tokyo, with whom I was discussing the question of the conference some days later, remarked bluntly that he could not understand what the British were up to, and asserted that Britain would have to bear the whole blame for the failure of the meeting if she refused to fall in with the American demands. One could only conclude from this that it was not *all* 'responsible American naval officers' who appreciated the British stand. As, however, the American demands, if accepted, would have entailed an all-round increase rather than a reduction in naval armaments, it was hardly surprising that a Japanese paper, the *Hochi*, remarked ruefully that the conference seemed to be heading for 'restricted armament expansion' rather than limited reduction. At the time it was made, this comment seemed extremely apt; but by the time the conference ended, it was being widely reported that the real sponsors of the American demands were certain American armament firms. These aimed, not at bringing about 'restricted armament expansion' but at ensuring the failure of the meeting by backing up these demands, knowing full well that they would be unacceptable and that the United States would then be free to expand their armaments without any restriction. It remained for President Hoover to confirm the truth of these reports when, two years later, in the autumn of 1929, he took the armament firms to task for having employed paid propagandists for this express purpose.

So blatant had this propaganda been, that the editor of the *Japan Advertiser*, himself an American, confided to me at the time that he had felt compelled to suppress some of the propagandist reports cabled to his office, as they were thoroughly mischievous and extremely tendentious. The aim was, in fact, to put forward demands, which the British were bound to reject, and then lay the

blame on Britain for the breakdown of the talks and the consequences that followed. It was little wonder, therefore, that the
First Lord of the Admiralty, who headed the British delegation,
publicly protested against 'the gross misrepresentation' of the
British position in reports circulated by interested parties.

While not openly admitting that they found the cost of their
armaments a serious burden, the Japanese became increasingly
perturbed by the growing clash between Britain and America and
the prospects of increased armaments if the conference proved
abortive. What Japan wanted above all else was actual reduction,
which would cut the cost, not just limitation and certainly not the
expansion implied by either acceptance of the American demands
or by failure to reach agreement. In a final attempt to stave off the
threatened collapse of the talks, Admiral Saito, the chief Japanese
delegate, therefore proposed a compromise. Under this, Britain
and the United States would have been allowed ten 10,000-ton
cruisers each, and Japan seven; small cruisers were to be considered separately. This would have suited the British, whose
defence requirements called for large numbers rather than large
size; but it made no appeal to the United States. There followed a
few more days of wrangling until 4 August, when the final
plenary session ended with heated exchanges between the heads
of the British and American delegations and a few well-guarded
words by Admiral Saito, in the combined role of benevolent
neutral and honest broker. So ended this abortive conference, and
the Japanese fears of what would happen if it ended in failure
seemed confirmed when, four months later, plans for a vast new
programme of naval construction were announced in Washington.

Regrettable as was this exhibition of Anglo-American disunity,
it would not have caused as much surprise as it did if the public in
general had remembered the bitter controversy on the subject of
auxiliary vessels, which had raged at the Washington Conference
six years earlier. The agreement reached there on capital ships
and non-fortification in the Western Pacific had been received
with such relief that it had tended to obliterate the memory of
everything else from the public mind. It was left to Hector
Bywater, in his *Navies and Nations*, to recall how near the Washington Conference had come to a breakdown over this very
question of cruisers and other auxiliary vessels, and how it was
only saved from rupture by the participants agreeing to postpone
all further discussion regarding their limitation until some later

occasion. The Geneva Conference of 1927 was, of course, the out-come of this decision.

In the early stages of that conference, the Japanese Press had accused both Britain and America of thinking only of their own interests, but towards the end this attitude had changed. Recog-nizing that the British problems of national defence were more akin to those of Japan than to those of the United States, the main blame was laid on America for demanding equality in numbers with Britain. For Britain, it was declared, a large navy was a necessity; for America it was no more than a luxury. Without ex-pressing himself so categorically, this view was reflected in what Admiral Saito said in the course of a talk I had with him shortly after his return from Geneva. Frankly admitting his sympathy with the British need for a large force of cruisers, he also ex-pressed himself strongly in favour of a British proposal for reduc-ing the size of capital ships. Such a proposal, he considered, should appeal to everyone, owing to the saving in expenditure that it would bring about. He regarded it as almost certain of acceptance if it was put forward again in 1931, when, in accor-dance with the agreements reached at Washington in 1921, a new conference was due.

As is now known, the projected conference to which he referred was, in fact, held in 1930, one year earlier than originally planned; it was to have tragic and fateful consequences, including, in-directly, the assassination of Saito himself some years later. It is of interest to recall, however, that on the occasion of my talk with him in 1927, Admiral Saito advocated that a preliminary con-ference should be held, in 1928 or 1929, to discuss this proposal for reducing the size of capital ships. The logic of his argument was convincing. If no further meeting was held till 1931, much money would have to be spent in the intervening years on experi-mentation and on drawing up plans for the replacement of ob-solete capital ships of the tonnage permitted by the Washington agreements; but all this money would have been wasted if it was then decided to reduce the size of capital ships. Instead, therefore, of waiting till 1931, acceptance of the British proposal ought to be sought at an earlier date by holding a preliminary meeting as soon as possible.

Although speaking in guarded terms, it was clear from other observations made by him in the course of this interview that Admiral Saito would have liked to support the British stand at

Geneva; for political reasons, however, he had felt compelled to adopt a neutral attitude in the Anglo-American controversy. Had he been given a free hand, he might well have given this support, but his failure to give it appeared to have been due to instructions from Tokyo, where it was feared that Japanese support of Britain would antagonize the United States and make matters worse. Be that as it may, Japan came under considerable criticism in British naval circles for 'sitting on the fence' and failing to adopt a more positive attitude on this occasion.

For the Japanese people as a whole, the bitterness of the clash between Britain and America over the question of naval armaments came as a surprise—a pleasant surprise in that it removed the fear that the two great Western Powers intended to combine against Japan, but a turn of events which left them somewhat bewildered. This bewilderment turned to anxiety when, as we have seen, Washington, four months after the close of the conference, announced plans for a vast new programme of naval construction. In the view of the Japanese Press at large, this programme went to show that the United States had been insincere in calling the conference and had been merely aiming to trick Britain and Japan. Sarcastic comments were bandied around at the inconsistency of proposing to spend $3,000,000,000 on an expansionist programme after professing to want armament reduction and, at the same time, putting out proposals for an anti-war pact. There was a renewal of this sarcasm when, in the autumn of 1928, the bitter controversy on naval armaments between Britain and America flared up once more. This was occasioned by an attempt on the part of Britain and France to straighten out their own differences in the matter of auxiliary naval armaments. The Japanese Press reflected the views held in Japanese naval circles by sympathizing with this attempt, and waxed sarcastic once more when the United States, after sponsoring the Kellogg Anti-War Pact, threatened to approve the Big Navy programme in its entirety if Britain and France went ahead with a separate agreement. Even in Britain, however, there was criticism, not so much of the agreement itself as of the somewhat bungling way in which it had been handled; but this was mild in comparison with the storm it created in America. This was reflected in a most untimely Armistice Day speech by President Coolidge, who used the occasion to urge the necessity of building more cruisers and to vilify Britain. The Japanese Press was shocked and held his remarks up to censure. But if it upset the Japanese, it delighted the Russians, who regarded the American outcry against Britain as a heaven-sent opportunity for creating trouble by circulating highly tendentious reports.

That the Russians were becoming victims of their own propaganda, in which the wish became the father to the thought, was brought home to me when, a few days after the Coolidge speech, the *Tass* correspondent in Tokyo came to see me. This was Vladimir Romm who, rather over eight years later, was to figure prominently as one of the accused in the Radek trial. The purpose of his visit, however, was to discuss the growing dispute between Britain and America and its probable consequences. His own belief, which reflected the views and hopes of the Soviet régime, was that Britain and the United States were about to fly at each other's throats and that war between them was all but inevitable. For an hour or more we argued over this matter, but nothing I said would convince him that the idea of an Anglo-American war over the question of armaments was utterly fantastic. Relations between the two countries were certainly embittered, but that this would lead to war was just ridiculous. The fact was that the Americans believed, or professed to believe, that the Anglo-French agreement included certain secret clauses detrimental to the United States, just as they had believed, equally without justification, that the Anglo-Japanese Alliance had contained similar stipulations; but in neither instance could this have led to war.

Unlike his predecessor Slapec, whom he had succeeded as *Tass* correspondent a year or so previously, Romm was a well-trained and highly intelligent journalist. It seemed extraordinary, therefore, that when Soviet hopes and wishes conflicted with rational reasoning, he always tended to give priority to the former in his assessment of any particular situation by believing what he wished to believe. During my years as a foreign correspondent in Japan, I came to know both him and Nagi, his successor, well, and I developed a real liking for both of them; but time and again I was struck by this curious dichotomy in the reasoning of these two extremely intelligent, well-informed and likeable men. Slapec, Romm's predecessor, on the other hand, was a very different type, a slimy, shifty little creature, who seemed more fitted for the role of a Communist agitator than for that of a foreign correspondent. That he did, in fact, assume this former role was asserted by Kagawa Toyohiko, the well-known Japanese social worker, who complained to me on one occasion that Slapec was continually carrying out Communist propaganda among the working classes. Kagawa was not the kind of man to make such a forthright accusation without first-hand knowledge of the facts, and his assertion seemed borne out when, in May 1927, Slapec was had up for examination by the police and was replaced by Romm a few months later.

That the attempts to spread the gospel of Communism among the workers met with little success was made clear in a talk I had towards the end of 1927 with Matsuoka Komakichi, General-Secretary of the Japan Federation of Labour. The workers themselves, he said, favoured evolution on the British Labour Party lines rather than revolution on those of Moscow. With the exception of the Printers' Union, which he characterized as 'loyal to anarchy', there was very little radical thought among them, extreme radicalism being confined largely to university professors and students. These he condemned strongly for trying to stir up trouble in the labour ranks and keeping safely in the background, instead of coming forward as genuine leaders of social reform. His words were borne out a few months later by developments which followed the general elections of February 1928, the first held since the grant of Manhood Suffrage three years earlier. Hoping to turn these elections to their own advantage, and being unable, on account of their illegal status, to put up candidates of their own, the Communist Party infiltrated some of their own members into the newly formed 'proletarian parties' and supported secret sympathizers standing for election. As part of their campaign, they circulated inflammatory pamphlets, demanding the abolition of the monarchy and the establishment of a government of workers and farmers. As a result of investigations into the origin of these tracts, large numbers of Communist suspects and their sympathizers were rounded up soon after, this being followed by orders for the dissolution of the Rōnōtō (Labour-Farmer Party) and of other radical organizations. All these, it was claimed, had been heavily infiltrated by Communists and Communist sympathizers and were, in effect, nothing more than Communist 'fronts'. Students and university professors were shown to have been strongly involved, and before long the anti-Communist drive was intensified by the dissolution of all radical student bodies and by the enforced resignation of a number of professors. Amongst these latter was Professor Oyama Ikuo, who had headed the Labour-Farmer Party and who, twenty odd years later, was to be awarded the Stalin Peace Prize for his part in the spurious World Peace campaign.

That the uppermost feelings of the Japanese at large, at this exposure of Communist activity, was one of annoyance and anger at the disloyalty shown to the throne rather than alarm, served to indicate that there was no great fear of Communism making much headway. At the same time, it was generally recognized that economic and social conditions were at the root of much of the trouble; until these were improved, the small but active hard-core of Communists would continue to exploit the resultant discontent. It was in the country districts that these conditions were at their worst; and it was because these districts provided the bulk of the recruits for the Army, and because a large proportion of officers came from these rural areas and sympathized with the hard lot of the tenant farmers, that the Army itself was later to become implicated in the extreme right-wing plots which so disfigured the 1930s and paved the way to war by stirring up emotional nationalism.

Rumbles of the approaching storm were already becoming evident by the late 1920s, with the right-wing extremists, in the sacred name of patriotism, attempting to counter Communism by violence, which the Communists themselves had hitherto eschewed. Barely a week after the Communist round-up in March 1928, self-styled patriots raided the Soviet Embassy compound and left a dagger with a note attached, accusing the Ambassador of providing funds to the proletarians in the recent elections. A month later, an armed raid was carried out on the offices of the *Tokyo Asahi*, the raiders terrorizing the staff and throwing sand into the machinery. This was done by way of retaliation for the refusal of that journal to insert denunciations of two leading statesmen for their alleged failure to take vigorous action against those holding and spreading 'dangerous thoughts'. One of these two statesmen was Count Makino, Lord Keeper of the Privy Seal, who was later to figure prominently as a target in a number of assassination plots.

The raids on the Soviet Embassy and the *Asahi* were typical of the melodramatically puerile activities of these self-styled patriots at this period, but they proved to be the prelude to the more violent and tragic assaults carried out a few years later. If the death sentence inserted in the Peace Preservation Law, when it was revised soon after, was intended to deter extreme left-wing offenders, it was fully as needful for curbing those of the extreme right-wing. It was significant that by this time some of the more extreme right-wingers were, in fact, former Communists or anarchists; it was a phenomenon that was to become increasingly noticeable in the nationalist upsurge a few years later. My attention was first drawn to this *volte face* by the *Tass* correspondent, Romm, when he came to see me in order to discuss the implications of the raid on the Soviet Embassy. The raid, he told me, had been led by Akao Bin, a former anarchist, who had switched over from the extreme left to the extreme right, from radical socialism to ultra-nationalism. Some six months later, in a talk I had with him on Communism in Japan, Romm brought up this subject again. Speaking more in sorrow than in anger, he remarked that the movement did not look very promising, as the Japanese were 'too unstable'; while remaining anti-capitalist, they were apt to be carried away by extreme nationalist fervour and by what he called 'idolatry to the Emperor'. In support of this contention, which subsequent developments served to confirm, he again mentioned Akao and added the name of Takabatake Motoyuki, who had compiled the best Japanese translation of Marx's *Das Kapital*, but had since turned from Communism to National Socialism. Had Romm remained in Japan until the 1930s, he would have been able to instance many more examples of this change of camp. By then, Takabatake's Fascist-like doctrines had taken a strong hold on an increasing number of former left-wingers, and Akao was figuring prominently in those extreme nationalist activities which led to the spread of anti-British sentiment and, ultimately, to the circumstances which brought the Army to power.[1]

At the time of this conversation with Romm towards the end of 1928, however, the feelings of the Japanese people at large were far more friendly towards Britain than to either the United States or Soviet Russia, and there was little or no sign of any pronounced anti-British sentiment. The Anglo-American clash over armaments had tended to evoke sympathy for Britain; and although British officers attached to Japanese military units were not given as great privileges as in the days of the Anglo-Japanese Alliance,

---

[1] For further light on this subject, the reader may be referred to *Militarism and Fascism in Japan* by the Marxist writers Tanin and Yohan, (Martin Laurence, 1934), and to Maruyama's *Thought and Behaviour in Modern Japanese Politics* (Oxford University Press, 1963).

Japanese officer friends, to whom I spoke about this, explained it as being due to the fact that they had now to treat British and American officers alike, lest the latter complained. Were it not for this, they said, they would be perfectly willing to give more information to the British and to let them see more than they did, as they had not the same distrust of the British as they had of the Americans. This may have been but a polite excuse on their part, but there were good reasons for believing that there was some truth in what they said.

While, however, British officers attached to Japanese units may not have had as much opportunity to see and hear what was going on in the Japanese Army as in the days of the Alliance, when they were granted privileges denied to others, they were still in a position to learn quite a lot and to draw deductions from what they saw and heard. A point that struck one of these officers was, he told me, that his Japanese brother officers, in studying the lessons of the 1914–18 War, showed little interest in the fighting on the Western front, as it had been largely static warfare. What really interested them were the operations in the Caucasus and the Balkans, where it was a war of movement. As the Japanese Army seemed never likely to be used anywhere other than in Manchuria and other parts of the Asiatic mainland, where static warfare of the kind waged in France and Belgium was unimaginable, this seemed natural enough. Their own operations from 1931 onwards were to show that their choice of campaigns to study had been justified and that the lessons drawn from their ponderings had been taken to heart.

CHAPTER X

First Rumbles of the Approaching Storm

Seen in retrospect after the passage of close on forty years, the Tsinan Incident of May 1928, when Japanese troops clashed with Chiang Kai-shek's Chinese Nationalist forces advancing on Peking, may be said to have started the train of events which led to Pearl Harbour thirteen and a half years later. Although the check to the Nationalist advance was only temporary and Chiang's ally, Yen Hsi-shan, was able to occupy the former Imperial Capital a few days later, Chiang himself, as we have seen, was left soured to such an extent that the Shidehara policy of peace and friendship, when reimposed a year later, was to prove a failure which played into the hands of the Japanese military. But that was not all. Recognizing that defeat was inevitable, Marshal Chang Tso-lin, the Manchurian warlord, who had striven to halt the advance of the victorious Nationalist forces, withdrew his troops into Manchuria and he himself left Peking by train for Mukden on 3 June. His journey ended in a tragedy which was to have far-reaching repercussions. As he drew near to the city, a bomb explosion wrecked his railway compartment and he himself received fatal injuries.

It was widely rumoured at the time that one or more Japanese officers were concerned in the outrage, and thirteen months later it was learned that a number of officers of the Kwantung Command[1] had been replaced. Amongst these was Colonel Kawamoto of the Divisional Staff, but it was not until the War Crime Trials of 1948 in Tokyo that his complicity in it was finally confirmed. It then emerged that Kawamoto, without the knowledge of his superiors, had planned the assassination and that it was to have been the signal for a *coup d'état* aimed at bringing Manchuria under direct Japanese control. The coup designed by Kawamoto was frustrated because the military authorities were not

---

[1] The Kwantung Army, which tended increasingly to become a law unto itself, had its headquarters at Port Arthur, on the Kwantung promontory, and was confined by treaty to the Liaotung peninsula and railway zone in South Manchuria.

behind it, but it foreshadowed the more successful coup, carried out with such fateful results in September 1931. What is also now known for certain is that Baron Tanaka, on learning the identity of the culprits responsible for Chang's death, wanted to have them brought to trial and punished with the utmost severity, but strong opposition from the Chief of the General Staff and others prevented him from taking this action. To do so, it was contended, would bring the Army into disrepute. His failure to insist on stern measures was, however, to have serious consequences; by providing a precedent, it paved the way for the serious deterioration in Army discipline during the years that followed.

While the authorities in Tokyo had no part whatever in the murder of the old Marshal, the Government had been increasingly worried for some weeks prior to it, lest Chang's forces, being unable to disengage themselves, should be driven back and the fighting spread into Manchuria. Their anxiety on this score had been stressed to *The Times* correspondent and myself in mid-May by Marquis Komura, who told us that a Cabinet conference was to be held to consider what steps should be taken to deal with any such eventuality. The Government, he said, would be guided in its decisions by the policy laid down at the China Conference held in Tokyo the previous summer. By way of indicating what that policy was, he showed us what purported to be a translation of the guiding rules drawn up at that meeting, and laid special emphasis on the final one. This dealt with Manchuria and Inner Mongolia and laid down most categorically that Japan would never hesitate to take whatever action she considered necessary to prevent the outbreak of disturbances in either of these areas. From the way in which he stressed the highly confidential nature of the paper and then proceeded to say we might quote the section on Manchuria on condition that no indication was given as to the source from which the information had come, it seemed obvious that he wanted it to be made known abroad that Japan was contemplating some definite action in the near future in accordance with these guiding principles. The first indication of what this might be came the following day, when it was announced that, as a precautionary measure for dealing with possible trouble in Manchuria and North China, a brigade of infantry had been ordered to return to Dairen from Shantung; another detachment of infantry and artillery, which was to have gone to Tsingtao, had been diverted to Tientsin. This was followed next day by the announcement that the Government had sent memoranda to both the Nationalists and to Chang Tso-lin, warning them that Japan was prepared to take any steps that might become necessary to prevent the fighting from spreading into Manchuria.

This warning was in line with the 'guiding rules' on which Komura had laid such stress to *The Times* correspondent[1] and myself two days before; but as Iwanaga remarked to me at the time, the government was taking a considerable risk in delivering it. Chang, he felt, was hesitating to evacuate Peking and fall back to Mukden because he still had hopes that Baron Tanaka would come to his aid, in the same way as he had been helped in 1925 when facing defeat by the rebellious Kuo Sung-lin in Manchuria. Iwanaga thought it likely that Chang would finally withdraw when he realized that Tanaka had no such intention, but he stressed the danger that would arise if he elected to hold on till the last moment before falling back. In that event, the retreating Mukdenites would have the Nationalists close on their heels and Japan would be faced with the task of disarming them in accordance with her warning, a task which would almost certainly lead to a far more serious clash than had occurred at Tsinan. Fortunately this contingency did not arise and there was a general feeling of relief when the news came through on 3 June that Chang had at last left Peking before it was too late and was on his way to Mukden. Twenty-four hours later, however, came the news of the bomb explosion, which left him a dying man. The momentary relief was therefore replaced by fresh fears, brought about by the realization that, if the 'Old Marshal' succumbed to his injuries, Japan would be deprived of one who had been generally regarded as a strong stabilizing factor in Manchuria and, on the whole, a valuable friend.

Relief that Chang had decided to withdraw without fighting had been shared by the foreign communities in North China. The British element in particular had feared a repetition of the excesses experienced in Nanking and Hankow if the Nationalists broke into Tientsin. They had braced themselves accordingly to resist any attempt to enforce a humiliating surrender of their Concession in Tientsin as had happened at Hankow. But the Nationalist forces, which replaced Chang's Mukdenites there and in Peking,

---

[1] This was Hugh Byas who, by entitling the book he wrote fourteen years later *Government by Assassination*, coined a phrase which aptly summed up the political situation in Japan in the 1930s.

I

had been purged in the meantime of their Communist elements, who had been mainly responsible for the outrages in the Yangtse cities. The change of régime in North China was therefore carried out smoothly.

Taken in conjunction with the Nationalist success in North China which, at least in principle, established Nationalist rule throughout China, Chang's death, which had been announced a few days after the bombing of his train, presented serious new problems for Japan. So long as Chang was alive, he had acted in such a way as to render Manchuria virtually independent of metropolitan China. He had handled his relations with Japan and Russia as he saw fit, without any reference to the Chinese Government, and he had entered into private agreements with them without the troublesome formality of seeking sanction for their conclusion. During the long years of civil war in China, when its nominal rulers wielded little more than local power, Chang had been left free to act in this way and had had Japan's full co-operation in maintaining peace and order in Manchuria. But now that the Nationalists were flushed with victory, they were determined to bring Manchuria under their control. With Chang out of the way, their aim was made all the easier by the fact that his son, the 'Young Marshal' Chang Hsueh-liang, who succeeded him, was bitterly anti-Japanese. So were some of his principal henchmen. By mid-July it was known that the Nationalists were negotiating with the new ruler to enter the Nationalist fold and there were rumours that Japan was pressing him to break off the talks. When first I asked Marquis Komura about these reports, he denied them; but three days later he admitted that the Japanese Consul-General in Mukden had 'advised' the Young Marshal against joining the Nationalists, although, according to Komura, Japan would have no objection to his doing so, provided that the agreements made by his father with the Japanese were respected. This was, of course, the crux of the whole matter, as these agreements gave them strategic and economic privileges which they regarded as vital. The Nationalists, for their part, expressed indignation at what they regarded as Japanese interference in Chinese domestic affairs and the Tokyo Government was denounced at the same time by the Opposition leaders in Japan for its clumsy handling of the situation.

The seriousness of the situation was reflected in remarks made to me on 10 August by Marquis Komura. The Government, he stressed, was extremely worried at the prospect of the Nationalists obtaining control of Manchuria; they had already abrogated the Sino-Japanese Commercial Treaty unilaterally and would almost certainly attempt to scrap the old agreements between Japan and Mukden if they gained control. In that event, he declared, Japan would be forced to resort to arms to protect her rights and interests. It was because she wanted to avoid armed conflict that Japan was so anxious to keep the Nationalists out of Manchuria—at least until she was satisfied that they would not attempt to tear up the existing agreements. This, he said, was the principal reason, but there was also another. The initial unity in the Nationalist ranks was already showing signs of breaking up and a fresh outbreak of civil war in China seemed likely, with Feng Yu-hsiang, the so-called 'Christian General', as the main disturber of the peace. He had already changed sides a number of times. If the Nationalists were in control of Manchuria and Feng rose against them, the resultant fighting might well spread into Manchuria, where it was a fundamental of Japanese policy to ensure the maintenance of peace and order. It was perhaps significant that, three days after this talk with Komura, it was learned that Chang Hsueh-liang had apparently decided not to join the Nationalists for the time being, as serious dissensions in the Nationalist ranks had been revealed at a plenary session of the *Kuomintang* held in Nanking and he had no wish to become embroiled if these dissensions should lead to a fresh outbreak of civil war.

Understandable as it was that the Japanese Government should feel worried about what would happen if Manchuria came under Nationalist control, the Opposition parties in the Japanese Diet exploited the Government's dilemma over Chang Tso-lin's murder to the full, by criticizing its failure to reveal all the facts concerning the bomb explosion and its handling of the situation brought about by the Nationalists' attempt to win his son over to their cause. In doing so, the Opposition was thinking primarily in terms of advancing its own interests; but it was evident from private talks with Japanese friends, with no particular axes to grind, that many thoughtful Japanese were doubtful of the wisdom of the Government's action in seeking to dissuade young Chang from negotiating with the Nationalists and in maintaining a veil of secrecy over the full circumstances of his father's death. Baron Hayashi, whom I had first come to know when he was

Ambassador in London at the time I was working at the War Office in 1921, expressed his belief, in a talk 'off the record' after attending Chang's funeral in Mukden, that the bombing had been the work of *Shina ronin*,[1] acting in conjunction with Chinese elements hostile to the old Marshal. Considering it essential that the full facts should be made known, he had, he said, been urging the Government to carry out a thorough probe into the whole matter in order to clear itself in the eyes of the world. But the Premier had rejected his advice on the grounds that the Chinese themselves were opposed to such a step. The reason given for Baron Tanaka's rejection of these proposals could hardly be accepted at its face value; it seemed clear that the real explanation was that, although the Government itself had a clear conscience, it feared that investigations might prove that other persons in high places were implicated.

While Hayashi's belief in the need for a thorough investigation into all the circumstances of Chang's murder, and of those responsible for it, was shared by many others, a talk I had in October that year with Iwanaga, the head of the *Rengo* News Service, threw an interesting light on the question of the attempt to dissuade Chang Hsueh-liang from linking his fortunes with those of the Chinese Nationalists. Tanaka, he considered, was no great statesman, but he was a man of genuine sincerity and extremely loyal to his friends. It was from a sense of loyalty to the memory of his old friend Chang Tso-lin that he felt compelled to caution his son about the dangers of subordinating himself to the Nationalist Government in Nanking. The turn-coat Feng, it seemed, had already made a secret approach to Japan for support against Chiang Kai-shek; and from this and other indications of dissension in the Nationalist ranks, he had serious doubts of the new régime's stability. Tanaka had therefore felt it his duty to warn young Chang against the possibility of being dragged into China's internal struggles if he placed himself and Manchuria under Nanking's control. By giving this advice, however, he had played into the hands of the Nationalists, who quickly learned of it and readily exploited the indiscretion by denouncing Japanese interference in China's internal affairs.

Considering the perturbation caused by the prospect of Man-

[1] Free-lance Japanese civilians of the adventurer type, who meddled in Chinese affairs and were not averse from violence in the sacred name of patriotism.

churia coming under Nanking's orders, it was surprising to note the calmness with which, at the close of 1928, the news was received in Japan that the Young Marshal had given his allegiance to the Nationalist Government and that the Nationalist flag had been hoisted over Manchuria. Nearly three years were to pass before the storm finally broke. When it did, Chang Hsueh-liang was to look in vain for armed assistance from his masters in Nanking and had to face Japan alone, with nothing more than their moral support to help him.

In the meantime, while the question of Manchuria had been attracting so much attention in Japan, the Japanese had been engaged in negotiations, which were to lead in June the following year to their own formal recognition of the Nationalist régime in China. At the start, the primary object of these talks had been to settle the issues arising out of the Tsinan affair in such a way as to enable Japan to withdraw her troops from Shantung, without exposing the lives and property of the local Japanese communities to further danger. When the negotiations first opened, there was no question of recognizing the Nationalists as the rulers of all China, and when, towards the end of July 1928, the United States sent a Note to Nanking implying *de facto* American recognition of the new régime, the Japanese Press was highly critical of what they construed as an attempt on the part of Washington to secure the leadership of the foreign Powers in China by showing what the *Asahi* characterized as 'uncritical and unconditional sympathy' towards the Chinese. Apart from occasional hitches, however, the Sino-Japanese negotiations continued with reasonable smoothness until January 1929, when a rickshawman was knocked down by a Japanese armoured car in Hankow and anti-Japanese demonstrations were staged in consequence. By the end of March, however, a settlement of the Tsinan affair had been reached and orders had been sent out for the withdrawal of the Japanese troops from Shantung to be started, but by then a new difficulty had arisen; this time it was in the form of serious internal troubles amongst the Chinese Nationalists. Faced with the likelihood of a fresh outbreak of civil war, the Nanking Government, which had previously been so anxious to see the last of the Japanese troops, requested that the evacuation of Shantung be postponed, as it could not guarantee the safety of Japanese lives and property there if fighting broke out. It was not, therefore, until the end of May that the withdrawal could be

completed, and by that time all the other outstanding issues between Japan and China had been settled amicably. Not least among
the results of the talks was the conclusion of a new Commerical
Treaty, to replace the one abrogated unilaterally by Chiang in the
previous July.

As there had been no less than three open splits in the Nationalist ranks since the beginning of the year, and as Chiang himself had been so exasperated by the dissensions and self-seeking proclivities of his followers that he had resigned from the
leadership of the party for a time during the previous summer, it
was perhaps understandable that Japan had hesitated to accord
formal recognition to a régime which was still so unstable; but
now that the main causes of dispute were at last out of the way,
she decided to do so. On 3 June Yoshizawa Kenkichi, who carried out the final negotiations so successfully and was to become
Foreign Minister some three or four years later, presented his
credentials at Nanking as Japanese Minister and gave the
Nationalist Government *de jure* recognition.

This seemed indeed a land-mark in the history of Sino-Japanese
relations, but it was an improvement which was not to last long;
and meanwhile the repercussions of Chang's murder the previous
summer were continuing, both in Manchuria and in Japan itself.
Within two weeks of 1929 being ushered in, news came that Yang
Yu-ting, formerly Chang Tso-lin's right hand man, had been
murdered. According to report, he had been invited to dine with
the Young Marshal, but during the dinner he and another official
had been suddenly seized and put to death. This may have been
true, but there were so many rumours circulating about Yang
himself, and about the reasons for his murder, that it was difficult
to confirm the actual facts. Some six months previously, however,
I had been told by a Japanese friend, a very knowledgeable political commentator who had just returned from a visit to Manchuria, that Yang was reputed to have known about the plans
for Chang's assassination and was unlikely to return to Mukden;
he would almost certainly share the fate of his former master if he
did so. Whether or no he had, in fact, been connected with Chang's
murder, the belief that he himself would be assassinated certainly
proved well founded and his death added to the Japanese Government's difficulties. Yang had often been critical of Japan, but he
had been at one with her in wanting to keep Manchuria semi-
independent and free from Chinese Nationalist control. With his

removal, Chang Tso-cheng, the Governor of Kirin, who had always been anti-Japanese, had become a leading figure in Manchuria. It seemed likely therefore that, with him and the Young Marshal working closely together, Chinese Nationalist control would be increased.

That Tanaka did not relish this prospect was indicated clearly when, in his capacity as Foreign Minister at the opening of the new Diet session later that month, he devoted most of his speech to outlining the Government's China policy and laid particular stress on 'Manchuria as distinguished from the rest of China'. There was nothing new in this, as Japan had always drawn a firm distinction between the two; but, coming so soon after the hoisting of the Nationalist flag over Manchuria, it was a definite warning that, while Japan was prepared to accept nominal Nationalist control over this territory, she would not tolerate any interference with the rights and interests she had obtained there under the terms of the Treaty of Portsmouth or from the agreements reached with Chang Tso-lin himself.

Apart from this warning to Nationalist China, the opening of the new Diet session was significant for the final attempt by Tanaka to dissuade the Opposition leaders from making political capital for themselves by bringing up the question of Chang's murder. In this he was unsuccessful, although a resolution, demanding that the Government reveal all available evidence, was defeated by a small margin. The failure of his plea was to play an important part in bringing about the downfall of his government six months later. When it came, it came with unexpected suddenness. Ever since the beginning of the year, the Government had been subjected to a barrage of criticism on a variety of issues, both foreign and domestic. Prominent among these had been the question of Japan's adherence to the Kellogg Anti-War Pact, strong objection being raised to the phraseology used in it. By the second half of June, however, the Privy Council had decided to recommend its ratification. This decision, which for long had hung in the balance, raised a great load off the Government's mind, and the prospects of prolonging its life by a reorganization of the Cabinet seemed bright. Then suddenly, out of the blue, came an unforeseen Cabinet crisis, brought about by a last-minute hitch over ratification of the pact. The crisis quickly worsened when, in addition, General Shirakawa, the War Minister, threatened to resign, in protest against the Government's intention to punish certain officers of the Manchurian garrison for alleged negligence on the occasion of the Chang Tso-lin bombing outrage just one year previously.

Enquiries I made at the time from both official and unofficial sources brought contradictory details of 'behind-the-scenes' happenings; but the general picture that emerged was of the luckless Tanaka being assailed on three fronts—by the Army leaders for trying to throw the blame onto the shoulders of certain officers, by extreme right-wing civilians for approving the phrase 'in the name of the people' in the Anti-War Pact, which was considered 'out of harmony with the National Constitution' on account of its 'violation of the Emperor's prerogatives', and by circles close to the Throne for inept handling of both issues. So far as the wording of the pact was concerned, it was asserted that the Privy Council disliked the controversial phrase, but had finally given its approval, owing to the bad effect that failure to sanction ratification would produce abroad. It seemed clear, however, that it was the clamour over the 'certain grave affair' in Manchuria—the euphemistic term used for the bombing of Chang Tso-lin—which brought to a head the growing dissatisfaction with the Tanaka régime felt in high quarters. It was this, and particularly the strong feeling aroused in leading Army circles by Tanaka's proposal to take stern measures against those concerned in the outrage, that precipitated the Government's resignation on 2 July, a bare three days after the storm had broken and just over a year since Chang's murder.

Although hardly foreseen at the time, the Government's failure to insist on strong disciplinary action marked the beginning of the rot which was shortly to result in the ever-increasing flouting of successive governments by the Army, the serious undermining of military discipline, the gradual transfer of power from the nominal Army leaders into the hands of relatively junior extremist officers, and all the other disastrous consequences that followed. On the day before the Government fell, however, it was announced that General Muraoka, Commander of the Kwantung Army, had resigned 'at his own request' and had been succeeded by General Hata Eitaro. Muraoka's resignation was said to be due to his desire to accept responsibility for his failure to take the necessary precautions to prevent the bombing of Chang's train, but it was also learned on good authority that Colonel Kawamoto of the Divisional Staff, Lieutenant-General Saito, Chief of Staff in

Port Arthur, and Major-General Mizumachi, Commander of the Independent Railway Zone Guards, had been removed from their posts. This was not officially admitted at the time, but a few days later an extremely provocative speech by Kawamoto, expressing strong views on the way to deal with the Manchurian military clique, was reported and seemed to bear out the suspicions concerning his complicity in the murder of the Manchurian warlord.

The news of the Cabinet crisis had broken on 29 June. Only as recently as the previous day I had learned from Saito Hiroshi,[1] who had just succeeded Marquis Komura as official Foreign Office spokesman, that the Government was to publish a statement next day, giving the results of its investigations into the circumstances of Chang's murder. Then came the unexpected news of the Cabinet crisis. When I asked him about it, Saito had been evasive and sought to minimize its seriousness, although he admitted that publication of the findings concerning 'the Manchuria affair' had been 'postponed indefinitely'. I lunched that day, however, with Shiratori Toshio, who was to succeed Saito a year or so later as Foreign Office spokesman. Unlike Saito, he was extremely outspoken. Far from evading my questions, he said quite frankly that the Government's days were numbered; and when we were joined by Kaneko, the Premier's private secretary, he remarked to him jovially, 'Well, it looks as though you will be out of a job in another day or two.' He was right. Three days later, Tanaka handed in the Government's resignation, and by the evening of the same day a new Ministry had been formed, with the ill-fated Hamaguchi Eizo at its head and the peace-loving Baron Shidehara back once more as Foreign Minister. Both Hamaguchi and the new Finance Minister, Inouye Junnosuke, were to be victims of assassination within little more than two years.

The new War Minister was General Ugaki who, when holding that same portfolio a few years previously, had incurred the unpopularity of many Japanese officers by reducing the main force of the Army from twenty-one to seventeen divisions. Just five months before his entry into the Hamaguchi Cabinet, I had had a curiously enlightening talk with him during an informal dinner given by Tsurumi Yusuke, an ambitious young politician, who clearly regarded Ugaki as the coming saviour of Japan. Apart from myself, the only other guests were *The Times* correspondent

[1] Recently Consul-General in New York and later Japanese Ambassador in Washington.

and the two principal American correspondents in Tokyo. It soon became clear that the main purpose of the gathering was to project abroad an image of the man who, in Tsurumi's opinion, would one day emerge as the great national leader of Japan, a commanding figure such as Tanaka's supporters had once believed that Tanaka would become.

Although, as War Minister in three successive cabinets between 1924 and 1927, Ugaki had been brought into close touch with parliamentary affairs, he had hitherto steered clear of party politics. It was something of a surprise, therefore, when Tsurumi introduced him to us as 'the future Premier of Japan'. It was even more surprising when Ugaki himself, after indicating that he was weighing up the merits and demerits of the two main parties in the Japanese Diet with a view to entering one or the other, remarked in all seriousness that he had taken the precaution of consulting a well-known fortune-teller, to find out what the future had in store for him. According to the sooth-sayer, he said, he came under the same heavenly signs as Hara[1] and Tanaka; but Tanaka's particular star was now on the wane, whereas his own was on the ascendant and he would succeed to the Premiership within the next five years.

It was obvious from the way he spoke that Ugaki had been much impressed by this prediction, and Tsurumi commented that, in point of fact, he would probably become Premier long before the five years had passed. Even if he did not head the next government, he would, he predicted, be either Foreign Minister or War Minister in it and would certainly emerge as Premier in the one that followed.

These predictions were to prove well-founded in part, but not wholly. Tanaka's star was certainly on the descendant, as he was forced out of office five months later and died before the year was up. Ugaki, on the other hand, returned to his old post as War Minister in the next Cabinet and some years later he became Foreign Minister; but although, in 1937, he was to receive the Imperial summons to form a new government, he never became Premier. The Army, which was by then in the ascendant, refused to support him and he failed in the attempt to carry out the Emperor's command.

Much as Ugaki had hoped one day to attain the Premiership, he was no self-seeking schemer. Believing that his country needed

[1] Hara had been Premier from 1918 to 1921, but was assassinated on the eve of the Washington Conference.

a leader who would place national interests before those of party, he believed it to be his duty to offer his services to whichever of the two principal parties, the *Seiyukai* or the *Minseitō*, seemed the more likely to advance the true interests of the country. Both had been angling for his support, and it only remained for the assurance of his sooth-sayer friend to convince him that it was his duty to enter politics. He had already served as War Minister under a *Kenseikai* administration and he had great respect for Baron Shidehara who, though non-party, had served with him in the same Cabinet. Now that the *Kenseikai* had been dissolved and reorganized as the *Minseitō*, it was perhaps but natural that he favoured that party.

A pleasant-looking military officer in his sixties at the time of the meeting at Tsurumi's dinner party, he was a small, stockily-built, rotund figure, with a white, clipped moustache, florid complexion and close-cropped hair, balding on the top. Though hitherto aloof from party politics, he had the reputation of being liberal and progressive in outlook, a fine administrator, extremely courageous, popular with the masses and with politicians and leading statesmen, and—an important asset—held in high esteem by the aged *Genro*, Prince Saionji, who was said to have great confidence in his abilities. Although he failed to gain the leadership for which he had hoped, this reputation was shown by subsequent events to have been largely merited. As Governor-General of Korea from 1931 to 1936, he was notably more moderate than most of his predecessors had been; as Foreign Minister at a critical period two years later, he was to win the respect and confidence of the British and other foreign diplomatic representatives in Japan. In between those two appointments, he had the support and sympathy of a large proportion of retired senior officers at the time he was invited to form a government in 1937. Due largely, however, to his liberal outlook, especially in foreign affairs, the Army leaders of the time forced him to give up his attempt to do so. For the same reason, he became the target of nationalist extremists and narrowly escaped assassination on more than one occasion.

The one apparent lapse from his normal advocacy of moderation was seen in the opening months of 1931, when he became involved in a plot known as the 'March Incident'.[1] From such

---

[1] The main details of this affair are given in Richard Storry, *The Double Patriots*, pp. 57–66.

evidence as has since come to light, however, it would seem that Ugaki was deliberately misled by the principal conspirators as to the true nature of their plans and that he withdrew his support and denounced those responsible when he learned what was really intended.[1] The plot proved abortive and no word of it was allowed to leak out to the general public at the time; but it marked a further stage in the deterioration of Army discipline—first revealed by the bombing of Chang Tso-lin's train in 1928—and was the prelude to the more serious and successful plots that followed. What was perhaps of even greater significance was that it marked also the emergence of intrigues involving both Army officers and civilian extremists. The latter had, for many years past, indulged in ultra-nationalist activities on their own, but it was not until the late 1920s that they had begun to win serving officers over to their own way of thinking. The first civilian body to do so and to establish working arrangements with some of them was the *Gyochisa*, the Action Society, an organization with terrorist proclivities and with 'national reconstruction' as one of its professed aims. Founded in 1925, it had suffered a split in its ranks two years later. It was shortly after this that it made its first active converts in the Army, and in 1927 the first body of politically-minded officers with strongly nationalist outlook was formed clandestinely. Under the name of *Kinkikai*, the Imperial Flag Society, it was to come into prominence a few years later.

In essence, the main aims of these civilian extremists and politically-minded officers at the start were to extend Japan's control over Manchuria and to bring about a fundamental social and political reconstruction of Japan itself; but in attempting to implement the first of these two objectives by force, they were to lay their country open to severe foreign censure. This, in turn, aroused strong national sentiment, even among those who had disapproved of the Army's actions at the outset—rather as foreign criticism had done in Britain at the time of the Boer War thirty odd years earlier. What, therefore, began as an attempt by the Army to carry out a relatively limited 'forward policy' quickly gave rise to serious international complications, in which Japanese resentment and anger, whipped up by extremist elements, was aroused against the Western Powers in general and against Britain and the United States in particular.

[1] See p. 164.

CHAPTER XI

The Calm before the Storm

Although the Tsinan Incident of May 1928, and the circumstances of Chang Tso-lin's murder a month later, may be said to have laid the train for the subsequent social and political upheaval in Japan and for the serious deterioration of Japanese relations with Britain and America which followed, there was little on the surface in 1928 and 1929 to indicate the approach of a violent eruption. Close observers, it is true, noted the growing symptoms of internal social and economic unrest and were beginning to wonder whether, in the event of an explosion, it would come from the left wing or the right, Communist in complexion or Fascist. Most observers would have put their money on the latter as the more likely of the two, and they would have been right. But apart from such speculations, the rejoicings over the young Emperor's enthronement[1] in the autumn of 1928, and the friendly welcome accorded to the Duke of Gloucester when he visited Japan in May the following year, seemed to indicate that the country as a whole was as united in its devotion and loyalty to its sovereign as ever and that Anglo-Japanese relations were on the surest foundations of peace and good will.

Impressive as the enthronement ceremony and its attendant jubilations were, they bear only indirectly on the developments with which these pages deal, but a few observations on them may not be out of place.

The Emperor was to leave his palace in Tokyo in the early morning of 6 November, on the first stage of his journey to the ancient capital of Kyoto, where the ceremony was to take place four days later. The foreign correspondents had been allotted seats in a stand, which had been erected facing straight up to the Nijubashi, the imposing double bridge by which the imperial cortège would emerge from the palace grounds. All was in inky darkness when I arrived and it was some minutes before I was able to recognize that my two next-door neighbours, both of them

[1] Sometimes incorrectly called his coronation; a misnomer, as there is no crown in Japan and therefore no crowning ceremony.

meticulously attired in 'tails' and top-hat, were Vladimir Romm, the *Tass* correspondent, and Bose, the Bengali terrorist, who was acting as special correspondent for some Indian paper. It seemed a curious anachronism, and set me wondering what was passing through their minds as the Emperor drove by, with his cavalry escort and imposing array of court ritualists in ancient ceremonial attire, princes and princesses in their glittering coaches, and the *Kashiko-dokoro*, the Ark of the Sacred Mirror or Place of Awe,[1] borne aloft on the shoulders of men clad, like the court ritualists, in the raiment of a remote past. Romm, as a representative of the régime which had murdered the Czar and Czarina a bare ten years before and still advocated the overthrow of all monarchies, could hardly have been expected to enthuse over the enthronement of an emperor; and Bose, on just such an occasion as this, had been one of those concerned in the murderous attack on Lord Hardinge when, as Viceroy, he was passing through Delhi in a State procession in December 1912. Bose, now a fugitive from justice, had no reason to indulge in similar terrorist activities against the Japanese monarch; but, as noted earlier, he was busying himself in trying to foment hatred of Japan's former ally and preparing the way for the outburst of anti-British sentiment that was to occur in Japan a few years later.

Having been instructed to cover the celebrations from Tokyo, I was unable to attend the actual ceremony of enthronement in Kyoto; but, together with some of the other accredited correspondents, I was able to pay a hurried visit there to see the full-dress rehearsal held a day or two before it took place. It was an immensely impressive sight, but what was particularly striking was the simplicity and solemnity of the setting in which the central act was to be performed. It was there, amidst the silent grandeur of towering great cryptomeria, that two primitive structures of rough unbarked pine and reeds, decreed by tradition from time immemorial, had been set up, with watch fires and lanterns of ancient design nearby to provide the only illumination on the great night when the Emperor would perform his solitary act of communion with the spirit of his ancestress, Amaterasu, the Sun Goddess. Little more than seventeen years later, under the shadow of his

---

[1] The Sacred Mirror is one of the three mystic emblems comprising the Imperial Regalia and is reputed to have been bestowed by the sun Goddess on her grandson, when he was sent down from Heaven to rule Japan. The other two are the Sacred Sword and the Curved Jewels.

country's defeat, the Emperor was to renounce his divinity and to declare himself a mortal like his stupefied subjects; but at the time of his enthronement in November 1928, he was still, in the eyes of his people, the heaven-descended representative of the gods on earth. His lone midnight vigil with the spirit of his divine ancestress was an integral part of the ceremonies surrounding his enthronement.

On 10 November, the actual day of the enthronement, Tokyo was in festive mood, with vast crowds gathering from an early hour at the principal vantage points throughout the city. With a friend, I made my way to the great plaza in front of the Nijubashi to see how the crowds were deporting themselves. They were in their thousands, bowing low and making obeisance to the dwelling place of their absent Emperor. Elsewhere there were similar gatherings, cheerful and well-behaved despite, or perhaps because of, the entire absence of police.

Exactly at three o'clock that afternoon, the moment timed for the Premier to lead the nation in *banzai* for the Emperor in Kyoto, a gun was fired and the crowds raised their voices in resounding *banzai*, while many of the more elderly among them bowed their heads and solemnly clapped their hands three times as though praying before a *Shintō* shrine. There was something strikingly impressive about it all. That evening, as I made my way once more to the Nijubashi plaza, vast processions of men, women and children, bearing paper lanterns in their hands, were converging from every direction, the mass of twinkling lights giving the appearance of a huge sea of fire, rising and falling rhythmically as their bearers swung them to and fro to the accompaniment of thunderous *banzai*. What struck one in particular was that the processions appeared to be composed largely of students in their uniforms and men of the labouring classes; it seemed to give the lie to the belief that 'dangerous thoughts' were rampant in those sections of the community. For the moment, at least, the nation seemed welded in one in its loyalty to the Throne.

Six months later, in May 1929, large crowds gathered once more, not on the same vast scale as before, but cheerful and good-humoured. The Duke of Gloucester had arrived, to invest the Emperor, already an honorary General in the British Army, with the Order of the Garter, and the welcome given to this royal prince of Japan's former ally seemed wholly genuine. For the time being, the lingering resentment over the abrogation of the Alliance appeared forgotten and this outward sign of a real attempt to 'keep alive the spirit of the Alliance' was reflected in the comments of the Japanese Press. Some months earlier, shortly after the enthronement ceremony, I had had a talk with our Ambassador, Sir John Tilley, about a reference to the strengthening of Anglo-Japanese co-operation in the Far East, made in a recent speech by the Foreign Minister, Count Uchida. The Japanese Press had jumped to the conclusion that a renewal of the Alliance was contemplated, but Sir John had emphasized to me that such a step was now out of the question. He readily admitted the desirability of closer co-operation, but flatly denied that any concrete plan had been put forward by either party. He hinted, however, that some sort of talks, in which both countries had recognized this desirability, had taken place. Some confirmation of this was given by Marquis Komura, to whom I spoke later in the day about Uchida's alleged veiled reference to a possible renewal of the Alliance. Although the Press reports, he said, were exaggerated, they were 'not groundless'; and he virtually admitted that Uchida, on a recent visit to London, had broached the subject of closer co-operation in China. He emphasized, however, that the aim was to obtain the co-operation of America and other Powers as well; but a day or two later I learned, through a friend in the American Embassy, that this hope was not likely to materialize. Uchida, he confided, had sounded out the United States Government when on his way through Washington after his visit to London, but, unlike the British Foreign Office, the American State Department had shown little interest in the suggestion and had been distinctly cool towards it.

From remarks made to me by Japanese friends, it seemed clear that, although there was no active hostility towards America at this time, there was a growing feeling of exasperation at the way in which the United States appeared to be buttering up the Chinese, to the disadvantage of the other foreign Powers, and refusing to co-operate with the latter for the purpose of safeguarding their rights and interests. General Ninomiya, whom I had known well since my Army days when he was still a Staff Colonel, was particularly outspoken in a talk I had with him on his return from a tour of inspection in China towards the end of 1928. Co-operation between Britain, Japan and the United States in China he considered was essential if the situation there was to be kept under control; but the Americans were refusing to co-operate and he expressed his surprise at having found, while in Tientsin, that American troops were holding joint manœuvres with the Chinese and were indulging in open criticism of both Britain and Japan for their alleged anti-Chinese actions and attitude.

With the arrival of the Duke of Gloucester the following May, the inevitable rumours of a new Anglo-Japanese Alliance began to circulate once more. Romm, the *Tass* correspondent, was amongst those who questioned me about them. What worried him in particular was a remark made by the Duke, in replying to a speech of welcome by the Premier at an official banquet. 'In peace as in war', he had said, 'Britain and Japan would always be friends.' To Romm, this signified that there was still some sort of alliance or secret understanding between the two countries, and nothing I said would convince him that the words used were no more than friendly rhetoric. In Soviet eyes, however, Britain was forever engaged in Machiavellian intrigue and when, later in the month, the Chinese carried out a raid on the Soviet Consulate-General in Harbin, for the alleged purpose of obtaining evidence of Bolshevik activities and of proving their connection with the 'Christian General', Feng Yu-hsiang, the Soviet Ambassador in Tokyo expressed his belief to a friend of mine that the raid had been instigated by the British Government. This, he maintained, had been done in the hope of working off another 'Zinoviev letter' coup on the eve of the General Elections, which were to be held in Britain a day or two later. It was a revealing commentary on Soviet mentality and utterly fantastic, but the raid itself was to have far-reaching consequences. Of these more will be said shortly.

The jubilations accompanying the enthronement of the Emperor in November 1928, and the Duke of Gloucester's visit six months later, were to prove the lull before the storm. Barely had the royal visitor left before the crisis over the issue created by Chang Tso-lin's murder the previous year forced the Government to resign. A week later came the news that the Chinese Nationalists, carried away by exuberance after their rise to power, had decided to challenge the Russians in North Manchuria by raiding the Soviet Consulate in Harbin, arresting all the leading Soviet officials in the Chinese Eastern Railway Administration, seizing the telegraphic and telephonic communications, deporting a large number of those arrested, and installing Chinese in their place. Ostensibly due to the belief that the Soviet representatives were engaged in fostering Communist activities, this action was followed a day or two later by the seizure of the whole railway and the forcible expulsion of all Soviet officials.

While having no great love for the Russians, the Japanese watched these developments with increasing apprehension. The situation, as they saw it, presented two dangerous possibilities. If the Russians left the Chinese in possession of the railway, the Chinese would be so puffed up with their success that they would then try to take over the South Manchuria Railway from the Japanese; if, on the contrary, the Russians tried to recover the railway by force, Japan might be compelled to take military action to protect the lives and property of her own nationals in the area of operations. As this would be in the Russian sphere of influence, an armed clash with the Soviet might result. This was, in effect, what Saito, the Foreign Office Spokesman, admitted when I discussed the matter with him at the time the news came through. On the other hand, a week or so later, at a farewell lunch to which General Hata invited me shortly before leaving for Manchuria to take up his new appointment as Commander-in-Chief, the general impression given by the other officers present was that war was unlikely. When, however, I asked him how he relished the prospect of going to Manchuria as C.-in-C. in the existing circumstances, he said he was quite looking forward to it, but wondered whether he would return to Japan with honour or with relegation to the retired list. Although this last remark was made jokingly, he clearly realized the difficulties with which he would be faced if things came to a show-down between China and Soviet Russia. In point of fact they did. The Russians finally lost patience with the Chinese, drove them back with little difficulty, and forced them to hand back the railway; but the Japanese were able to stand aside. Poor Hata himself never returned to Japan, either with honour or in disgrace, as he died at his post a year or so later.

From early July 1929, when the Chinese started arresting Soviet officials in Harbin as a preliminary to seizing control of the whole railway, until the end of the year when the Russians, having forced the Chinese to relinquish their hold on it, were withdrawing their troops from Manchuria, the Japanese had maintained what Saito described to me as 'closest watchful waiting and strict neutrality'. This policy, he had said, did not preclude readiness to act if Japan's own interests were endangered; action would certainly be taken if the fighting spread south of Changchun. This was the junction of the South Manchuria Railway and of the Chinese Eastern Railway extension southward from Harbin, and marked the dividing line between the Japanese and Russian spheres of influence in Manchuria.

While the Japanese Government maintained this stand throughout, it was noticeable that the Japanese Press, normally none too well disposed to Soviet Russia, was virtually unanimous in condemning China's action in seizing the railway in violation of agreements; but a new development in the situation was introduced later in July when Stimson, the American Secretary of State, was reported to have drawn the attention of the two disputants to the need for avoiding war, as both of them were signatories of the Anti-War Pact, which was due to go into effect a few days later. The initial reaction of the Japanese Press to this attempt to preserve peace was one of mild reproof to the United States for interfering in a dispute concerning Manchuria, the special preserve of Japan, China and Russia. It was up to Japan rather than to anyone else, the papers contended, to make the first move, if any move was required. Ruffled feelings continued for some days, but finally calmed down when it became known that Stimson had made informal approaches to Britain, Japan, and France to do what they could, in an informal way, to remind the two disputants of their obligations under the Kellogg Pact and had not just acted on his own. Japanese Press reaction, however, served to underline the touchiness of Japan on any sign of outside interference, especially of American interference, in matters concerning Manchuria. The main credit for preventing an open clash at this stage seemed, nevertheless, to be due to Baron Shidehara, the Japanese Foreign Minister, for his refusal to say anything that might be misconstrued as support for either side. Added to this was Japan's well-known determination to act if her vital interests were jeopardized.

For the moment, the danger of armed conflict appeared to have been removed; but although China had sent a conciliatory reply to the ultimatum delivered by Moscow, the Russians considered it evasive. Relations between the two countries had accordingly been severed and the Russians continued to press for the return of the railway. It was significant, therefore, not only of Soviet intentions if the Chinese remained obdurate, but also of the future balance of power in the Far East, that on 6 August a decree was issued in Moscow, providing for the formation of a 'Special Far Eastern Army' under command of General (later Marshal) Blucher.[1] It was the initial step in a plan to make Russia's possessions in the Far East self-supporting, both militarily and economically, in the event of war. Mainly a defensive measure at the time it was announced—to ward against further acts of Chinese nationalist exuberance and against the potential threat posed by the expanding network of railways in South Manchuria and their availability to Japan for rushing troops to vital points in the event of some future war—the formation of a Soviet Far Eastern Army nevertheless could not but arouse suspicion and some apprehension in the minds of Japanese military leaders. This anxiety was increased when, late in November, Russian patience with China's intransigence and procrastination became exhausted and Soviet troops launched an offensive against the western terminus of the Chinese Eastern Railway. Driving the Chinese troops back to the Khingan mountains and beyond, they had little difficulty in forcing them to sue for peace and relinquish their hold on the whole railway—925 miles from east to west, together with the 150-mile branch line southwards from Harbin to Changchun.

The ease with which the Russians overcame the Chinese, and the skill and efficiency with which they conducted the operations, did not come as a complete surprise to the Japanese Army. Coupled, however, with the recent announcement of Moscow's intention to establish a separate army in the Far East, it brought home to the Japanese—and especially to the Japanese people at large, who had tended to under-rate the military ability of Soviet Russia—that Russian military power in the Far East was becoming a potential threat to Japan's position in Manchuria.

If this demonstration of Soviet capabilities served to alert Japanese apprehensions about the future, Moscow's readiness to ignore its obligations under the Anti-War Pact, and to flout its co-signatories with impunity, provided a lesson which was not lost on the Japanese Army. Three years previously the Chinese had seized the British Concession in Hankow by force and had then, by a system of virtual blackmail, persuaded Britain to retrocede it to them. Having extorted it from the British by threats and coercion, they imagined that, by similar means, they would be

---

[1] It was Blucher, posing under the pseudonym of Galen, who had been seconded to Canton in 1924 to help in training and organizing the Chinese Nationalist Army, which was being prepared for the mastery of China.

equally successful in forcing other countries to give up their rights and privileges; but when they tried similar methods in order to possess themselves of the Chinese Eastern Railway, the Russians, ignoring the Anti-War Pact, had hit back. To the Japanese, or at least to the Japanese Army, the lesson was clear-cut. The Chinese might try to hide behind the provisions of the Kellogg Pact and the League Covenant, as they did after the Russians launched their offensive, but neither of these instruments for preventing war possessed 'teeth'. If, therefore, necessity arose, these devices for averting resort to arms could be disregarded with equal safety by Japan, and armed force could be used to counter any attempt by the Chinese to recover their 'rights' from the Japanese in Manchuria. This, of course, is exactly what did happen two years later when the Japanese Army, nettled by the Chinese 'Rights Recovery Movement', and determined to ensure the retention of Japan's vital interests, took the bit between their teeth and seized control of the whole of Manchuria. As a British diplomat in Tokyo had remarked to me shrewdly, at the time when Stimson first sought to prevent an armed conflict between China and Russia over the Chinese Eastern Railway, 'The Anti-War Pact may be all right where countries like our own are concerned, but, depending as it does on moral suasion alone, it is not likely to deter many others.' How right he was!

To conclude this chapter in lighter vein, it may not be out of place to record an incident which occurred shortly before the Russians launched their offensive to recover their rights over the Chinese Eastern Railway. Early in November 1929, a Conference on Pacific Relations had been held in Kyoto. The British delegation attending it had been headed by Lord Hailsham, the former Lord Chancellor. While the conference was in progress, news came in that Anglo-Soviet diplomatic relations, which had been severed at the time of the Arcos raid in May 1927, had been restored by the British Labour Government, which had recently come into power. Romm, the *Tass* correspondent, who was attending the meeting as the official Soviet 'observer', was delighted with the news. Thinking that Lord Hailsham would be equally pleased, he went up and congratulated him on the restoration of relations between their two countries. 'Well', replied Hailsham with a grim smile, 'I congratulate you too, but I will be quite frank. I did everything I could to oppose the restoration of relations with your country when I was in the Conservative Government; I would have done so again if I had been in the present government.' It was Romm himself who told me of this little exchange of pleasantries; to his credit, he told it with great glee and was clearly not put out in any way by the bluff rejoinder.

It was, incidentally, at this conference that Matsuoka Yosuke, who was to gain considerable notoriety later, delivered a speech on Manchuria, which made a great impression on all the delegations present and was described to me later by Lord Hailsham himself as 'a most masterly exposition'. Matsuoka, whom I had come to know well, always struck me favourably until after the outburst of nationalist fervour, to which foreign censure of Japan's incursion into Manchuria in September 1931 gave rise. At first but grumblingly resentful of this criticism, his resentment soon turned to anger and bitterness, and he became bluntly outspoken in his denunciation of the League of Nations in general and of Britain and America in particular. A squat, thick-set, bullet-headed little figure, he had always been inclined to bluntness of speech, a characteristic which had rather appealed to me, since most Japanese tend to avoid saying things that might displease the hearer; but as the years went on, he became increasingly aggressive and bombastic in his actions and utterances. This was particularly noticeable during his year of office as Foreign Minister from July 1940 to July the following year. It was then that his bitterness towards Britain and the United States was given full rein, in his vigorous advocacy of an all-embracing alliance with Germany as the best means of holding those two countries at bay. The conclusion of the Tripartite Pact of Mutual Assistance with Germany and Italy in September 1940 was largely the result of his manœuvres and, for his part in bringing it about, he was to figure as one of the twenty-eight Japanese designated as major war criminals at the War Crime Trials which opened in May 1946. It was perhaps fortunate for him that he died during the course of the trials, before he could be sentenced for his misdeeds.

CHAPTER XII

The London Naval Conference and Internal Unrest

The abortive conference for the limitation of naval auxiliary vessels held at Geneva in 1927, it will be recalled, had been followed four months later by the announcement of a projected American programme, envisaging an expansion of naval armaments rather than a reduction. A renewal of the bitter Anglo-American controversy had broken out in the autumn of 1928 and President Coolidge's untimely Armistice Day speech had served to add fuel to the flames. It came as a pleasant surprise, therefore, when, towards the end of April the following year, Hugh Gibson, the chief American delegate at the Preliminary Disarmament Conference at Geneva, put forward proposals which seemed to hold out a chance for a further measure of naval armament restriction. The proposals were well received both in Tokyo and London, and three months later the Japanese Government intimated its readiness to participate in a conference, provided it sought positive reduction and not merely limitation. Within a week this was followed by the news that Ramsay MacDonald, the British Premier, had announced the suspension of work on two cruisers and that President Hoover had stated that the keels of three projected cruisers would not be laid for the time being.

These gestures were welcomed in Japan, where it was hinted that a similar gesture would probably be forthcoming. Instead, a month later it was reported that the Japanese Navy Office had drawn up an auxiliary replacement programme, which included four eight-inch cruisers, for completion in six or eight years. In view, however, of the government's policy of economy and retrenchment, it seemed unlikely that the necessary funds would be sanctioned; it was generally believed—probably rightly—that the main object of the proposed programme was to enable the Navy to present a blue-print with which to bargain when the conference was convened. From then on, until the conference finally opened in January 1930, the indications were that all five of the countries concerned—the other two being France and Italy—were jockeying for position.

During those intervening months, the initial feelings of optimism and good-will, aroused by the proposals for a new naval conference, were wearing thin; the bitterness, which had marked the abortive meeting of 1927, was building up once more, but this time with a difference. Britain and America were still at variance with one another, but their attempts to reach a preliminary understanding between themselves served to revive Japanese suspicions that they were planning to 'gang up' against Japan. Although it was made known in the latter part of September that Matsudaira, the Japanese Ambassador in London, was being kept fully informed, by Downing Street, of the progress of the preliminary talks between MacDonald and the American Ambassador, Charles Dawes, it was clear from remarks made in Japanese official circles that some apprehension about these discussions was felt.

As I myself had been told in strict confidence that Matsudaira had been shown the draft of a tentative agreement between Britain and the United States and had been asked to obtain his government's views on it, these fears appeared, at first sight, unwarranted; but in the course of a talk I had a few days later with Captain Koga, the Navy Office spokesman, he expressed concern lest MacDonald, being a pacifist by nature, might be allowing himself to be 'led by the nose' by the Americans; in his desire for peace and goodwill, he might be pledging himself to give away too much and agreeing to matters of disadvantage to Japan. Did I think, Koga asked more than once, that the British had confidence in MacDonald's ability to safeguard their own interests in the matter of national defence? What concerned him most, however, was the question of cruiser strength. Only a week or so previously, the Navy Minister, Admiral Takarabe, had told an American correspondent that he favoured a 70 per cent ratio for cruisers, though he would not commit himself to saying that Japan would insist on that ratio; but Koga was rather more outspoken. He kept harping on the theme that America was 'egoistic and self-centred' and maintained that the general feeling in both naval and military circles was one of sympathy for Britain; it was considered that she was being made to sacrifice everything and the United States nothing. Japanese officers, he asserted, were unanimous in their opinion that America had no right to demand parity in total cruiser strength with Britain and superiority in eight-inch cruisers; they were fearful of the effect this would have on Japan's need for a 70 per cent ratio in heavy cruisers with the United States if Britain gave way to American demands.

This feeling of sympathy with Britain and hostility towards the United States became increasingly marked as the time drew near for the opening of the conference; with it were coupled the growing demand for a 70 per cent ratio with America and the lurking fear that Britain would give way to the Americans to Japan's disadvantage. There was some momentary relief when, early in October, the British invitation to Japan to attend the conference in London, and to hold informal talks with her until it opened, was received in Tokyo; it seemed to show that there was no intention of trying to force an Anglo-American agreement on Japan or on either of the other two participants. But the feeling of relief was short-lived.

In her reply, Japan had gladly accepted the invitation and had emphasized that actual reduction of naval armaments, not just limitation, should be the goal for which to strive. In a statement issued at the same time by way of amplifying the gist of this reply, Baron Shidehara had stressed a number of points. Amongst them was the assurance that the proposed preliminary conversations envisaged no agreement or understanding prejudicial to any third party, but was intended to prepare the ground for the conference itself; Japan, he said, was willing to hold similar talks with any of the participants. It came as something of a jolt, therefore, when, in mid-November, it was reported in the Press that Matsudaira had cabled to the Government that MacDonald was prepared to accept Japan's demand for a 70 per cent ratio in eight-inch gun cruisers *vis-à-vis* Britain, but was absolutely opposed to her having this ratio towards America, as this would give her more than 70 per cent compared with Britain and might even give her a larger total tonnage of heavy cruisers than Britain. It seemed clear, therefore, that MacDonald, who had paid a personal visit to the United States in September for talks with Hoover at Rapidan, had, in fact, come to some preliminary agreement or understanding with the Americans prejudicial to Japan, who had no fears of Britain but considered a 70 per cent ratio with the United States to be the minimum essential for the needs of national defence.

Although, as I learned on enquiry, the news had been 'leaked' to the Press by someone in official quarters, the Tokyo Foreign Office, fearing that it might embarrass Matsudaira in his conversations with MacDonald, hurriedly issued instructions to have it suppressed, but it was too late; the news had already been published and the damage was done. From talks with Japanese naval officers and others during the next few days, it seemed clear that their faith in Britain had been badly shaken. The fear was expressed that the old traditional friendship between the British and Japanese navies might be seriously impaired at the coming conference as a result of Britain's tentative agreement to let the United States have a larger force of eight-inch cruisers than herself, as this would make her bound to oppose the Japanese demand for a 70 per cent with America. There was, however, another unfortunate aspect of the matter and it was first brought to my notice by Sir John Tilley, the British Ambassador, when he questioned me as to how the report had come to be published. What worried him was the way in which it had been written up in the *Japan Advertiser*, an American-owned paper; he considered that it smacked strongly of American propaganda, an attempt to make it appear as though it was Britain, not America, that was trying to block the Japanese demands. In support of his belief, he recalled the case of Shearer, the propagandist employed by certain American armament firms at the abortive conference of 1927. By means of large bribes, Shearer was said to have been used by these firms to influence the American Press to prevent agreements. Sir John thought that there might be another attempt of the same kind to 'make Britain the goat', as he put it. He was, I think, wrong about the *Japan Advertiser*, but, as subsequent events were to show, he was quite right in fearing that American propaganda was once more at work.

Although the Tokyo Foreign Office had failed to suppress the news, it had succeeded in its attempt to prevent editorial comment on it in the Japanese Press. Having received 'off the record' confirmation of the report from Shiratori, who had recently replaced Saito as Foreign Office Spokesman, I was amused when Admiral Yamanashi, the Navy Vice-Minister, assured me that the Press reports were 'largely imaginative'. It seemed clear that he was trying to clamp down the facts. He did, however, admit that there was 'a certain amount of pessimism' in some quarters, though he professed to consider this a good sign; over-optimism might do harm and bring about an undesirable reaction at the conference itself if things did not turn out as well as hoped. Like others, he sympathized with Britain for being more or less forced to concede to the American demands on the cruiser question and said he realized the difficulty of adjusting cruiser ratios in such a way as to be acceptable to all concerned; but he seemed hopeful that some way would be found to satisfy the conflicting claims, and emphasized that one of Japan's main desires was to find a way by which to reduce the cost of armaments without sacrificing her requirements in regard to national defence.

While this talk was mainly concerned with the cruiser question, he mentioned also the question of the Singapore base. This, he said, might have to be brought up for discussion at the conference, but the naval authorities were anxious to avoid any mention of it for the time being. It was, he stressed, 'a very delicate question'; the Navy understood the position, but the Japanese people as a whole failed to do so and were apt to get unnecessarily worked up about it. From all he said, it seemed clear that the Japanese author-ities were genuinely anxious to do or say nothing that might stir up anti-British sentiment, a great contrast with the attitude that was to be adopted a few years later. His remark about Singapore, however, had a bearing on what a party of Japanese naval officers had said a few days before to a British naval friend of mine, whom they were entertaining. They were not worried about Singapore, but they hoped that Britain would never give up Hong Kong, as they regarded it as a help in keeping America from 'butting into South China'. Like many other Japanese officers, they also main-tained that Japan should walk out of the conference if her demands for the 70 per cent ratio were refused. As events were to show, the Government's failure to insist on acceptance of this particular demand was to provide the first victim in the long series of assassinations that followed.

While many of the Americans in Japan were inclined to sym-pathize with the Japanese stand, there were others who did not. The American Naval Attaché in Tokyo was one of these latter; he made it clear to a mutual friend that he agreed wholeheartedly with the views of the American Admiral Fiske, who had written an article, which had been reproduced in a Japanese paper about this time. Ranting against President Harding and others for 'letting down' their own country at the Washington Conference, he had derided them for sacrificing America's interests without getting anything in exchange.[1] It seemed an incredible assertion,

[1] Compare this with the assertion of Whitney Griswold, a former President of Yale University: 'The forts, the ships given up by Mr Hughes were the

but it was a view firmly held by many Americans and helped to explain the American demands made on Great Britain in the autumn of 1929 and the reaction to them in Japan.

It was in this atmosphere of growing irritation that the Japanese delegation—consisting of Baron Wakatsuki and Admiral Takarabe, who were to be joined in England by Matsudaira—left Tokyo on 30 November to attend the London Naval Conference in January. In and around the station, tremendous crowds had gathered to wish them good luck, and there was much cheering and shouting of *Banzai*. On the surface, all seemed well, and the scene reminded one of a football team, confident of victory, being seen off to some important match by enthusiastic supporters; but a remark made to me by Admiral Kobayashi, with whom I had been on friendly terms since 1921—when he was Japanese Naval Attaché in London and I was at the War Office—reflected the anxiety felt by those in a position to appreciate the dangers that lay ahead. The day was cold and cheerless and, seeing me on the platform, he hailed me cheerfully with the remark, 'Looks like snow'; then, after a brief pause, he added, 'It will help to keep our delegates cool-headed.' His words were said jokingly, but they made me wonder what sort of reception the delegation would receive on its return, if it failed to get Japan's demand for a 70 per cent ratio accepted. The answer was to come before another year had passed. The demands were rejected, Admiral Kato Kanji, Chief of the Japanese Naval Staff, resigned in protest against the signing of the London Naval Treaty contrary to his advice, and Hamaguchi, the Premier, who was held responsible for the signature, was shot and fatally wounded by a fanatical nationalist. The shot from which Hamaguchi died a few months later was to prove as shattering in its consequences as the pistol shot at Sarajevo in 1914.

During the weeks between the departure of the Japanese delegation for London and the opening of the conference on 21 January 1930, the clouds heralding the approaching storm were clear to all close observers in Japan; they deepened perceptibly as the conference proceeded on its way. Nationalist extremists began voicing demands that the Diet should tie the Government's hands from the start, by passing a resolution insisting that Japan should

---

merest potentialities . . . nothing but a few blueprints which . . . stood no chance of Congressional approval.' (*The Far Eastern Policy of the United States*, p. 321.)

walk out of the meeting unless the 70 per cent ratio was conceded to her. The Government, however, was already coming to realize that there was little likelihood of obtaining acceptance of the proposed ratio, and Shiratori admitted in strict confidence, a few days before the conference assembled, that Japan could only continue to insist on acceptance at the risk of wrecking the conference; this, he said, the Government could not afford to do. In the meantime, the growing feeling of exasperation with America was reflected in a talk I had with Count Soyeshima, an ardent Anglophile and a close friend since my days with the Japanese Army. America, he maintained, was the real stumbling block to a successful outcome of the conference, as her demands were 'based on vanity and not on defensive requirements'. It was a view I had heard expressed by others and was to hear on a number of subsequent occasions; but what interested me in particular about this talk with Soyeshima was a revealing remark he made about Baron Shidehara, to whom he had made a similar observation a few days earlier. Shidehara had agreed with his comment, but had gone on to say that, as America was suffering from a '*narikin*'[1] complex, none of the other Powers could do anything but let her have her own way, 'like a spoilt child'. She had the money and could spend as much as she liked on armaments. The other Powers were in the position of 'poor relations'.

Shidehara would never have been so outspoken in public, but he did, in effect, administer a mild rebuke to the United States a few days later when speaking in the Diet. This was on 21 January, the day the conference opened in London. Commenting on it he remarked that 'certain Powers were basing their claims on national prestige, whereas the fundamental principle, if success was to be achieved, should be the minimum requirements of national defence'. The Powers in question were left unspecified, but the words were clearly directed at America; Japan's own stand was summed up in his slogan, 'We offer no menace to any nation. We submit to menace from none.'

That the view, that the Americans were basing their claims on prestige rather than on defence requirements, was shared by others besides the Japanese was made clear in a private talk I had with Captain (later Admiral Sir Varyl) Robinson, the British Naval Attaché, in February. After expressing his belief that Japan was the only country with a real naval policy based purely on

1 *Nouveau riche.*

defensive requirements, he spoke very forcibly of the 'hypocrisy and unreasonableness' of the American claims and said it was impossible to construe them as being based on anything but plans for offensive action. Though not quite so forthright, Sir John Tilley was equally critical of the claims put forward by the United States, and both he and Robinson spoke with considerable heat about the way in which the Americans were trying to saddle Britain with the blame for blocking Japan's demands and making it appear that they, the United States, were trying to mediate between the two. Robinson had queried the Admiralty in London about American reports in the Japanese Press, laying the blame on Britain, and had received the reply that there was not a word of truth in them; Britain had no objection to Japan being allowed a 70 per cent ratio with America, provided the United States would reduce their demands in the matter of eight-inch cruisers to the same level as Britain. Robinson put his finger on the mark when, after saying 'it was time that someone spoke straightly to the Americans', added, '*We* can't do so, because our hands are tied by the tentative agreement made by MacDonald with Washington during his talks with Hoover at Rapidan, allowing the Americans more eight-inch cruisers than ourselves'.

It was this tentative agreement that was at the root of the trouble. So long as it existed, it was impossible for Japan to have 70 per cent with America without having a still larger ratio with Britain, and to this Britain could not agree; but it was little short of sophistry for the Americans to claim that it was Britain who was blocking Japan's demands. The Japanese authorities recognized this, but were angry with MacDonald for having tied Britain's hands in this way. Captain Koga, in a talk I had with him at the Navy Office shortly after the opening of the conference, declared quite frankly that the opinion in naval circles, and among thinking Japanese in general, was that MacDonald had made 'a grave error' in ever agreeing, even tentatively, to Britain having fewer eight-inch cruisers than America, as this was bound to bring Japan into conflict with Britain over her demand for 70 per cent with the United States. At the Foreign Office a few days later, a similar view was expressed by Shiratori, who added, 'I wish someone would make it clear to him how much, and why, we regret this action of his'. That MacDonald, in his ardent desire to prevent useless competition in armaments between Britain and America, had acted over-hastily and had overlooked the effect it would have on Japan, was, in fact, the general opinion in Japanese official circles.

While the Japanese authorities appreciated the difficulty into which the British had been brought by MacDonald's action, the general public in Japan was far more inclined to accept the American line that Britain was the nigger-in-the-woodpile. It was even suggested in the Japanese Press that Britain was acting in collusion with America, and she was accused of conniving with the United States to force Japan to accept a 60 per cent ratio. This was in February, and some two months later, as the conference neared its end, it looked almost as though the accusation had been merited. On 1 April came a despatch from London, reporting that Mac-Donald had gone behind the backs of the Japanese delegation and had communicated with the Japanese Government direct. Responsibility for the failure of the conference, he was quoted as saying, would devolve on Japan if she refused the terms of a proposed compromise.

This attempt to browbeat Japan was received with indignation, which was temporarily allayed by a London denial of the report. Later that day, however, I learned, on what seemed very good authority, that not only had MacDonald communicated direct with Tokyo through Sir John Tilley, but that Stimson had sent a similar communication to the Japanese Government through Castle, the American Ambassador in Tokyo. In the rather slender hope of obtaining confirmation at the Foreign Office I asked Shiratori about it. To my surprise, he admitted that the report was, 'in the main, correct', and added (but not for publication) that he considered it 'a serious blunder' on the part of MacDonald. Sir John and Mr Castle, he said, had been instructed to deliver their respective communications separately to Shidehara and leave it to his discretion whether or not they should be passed on formally to the Prime Minister. As Shidehara decided that it would be inadvisable to do so, the London denial of the story was clearly in the nature of a diplomatic half-truth, in the sense that no communication was sent direct to the Premier. It was doubly unfortunate, nevertheless, as it served to play into the hands of those who asserted that the Anglo-Saxon Powers were co-operating against Japan and, as no mention of the simultaneous and rather milder American communication had been made, Britain got all the blame. There was, however, a curious sidelight to the whole affair. Byas, *The Times* correspondent, who had been with me when

Shiratori made the admission, promptly went off to the Embassy to ask Sir John about MacDonald's communication. Being unaware till then, that the news had leaked out into the Japanese Press, Sir John, normally quiet-spoken and unemotional, burst out in fury against the papers for publishing the story, against Shiratori for admitting to it, against MacDonald for putting him in the invidious position of having had to deliver the communication, and against the luckless Byas for asking him about it. I had intended going to see him about it myself, but as Byas had promised to let me know the outcome of his interview, I had left it to him. In view of the reception accorded to him, I was glad I had not done so!

Sir John's reaction was understandable, but it was fortunate that the news had not leaked out two or three days earlier, when the instructions were actually received; it would have raised a storm of indignation at a highly critical moment, just when Japan was about to reply to the proposed compromise plan. This plan, submitted to Tokyo on 15 March, had been the subject of extremely heated discussion between the naval authorities and the Foreign Office, the former opposing it, the latter urging its acceptance. The Foreign Office finally won and Japan's reply, accepting it with reservations, was despatched on 1 April, the same day as the news of MacDonald's barely-veiled ultimatum broke. It had been touch and go till the last moment, and the decision might well have been reversed if the news had leaked out sooner. Under the compromise, Japan was to be allowed 70 per cent in total tonnage of auxiliary craft, but her demand for 70 per cent in heavy cruisers was refused. In deciding to accept the proposal, the Government had had to consider the conflicting claims of national defence, of international relations and of economy and finance; each had to be weighed up against the other. The claims of the Navy were considered by no means unreasonable, but the good results arising from acceptance were felt to outweigh any disadvantage that might be incurred by insisting on what the naval experts regarded as the minimum necessary to ensure the security of the Japanese Empire. It was a decision hailed abroad as reflecting true statesmanship, but the consequences were to prove disastrous.

It was their recognition of the offensive capabilities of the 10,000-ton cruisers with eight-inch guns that had made the naval authorities so insistent on the 70 per cent ratio. As a Japanese officer put it to me, a 70 per cent ratio would be insufficient to enable Japan to carry out an offensive in American waters, but it was the minimum required to ensure that the United States could never attempt an offensive, with any prospects of success, for the purpose of dictating to Japan and threatening her interests in the Far East. The Washington agreements on capital ships and non-fortification in the Western Pacific had been drawn up in such a way as to rule out the possibility of either country launching an attack against the other; but if America was to be allowed a greater preponderance of heavy cruisers than the 70 per cent ratio with Japan would give her, 'the whole position', he asserted, 'would be changed to our disadvantage, as we Japanese would be left without this safeguard'. When I asked Captain Robinson, the British Naval Attaché, if he thought this was a fair appreciation of the situation, he replied, 'Absolutely, and my sympathies are entirely with Japan in this matter. America's demands can only be regarded as aiming at sufficient strength to interfere in Far Eastern waters if ever she wishes to do so, and this just makes nonsense of the principles worked out at Washington in 1921.' He had tried, he said, to get an explanation from Captain Ogan, the American Naval Attaché, as to why they wanted so many heavy cruisers, but all he could get out of him was, 'We want them because we have no bases for capital ships in Far Eastern waters'. 'That', retorted Robinson, 'can only mean that you want them for use in distant waters and therefore for aggressive action.' Ogan merely shrugged his shoulders.

It was because the Japanese recognized this potential threat that the naval authorities were building up large reserves of oil. An indication of their plans in this respect had been given by Admiral Takarabe, the Navy Minister, in a talk with a friend of mine in the oil business some months earlier. Commenting on Japan's de-pendence on outside sources for the bulk of her requirements and on the need to build up adequate reserves to meet all contingencies, Takarabe had said quite frankly, 'I consider we ought to have enough for two years.' Twelve years later, it was the diminishing reserves of oil, resulting from the embargo placed on the supply of oil by Britain, America and Holland, that finally drove Japan to war.

Although the question of oil supplies did not arise, there were, of course, heated discussions at the conference on a wide variety of matters besides cruisers—on the abolition or reduction of sub-marines, on the abolition of capital ships, on gun calibres, on

Italy's claim for equality with France, and so forth—but the most significant and bitter dispute was over the question of eight-inch cruisers. As a result of this dispute, the old suspicions of America and of Anglo-American collusion against Japan, which had been largely dissipated by the Anglo-American rivalry witnessed at Geneva in 1927, were revived once more, and a feeling of bitterness was engendered in the Navy against the politicians and the civilian officials in the background, who had disregarded the advice and warnings of the naval authorities. The Army, too, was feeling disgruntled over the way in which the question of Chang Tso-lin's murder had been handled and, as we have seen in the previous chapter, was beginning to meddle with politics and forming clandestine bodies, aiming at a military coup and seizure of control over Manchuria. Resentment against the politicians and against civilian control was becoming as rife in the Army as in the Navy, although in other matters the two fighting services were at loggerheads with each other. Stemming from the days when the two great clans of Chōshū and Satsuma—which later had become the patrons of the Army and Navy respectively—were rivals for power, this friction between them was to have a profound effect in the years ahead.

Although the extent to which discontent and dissatisfaction in the two services had spread was not to come into the open until later, a remark made to me by a liberal-minded Japanese friend reflected a widespread feeling of apprehension among thoughtful Japanese at this period. We had been discussing the political situation in Japan and the need for some strong outstanding personality to put a stop to all the unseemly squabbling and bickering in the Diet and in the country in general. I asked him what he thought of General Ugaki as a possible Premier or party leader. He shook his head and, screwing up his face, replied, 'We don't want any more soldier politicians'. It was a sentiment somewhat akin to the residue of distrust left in England ever since the days of Cromwell's major-generals.

The rumbles of discontent in the Army and Navy, however, had their counterpart in the country at large. Left-wing radicals and right-wing extremists were becoming increasingly vociferous, and in March 1929 a young reactionary had assassinated Yamamoto Senji, one of the proletarian members of the Diet. A few days later, another reactionary youth had attempted to commit *harakiri* in front of the Premier's official residence, by way of emphasizing his disapproval of the Government. Both incidents were reflections of the prevailing social and political unrest. The disorderly scenes, so frequent in the Diet at this time, reflected the same *malaise* and served to increase the contempt in which the politicians were held by the armed services and others. In the country districts, disputes between peasants and landlords were endemic; and although not generally realized until later, the changing composition of the officer class in the Army was bringing about a special bond of interest between politically-minded young officers and the peasants. Up to the time of the 1914–18 War, the great majority of officers had been of *samurai* stock, or could at least claim some connection with the old warrior class; but since then the commissioned ranks had included an increasing number of officers, both serving and reservist, from the tenant farmer communities, men with no *samurai* background whatsoever. These officers, especially those on the reserve, understood and sympathized with the hard lot of the peasantry, on whom the Army relied for the bulk, and the most hardy, of its recruits. While strongly monarchical in outlook, they tended, therefore, to align themselves with the more radically-minded peasants against the urban capitalists, industrialists and politicians, who were held responsible for their grievances.

It was not only in the Army and among the rural communities that changes in life and outlook were taking place; they were evident in the country at large and, more particularly, in the towns and cities. How rapid was the change was brought home to me by a conversation with the liberal-minded Quaker philosopher, Dr Nitobe, in the early summer of 1929. On asking him if he was thinking of writing another book, he replied with a smile that, shortly before leaving Geneva, where he had been Assistant Secretary-General of the League of Nations for five years, he had been asked by a London publisher to write a book on present-day Japan. Thinking this would be a task of no great difficulty, he had agreed to do so; but on returning to Japan he had found that such great changes had taken place in his absence that it was impossible for him to carry out his undertaking until he had had time to study the changed conditions. He had been away since 1921 and there had been changes in the very fabric of Japan in the intervening years. The old relations between master and man, a legacy of the not very distant feudal past, had already changed to a large extent even before he left, but the pace of the change had been accelerated and had become more marked. There was, too, the disturbing phenomenon of aggrieved 'unemployed intellectuals', caused by the ever-growing supply of university graduates in excess of demand. Some of the other more noticeable changes were summed up in the following passage from a book of mine published in 1930:[1]

Old standards of conduct and morality are being replaced by new; the family system, which has played so important a part in the social organization and welfare of the country for more than twelve hundred years, is breaking down under the pressure of modern economic conditions; the good of the community above the good of the individual, which has been the rule in the past, is giving way to the promotion of personal considerations which, while assisting in the creation of individuality, is likewise tending to inculcate a spirit of selfishness; class consciousness which, in so far as bitterness and discontent are concerned, was formerly non-existent, is coming into being and a spirit of social unrest and uncertainty is spreading countrywide.

Being mainly under the surface, these changes were not so readily discernible to the transient visitor or casual observer as were the more spectacular outward changes. These were plain for all to see; but they were more significant and, like many of the surface changes, were causing serious misgivings to conservative-minded Japanese. These changes had become particularly marked since the Great Earthquake of 1923—the growth of what was dubbed 'the café civilization of Japan', a proliferation of tawdry cafés, cinemas and dance-halls in the larger towns and cities, where young men and maidens, to the dismay of their elders, mixed freely and danced together to the latest Western jazz tunes; it was a practice never tolerated before in a country which kept the sexes strictly apart, except in the confines of the 'gay quarters', where the feminine element was restricted to professional entertainers and licensed prostitutes. These were perhaps but manifestations of the ill-digested ideas of democracy, with its emphasis on freedom and equality, which had become so popular, especially with the youth of the nation, since the close of the World War; but the sight of young girls with bobbed hair, strolling hand-in-hand with young students and sitting with them in the garish bars and cafés, was beginning to arouse the ire of the super-patriots, who regarded it as degrading and out of keeping with 'the Spirit of Old Japan'.

[1] *The Changing Fabric of Japan*, p. 4.

Equally noticeable, though less objectionable to outraged conservatives, was the growing enthusiasm for Western sports and
good Western music, the ousting of the *rikisha* by taxis and motor
buses, the replacement of bullock carts by motor lorries, and the
remarkable reconstruction and modernization of Tokyo and
Yokohama since their destruction by earthquake only a few years
before. These were but some of the more outward and visible
signs of change taking place, but along with them went the
changes brought about by the introduction of manhood suffrage,
by the growth of a young and vigorous proletarian movement
extending its influence in both national and local politics, by the
spread of Marxism and its subversive doctrines, by the growing
demands of women for equal civil and political rights with their
men-folk, and by an enterprising and energetic vernacular Press
with daily circulations, in some instances, of a million or more.

It was in this atmosphere of rapid change that, in October 1929,
Inukai Tsuyoshi, a veteran politician who was to fall victim to
assassination at the hands of self-styled patriots less than three
years later, succeeded the deceased Baron Tanaka as President of
the *Seiyukai*, the main Opposition party at the time. A week later,
the Government raised a hornet's nest, which was to add to the
prevailing spirit of social and political unrest. In an attempt to
implement its policy of economy and retrenchment and to ease the
serious economic crisis facing the country, it ordered a ten per
cent reduction of salaries for all government servants earning
more than 100 yen[1] a month. By doing so, it hoped to set an
example which the rest of the country would follow. If they did,
overhead charges and commodity prices would be lowered and
the cost of living cut. It was a vain hope, and all it did was to
produce such a storm that the Government felt obliged to revoke
its decision—a wise move in the circumstances, but a sign of
weakness, which did nothing to restore confidence. As Britain was
to discover two years later, when faced with mutiny at Inver-
gordon, it does not do to tamper with pay rates in this way,
especially when those primarily affected are not amongst the more
wealthy sections of the community and are men on whose loyalty
so much depends.

[1] Equivalent to about £10 at that time.

CHAPTER XIII

Ominous Portents

Apart from the question of immigration, which had rankled with the Japanese ever since the passage of the American Immigration Law in 1924—an enactment closely associated with the colour question and with its off-shoot, the Pan-Asiatic movement—the two main bones of contention between Japan and the United States were the cruiser ratio and Japan's claim to a special position in China and the Far East. The two bore closely on one another.

The rise of the Chinese Nationalists to power had faced Japan with serious new problems; but although the new rulers of China were demanding the restoration of their country's sovereign rights, they were racked with disunity among themselves and, in the closing weeks of 1929, the civil war then raging looked like bringing the Nanking régime to an end. So threatening was the situation becoming in the Yangtse area that the Japanese hurriedly despatched a cruiser to Shanghai early in December in case it was needed for protective purposes, while the foreign Powers in general were making preparations to evacuate their women and children from Nanking and other threatened cities and taking sundry similar precautionary measures. On top of all this, Japan found herself unexpectedly faced with last-minute Chinese objections to the appointment of a new Japanese Minister in Nanking and was hinting that, if China continued her refusal to accept the Japanese nominee, the Japanese Government might be compelled to ask for the withdrawal of the Chinese Minister from Tokyo.

A further complication arose when, on the advent of the New Year, China took yet another step towards her goal of rights' recovery by issuing an edict demanding the immediate abolition of extraterritoriality. It was an action affecting all the Powers with extraterritorial rights in China and could not be accepted lightly by them; but a temporary solution was achieved by Britain agreeing, not to grant immediate abolition but to consider 1 January 1930 as the day on which 'the process of abolishing extraterritoriality' would begin. It was a clever diplomatic move and was recognized as such by Japan; it saved China's 'face' by avoiding outright rejection, but, in effect, postponed acceptance until such time as conditions in China had been improved sufficiently to ensure the proper administration of justice in cases concerning foreigners.

That these conditions were still far from being fulfilled was all too apparent to foreigners living in China, and shortly before the issue of this edict I had an indication that even some Americans, who had hitherto viewed the Nationalist régime and its achievements through rose-coloured spectacles, were becoming sadly disenchanted. An American friend had invited me to dinner at his house to meet three young American journalists, who had been on a tour of China and Mongolia. They had enjoyed their trip, but they spoke bitterly of what they had seen and heard, and confessed to having become completely disillusioned of the beliefs they had held formerly about the good work of the Chinese Nationalists. They had been disgusted, they said, with the arrogance, brazen lying, bribery and corruption, and incompetence, and with the puerile attempts at anti-Japanese and other propaganda they had encountered. As one of them put it, 'We went to China prepared to sympathize and applaud. We have come back, firm in the conviction that no greater liar or incompetent bully than the Chinese official exists anywhere.' They had been assured by leading Nationalists that China was now unified, that opium had been abolished throughout the country, that foot-binding was no longer tolerated anywhere, and that peace, prosperity and happiness reigned supreme. They had very soon seen for themselves, however, that this Utopian picture was a complete myth; it was based on nothing more substantial than wishful thinking. Without in any way condoning Japan's subsequent actions, it was this Chinese predilection for self-delusion, and ability to delude others who lacked on-the-spot knowledge, that so infuriated the Japanese when, two years later, they were to be arraigned before the League of Nations at Geneva.

It was not only in China that Japan found herself faced with difficulties in the opening months of 1930. In Korea, too, she was confronted with the problem of student unrest and other troubles. Commenting on this, a Japanese friend, with whom I was lunching, drew what he regarded as a parallel between Japan's problems in Korea and Britain's in India, where the All-India Congress had been passing resolutions, calling for complete independence as its goal. Japan, he remarked, could sympathize with Britain in her dilemma over India, as she had similar, albeit smaller-scale difficulties, in Korea. Because of this similarity, the Japanese Government was anxiously watching to see how Britain would handle her problems. It was not, of course, an exact parallel, as the Indians had already been given political rights and privileges still withheld from the Koreans; but it had sufficient semblance to account for the way in which Japanese officialdom, at this period, still tended to frown on the Pan-Asiatic movement on account of its pronounced undertones of hostility towards British rule in India. What was sauce for the British goose, it was feared, might become sauce for the Japanese gander.

It was this same Japanese friend, Zumoto Motosada, who, later that year, told me of the embarrassment to which he had been put by two visiting American Y.M.C.A. officials, whom he had invited to lunch to meet some of the leading members of the Japanese Press. Instead of confining themselves to a friendly exchange of views, they had launched forth on a violent diatribe against the British in India and had expressed the hope that the British Raj would soon be overthrown. It was the kind of anti-British propaganda that one might have expected from Bose or any other Indian malcontent, but not from an American Y.M.C.A. representative on a visit to Japan. It was, therefore, revealing of the attitude of thoughtful Japanese towards the question of India that Zumoto followed up his account of this luncheon party by lending me a copy of *India in Bondage*; it was a book written by an American named Sunderland, and had pencilled comments in the margin by Count Soyeshima, contradicting the more virulent anti-British statements made by the author.

Critical as many Japanese had been about Ramsay MacDonald's agreement with the United States on the cruiser question at the London Naval Conference, there was still but little deep-rooted anti-British sentiment in Japan at this time, and the determination of the Japanese Imperial Family to strengthen the bonds of friendship with the British Royal Family was clearly reflected in April 1930, when Prince Takamatsu, one of the Emperor's three younger brothers, left for England on a friendly visit. It was my good fortune to travel home on leave in the same ship and to find how friendly and unassuming he was.

It was shortly after my return to England on leave that the first serious outcome of the naval conference was reported. On

12 June came the news that Admirals Kato Kanji and Suetsugu, Chief and Vice-Chief of the Naval Staff respectively, had resigned in protest against the signing of the Treaty. Their places had been taken by Admiral Taniguchi, Chief of the Kure Naval Station, and Admiral Nagano, head of the Etajima Naval College.

Other resignations were announced at the same time as those of Kato and Suetsugu, although their exact bearing on the Treaty was not wholly clear. Admiral Yamanashi, the Navy Vice-Minister, who had supported the delegation from the very start of the London negotiations, was replaced by Admiral Kobayashi, whose comment on the occasion when the delegation set out from Tokyo the previous November was noted in the last chapter. General Ugaki, the War Minister, was also reported to have resigned and to have been replaced by General Minami, who was to figure prominently at the time of Japan's incursion into Manchuria in September 1931. This report, however, proved strangely premature, as Ugaki's replacement by Minami did not take place until April the following year.

To close observers, Admiral Kato's resignation did not come as a complete surprise. As far back as February, when the conference had been in progress a bare month, I had learned that he had threatened to resign if the delegates agreed to less than 70 per cent of the American strength in heavy cruisers; there were unconfirmed reports, too, of his intention to resign at the time of Japan's reply accepting the compromise plan with reservations. When he and Suetsugu did, in fact, resign in June, however, the general belief was that the main obstacles to Japan's ratification of the Treaty had been removed; it was recognized nevertheless that naval diehards would probably do their best to prevail upon the Privy Council to refuse to recommend its ratification. In the event, the diehards acted as anticipated and a prolonged struggle between the Government and the Privy Council ensued; but on 18 September, while I was on my way back to Japan, it was finally agreed that the Treaty be ratified, and six weeks later the ceremony of depositing the ratifications of Britain, America and Japan was held in London. It was, incidentally, an event marked by the first real attempt to link up the world by means of wireless broadcasts on such felicitous occasions, Hamaguchi broadcasting to Europe and America, and President Hoover and Ramsay MacDonald making similar orations over the air; the speeches were picked up reasonably clearly in Tokyo.

This was on 27 October, and it seemed a happy omen; but barely a fortnight later came the first clear indication of the explosive situation in Japan. On the morning of 14 November, as he was about to board a train for Okayama to attend the Army's annual Grand Manœuvres, Hamaguchi, the Japanese Prime Minister, was shot in the stomach by a young nationalist extremist with a warped sense of patriotism. A ban was placed on any mention of the' assailant's motive, but it was obvious to everyone that he had committed the crime as a protest against the ratification of the Naval Treaty, for which he held the Premier responsible.

It was not until 10 December that the ban was removed and details given out. These revealed that, unlike in previous instances of actual or attempted political assassinations, the assailant, Sagoya Tomeo, had acted in collusion with other extremists. In all, twenty-seven arrests had been made; although all but four of those taken into custody had since been released, there was sufficient evidence to show that Sagoya, a weak-minded youth like the murderer of the Premier, Hara Kei, in 1921, had been the tool of the other three and possibly of others as well. One of these, Iwata Ainosuke, President of the *Aikokusha* ('Patriotic Society'), had previously served twelve years in prison for the assassination of Abe Moritaro, a Foreign Office official, in 1914; another was Matsuki Yoshikatsu, a member of the same extremist organization, although, like an increasing number of such men, he had formerly been a left-wing radical. He was said to have helped Sagoya to carry out target practice with the Mauser pistol used in the attempt on Hamaguchi. The third was Yamamoto Iwao, the *Aikokusha* Vice-President, but no further details about him were available for the time being.

Although the *Aikokusha*, as a separate organization, did not figure in any of the subsequent assassination plots, its members had links with similar terrorist bodies formed since 1919; in outlook it was akin to the far older *Genyosha* and *Kokuryūkai* (Black Dragon Society), from which so many of the other extreme nationalist organizations of the 1930s were spawned.[1] Hamaguchi was to live for another ten months, but this attempt on his life proved to be the prelude to the explosion of fanatical nationalism which played so insidious a part in the years ahead. For the time

---

[1] The links between these bodies are well set out in Appendix III of Richard Storry, *The Double Patriots*, Chatto & Windus, 1957.

being, however, the repercussions of the Naval Treaty were confined to the more harmless field of polemics, in which the Ministers of Navy and Finance wrangled together over the disposal of the somewhat conjectural savings resulting from the limitations set on armaments by the London agreement. These accruing savings were estimated at around 500,000,000 yen and the Navy wanted them set aside for a projected replenishment programme; but this would have left nothing for the reduction of taxation promised by the Government. After prolonged discussions, a compromise was finally reached for a six-year programme at a cost of 373,000,000 yen, the balance of the conjectured savings going to the Government. It was a compromise which was also to have its repercussions, in that the Finance Minister, in consequence of it, incurred the wrath of the super-patriots. Six months later, on 3 May 1931, a bomb was thrown at his house; only minor damage was done, but in February the following year he was to fall victim to assassination.

In the meantime, with Hamaguchi confined to hospital, Baron Shidehara had been appointed Acting Premier. Like the wounded Hamaguchi, he was a man of the highest principles and proof against the intimidation which was now so much in evidence. Being entirely without fear in this respect, he was said to be a bit of a trial at times to some of his more nervous colleagues; they, like so many of their countrymen, feared nothing more greatly than the risk of having their words or actions stigmatized as 'unpatriotic', however unmerited the accusation might be. His appointment brought strong protests from the Opposition parties in the Diet, on the grounds that it violated the principles of party government, he being a non-party man. It was not, in fact, until after the War—when he became Premier in October 1945—that he was finally persuaded to enter party politics and became President of the Progressives, the resuscitated *Minseitō*, which had been dissolved in 1940. With the advent of 1931, however, he was faced with an increasingly ominous situation—with the long-smouldering internal unrest beginning to burst into flame, with the ever-growing need for economy and retrenchment, and with the Chinese obstructing his attempts to implement his policy of peace and friendship towards China. In turn, the frustration of his China policy was playing into the hands of the Army and right-wing extremists, who were urging stronger measures.

It was the provocation and obstruction encountered in

Manchuria that was causing particular concern, as the Chinese Nationalists were ignoring the railway agreement concluded between Japan and Chang Tso-lin in the days of the former régime and were acting as though they had never existed. When I asked Shiratori about this in the closing days of 1930, and about the rising anger expressed by the Japanese Press, he asserted that the papers were unduly excited, but admitted that the Foreign Office, through the medium of the South Manchurian Railway, was about to take the matter up with the Nationalist authorities in Mukden. Protests against Chinese violation of the railway agreements, he recalled, had been made before, but had gone unheeded; further protests were therefore considered useless, so an attempt was to be made to persuade Mukden that there was plenty of room in Manchuria for both Chinese and Japanese development and that it would be of mutual benefit to co-operate instead of competing.

Although the news was hushed up at the time and known only to a limited circle in the Army, the early spring of 1931 witnessed the first serious, albeit abortive, plot by Army officers to substitute military government for civil. Known as the 'March Incident', the handful of officers concerned in this plot were members of the *Sakurakai* ('Cherry Society'), a clandestine organization formed the previous year. Their aim was to carry out, in conjunction with civilian extremists, a *coup d'état* to put an end to government resistance to military plans and to ensure independence from cabinet control for the Army. As General Ugaki had already indicated his readiness to form a new government if, as seemed probable, Hamaguchi died of his wounds, he was sounded out about his willingness to take over the reins of government if a new cabinet had to be formed. The full objectives of the plotters and the methods to be employed, however, were withheld from him; and although the detailed plans have remained obscure to this day, Ugaki was apparently led to believe that the conspirators were men of relatively moderate views, anxious like himself to ensure strong and stable government for the country. It was only later, when he learned the true nature of the plot and the violent means proposed, that he withdrew his initial acquiescence and took steps to put a stop to it.

So secret was the whole affair kept at the time that it was not until several months later that it became known even in the inner circles of Japanese officialdom; but some indication of it must have leaked out at an early stage. As early as 16 December the previous year, a Japanese journalist friend told me that the leading vernaculars and news agencies had made a combined protest against the arrest of a Press reporter by the police, who had subjected him to a rigorous cross-examination about a report concerning Hamaguchi's condition and about Ugaki's intentions. Some two or three weeks later, Ugaki himself was said to have been questioned by the Home Minister—to whom the police were responsible—concerning rumours that officers on the active list had formed a secret society and were engaging in political manœuvres behind the scenes. Subsequently, when lunching with Colonel Furujo, a friend of my army days, I was told that Ugaki was likely to become Premier before long. Viewed in retrospect, these comments—although the last of them proved incorrect—would seem to have been of more significance than they appeared to be at the time; clearly the police must have sensed that something was in the wind.

It was while this small group of Japanese officers and civilian extremists were planning their abortive coup that Shidehara, replying to a criticism about the London Naval Treaty, retorted that its ratification was, in itself, sufficient proof to show that national defence was not considered to be endangered by it. It seemed a harmless enough remark, but it caused an uproar in the Diet; it was interpreted as an attempt to shift responsibility onto the shoulders of the Emperor, who had sanctioned the ratification. Despite his assurances to the contrary, demands were made for an apology from Shidehara, a retraction of the offending words, and even his resignation. 'Traitor' was but one of the abusive epithets hurled at him by Opposition members.

Similar tumultuous scenes had been enacted in the Diet earlier in the week and culminated the following day in a virtual free-for-all fight; during it, two members and a number of onlookers were injured, one of them by a dagger thrust. Six weeks later, when the session was drawing to a close, the stormy scenes, both inside and outside the Diet, came to a climax in a series of mass demonstrations and clashes with the police. These started on 18 March, when the luckless stenographers employed in the Diet building were beaten up by a band of roughs. This was followed next day by further hooliganism, and a force of 3,000 police had to be called out to deal with a riotous demonstration staged by the *Seiyukai*; in the violent clashes that resulted, some sixty or seventy persons were injured. Not to be outdone, the proletarian parties held a mass demonstration the following day, when there were further clashes with the police, who again had to be mobilized in force.

The Diet session finally ended on 27 March, but some two weeks earlier Hamaguchi, having recovered sufficiently from his wounds, had returned to his post as Premier. The strain of dealing with these disorders, however, was too much for his weakened condition and he had to return to hospital early in April. Four months later, after a series of operations, he died, and the removal of his strong, firm hand at so critical a period left the country bereft of anyone capable of weathering the rapidly approaching storm.

Much against his will, Baron Wakatsuki had been persuaded to take over both the Presidency of the *Minseitō*, the Government party, and the premiership on 11 April; three days later he formed a new Cabinet. Only a high sense of duty had induced him to return to the parliamentary arena; but although a fine administrator, he lacked the strength and force of character of his predecessor and was not the man for such a crisis as now faced the country. Within a week of his coming to office, indications of the growing discontent and general state of unrest throughout the country were reflected in reports of radical activities of various kinds—alleged plots to create disturbances on May Day, round-ups of students and others by the police, anti-religious movements by leftists, and much else besides. Careful handling of the situation was clearly required if worse was to be avoided. A month later, with the removal of the police ban on the news of the Communist round-up of the previous year, it became known that the Communists, who had previously left violence to the right-wing extremists, were themselves resorting to violent measures. Many of those arrested were said to have been armed and, in resisting arrest, had caused the death or injury of several policemen. An attempt to set fire to the Diet building had been frustrated, but this resort to violence and the use of weapons was a new and disturbing feature of the Communist problem.

Coincident with these signs of left-wing unrest, indignation was aroused in Japanese officialdom by the Government's decison to resuscitate its proposal for salary cuts. Not only amongst the lower-grade government servants was there a countrywide outcry, but amongst higher officials as well. The intensity of feeling amongst some of these latter was reflected by Shiratori who, when lunching with me towards the end of May, launched forth into bitter condemnation of the Government's action and told me that a number of officials in government departments, high as well as low, were threatening to resign. A government statement issued three days later did little to abate the rising indignation, though it explained the urgent need for effecting economies in order to make good the anticipated deficit in revenue; it also stressed that, whereas the non-official classes had been suffering loss of income from the prolonged economic depression, officials had been receiving the same pay as in times of prosperity. Like the previous attempt to reduce salaries, however, the Government gave way at the last moment. The reversal of its decision was due, not only to the threats of resignation but, more particularly, to threats of a general strike by railwaymen and others; although not directly affected by the projected reduction of pay, they were fearful that the next step in the economy campaign would be a reduction in personnel. With all these threats in view, the Government was brought to realize that its action might well precipitate a dangerous national crisis, which the radical elements in the country would exploit for their own purposes. So far as the threatened railway strike was concerned, these fears were probably not unfounded, but prompt action by the police in arresting a number of agitators and trouble-makers prevented it from materializing.

With social and political unrest on the increase in Japan itself, the situation in Manchuria was also showing disquietening signs. The Young Marshal, Chang Hsueh-liang, was seriously ill; and although he was no great friend of Japan, the Government was worried about what would happen if he died; there was no one to succeed him and his death would probably precipitate a struggle, bringing civil war to Manchuria, between those who wished to take his place. This was the last thing Japan wanted to see. The indiscreet Shiratori, however, put a different complexion on the matter. Manchuria's alliance with Nanking, he assured me, was a purely personal arrangement between Chang Hsueh-liang and Chiang Kai-shek; if Chang died, Manchuria would probably break away from Nanking and thereby add to Chiang's troubles, which at that time included Communist guerrillas and a dissident Canton. He seemed to think that this might be all to the good for Japan. It was, nonetheless, an indication of the growing concern felt by the Government about developments in Manchuria that on 12 May they appointed, as President of the South Manchurian Railway, a veteran statesman of international repute, a man who might have been thought to be of too high a calibre for such a post. This was Viscount Uchida, who had served as Ambassador both in Washington and Petrograd in pre-War days and had been Foreign Minister three times. His appointment came as a complete surprise to everyone and, as he had always been regarded as being in the *Seiyukai* camp, it showed the Government's determination to keep the S.M.R. Presidency out of the realm of party politics. Five days later, General Ugaki retired from the Army and was appointed Governor-General of Korea, a further indication that the Government was seeking to strengthen its hands on the neighbouring mainland and to maintain its control there.

The close link between the situations developing in Manchuria and Korea was made evident two or three weeks later. For some years past, the presence of several hundred-thousands of Koreans in Manchuria had been a cause of frequently recurring friction between Japan and China. Many of these Koreans had left their own country in order to get away from Japanese rule, but they were still technically Japanese subjects; as such, they were entitled to extraterritorial rights. This meant that they came under Japanese consular jurisdiction and also under the supervision of Japanese consular police, who performed the dual task of helping them when necessary and of keeping a close watch on those suspected of anti-Japanese activities. With the extension of Chinese Nationalist control over Manchuria at the close of 1928, Sino-Japanese friction over the Korean question in Manchuria had increased and the Chinese objection to the purchase or lease of land by Koreans led to Chinese attempts to evict Koreans from the land they had acquired. Occasional clashes occurred in consequence, the Japanese being angered by what they regarded as Chinese oppression and persecution of Koreans, and the Chinese indignant at the use of Japanese consular police to protect them. Tempers became aroused to boiling point on 1 July 1931, when a body of some four hundred Chinese farmers tried to prevent Korean settlers at Wanpaoshan, some miles north of Changchun, from constructing an irrigation canal; Japanese consular police went to the help of the Koreans and dispersed the Chinese. There were no casualties, but sensational accounts of the affair reached Korea and inflamed Korean sentiment to such an extent that serious anti-Chinese rioting broke out in Chemulpo two days later and quickly spread to other towns and cities in Korea. According to Chinese accounts, over one hundred Chinese were killed and close on four hundred injured. Japanese indignation over the alleged massacre of Koreans at Wanpaoshan was only equalled by the fury aroused in China. There the anti-Japanese boycott was revived and the Japanese authorities in Korea were accused of failing to take proper action to suppress the anti-Chinese riots. The accusation was strenuously denied by the Japanese Government who, however, offered to pay compensation to the families of those killed; but the anger on both sides continued unabated.

In itself, the Wanpaoshan incident was of no more consequence than others that had occurred previously; but, in its sensationalized form, and in the bitterness aroused by the Chinese accusations concerning the resultant riots in Korea, it served to play into the hands of the Army and of the nationalist extremists in Japan. These elements were tiring of the failure of the Chinese to respond to the Shidehara policy of peace and good-will and were demanding more forceful measures to ensure Japan's 'special position' in Manchuria.

In the meantime, the situation in China itself was becoming increasingly confused. In the south, a newly-formed Canton Government was in open revolt against Nanking; in Central China, Chiang Kai-shek was engaged in operations against the Communists; in the north, heavy fighting was in progress between Shih Yu-san's troops and Chang Hsueh-liang's Mukdenites; elsewhere, Feng Yu-hsiang and others were sitting on the fence, watching developments before deciding how best to benefit themselves. To complete the picture, an unsuccessful attempt had been made on the lives of the Nanking Foreign Minister and Shigemitsu, the Japanese Consul-General, with whom he had been conferring in Shanghai; anti-Japanese boycotts had been launched in Shanghai and other cities; and Chang Hsueh-liang was said to have sought, without success, to obtain America's aid to curb Japanese policy in Manchuria.

This was the position when, towards the end of July, Eugene Chen, a former Chinese Foreign Minister and unscrupulous intriguer, arrived in Japan for the alleged purpose of seeking aid for the Cantonese. In a talk I had with him two weeks later, he denied that he had any such intention and denied, too, that there was any truth in the report that he had offered concessions in Manchuria in return for Japanese assistance. His main object, he said, was to study at first hand the situation in Japan and to find out the

M

real feelings and intentions of the Japanese towards China; Canton would then be able to formulate its foreign policy on the basis of his findings. While strongly censuring Chiang Kai-shek for 'treating China as though it were his own personal property, selling all the most lucrative posts, and being subservient to the chief of the Chinese underworld in Shanghai',[1] he asserted that the Canton defection was not a separatist movement but a national one, aimed at establishing a new national government to carry out the principles of the 1911 Revolution, which Chiang had ignored.

Denying though Chen did, that he had offered concessions to Japan in Manchuria in return for Japanese assistance, Baron Shidehara confided to a friend of mine some time later that he had, in fact, done so. Recalling the incident, Shidehara described the amazement he had felt when Chen called on him and revealed the purpose of his visit. He had been empowered by Wang Ching-wei, he said, to notify him that if, as he expected, the Canton clique came into power in Nanking, it was prepared to turn Manchuria into an autonomous state under Japanese protection, demilitarize it, and appoint Tang Shao-yi as Chinese High Commissioner. Chen, of course, was never in a position to implement his promises, even if Japan had agreed to help him; but it may be recalled in passing that Wang, for whom he claimed to speak, was to break away from Chiang Kai-shek in March 1940. Having then established a government of his own in Nanking, he later concluded a treaty with Japan. From that treaty was to spring the Alliance with the Japanese, into which his government entered in June 1943, at the height of the Pacific War.

From what Shidehara said, it was clear that Chen's denial was not strictly correct. The confidences he retailed to me, about secret promises of active support for Canton from prominent Chinese generals and politicians, proved of equally little substance. On the other hand, a talk I had, close on two years later, with Komai Tokuzo, a member of that body of independent Japanese political adventurers known as *Shina ronin*[2] seemed to indicate that there were other Chinese besides Wang Ching-wei and Eugene

[1] This was the notorious Tu Yueh-sen, whose henchmen had carried out the slaughter of the Chinese Communists in Shanghai in April 1927 on his orders, apparently at Chiang's instigation.

[2] Although I was unaware of it at the time, Pu Yi, in his autobiography *From Emperor to Citizen*, says Komai was head of the General Affairs Office of State Control in the Manchoukuo Government until July 1933; as such, he was the virtual Premier.

Chen, willing to recognize Japan's rights and interests in Manchuria. By April 1933, when this talk took place, Japan had already taken control of that area; but Komai, expressing his regret that the Japanese had been compelled to resort to armed action, asserted that force would not have been necessary if his advice had been followed at the time of Kuo Sung-lin's revolt against Chang Tso-lin in December 1925.[1]

Kuo's aim, he said, had been to rid Manchuria of the corruption and maladministration of the Chang régime and to establish an autonomous government in Mukden, guaranteeing Japan's rights and interests. Both C. T. Wang and Feng Yu-hsiang, he maintained, were behind him in this and were prepared to support him. Komai had tried to persuade the Japanese authorities to back Kuo, morally if not actively, as he had felt convinced of Wang's sincerity and that a well-administered Manchuria friendly to Japan would be of immense benefit. The Japanese authorities, however, had rejected his suggestion and had adopted a neutral attitude which, in actual fact, had helped Chang and handicapped Kuo.

Chang, in the meantime, had made all kinds of promises in the extremity of his distress, but forgot them all when the danger was past. By then, of course, it was too late to remedy the situation, although Count Kodama, Governor of the Kwantung Leased Territory, apologized subsequently to Komai for the mistake he had made in rejecting his advice, Komai's comment in recalling all this was that, had his advice been followed and Kuo had thereby achieved his aim, the developments since September 1931 would never have occurred and Manchuria would have become an autonomous state on much the same lines as recommended in the Lytton Report.

If Kuo had, in fact, been able to bring about this satisfactory condition of affairs, the Japanese Government's policy of seeking to ensure Japan's rights and interests in Manchuria by peaceful means might well have succeeded; but much had happened since December 1925, and by the summer of 1931 the situation created by the Chinese Nationalists' demands for the recovery of Chinese rights in Manchuria had become explosive. The ominous shadows being cast were reflected in the growing signs of uneasiness in Japanese official circles.

Coming on top of the indignation aroused by the Wanpaoshan affair and by the anti-Japanese boycott in China, the news that a

[1] See pp. 86–7.

Japanese officer, Captain Nakamura, and his three companions had been shot by Chinese soldiers near Taonan, on the borders of Manchuria and Inner Mongolia, added further fuel to the fire. The shooting, and the subsequent cremation of the four victims for the purpose of removing all trace of the outrage, had occurred late in June; but it was not until 17 August that news of the incident was released for publication. From later information, it was clear that Nakamura had been engaged in some kind of secret mission; but the fact that he, a serving officer, had been murdered by Chinese soldiers was regarded as an affront to the Japanese Army, who demanded stern measures accordingly. Attempts were made to settle the matter and other outstanding issues amicably, but it was clear from talks with Foreign Office officials and Japanese officers that the Foreign Office and the War Office were at loggerheads about this; the former urged patience and restraint, the latter demanded more forceful measures. To make matters worse, anti-Japanese rioting broke out in Tsingtao on the day after the murder of Nakamura was announced and added to the rising feelings of resentment and frustration.

It was while the situation was boiling up in this way that I had a visit from an American friend, who had just come over from Manchuria, where he had been in the employ of the South Manchurian Railway for some years. His comments were revealing. According to him, there had always been a certain amount of criticism, by Japanese traders and small businessmen there, of the Government's failure to take strong action against Chinese misdeeds, but the Japanese official classes and the more responsible residents normally took little heed of these murmurings. He had noticed, however, a distinct change of late; even the higher officials, he said, were beginning to feel that something ought to be done without further delay if the situation was not to drift from bad to worse. Not only were the Chinese continuing their old practice of procrastination but, puffed up with their own conceit and taking advantage of Japan's declared policy of conciliation and leniency, which they interpreted as a sign of weakness, they were resorting to a provocative policy of irritation and pin-pricks, much as they had employed against Soviet Russia until the Russians had turned round on them in 1929. What he feared was that, if the Chinese continued in this way much longer, the Japanese, their patience exhausted, would eventually hit back as the Russians had done. The Chinese, however, counted on

America and the West to side with them against Japan if this happened, he said, and they imagined that, because Japan was afraid of this and also feared the outbreak of revolution in her own country if she resorted to armed action in Manchuria, she would not dare to strike. His personal view was that the Chinese, in counting on the Western Powers rallying to their support if Japan hit back, overlooked the fact that they themselves had forfeited any such sympathy by their actions since 1920.

Apart from this final observation, which was soon to be proved unjustified, the fears expressed by my American friend were shown to be well-merited. On the night of 18 September, a bare fortnight later, a bomb explosion on the railway line just outside Mukden brought on an exchange of shots between a Japanese patrol, which went to investigate the cause of it, and a party of Chinese soldiers. The fighting spread rapidly, the local Japanese military authorities took action, and by dawn the following day Mukden was under Japanese military occupation. The Army had taken matters into their own hands, the Government in Tokyo was, from then on, to be increasingly ignored and, though hardly foreseen at the time, the way was set for 'government by assassination', for Japan's alliance with Germany, for Pearl Harbour, for the ending of colonialism in South-East Asia as a result of Japan's espousal of Pan-Asianism during the War that followed, and for the rise of Communist China as a great world problem.

CHAPTER XIV

The Manchurian Eruption and its Reverberations

In acting as they did and thus forcing the Government's hand, the military authorities in Manchuria claimed that the bombing of the railway line, and the firing that followed, had created a situation calling for prompt and effective action, to prevent more serious developments. Later, when censured abroad for failing to appeal to the League of Nations before resorting to force, the Japanese reply was, that there was not time to do so; the situation would have got completely out of hand, to Japan's disadvantage, long before the slow-moving machinery of the League had even got into gear. It was much the same argument that Britain was to use twenty-five years later at the time of the Suez crisis, when she was upbraided for failing to bring the dispute before the United Nations. Whatever the legal and moral aspects of the two affairs may have been, the purely tactical reasoning in both instances was perfectly logical.

Up to the time of the Mukden incident, Japan's fundamental policy had been to maintain and develop her rights and interests in Manchuria by peaceful means. Not only was this considered essential for the economic welfare of Japan and for building up the area, both as a bulwark against Soviet Russia and as a supply source in the event of some future clash with the United States; it also had a strong emotional appeal for the Japanese people at large, who dwelt sentimentally on the 'blood and treasure' expended in recovering these rights and interests from Czarist Russia in 1905. By striving, therefore, for friendly relations with her immediate neighbours and with the West, Japan sought to avoid any outside interference with this policy; by her determination to prevent either Chinese civil war or Muscovite subversion from spreading into her sphere of influence in South Manchuria, she strove to ensure the peace and stability that were essential for the development of that region. That she aimed to carry out her development schemes by peaceful means was indicated by her strong support of the League of Nations and its Covenant and by her advocacy of international co-operation in general; but the events which took place on that September night in 1931 marked the end of these peaceable attempts and their substitution by resort to force.

What was not known at the time, either to the Japanese public or to the outside world, was that preparations for the doings of that night and for the developments that followed quickly on them, had been made by a handful of politically-minded officers of field rank in the Kwantung Army, the military force based on Port Arthur and responsible for the protection of both the Kwantung Peninsula and the South Manchurian Railway zone. They had intended to start the incident ten days later, but they had got wind of the fact that conversations between Shigemitsu, Chiang Kai-shek, and T. V. Soong in Nanking had resulted in a decision to send Soong to Manchuria to confer with Count Uchida and Chang Hsueh-liang on an overall settlement of the Sino-Japanese issues in Manchuria. They decided, therefore, to forestall the meeting by starting the incident on 18 September instead of the 28th as originally planned. Even so, there was nearly a hitch at the last moment. Both the Government and the military authorities in Tokyo had been apprehensive about the highly charged atmosphere in Manchuria. The War Minister had accordingly sent Major-General Tatekawa as his representative to Mukden to urge prudence. Determined to precipitate matters before he had had time to pass on his message to the Commander-in-Chief, the plotters contrived, therefore, to put him into a drunken slumber. It was while he was in this condition that the explosion took place on the railway line, a few miles north. Developments followed in rapid succession.

On receipt of the news that fighting had broken out, both the Chief of the General Staff and the War Minister sent orders to prevent any extension of the operations, but their orders were ignored. The C.-in-C. in Manchuria wished to comply with Tokyo's instructions, but he was over-ruled by his subordinates, who persuaded him that it was his duty to take action to deal with the unrest reported in Harbin and Kirin. As the Japanese had a force of only some 10,000 men in Manchuria at the time as against 260,000 Chinese troops, the C.-in-C.'s action was perhaps understandable; but it marked the first open act of defiance to the central authorities in Tokyo and a further deterioration in military discipline. Other acts of defiance followed, even the Emperor himself being defied when troops from Korea were rushed to Kirin, in spite of his refusal to sanction their despatch.

Rather than reveal the intransigence of the Kwantung Army and the lack of unity in the Army as a whole, the military authorities in Tokyo, after failing to obtain compliance with their orders, accepted the initial *fait accompli* with as good grace as possible, but continued to do what they could to localize the operations. They had no love for Chang Hsueh-liang, and in his place they would have liked someone who would establish a régime friendly to Japan; but they were opposed to annexation or to the creation of a new state severed from China. They were particularly anxious to avoid any extension of the operations into North Manchuria, as they were fearful of antagonizing the League and provoking the Russians into action. Instructions to this effect were sent to the Kwantung Army but, after initial acceptance, they were again ignored. It was, in fact, significant that on only three occasions were their orders obeyed and in each instance these concerned primarily military considerations—on 23 September forbidding an advance on Harbin, on 24 November ordering the evacuation of Tsitsihar, and on 27 November halting the advance on Chinchow. Orders with a political content were ignored completely; and so it came about that, contrary to the opposition of both the Government and the military authorities in Tokyo, Manchoukuo was brought into being in February 1932, with the former 'Boy Emperor' of China, Pu Yi, as its Chief Executive. Like the War Office and General Staff, the Government had been totally opposed to severing Manchuria from China in this way. What it would have liked was an autonomous or semi-autonomous régime friendly to Japan, combined with a measure of control from Tokyo—something on the lines of Outer Mongolia *vis-à-vis* Soviet Russia. But this is looking ahead.

What is perhaps not generally known is, that Baron Shidehara had apparently given serious consideration to taking up with the League the question of China's constant violations of treaty rights and general provocation, but had waited too long. It was a parallel, in some respects, to Sir Edward Grey's failure in 1914 to warn Germany in time that she would have to reckon with Britain as an active belligerent against her in the event of a European conflagration.

That Shidehara had been warned of the dangers of continuing his policy of friendship and conciliation too long was confided to me by Iwanaga some weeks after the outbreak of the Manchurian trouble in September 1931. As early as March that year, he said, he had urged him to lay the whole matter before the League, with a view to bringing China to task. Unless some such step was taken before the situation got any worse, national sentiment in Japan, already highly charged and critical of the Government for being too weak-kneed towards China, might erupt and force his hand. Shidehara had admitted to him that such a danger existed, but had stressed that he was simply pursuing the tactics of his two greatest predecessors as Foreign Minister, Count Mutsu and Marquis Komura. They had come in for similar criticism in the days leading to the wars with China and Russia, in 1894 and 1904, but had refused to be diverted from their policy of patience, forbearance and conciliation until they were assured of the moral support of the world in general for whatever action they might take. He, too, was determined to make concessions to the limit of endurance so that, when finally the time came to take action, world opinion would be on Japan's side.

Had he taken the advice proffered by Iwanaga and others, the tragedy might have been averted, but he waited too long and his hand was forced in such a way as to nullify the policy he had carried out so persistently with such patience and tolerance. Even so, the Government did its best to localize the fighting and put an end to it, and the Japanese Press, while showing its approval of the initial action taken by the Army, urged the need to prevent unnecessary extension of the military operations and expressed the hope of a speedy return to normal conditions. In contrast to the reaction in China, where violent anti-Japanese outbursts occurred, there was, in fact, very little bellicosity in Japan at the start amongst the people at large. The Kwantung Army, however, viewed the situation in a different light; ignoring orders from Tokyo, they despatched reinforcements from Korea. From a strictly military point of view, their subsequent actions in extending the area of operations were probably justified, but their increasing disregard of the Government's instructions caused acute embarrassment to the authorities in Tokyo.

In the meantime, within three days of the Mukden incident, China had appealed to the League and the very efficient Chinese propaganda machine was soon in full swing. The consequent criticism of Japan, which began to pour in from abroad, caused growing resentment amongst the general public who, during the opening days, had welcomed the Government's attempt to regain control of the situation and hold the Army in check. As a Japanese friend remarked to me at the time, 'It is all very well for us Japanese to criticize our own Government, but we are not prepared to be told by foreigners what we should and should not do.' It was a reaction similar to that in Britain at the time of the Boer War.

In view of American actions in Mexico, Nicaragua and elsewhere, American criticism was particularly resented; it seemed to imply a double standard of what was right and what was wrong. Japan had never questioned or interfered with the American Monroe Doctrine; why, then, should the United States interfere in East Asia, where Japan's political, strategic and economic interests were just as vital as America's were in the Western Hemisphere? Had not Theodore Roosevelt himself, at one time, advocated some kind of Monroe Doctrine for Japan in the Far East? So ran the argument; but before long, strong resentment against Britain and the League of Nations was also being voiced. Not only had criticism of Japan come from British spokesmen at the League Council but, barely a week after the outbreak in Manchuria, anti-Japanese riots had broken out in Hong Kong. Wild and grossly exaggerated reports about them had circulated freely and the local British authorities were accused, quite unjustly, of having failed to provide adequate protection for the Japanese residents in the colony. It was, however, the criticism made by Lord Reading and Lord Cecil at Geneva, and alleged criticisms by Sir Miles Lampson and others in China and elsewhere, that caused the greatest umbrage.

How deeply this resentment was felt, even by the most fervent Anglophile Japanese, was indicated by a remark made by Count Soyeshima towards the end of October. Half-jokingly, but with obvious reproach, he shook his fist at me and said, 'You British! You have stabbed Japan in the back at Geneva and in China, and are likely to lose even your best friends in Japan.' Always an ardent admirer of Britain and a keen advocate of Anglo-Japanese friendship, it had come as a shattering blow to him to find Britain seemingly turning against Japan and siding with China at Geneva, while Lampson appeared to be as thick as thieves with Chiang Kai-shek and Chang Hsueh-liang and hob-nobbing with them to the detriment of Japan. That it was Lampson's duty, as British Minister to China, to maintain close and friendly relations with the leading Chinese officials was, to Soyeshima, beside the point;

but there was every reason to believe his assertion a few days later, that he had never known anti-British sentiment so wide-spread or so deeply grounded as it then was. In part this was due to sensational, and often misleading, Press reports and to Pan-Asiatic propaganda, but it was something of a shock to find that even so level-headed and well-informed a man as Soyeshima was giving credence to the wild reports circulating at the time.

A good example of Pan-Asiatic fulminations appeared in a fiery article in the right-wing paper *Nihon* on the same day as Soyeshima made this assertion. In it, Dr Minagawa, a violent reactionary and fervent supporter of the Pan-Asiatic movement, urged that, if the League attempted to apply sanctions, Japan should proceed to conquer the whole of China and expel all Western influence, first from East Asia and ultimately from all Asia, in order to release Asiatics from 'the bondage of the proud and arrogant Whites'. Britain he dubbed as the 'arch-fiend', obstructing Japanese expansion on the mainland, and he ended with the pious hope that India would rise and deal her a mortal blow.

Articles and letters on similar lines, written by Japanese right-wing extremists or by Indian malcontents, were by no means uncommon, but normally they carried little weight with the Japanese reading public; from the autumn of 1931 onwards, however, it was clear that the little handful of Pan-Asiatic enthusiasts was doing its best to exploit the growing feeling of resentment aroused by the criticisms of Japan in the countries of the West, the 'proud and arrogant Whites' castigated by Dr Minagawa and others. The dire effect of this campaign was not at once apparent and was not, in fact, taken seriously at the start; but as the 1930s went by, its results became all too apparent and Minagawa's tirade, with its appeal for the expulsion of Western influence and the release of Asia from White bondage, fantastic as it seemed at the time, became gradually an article of faith with the Japanese people at large.

Understandable as was the Japanese reaction to the criticisms made abroad, the resentment was due, at least in part, to the mischievous nature of so many Press reports and rumours. Even Sir Francis Lindley, who had succeeded Sir John Tilley as British Ambassador in the early summer, was accused of being pro-Chinese and of sending reports unfavourable to Japan to London. As I had good reason to know, the accusation was both unfair and unfounded. Throughout the Manchurian trouble, he made a point of inviting me along to his study for private talks at frequent intervals; his remarks were not, as a rule, for publication, but it was perfectly clear that, on the whole, his sympathies lay with the Japanese and he spoke bitterly at times of the way in which his advice had been ignored in Downing Street. This was particularly so up to the time when Sir John Simon took over from Lord Reading as Foreign Secretary in November that year. His Military Attaché, Lieutenant-Colonel Hugh Simson, a friend of mine from Army days, was even more outspoken in his condemnation of the way in which the League and sections of the British Press 'fell for Chinese propaganda'. Generally speaking, in fact, the whole staff of the British Embassy in Tokyo was sympathetic towards Japan, even when critical of some of her actions.

What was perhaps surprising, after all the criticism that had come from Geneva, was the moderation in which Walters, one of Sir Eric Drummond's secretaries in the League, spoke during a visit he made to Japan in November. I had a number of private talks with him and was struck by his frank admission that the League had blundered badly on several occasions and that their handling of the whole question had been 'unlike the usual methods of the Council'. This, he felt, was largely due to 'a bad attack of nerves', everyone being 'scared stiff' lest the situation should develop in such a way as to bring on another world war. Although he did not put it so bluntly, the implication was that the Chinese, whom the Japanese accused of manipulating the League Secretariat for their own ends, had sought to stampede the League into action and had succeeded.

Sir Francis Lindley, who had invited me to a private lunch on this occasion to meet Walters, was particularly critical of the League for inviting the United States to attend the Council meetings. America was not a member and it seemed to him preposterous, especially in view of the mutual suspicions between her and Japan, that she should take part, even as an observer; it was bound to play into the hands of the reactionary extremists. Walters was inclined to agree, but suggested that Japan ought to have seized the initiative and proposed America's inclusion herself; she should also, he felt, have proposed the despatch of a League commission to Manchuria. Instead, she had placed herself in the position of being considered unconciliatory by opposing both these proposals so vigorously when they were put forward. Perhaps he was right, although his suggestion tended to overlook

Japan's innate suspicions of the United States and the intensity of her feelings about outside intervention of any kind in Manchuria. The League's apparent failure to appreciate Japanese national sentiment on these two scores, and on the reasons for her repeated insistence on direct negotiations with China, undoubtedly accounted for much of the trouble that arose from the outset. There seemed to be a similar failure on the part of the British, American and French governments a few weeks later, when their ambassadors in Tokyo were instructed to present notes expressing apprehensions about the Chinchow situation. Though couched as expressions of 'friendly concern' rather than as actual warnings, the action of the three governments in making this joint approach reminded the Japanese all too forcibly of the Triple Intervention of 1895 and all its consequences. I was amused, however, when, a few days after this talk about the League, Iwanaga, at a private dinner at his house, invited Walters to a game of golf the following day. On Walters saying he had brought no clubs with him, Iwanaga twitted him about coming to Japan without any. 'You are just like the League,' he said, with a twinkle in his eye. 'You fail to understand Japan. No golfer, if he knew anything about my country, would come here without his clubs, and the League would never have made such blunders if it had had any real knowledge of Japan.'

Without in any way minimizing the gravity of the operations launched by the Japanese Army, the term 'Japan's incursion into Manchuria' is apt to conjure up the picture of a large-scale invasion and to overlook the fact that the initial action was taken by Japanese troops stationed there in accordance with treaty rights. Under the terms of the Portsmouth Treaty, Japan was entitled to maintain fifteen officers and men for every kilometre of the railway, or some 16,500 in all. Even including the reinforcements rushed in at the start, this number was not exceeded and was minute compared with the forces available to the Chinese in Manchuria; but the Government, being anxious to localize the fighting, had promptly issued orders for the recall of the reinforcements and had ordered that no more were to be sent, as they were fearful of increasing the total beyond the limit allowed by treaty. In this, and in their attempt to check any further extension of military operations, the Government appeared momentarily to have been successful; but soon there were ominous signs that they were playing a losing game. From information made available since the War, it is clear that the bomb explosion outside Mukden was the work of Army plotters; but, at the time, the Japanese contended it had seemingly been the work of Chinese hot-heads annoyed with their superiors for having agreed to the punishment of Nakamura's murderers,[1] while the Chinese maintained that the Japanese themselves had staged the whole affair in order to provide a pretext for military action. Be that as it may, with both sides itching for a fight, the bomb incident merely provided the spark that set off the powder magazine and the Japanese acted with clock-like precision in occupying strategic points along the railway line over an extended area. For the first two or three weeks this appeared to satisfy the Army's requirements; but from early October, for seemingly valid military reasons, one thrust forward followed another. Each of these was to have far-reaching consequences, as also had an outbreak of disturbances in Tientsin.

The first of these thrusts had actually been launched within thirty-six hours of the explosion on the railway line outside Mukden, when troops had been sent to secure the town of Kirin, eighty miles east of Changchun; ostensibly this was to ward off a threatened attack from that direction. It soon became clear, however, that the Japanese were availing themselves of this opportunity to link it by rail with Kainei, on the north-east border of Korea; this was a strategical line, projected ever since 1909. The Chinese had agreed to its construction with Japanese capital 'at an opportune time', but had procrastinated and placed obstacles in the way ever since. The importance of this line for the Japanese lay in the fact that, in the event of a clash with Russia, it would enable them to rush troops much more quickly from Japan to North Manchuria, by sending them across by sea to north-east Korea and from there to Changchun, via Kirin, which was already linked to that city by rail. The outbreak of the Manchurian trouble in September, therefore, provided the pretext for occupying Kirin and setting to work to complete the long-projected line; but it had Russia rather than China in mind.

The next extension of operations was south-westward towards

---

[1] It may not be out of place to recall that my telegram, quoting this official Japanese view, was sent via Shanghai, where the Chinese censors proceeded to re-word it, so as to make it appear that Japanese, not Chinese, hot-heads were responsible. These distortions are recorded in J. N. Penlington, *The Mukden Mandate* pp. 108–9, Tokyo, Maruzen, 1932. Mr Penlington was *The Daily Telegraph* Correspondent at the time.

Chinchow, on the line from Mukden to Shanhaikwan, the gate-way to North China. There, Chang Hsueh-liang had established his headquarters and concentrated the main body of his troops. Inferior in quality, they were nevertheless vastly superior in numbers to the Japanese, who therefore regarded them as a serious threat and demanded their withdrawal. On 8 October came news that Japanese Army planes had bombed the city, preparatory to launching an attack on it. The news came in while Shiratori was talking to a group of foreign correspondents at the Foreign Office and his immediate comment was, 'That means the resignation of the Cabinet if true, as it shows that the Army is openly flouting the Government's orders.' Later in the day, however, the report was modified. There was no question of an attack being contemplated, it was stated, and the bombing had been unpremeditated; the planes had been fired on by the Chinese while reconnoitring over the city and had dropped the bombs in retaliation. The reaction abroad, however, was immediate and from then on until the end of December, when the Chinese finally withdrew, there was a series of alarums and excursions and an exchange of vituperation between Japan and her critics in Geneva, London and Washington.

Some light on the situation in Manchuria during this period was thrown during a talk I had, early in December, with Colonel Simson, who had just returned from a tour of inspection with a party of other foreign military attachés. He had been particularly impressed by the frank replies given by the Japanese military authorities on the spot and by their readiness to let the military attachés see whatever they wished to see. It was an impression that I myself was to have, rather surprisingly, some three years later, when studying the situation during a visit to what was by then known as Manchoukuo. Simson was very critical, however, of the anti-Japanese attitude of the foreign military observers from China, who had taken up their quarters in the building housing the Chinese headquarters in Chinchow. He was not alone in this; the French Military Attaché from Tokyo, he said, had nearly come to blows with his 'opposite number' from Peking on the attitude adopted by him. It was, in effect, an example in miniature of the curiously strong partisanship so often displayed by foreigners in Japan and China respectively.

While the Chinchow dispute was taking place, two other de-velopments of far-reaching importance served to bedevil the situation still further. On 3 November, a party of Japanese engineers was sent under military escort to repair the Nonni River bridges, which had been destroyed in operations between opposing forces of Chinese irregulars. After a number of minor incidents, including an exchange of shots resulting from Chinese attempts to prevent the repairs, the Japanese finally decided to use force and drove the opposing Chinese under Ma Chan-shan back northwards, as far as Tsitsihar on the Chinese Eastern Railway. The significance of this action was that it took the Japanese, for the first time, into the Soviet sphere of influence in North Manchuria. Lest the Russians should be frightened into taking some positive action, Japan sent a reassuring Note to Moscow; but a few days later, when replying to a Soviet protest, she followed this up by criticizing the Kremlin for allowing the Chinese to use the C.E.R. for sending reinforcements to General Ma. This, it was pointed out, was in strong contrast to Japan's strictly neutral stand in 1929, when she refused permission for Chinese reinforcements to use the South Manchurian Railway at the time of the Soviet operations to recover the Chinese Eastern Railway. This exchange of acerbities, brought about by the advance on Tsitsihar, marked the start of open friction with Russia; after periods of mounting tension, it was to lead to serious armed clashes in 1938 and 1939 and to culminate in Russia's entry into the War against Japan in 1945, a bare week before it ended.

Almost simultaneously with the Nonni River developments, disturbances had broken out in Tientsin and reports were soon circulating that the Chinese 'Boy Emperor', Pu Yi, who had been living in the Japanese Concession there ever since his escape from the Forbidden City in 1924, had been 'spirited away' by the Japanese and taken to Manchuria, his ancestral home. A Chinese assertion that he had been abducted and conveyed there in a Japanese warship was officially denied. From what his former British tutor, Sir Reginald Johnston, said later in his *Twilight in the Forbidden City*, and from the very confusing evidence given at the War Crime Trials in Tokyo in 1946, it would seem that the denial was justified and that he went to Manchuria of his own free will.[1] Be that as it may, his flight to Manchuria, which was officially admitted on 15 November, was to have a profound effect on the whole situation, although this was by no means clear at the start.

[1] This has now been confirmed by Pu Yi himself in his autobiography, *From Emperor to Citizen* (Peking, 1964).

When I questioned Shiratori on what Japan's policy would be if Pu Yi was proclaimed ruler of Manchuria, he maintained that the question had not been seriously considered, as such a contingency was not anticipated.

During the weeks that followed, the situation developing around Chinchow was the main centre of attention, and wide-spread indignation was aroused in Japan when Press messages reported that Henry Stimson, the American Secretary of State, had accused Japan of breaking her pledge and letting the Army 'run amok'. His outburst had been occasioned by a temporary advance of Japanese troops towards Chinchow, after assurances had been given that no attack was contemplated. Apart from the use of the words 'run amok', which were considered highly offensive, the main cause for indignation was that Stimson had revealed Japan's assurances, given in confidence, that no attack on Chinchow was intended. By his revelation of this undertaking, it was feared that Chang's attitude would be stiffened; safe in the knowledge that Japan was not planning to drive his troops out of the city, he would revoke his proposal to evacuate it. Although it subsequently transpired that the offending words, 'run amok', had never been used by Stimson, Shiratori confided to myself and other foreign correspondents that Stimson had apologized to Debuchi, the Japanese Ambassador in Washington, for having inadvertently revealed the assurances given confidentially by Japan. The main sufferer from this unfortunate slip, however, was the luckless Baron Shidehara, who was denounced in scathing terms by nationalist extremists for giving away the 'strategic secrets' revealed by Stimson.

With the advent of 1932, the situation appeared to have been eased; the Chinese had finally withdrawn from Chinchow and on 2 January the Japanese had taken over control of the city. Acting on the principle laid down by the Chinese strategist Sonshi more than 2,000 years earlier, the Japanese had kept up steady pressure to show that they were prepared to use force if necessary, but had left a loop-hole for escape, so as not to drive the enemy to fight with desperation. The situation was not, however, to remain eased for long. Before the month was up, developments in both Harbin and Shanghai were casting ominous shadows, which were to materialize to a serious extent in the weeks ahead. The situation in Harbin—like Tsitsihar, it was within the Soviet sphere of in-fluence—began to show disquieting signs early in January when,

N

as in the instance of the Nonni River bridges two months earlier, trouble arose between two opposing groups of Chinese irregulars. Looting and disorder broke out, followed by fighting, and fears were felt for the safety of the Japanese community there. On the 27th came reports that two Japanese and sixteen Koreans had lost their lives and that a Japanese aircraft, while reconnoitring over the city, had been shot down and one of its occupants murdered. That evening, when dining with Colonel Simson, I remarked half-jokingly that it looked almost as though the stormy petrel, Colonel Doihara, must be somewhere in the background, as he always seemed to be around where trouble was brewing. Smilingly Simson replied, 'You are quite right. I heard today that he is in Harbin.'

By the 28th, a small force of infantry and artillery was on its way there to protect the lives and property of the 6,000 Japanese residents. The Japanese Ambassador in Moscow was instructed to explain to the Soviet Government that it was a purely protective and temporary measure, but the Russians responded by refusing the use of the C.E.R. branch line from Changchun to Harbin for the transport of the Japanese troops. To the Japanese warning that refusal of railway facilities would be regarded as 'an unfriendly act', the Russians retorted that they were resolved to observe strict neutrality by denying the use of the line to Japanese and Chinese troops alike—a boomerang from the Japanese protest, lodged two months earlier, against the transportation of Ma Chan-shan's reinforcements to Tsitsihar. The upshot was that the Japanese decided to take temporary control of the line and, after heavy fighting with the Chinese on the outskirts of the city, they entered it on 5 February.

With Japanese forces now in North Manchuria, in the Soviet zone, at two points along the main Chinese Eastern Railway—at Tsitsihar and Harbin—Japanese-Soviet friction became increasingly noticeable; but Moscow, intent on completing its Five-Year Plan, was clearly not anxious to engage in warlike operations with Japan or with anyone else at that juncture. The Kremlin had, in fact, broached the subject of a non-aggression pact with Japan to Yoshizawa, when he was passing through Moscow on his way home from Geneva to take up the appointment of Foreign Minister in place of Shidehara. In making the proposal public, before the Japanese Government had had time to consider it or to prepare the ground for its favourable reception, however, the

Russians had, as Shiratori put it, 'blundered badly'. As, moreover, Japan considered the Kellogg Pact sufficient for the purpose and had no non-aggression pact with any other Power, the proposal was rejected, the Japanese asserting for good measure that they had no intention of violating Soviet territory anyway.

In the meantime, trouble of a far more serious nature had been brewing in an unexpected quarter and was certainly not stirred up deliberately by the Japanese; they were far too preoccupied with Manchuria to hanker after military operations elsewhere, least of all in an area of such international importance as Shanghai. Following the indignation aroused by the publication of insulting remarks about the Japanese Emperor in a Chinese newspaper and the assault on five Japanese monks by a Chinese mob in Shanghai on 18 January, a group of Japanese civilian hot-heads carried out an attack two days later on a factory, at which those responsible for the assault were said to be employed. Coming close on the heels of the murder of a Japanese teacher and his wife by a Chinese mob in Foochow, and in combination with a number of other incidents involving violence, tension rose rapidly. In the belief that a display of naval force would be sufficient to bring the situation under control, the Government ordered the despatch of a number of warships to Shanghai, together with detachments of bluejackets to serve as landing parties. Demands made to the local Chinese authorities for the suppression of the organized anti-Japanese movement remained unanswered. With the situation becoming increasingly tense, the Navy Office in Tokyo accordingly issued a statement on the night of 27 January. Characterizing the prolonged anti-Japanese agitation as virtually 'warfare without arms', it went on to say that, if the Chinese failed to put a stop to such activities, the Navy would be compelled to take steps to protect Japanese lives and property. These were ominous words. On the following day, therefore, the municipal authorities in the International Settlement, fearing the rising tempers of the Chinese mobs roaming about the city, declared a State of Siege and called out the volunteers to man the defences.

For the next few days, the common danger threatening Japanese and other foreigners alike, tended to bring them together, and there were even reports of plans afoot for closer co-operation between Britain and Japan. Although this turned out to refer only to conferring together about the steps to be taken in the event of China carrying out her threat to abolish extraterritoriality,

London's action in declining to join Washington in a recent minatory Note on Manchuria had helped very considerably to restore more friendly Japanese feelings towards Britain, a friendship which had been sadly impaired for a time by the British attitude at the League session in October. The question of Anglo-Japanese co-operation cropped up again a few days later, after regular forces of the Chinese Army had fired on Japanese bluejackets on 29 January. The latter were taking up their positions in the defence sector of the International Settlement at the time and had hit back. For doing so, they were roundly denounced in the United States, and sensational Press telegrams from America, hinting at war with Japan, implied that Britain and America were determined to act in concert against her. On my speaking to Iwanaga about these reports, he told me that some of the Press messages from the United States coming in through his organization were of so inflammatory a nature that he had felt obliged to suppress them; then, turning to Anglo-Japanese relations, he added sorrowfully, 'The situation has been rendered so delicate by American suspicions of Anglo-Japanese co-operation that both Britain and Japan have felt it necessary to remove those suspicions by refraining from co-operating as closely as they would like to do. By holding back in this way, misunderstandings have arisen and the Chinese, of course, are delighted.'

The fact that soldiers of the Chinese regular forces had fired on the Japanese bluejackets aroused grave apprehensions in Tokyo. As Shiratori explained it on the day the news came, the possibility of trouble with Chinese students and irregulars had been foreseen, but the participation of Chinese regulars was wholly unexpected. There were, he said, some 30,000 of them concentrated around Shanghai; if they took concerted action, the small Japanese force of 2,000 bluejackets, or less, faced the risk of being overwhelmed by sheer weight of numbers. To prevent such a disaster, Japan might therefore be compelled to despatch a strong military force or even bombard the city, though this step, he added, would only be taken in an extreme emergency, like in the case of the British at Wanhsien in 1926.

Similar comparisons with British actions in China were to become frequent and when, later that same day, the Government issued a formal statement, explaining its action in despatching more warships to deal with the increasingly dangerous situation, it was stressed that the sole aim was the protection of Japanese lives and interests, a move likened to the British action in despatching the Shanghai Defence Force in 1927. Apart from this, it was becoming clear that both the Japanese and the municipal authorities in the Shanghai International Settlement had miscalculated badly. They had assumed that a display of force on the part of the Japanese Navy would have sufficed to overawe the Chinese and bring them to their senses; but the Chinese, instead of climbing down, had seemingly seized the opportunity to force the Japanese into a false position, by compelling them to take action likely to embroil them with the other Powers, whose interests would be threatened by fighting. The comment of a Shanghai journalist, who happened to be in Tokyo at the time, seemed apt; the Shanghai trouble, he considered, had been brought to a head by China's determination 'to force the Powers to take a hand in the final settlement of the dispute in Manchuria, as she dares not face Japan alone in the direct negotiations on which the Japanese are insisting'. China, he maintained, had hoped to drag in the other Powers by her appeal to the League, but had failed, so she had fixed on Shanghai, with all its international complications, to compel them to intervene. It was an explanation which seemed plausible, since it was Japan's insistence on direct negotiations with China, and her belief that intervention by the League and others merely encouraged the Chinese to refuse to negotiate direct with her, that aroused so much resentment in Japan against the Western Powers.

With the situation in Shanghai rapidly worsening, Yoshizawa, who had recently returned from Geneva to take up the appointment of Foreign Minister, invited the foreign correspondents in Tokyo to an interview on the evening of 31 January. A small, thin, rather delicate figure, puffing incessantly at a cigar, he looked tired and pale and made no attempt to hide his anxiety. Stressing the extreme gravity of the situation and the heavy responsibilities resting on his shoulders, he said he had just seen the British, American and French ambassadors and had explained to them that, unless the Chinese stopped pouring in troops or withdrew to a safe distance from the city, not only would the position of the Japanese marines be exposed to the gravest danger but so, also, would the International Settlement itself. He had requested the three ambassadors, therefore, to ask their respective governments to use their influence to persuade the Chinese to withdraw voluntarily. He had done his best, he said, to remove the misapprehensions and misunderstandings that had arisen and had warned them that the Army would probably be compelled to despatch troops if the Powers failed to induce the Chinese to withdraw; Japan was not prepared to risk the annihilation of her naval landing parties.

It was a solemn meeting and a solemn warning of what was shortly to happen; and as he spoke, he outlined the developments leading to the outbreak of the fighting two days earlier, making clear the results of the miscalculations of the Japanese and the International Settlement authorities alike. The clash on the 29th had occurred when the Japanese bluejackets were taking up the positions allotted to them in the plan for the joint defence of the Settlement, a plan drawn up by the commanders of the foreign armed forces at a meeting on the 27th; but, as a result of this clash, the municipal authorities had, quite understandably, become alarmed at the prospect of being dragged into what was primarily a Sino-Japanese dispute, and at the consequent danger to the lives and property of their own countrymen in Shanghai.

In view of these circumstances, it was perhaps but natural that Japan was being blamed for the serious predicament in which Shanghai now found itself. In the United States in particular, anti-Japanese sentiment was being whipped up by glaring and often misleading headlines in the American Press, and by sensational reports from American correspondents in Shanghai; many of these latter were so anxious to file a 'good story', and to file it without delay, that the bare truth and explanatory background received but secondary consideration or none at all. To their credit, however, Senator Borah and other responsible Americans were speaking out strongly against the so-called 'peace societies', which were advocating an economic boycott of Japan. In England the *Daily Mail*, not inaptly, was dubbing such bodies as 'bloodthirsty pacifists'.

From private talks with him during the next few days it seemed clear that fundamentally Sir Francis Lindley's sympathy lay with Japan. He was very critical of the Japanese resort to bombing from the air and was annoyed at the way in which the Japanese were aggravating the situation, but he was equally critical of the Americans for being 'so damnably swelled-headed and itching for a fight in their belief that their interests in China require it'. It was this American attitude, and the apparent attempt by Washington to line up Britain and France against Japan, that was arousing so much ill-feeling against the United States among the Japanese.

That resentment was rising once more against Britain and the

League, as well as against America, was reflected in the comments of the Japanese Press, the *Mainichi* accusing them of 'encouraging China and discouraging Japan just enough to prolong the trouble'. In much the same vein, the *Asahi* stressed the danger of the Powers encouraging China to continue flouting each country in turn, if she thought she could rely on others to fight her battles for her and if misplaced sympathy should permit the Chinese to escape the penalty of their own follies. In 1926 and 1927, Britain had been made the scapegoat for these follies; now it was Japan that was being made to suffer. Even as late as the eve of the Manchurian outbreak in September 1931, it was recalled, British indignation against China had been aroused by the murder of Thorburn, a young Englishman; China's refusal to give satisfaction for the outrage had resulted in growing tension. Chinese readiness to change rapidly from one target to another, however, had been demonstrated by the way in which she had suddenly made amends and put an end to anti-British provocation in order to concentrate on Japan as the new scapegoat.

So inflamed was national sentiment becoming as a result of the reactions abroad to the developments in Shanghai that on 4 February Sir Francis called a meeting of the senior members of his staff to consider the situation and invited me to join in the discussions. Emphasizing the extreme gravity of the situation, he said he had strongly warned the Government at home of the danger of bringing further pressure on Japan, as it would only play into the hands of the civilian extremists; if economic sanctions were applied, they and the Army would very possibly insist on a gamble rather than throw up their hands in surrender. This would probably entail their seizure of important strategic points in China, in order to control sources of supply for the food and raw material required in Japan. The Powers would then be faced with the alternatives of a devastating war to bring Japan to heel or a complete and humiliating climb-down. No doubt Japan would lose in the long run, but she could 'play merry hell' at the start. She could, as a first step, mop up the British and American warships up the Yangtse, together with the military detachments sent to Shanghai from Hong Kong and Manila; she might even get Hong Kong itself by a sharp, swift stroke, as the garrison was much under strength at the time. It was a grim picture, which fortunately did not materialize on this occasion; but it foreshadowed what did, in fact, take place rather less than ten years later, when the embargo imposed on oil and other essential materials in the summer of 1941 led to Japan's desperate gamble which, for a while, looked like succeeding.

While Sir Francis was outlining the dangers as he saw them, a sealed envelope was brought in. He opened it, read the enclosure with a worried look, and then carefully burned it, after noting its contents and drafting a cable to be encyphered and sent to London. The letter, he told us, was from Baron Hayashi, a former Ambassador to Britain, and was to the effect, 'What I told you this morning that I feared, has taken place. One division has already sailed.' It was a terse and ominous message, and Sir Francis was much perturbed as to the effect it would have when it reached London, though he was hopeful that his previous warnings would serve to check any action that might otherwise be taken. Simson, on being asked for his views, replied bluntly with the advice that all the Powers should 'shut their eyes for a week or two' while the Japanese drove back the Chinese from around Shanghai. Later, producing a large-scale map of the district, he pointed out that the recent Japanese bombardment of the Woosung forts was almost certainly intended to clear the way for the passage of troop transports and for a landing at Woosung, with the object of carrying out a sweeping movement from there against the Chinese 19th Route Army outside Shanghai.[1] His appreciation of the situation was to prove correct.

Sir Francis was inclined to agree with him about the need for the Powers to adopt a policy of 'masterly inactivity' for the time being and to trust to it that, in the meantime, the Japanese would be able to clear up the whole mess; he feared, however, that it might be difficult to get everyone to take this view, and he mentioned a private letter he had had from a prominent British statesman some time before, upbraiding him for his advocacy of a policy of non-interference by Britain in the Manchurian dispute. Such an attitude, his correspondent considered, was grossly immoral. Sir Francis's own view was that, in the existing circumstances, it would be far more immoral to bring such heavy pressure on Japan as to precipitate a world war, in which millions might be killed and civilization dealt a blow even greater than in 1914-18.

[1] The 19th Route Army, commanded by Tsai Ting-kai, was not under Chiang's direct control. Its nucleus, the 67th Division, had been responsible for the Nanking outrages of March 1927. (See pp. 99-100).

Although the news of the division being sent to Shanghai had been passed to Sir Francis in strict confidence, Shiratori gave the same information to the foreign correspondents attending a Press conference later that day, but said we would be unable to cable the news, as a strict censorship on all military movements had been imposed.

On mentioning this to Sir Francis later that morning, he asked me to go along with him to see Colonel Simson. In the discussion that followed, he made no attempt to hide his continuing anxiety about the possible consequences of Japan's action in sending land forces to Shanghai, and asked me to do my best to explain the Japanese viewpoint as favourably as possible in my cables; this, he felt, was necessary in order to lessen the likelihood of the British public demanding further pressure on Japan. With Japanese troops on their way, it was now, he stressed, more than ever essential to avoid any action that might arouse national sentiment in Japan to the extent of challenging the world. 'If that happened', he added, 'they would simply have our people in Shanghai at their mercy.'

That Japanese officialdom was equally apprehensive was made patently clear when, after attending another Press conference at the Foreign Office that afternoon, I was walking back to my office with Byas, the *Times* correspondent. A taxi drew up and out jumped Captain Takahashi of the Navy Office. He had been sent by Admiral Osumi, the Navy Minister, to ask us to see him without delay. On our reaching his office, Osumi told us—without any beating about the bush—that very disquieting reports had been received regarding a change in Britain's attitude towards Japan since the outbreak of the trouble in Shanghai. One such report, which he said had just come from a very reliable source—neither British nor Japanese, he stressed—was to the effect that the British Government had decided to take drastic action if Japan despatched any land forces. As Japanese troops were already on the way, this report, he said, had caused the gravest concern; he begged us, therefore, to do what we could to remove the suspicions as to Japan's motives and to make clear her reasons for deciding to send Army reinforcements. We could quote him as authority for declaring that Japan had no other aim than to relieve the handful of bluejackets, who were worn out by continuous fighting against an enemy ten-fold superior in numbers, and to drive back the Chinese from the immediate vicinity of the city. Japan, he emphasized, had absolutely no intention of carrying out anything in the nature of a permanent occupation or of menacing British interests in the Yangtse valley, but would withdraw her armed forces as soon as their immediate task was completed.

Frankly admitting his anxiety lest the Japanese action in despatching troops should be misinterpreted abroad, he expressed the hope that the arrival of land forces might, in itself, lead the Chinese to withdraw voluntarily; even if fighting was unavoidable, he said, Britain could rest assured that the area of operations would be strictly limited—possibly extending twenty to thirty miles but certainly no further, he added in reply to my query. If Britain would only recognize that Japan regarded the Shanghai trouble in an entirely different light to the Manchurian affair, she would realize that there was no need to question Japan's intentions, he declared. 'Manchuria', he added, 'is a matter of life and death to Japan. Shanghai is only a passing incident, which we are anxious to close as soon as possible.' This clear distinction between Manchuria and China Proper did, in fact, sum up the general sentiment in Japan up to that time and for a few years more.

After suggesting that future trouble in Shanghai might be avoided by some sort of international agreement similar to the Boxer Protocol concerning Tientsin, under which no Chinese troops were permitted within a specified number of miles, the Navy Minister expressed the hope that the appointment of Admiral Nomura to command the naval forces in Shanghai would ensure better co-operation and understanding, as he was trusted by the Americans and had the reputation of being a statesman as well as a fine sailor. As future developments were to show, this reputation was well merited, though it was to be Nomura's misfortune that he was Ambassador in Washington at the time of Pearl Harbour.

From the candour with which Admiral Osumi spoke, and from the appeal he made to us to be absolutely candid in any criticisms we cared to make and in any suggestions we could offer for helping to remove misunderstandings and misapprehensions abroad, it was clear that he was deeply worried and genuine in his assurances. Sir Francis Lindley, to whom we reported the interview, assured us, however, that the report of Britain's intentions, to take drastic action if Japan sent land forces to Shanghai, was wholly unfounded; his latest information was that the British Government had come to recognize that further pressure on

Japan would be sheer folly. Rightly or wrongly, he suspected that the 'outside source' responsible for the report was his Italian colleague. From a number of talks I had subsequently with this colleague of his—a friendly but somewhat cynical diplomat—it seemed probable that he was right. When, some years later, Italy joined Japan and Germany, first in the Anti-Comintern Pact and ultimately in the Tripartite Pact of Mutual Assistance, the gist of these talks took on a significance which had not been apparent at the time. They seemed to mark the initial indication of Italy's attempt to prepare the ground for future co-operation with Japan.

CHAPTER XV

Internal Convulsions and Birth of Manchoukuo

During the weeks following the despatch of Japanese troops to Shanghai, Britain sought, with varying success, to assume the role of honest broker and to withstand those who urged her to take on the task of chastising her former ally; but before dealing further with developments in the Shanghai situation, it is necessary to turn back to the previous autumn in order to consider the internal convulsions which had taken place in Japan in the meantime. Their bearing on Japan's actions in the international field requires no emphasis.

The 'March Incident' of 1931, though nipped in the bud, had shown very conclusively that politically-minded young officers were engaged in dangerous intrigues with civilian nationalist extremists. The outbreak of the Manchurian trouble six months later served further to indicate that the Army was becoming restive and inclined to take matters into its own hands. It came as something of a shock, however, to learn in confidence from a Japanese journalist friend on 17 October that General Minami, the War Minister, had sent for the heads of the principal Japanese news organizations in order to impart secret information about the arrest of ten junior officers of the General Staff. All ten, he revealed, had been implicated with certain civilian reactionaries in a plot to assassinate some of the leading statesmen, whom they considered to be acting contrary to the country's interests by being too moderate. The intended victims were said to be Baron Shidehara, the Foreign Minister, Count Makino, Lord Keeper of the Privy Seal, Inouye Junnosuke, the Finance Minister, and Baron Wakatsuki, the Premier. Although the ageing *Genro*, Saionji, was not included, he and Makino in particular were reputed to have incurred the Army's wrath by bringing strong pressure to bear on the military authorities to curb their actions. According to my informant, the aim of the plotters was to set up a military dictatorship so that, if the League tried to invoke Article XVI of the Covenant for the imposition of economic and financial sanctions, steps could be taken without delay to ensure control of essential sources of supply by extending control over the Malay Peninsula and other strategic points in the Far East.

Although an attempt was made to suppress the news of the plot, it soon leaked out and was followed by sensational rumours. One of these maintained that army hotheads planned to get the Emperor into their hands during his attendance at the annual Grand Manœuvres in Kyushu in November and force him to abdicate in favour of Prince Chichibu. As, however, the Prince was far too advanced in his views and much too independent for the liking of the more conservative elements in Japan, the rumours seemed too fantastic to merit attention. His name, never-theless, was to be linked, albeit without any justification, with similar plots later; but from information that has become avail-able since the War, it is now known that there were extreme elements in the Army who, because the Emperor was constantly urging restraint, sought to have him removed.

From what I learned some weeks after news of the plot had leaked out, the plotters had planned to set up General Araki as dictator; but he himself was utterly opposed to anything in the nature of a military coup. On hearing what was in the wind, he had promptly taken action and put a stop to it. The officers re-sponsible, however, had since been released with nothing more than a severe reprimand as punishment. It was another instance of the typically Japanese attitude towards crimes of violence, com-mitted or projected out of a distorted sense of patriotism; the patriotic motive was regarded as more important than the criminal act or intention and therefore leniency had to be shown. It was an attitude which was to be displayed again and again in the assassin-ation plots that followed and was to undermine military discipline to an ever-increasing extent. The *Kinki Kakumei* (Imperial Flag Revolution), or 'October Incident' as the plot came to be known, was to be linked with subsequent and more disastrous plots, as the civilian participants in the 'incident' were to figure promin-ently in these later affairs.

Barely a month after the revelation of this plot, a sensation was caused by the action of Adachi Kenzo, the Home Minister, issuing a statement advocating the formation of a national or coalition government. This statement was followed later the same day by an announcement that Wakatsuki, the Premier, while agreeing that it was justified in principle, considered it difficult of realiza-tion in the existing circumstances. That seemed to settle the matter; but Adachi continued to agitate for a coalition and some three weeks later, on 11 December, after a final unsuccessful attempt to persuade him either to hand in his resignation or cease his active advocacy of a coalition cabinet, the Government resigned. Adachi was strongly criticized at the time, but a close friend of his assured me that his aim was to forestall the possibility of a military dictatorship, as he feared that the riotous scenes, which he anticipated in the coming Diet session if the Wakatsuki Government remained in power, would so sicken the country at large (which was already disgusted with the antics of the political parties) that the people might welcome a dictatorship as a preferable alternative to the continuance of party government. This may well have been true. Certain it is that increasing contempt for party politicians became evident under the new *Seiyukai* government formed by Inukai Tsuyoshi, whose first and immediate action was to reimpose the gold embargo, which had been raised by the previous government two years before. As a result, not only were all the sacrifices made by the country in order to return to a full gold basis rendered vain, but fortunes were made by speculators on the yen exchange at the expense of the millions living on the border line. Between corrupt politicians and speculating financiers there seemed little to choose, and before long, leading politicians and financiers were being lumped together with 'weak-kneed' statesmen and 'evil advisers' around the throne as targets for attack by Nationalist extremists.

The resignation of the Wakatsuki Government had marked the final death-throes of the Shidehara policy, which had been dealt such a fatal blow by the events of 18 September and all that followed. Some weeks later, when I met the former Foreign Minister at a private dinner party, I found him looking well and seemingly care-free, in spite of all he had gone through during his last three months in office. One remark of his, however, appeared to reflect his inner feelings. Great as was the relief he felt at being no longer responsible for his country's foreign policy at such a critical period, he now always opened his morning papers, he said, in fear and trepidation as to what blunder he might find had been committed by the new government. This was but one aspect of Shidehara's reaction. Another was shown in a talk he had, a few days after his resignation, with a Chinese friend, who had called on him to express his sympathy. Iwanaga, who told me about it, had learned of it from Shidehara himself.

In view of the way in which he had been treated, his Chinese visitor had assumed that he would lend a willing ear to anything said against the Army. He therefore launched out into a tirade against the Japanese military authorities and their actions. But instead of finding a sympathetic listener, he had met with a stern rebuke from Shidehara, who turned on him in anger and told him that the things of which he had complained would never have happened if the Chinese had not so consistently scorned all his, Shidehara's, proffers of friendship and conciliation in the past and treated them as signs of weakness.

It was Shidehara's misfortune that Chinese intransigence had served only to foster the intransigence of the Japanese Army in Manchuria; but in expressing his fears of blunders by the new government in Tokyo, he had been rather less than fair to Inukai, the new Premier, and his Foreign Minister, Yoshizawa. Inukai, it is true, had always had strong nationalist leanings and, at the time of the Chinese Revolution in 1911, he had dabbled in Chinese affairs; among other things, he told me on one occasion, he had sought to dissuade Sun Yat-sen from replacing the monarchy with a republican form of government. But he had always been an advocate of friendly Sino-Japanese co-operation and, like Wakatsuki and Shidehara, he was opposed to severing Manchuria from China completely and attempted to forestall the creation of an independent régime. In this he was strongly supported by Yoshizawa, whose recent tour of duty as Japan's chief spokesman at Geneva had made him keenly aware of the dangers of flouting world opinion. By making his views on this clear and seeking to curb the military hot-heads in Manchuria, Inukai had, in effect, signed his own death-warrant; but he was undeterred and, through his close and long-standing contacts with leading Chinese, he had hoped to settle the Manchurian dispute by peaceful negotiations with them. That he failed in his attempt was in no small part due to the disloyalty of his chief Cabinet Secretary, Mori Kaku, and others, who intrigued behind his back and foiled his plans.

It was shortly after Inukai's appointment as Premier that, with a view to placing the Army beyond criticism, an Imperial prince was appointed to succeed General Kanaya as Chief of the General Staff. This was Marshal Prince Kanin, who had made a fine reputation for himself as a cavalry commander in the Russo-Japanese War nearly thirty years earlier and was reputed to be a first-class soldier. Little more than a month later, on 2 February, the Navy, too, was to be placed beyond criticism by the appointment of Admiral Prince Fushimi as Chief of the Naval Staff. This was in succession to Admiral Taniguchi, who had made himself unpopular with the nationalist elements by demanding stern disciplinary measures against certain young naval officers engaged in extreme nationalist activities in the Tsuchiura naval air-training station. Of this, more will be said later.

With the advent of 1932, a further serious crisis was brought about when, on 8 January, a malcontent Korean threw a bomb at the Emperor, who was on his way back from attending a military review. The Emperor escaped injury and only minor damage was done, but the outrage caused intense indignation and the recently-appointed Premier, Inukai, tendered the resignation of himself and his whole Cabinet. This was in accordance with the precedent set in December 1923, when a similar attempt on the life of the Prince Regent—as he was then—had been made by a Japanese radical. The resignations, however, were declined and Inukai and his Cabinet were prevailed upon to continue in office; but for doing so, they were strongly denounced by nationalist extremists, who urged them to commit *harakiri* by way of expressing a sense of responsibility for failing to provide adequate protection for the Emperor. In order, therefore, to prevent an anticipated uproar in the House and the probable introduction of a vote of non-confidence, the Diet, barely an hour after its first session under the new government had been opened on 21 January, was dissolved as soon as the Premier, Foreign Minister and Finance Minister had completed their speeches outlining the policies they intended to follow. The consequent general elections, held on 20 February, resulted in an unexpected sweeping victory for the Government party and seemed, accordingly, to stabilize the political situation. It seemed clear, however, that the victory was by no means a reflection of the party's popularity; it was due to a feeling that, in the existing national crisis facing the country, patriotism demanded support for the Government, irrespective of its political complexion, rather than to any great confidence in its leaders.

The crisis, which brought this rallying to the support of the Government, was the outcome of developments, not only in the international field but also in the internal situation. The dangerous potentialities of the latter had been underlined a week or so earlier by the assassination of the former Finance Minister, Inouye

Junnosuke. Inouye, it will be recalled, had been one of the four statesmen marked out for assassination in the abortive 'October Incident', and his house had been bombed in the previous May. As however, his term of office as Finance Minister had ended when the Inukai Government came into power in December, it might have been thought that he was no longer in danger of attack; but on 9 February, while about to address an election meeting he was shot by a fanatical nationalist, Konuma Tadashi, who claimed to have been actuated by his conviction that the retrenchment policy, carrried out by Inouye when Minister of Finance, had been responsible for the poverty-stricken condition of the peasantry. He maintained, too, that he had acted on his own, but this was soon disproved. When Inouye's murder was followed a month later, on 5 March, by the assassination of Baron Takuma Dan, head of the powerful financial and industrial Mitsui combine, it was found that Dan's assailant, Hishinuma, was a personal friend of Konuma's. They and three other youths, it was revealed, had pledged themselves at the time of the London Naval Conference in 1930 to sacrifice their own lives, in what became known as the 'death pact', in order to remove any prominent persons whom they considered to be imperilling the safety of Japan.

They themselves, however, were only pawns in the game; behind them were others who were planning assassination on a grand scale. Of these, only one need be mentioned for the moment. This was a young naval aviator, Lieutenant-Commander Fujii, who had subsequently been killed during the Shanghai operations. The discovery that he and other young naval officers had been engaged in political intrigues of a violent nature came as a considerable shock. What was particularly disturbing was that the Navy, in contrast to the Army, had previously held aloof from such activities. Admiral Kato Kanji, it is true, had resigned in protest against the signing of the London Naval Treaty, but that was a perfectly legitimate action and was in an entirely different category.

Of the revelations which followed Takuma Dan's murder, more will be said later, but a comment made to me by Iwanaga on the day of Inouye's assassination was, in itself, revealing. Inouye had been a close friend of his and he was very upset at the news of his death; but he confided to me that what distressed him in particular was, that he himself felt indirectly responsible

o

for what had happened. Inouye, he said, had upbraided him and the Japanese Press in general some months earlier for failing to reveal all the facts behind the Army's actions in Manchuria and for failure to try and put a check on the Army by articles in the Press. He, Iwanaga, recognized that these strictures were, at least in part, well merited and that the Press had, at times, failed to reveal what it knew and had helped to stir up national sentiment by its sensational and often misleading reporting.

Apart from these assassinations and plots, whose widespread ramifications were to become startlingly clear after the murder of Inukai, the Premier, some two months later, a further indication of the dangerous extent to which extreme nationalism was growing among Army reservists was seen about the time of Inouye's murder. On 4 February, Dr Nitobe, former Assistant Secretary to the League of Nations, gave a private talk on the world situation to a small group of friends and others at Matsuyama. In order that he might speak quite freely, he asked that he should not be quoted in the Press and was assured that nothing he said would be published. The gist of his remarks was that, in his view, the world was menaced by two forces, Communism and militarism, and that the latter was probably the more harmful. Despite the promises given, his words were reported in a local paper and were passed on to the headquarters of the *Zaigogunjinkai*, the Reservists' Association, which interpreted them as aimed at the Japanese Army. They called for his chastisement accordingly. The subsequent developments, though incorrectly reported in the Press, were described to me soon after by his son, whose mother confirmed and amplified the details later in a private letter, which is still in my possession.

As a result of the alleged insult to the Army, his father, he said, had received so many threatening letters that he had to be placed under police protection on his return to Tokyo and had been asked to remain indoors until things had quietened down a bit. The Reservists' headquarters in Tokyo, however, asked him to appear before a gathering of their members in order to explain himself and apologize. His alleged apology was broadcast throughout Japan and abroad; but both his son, who was at the meeting, and his wife denied that he had made any apology. All he did was to explain just what he had said and why he had said it. The higher naval and military officers present accepted his explanation and treated him courteously, as they respected him as the author of the

well-known work on *Bushidō* and knew of his intense devotion to
the Emperor and to his country; but the young reactionary hot-
heads among the reservists proceeded to inveigh against him, calling him a traitor and refusing to accept anything but an unqualified
apology. This he declined to give, as his explanation, he said,
proved that there was nothing for which to apologize. The agitation therefore continued, but what was particularly interesting and
revealing in his son's account of what happened was his assertion
that the prime instigators of the virulent nationalist movement in
the Reservist's Association—a body which had previously steered
clear of politics and had interested itself mainly in the welfare and
morale of its members—were the *yobi shōi*,[1] the reservist second-
lieutenants. These young men, after completing their service with
the colours, tended, he said, to blossom forth as local 'bosses' on
their return to their rural communities and to lord it over their
fellows. They did useful work in inculcating loyalty to the throne
and in maintaining high standards of morale and comradeship,
but they were apt to develop an extremely narrow form of radical
nationalism. Combining this with distorted ideas of patriotism and
anti-capitalism, it was they who took the lead in denouncing the
big capitalists and wealthy landlords, along with party politicians,
and holding them responsible for the serious economic distress in
the country districts. While, therefore, they were loyal to the
throne and helped also to keep the local communities loyal, their
denunciations and exploitation of grievances served to stir up the
peasantry against the hated capitalists and their allies, the corrupt
politicians. The insidious part they played in this respect was to be
seen shortly after, when young reservist officers and farmers
figured prominently in the succession of assassination plots that
followed. The more senior officers on the reserve took little part
in such activities, but, having been brought up in the armed
services to despise both wealth and party politics, they had a great
deal of sympathy with these younger men and were all too ready
to show leniency towards them, even when disapproving of their
actions.

While it was Dr Nitobe's alleged insult to the Army that had
aroused the wrath of the reservists, his former connection with

---

[1] The *yobi-shōi* came from the One-Year Volunteers, men who, for educa-
tional or other valid reasons, were allowed to postpone their conscript service
with the colours on condition that they would undergo special training later
as candidates for reservist commissions.

the League of Nations had also told against him. From the outbreak of the Manchurian trouble in September 1931 onwards, the
League's actions had caused increasing resentment. The fact that
the United States, though not a member, supported it against
Japan was particularly resented; so, too, was the fact that Japan
was under constant censure for her actions in Manchuria, whereas
no complaint had ever been raised against the Soviet Union for
seizing control of Outer Mongolia and virtual control of Sinkiang.
As the increasingly dangerous situation developing in Shanghai
gradually attracted the lime-light which had previously been
focused on Manchuria, resentment against the League began to
flare up once more and nationalist demands that Japan should
withdraw from it, which had been voiced earlier, were heard once
more.

In these circumstances it was perhaps not surprising, therefore,
that views expressed by Lord Grey had met with approval. This
was when, some weeks before, he had been quoted as saying that
the League had been organized for dealing with disputes between
two countries that were masters in their own houses; its whole
machinery broke down when faced with a situation in which, as
in the case of China, one of the disputants was not in that position.
The weakness of the League in this, and in other respects, was,
in fact, aptly expressed by Sir Francis Lindley in talks I had with
him later. One of these weaknesses, he stressed, was the danger
it created by giving a false sense of security, a view expressed also
by other foreign diplomats to whom I had spoken; most of them
had been very critical of the League's actions and some of them
extremely cynical. Sir Francis's main criticism at the time of the
Shanghai trouble, however, was that the League's actions tended
to prejudge Japan as being in the wrong and seemed calculated
to strengthen China's determination not to withdraw its troops
from the area voluntarily; Chinese tactics were, in fact, to utilize
the League's machinery to serve China's own purpose and, thanks
to the encouragement given by the League to refuse direct negotiations with Japan, Nanking's refusal to negotiate was based on
the belief that help would be forthcoming. Added to this was the
fact that it was the small nations, with no direct interests or responsibilities in the Far East, that were urging strong measures
against Japan; the big Powers in the League, on the other hand,
having far more at stake, were doing their utmost to prevent the
application of further pressure. In saying this, Sir Francis illus-

trated his contention by mentioning a visit he had had from the Cuban Minister, who had urged him to do what he could to see that the League 'put Japan in her proper place' by employing force against her. When Sir Francis pointed out to him that it would be Britain's Army and Navy and Britain's money that would be called upon to do the main work, the Cuban Minister had replied blandly, 'Oh yes. But you would have the full moral support of my country and of others.' Sir Francis, who never minced his words, told him exactly what he thought of the promise of 'moral support'; he saw no reason, he said, why Britain should be made the cat's paw of those who were prepared to contribute nothing more practical than oratorical 'noble gestures' of a platitudinous nature, which did far more harm than good.

While most foreign residents in Japan, including the diplomatic representatives of Britain, France, Italy and Belgium, were generally more sympathetic towards Japan than to China, the League's attitude towards the Shanghai situation was arousing national sentiment once more, and on 14 February the *Asahi* came out with a slashing attack on those urging strong measures against Japan. Actions which overlooked the genesis of the dispute, it declared, not only served to arouse resentment and inflame Japanese national sentiment, but served to aggravate the situation in Shanghai still further by stiffening Chinese resistance against voluntary withdrawal. Four days later, intense annoyance was expressed when the League appealed to Japan to curb her actions, but made no similar appeal to China. To ask only Japan to withdraw was considered grossly unfair and unreasonable, as the Chinese, despite lip-service to peace, were committing outrages and acts which were undermining Japan's rights and interests. Moreover, if the despatch of Japanese troops to Shanghai and Manchuria was held to infringe the territorial and political independence of China, surely this charge was equally applicable to the troops of other foreign Powers in China and amounted to withdrawing the right of self-defence. Reports that America and/or the League might impose an economic blockade of Japan inflamed public opinion still further, and articles in Japanese papers and magazines left little doubt that the Japanese, if this were done, would take up the challenge to their national existence by occupying strategic points on the mainland; this they would do in order to secure sources of supply, while the Navy would ensure the safety of Japan's maritime communications in Far Eastern waters. As no blockade was instituted, however, the tension began to ease, only to be revived a few weeks later, when representatives of the South American states and other lesser countries in the League Assembly made fiery speeches demanding stern measures against Japan. The only result—of what was described as 'the irresponsible attitude of those with no interests at stake in the Far East in dealing with such vitally momentous issues'—was to strengthen the hands of the extreme nationalists and of those advocating Japan's withdrawal from the League.

The Government, however, had no intention of being hustled into any such action, and on 21 February Yoshizawa, the Foreign Minister, issued a statement stressing that it would be folly to quit the League and that Japan had no intention of repudiating either the Kellogg Pact or the Nine-Power Treaty, or of abandoning friendship with Britain and America, 'which hitherto had been such a conspicuous feature of Japan's foreign policy.' Another year was to pass before Japan did, in fact, leave the League and another six years before she repudiated the Nine-Power Pact; but, by a curious coincidence, on the same day that this statement was made confirming the policy of friendship with Britain and America, Sir Ian Hamilton, who had headed the British military mission with the Japanese Army during the Russo-Japanese War, was quoted as criticizing the League and declaring that 'all the trouble in the Far East is the fault of those who forced us to break our alliance with Japan.' The League, he was reported as saying, 'has done much, doubtless unwittingly, to blow fire into the blaze by first irritating the Japanese, then encouraging the Chinese, and now it wants us to pull their chestnuts out of the fire.'

This was largely in line with the Japanese view and was warmly welcomed accordingly. In spite of the outspoken criticisms made against Britain at times, there was still, in fact, a strong undercurrent of nostalgia, especially among the older generation of Japanese, for the days when Britain and Japan had been allies and Japan had a firm friend; and only a few days earlier, when discussing the situation with Matsuoka and Iwanaga at a private luncheon, the former had remarked sorrowfully that one of the most regrettable aspects of the Twenty-One Demands in 1915 had been that it had sounded the death-knell of the Anglo-Japanese Alliance. As a result, he said, Japan was left with only two alternatives in regard to her China policy—co-operation with

Britain and the United States or with the Soviet Union; she could not afford to try acting on her own. It was a comment that I was to recall later when, after leading the Japanese delegation out of the League of Nations in March 1933, Matsuoka became increasingly anti-British and anti-American until the point was reached when his hatred became a veritable phobia and obsession with him. Similar changes in attitude became increasingly marked in other Japanese in the years ahead and served to illustrate the Japanese characteristic of vindictiveness towards those considered to have treated them scurvily, in contrast to genuine gratitude for little acts of kindness.

In the meantime, with the situation in Shanghai becoming increasingly serious, the reasons for despatching troops there, and the need to drive back the Chinese 19th Route Army to a safe distance if it failed to withdraw of its own accord, had been explained by Yoshizawa to the British, American, French, Italian, and German ambassadors. It had become known, however, that when the question of sending land forces had first been raised, Takahashi Korekiyo, the Finance Minister, had opposed the suggestion, partly on financial grounds and partly because he believed the Chinese were already on the point of collapse. Later developments had convinced him of the necessity and he had withdrawn his opposition. By 7 February, therefore, a landing had been made at Woosung, as Colonel Simson had foreseen, the Government having issued a statement some hours previously, pledging the withdrawal of the Army as soon as the object in view had been accomplished. Two days later I learned from Iwanaga that General Sugiyama had assured him that the Army had no intention of going further afield than twenty kilometres or so at the most and that it was anxious to withdraw as soon as possible on account of the expense involved and because any money available was required for Japan's more vital interests in Manchuria. This same concern about the financial situation was expressed soon after in a private talk with Colonel Furujo, who said that reinforcements were required, but there were no funds to spare. This followed the rejection of a Japanese ultimatum demanding the withdrawal of the Chinese forces within a specified time and reflected the anxiety felt lest the troops already despatched should prove too few. The Army was, in fact, faced with the alternatives of a possible reverse—with serious consequences—through insufficient numbers, or the despatch of reinforcements entailing further expense and the liability of increased apprehensions abroad. The latter alternative was finally put into effect after the Japanese had launched their offensive on 20 February, when it became clear that reinforcements were essential if a set-back was to be avoided.

That the Japanese were not alone in feeling apprehensive was shown by reports from Shanghai indicating that the arrival of more Japanese troops would be welcomed by the foreign communities; it was indicated, too, in a talk with Sir Francis Lindley, who expressed the gravest concern lest the Japanese should meet with a set-back at Shanghai; the results, he feared, would be serious for everyone, with the Chinese becoming more arrogant and more difficult than ever.

It was at this juncture that the rivalry and jealousy between the Army and the Navy, which was to prove such a serious handicap to proper co-operation between the two services at times in the Pacific War, began to come into prominence. Up to this time, there had been a kind of tacit agreement between them that the Army would confine its activities to Manchuria and the Navy to coastal China. When, on 1 February, it was announced that Prince Fushimi had been appointed Chief of the Naval Staff in place of Admiral Taniguchi, who was said to have been strongly opposed to the Army taking a hand in Shanghai, it was stated that this had been done in order to facilitate 'more intimate co-operation' with the Army General Staff, now that Prince Kanin was head of the latter. From subsequent developments it became clear that 'more intimate co-operation' was, in fact, badly needed between the two services in general. The naval forces in Shanghai would have welcomed the Army's assistance at an earlier stage, but had not been prepared to admit that they were incapable of handling the situation by themselves. Many Army officers, on the other hand, had been openly critical of the Navy for sending too small a force to Shanghai and made no bones about jeering at their naval friends for having had to be rescued by the land forces. Subsequently, when the Army got into difficulties during their operations around Woosung and had to send for reinforcements because Chiang Kai-shek's troops had gone to the help of the 19th Route Army,[1] it

---

[1] That the 19th Route Army had hitherto been left to fight unaided was said to be due to serious friction between its commander and Chiang Kai-shek, who had reason to doubt the Route Army's loyalty to himself. If it received a severe mauling from the Japanese, so much the better; the threat to his own position would then be largely removed.

was the Navy's turn to scoff. Knowing that this would be so, the Japanese Army commander, General Uyeda, had hesitated to ask for reinforcements, as he considered it distasteful to admit that the troops under his command were insufficient to carry out their allotted task; it was apparently, therefore, on the recommendation of Admiral Nomura, who had recently been sent out from Tokyo, that they were sent.

While world attention was centred primarily on events in and around Shanghai, a new and significant development was taking place in Manchuria. Ever since the outbreak of the trouble there in September, there had been indications that the Japanese Army had been striving to provide a legal basis for their actions and for their future plans. Chang Tso-lin, it will be recalled, had always regarded Manchuria as at least semi-independent and had acted accordingly. His successor, the Young Marshal, had given his allegiance to Nanking, but there were still certain elements in both Manchuria and Inner Mongolia who dreamed of independence from China. It was perhaps not surprising therefore, that, with the outbreak of fighting, they had sought to utilize the situation for their own ends. They lacked any outstanding leader and, at the start, had little or no support from the people at large; but within a few days of the outbreak, reports of independence movements began to circulate. The Chinese accusation that Japan was fostering them brought a prompt denial from Tokyo where, only a few days earlier, the War Minister had issued instructions that no negotiations with the leaders of these movements were to be permitted. While, however, the Japanese Government itself was opposed to giving any assistance or encouragement to the advocates of independence, it welcomed the setting up of local peace maintenance organizations. When questioned on this, Shiratori had declared that Japan was prepared to negotiate a local settlement with anyone capable of maintaining peace and order in Manchuria if Nanking refused to enter into negotiations, but a final settlement, he added, would have to be reached later with the Chinese Central Government.

The local peace maintenance organizations welcomed by Tokyo had been established in the principal towns and cities under Japanese guidance for the purpose of carrying out the normal duties of local civil government. So far as the Japanese Government was concerned, they were only intended as a temporary measure; but it soon became evident that politically-minded

Japanese officers on the spot were giving active assistance and encouragement to a general movement for independence and regarded these bodies, and the subsequently established self-governing administrations in the three provinces comprising Manchuria, as part and parcel of the movement. What was needed, however, was a figurehead, and this was duly forthcoming in the person of Pu Yi, the former boy Emperor of China, whose forebears had founded the Manchu dynasty. On 4 October, barely two weeks after the outbreak of the Mukden 'Incident', reports had reached Tokyo that an attempt was being made to restore him to the Dragon Throne and that he was already in Manchuria. The reports proved premature but, little more than a month later, he did in fact leave Tientsin by sea and returned to the home of his ancestors, landing at the Manchurian port of Yinkou on 12 November. As noted in the previous chapter, his arrival was officially admitted three days later, but apart from occasional cryptic references in the Japanese Press to a mysterious Maru Maru Sama (Mr Blank Blank)—a cloak of anonymity intended to conceal the identity of the distinguished visitor—nothing more was heard of him or of the developments taking place until 14 February, when Press reports from Mukden indicated that the birth of Manchuria as an independent state was about to be witnessed.

On being questioned about this, Shiratori professed scepticism, but four days later came the news that the independence of Manchuria had been proclaimed and this was followed within twenty-four hours by the announcement that Pu Yi had been nominated Chief Executive.[1] This time, Shiratori was more forthcoming; but, when asked at a Press conference whether Japan would recognize the new State, he replied somewhat evasively that it would all depend on whether it proved to have the necessary attributes of an independent country. On being pressed by an American correspondent to say how long it would take to decide whether it possessed all these essentials, he replied somewhat testily, 'You can assure your people in America that we shall not be in too much of a hurry to grant recognition', adding caustically after a short pause, 'You see, we have no canal to build, so we can afford to wait.' It was a sly dig at the haste in which the United

---

[1] It was not until 1 March that the new independent state was officially founded under the name of Manchoukuo, with Changchun (renamed Hsinking, meaning New Capital) as its capital, and not until 9 March that Pu Yi was formally installed as Chief Executive.

States had recognized Panama twenty-nine years earlier and aroused intense indignation when reported in the American Press.

Only a few hours before news of the declaration of Manchurian independence had come in, I had spoken to Sir Francis Lindley about the likelihood of independence being proclaimed shortly. He had viewed the prospect with considerable misgiving and feared it would have a bad reaction abroad on account of its implications. Autonomy, he considered, would probably pass muster, but not independence. The latter would run counter to the pledges given to preserve the integrity of China and would, moreover, bring about international complications on account of its bearing on the Chinese Customs Service, the Salt Gabelle, and other matters.

That many thoughtful Japanese held similar views was made clear in a private talk I had with Iwanaga a day or two later. Even in Army circles, he said, there were conflicting opinions about the pros and cons of Manchurian independence, whilst business circles, though fully behind the Army in wanting to see the Chinese brought to task for disregarding their treaty obligations and for hampering legitimate trade, had never contemplated or advocated the establishment of Manchuria as an independent state; they were extremely dubious concerning the advisability of this latest development. In strict confidence he added that Saionji, Inukai and Yoshizawa held the same view, although Matsuoka had always favoured independence. Japan, he went on to say, would find it very difficult to contend that she had had nothing to do with the declaration of independence, as no one would believe her. She would therefore stand charged with having broken her promise to respect the administrative integrity of China and would only make matters worse if, as was being suggested, she should try to defend herself by quibbling over the difference between 'respecting' and 'guaranteeing'.

This, however, was not the only difficulty that he foresaw. Pu Yi had been appointed Chief Executive, but Iwanaga had learned that he was trying to insist on being made Emperor and that he was strongly supported in this by some of his henchmen, although others were absolutely opposed to the restoration of the ancient monarchy. What Iwanaga feared was that Doihara and other Japanese officers, who had manœuvred the whole affair, might have committed themselves to having Pu Yi elevated to the

Throne in order to induce him to accept the post of Chief Executive as a temporary measure. If this was so, it would lead to further complications. His forebodings were to prove justified when, two years later, Pu Yi was proclaimed Emperor.

CHAPTER XVI

Increasing Tensions

While Manchuria was being transformed into a nominally independent state, with Pu Yi as its figure head, the unexpectedly stubborn resistance of the Chinese 19th Route Army on the outskirts of Shanghai had necessitated the despatch of reinforcements from Japan. These had been sanctioned, on 23 February, after urgent representations from the military authorities, who had stressed that without them the situation would become aggravated and the operations prolonged. At the same time, it was decided to send General Shirakawa to Shanghai as Commander-in-Chief of the whole expeditionary force, although the announcement of his appointment was withheld for the time being.

At the time that these developments were taking place, foreign critics, noting the slow progress made in driving back the Chinese, tended to draw false conclusions about the fighting abilities of the Japanese troops. From this misjudgment grew the unfortunate myth that the Japanese Army was of far less consequence as a fighting force than formerly imagined, a myth that was to continue, with disastrous results, until the outbreak of the Pacific War nearly ten years later. What was overlooked was that the original force under General Uyeda was labouring under a twofold handicap. Not only was it necessary for Uyeda to avoid the risk of serious losses to his relatively small body of troops; there was also the necessity of avoiding action liable to damage the International Settlement. Japan had already been strongly criticized for the bombing of the Chapei sector of the city; she had no wish to incur further odium by bringing the International Settlement into the area of active operations. In view, therefore, of these considerations, the Japanese were unable to adopt the tactics best suited to compel the Chinese to withdraw or to strike sufficiently vigorously to ensure rapid and complete victory. In the existing circumstances, the tactical obstacle imposed by the Settlement was unavoidable, but the numerical impediment could be largely overcome if reinforcements were rushed out without delay. Failing this, Chiang Kai-shek, who had so far sent only a token force to the assistance of the 19th Route Army, might be compelled by popular clamour to throw his entire strength into the conflict and thereby transform the local battle into an all-out war.

This was the problem outlined to me by a well-placed Japanese friend on the day that the despatch of reinforcements was sanctioned; three days later Uyeda's avoidance of action liable to damage the International Settlement was rewarded. This was made clear by a visit from the British, French and Italian ambassadors to the Foreign Office in Tokyo to express their appreciation of the Japanese Commander's efforts to confine the fighting to outside the International Settlement. At the same time, they requested that the reinforcements being sent to Shanghai should be landed elsewhere than in the Settlement, lest the Chinese should endanger it by shelling the wharfs. It was considered significant, however, that although the American Ambassador also called at the Foreign Office and made a similar request, he had omitted to express any appreciation of the Japanese efforts to spare the Settlement. He had, moreover, asked that *all* Japanese warships be withdrawn from the vicinity of the waterfront. This was in contrast to the British, French and Italians, who recognized that this might be too much to ask and had indicated that they would be satisfied if the flagship *Izumo* could be moved, as it was drawing most of the Chinese shelling.

With reinforcements already on the way, it was learned that instructions had been sent, both to Matsudaira in Geneva and to Shigemitsu in Shanghai, to make it known that Japan was ready to halt hostilities whenever the Chinese gave convincing proof of their willingness to withdraw from the 20-kilometre zone; the Japanese troops would be withdrawn as soon as the Chinese had done so. The response was immediate and favourable. Next day came the news that private talks had been held on board the British cruiser *Kent* between Admiral Nomura, Matsuoka, Wellington Koo and General Tsai's Chief of Staff in the presence of Admiral Kelly, who had arranged the meeting.

The rapid developments that followed can be summarized briefly. While discussions continued with the aim of producing a satisfactory formula for ending the fighting, the Japanese 11th Division, which had been despatched as reinforcements, landed on 29 February at Liuho, up the mainstream of the Yangtse above Woosung, and quickly had the Chinese on the run. Three days later, on 3 March, came the welcome news that Shirakawa had ordered the cessation of hostilities, as the Chinese had been driven back the required distance. This was followed on the 14th by the announcement that the troops sent out as reinforcements were already under orders to return to Japan; but although further withdrawals had been carried out in the meantime, another two months were to pass before the situation was considered sufficiently satisfactory to enable the Government to order complete withdrawal within a month. This decision was reached a few days after the signing of a truce agreement in Shanghai on 5 May. Under it the Chinese agreed to maintain no troops within twenty kilometres of the city, while the principal Powers guaranteed to see that the Chinese kept to this undertaking.

That the Japanese should have insisted on some such guarantee before agreeing to withdraw completely was understandable, but it required two months of hard wrangling before this agreement was finally concluded. The Chinese, for their part, strove their utmost to avoid direct negotiations on the spot with the Japanese for a local settlement and sought to induce Geneva to deal with the matter; but the Japanese remained adamant and eventually got their way. It was perhaps inevitable, however, that Japan's insistence on a local settlement was interpreted in some quarters as proof positive that she had no intention of withdrawing and was merely seeking a pretext for maintaining her hold on Shanghai indefinitely, with a view to using it as a base for further aggression. Wild rumours to this effect circulated freely and it was even reported that troops were being poured into Formosa in preparation for an attack on Fukien and/or Manila. Although most foreign diplomats in Tokyo with whom I discussed these rumours at the time were extremely sceptical about them, a Scandinavian diplomat expressed his conviction that they were well founded and that Japan was about to seize great chunks of China.

Amongst those who had refused to accept these rumours at their face value was Majoni, the Italian Ambassador, who told me with great glee a few days later of a comment made to him by Yoshizawa, the Japanese Foreign Minister. Majoni, it seemed, had had a query from his government about a Press report, alleging that Japanese troops were being sent to Manila. Though convinced that the report was utterly ridiculous, he made official enquiries about it in accordance with his instructions. Yoshizawa had listened attentively as he read out the report to him and then, asking Majoni to repeat what he had said, remarked drily, but with a twinkle in his eye, 'I thought at first that you must have meant Sicily. I feel relieved that it is only the Philippines'.

Sceptical though most of the foreign diplomats in Tokyo were about these rumours of Japan's aggressive intentions, there was a wide-spread belief that Japan had no intention of withdrawing from Shanghai and that she would find some good excuse for retaining her troops there. There was considerable surprise, therefore, when the Japanese carried out a partial withdrawal even before any definite agreement had been reached. There was, however, a dramatic and tragic last-minute hitch in the truce negotiations, a hitch which could well have been used as a pretext for staying on if Japan had really wished to do so. This occurred on 29 April when, during the official celebrations in Shanghai for the Japanese Emperor's birthday, a Korean terrorist hurled a bomb onto the platform on which the leading Japanese naval, military and civil representatives were standing to attention while the national anthem was being played. General Shirakawa, the military Commander-in-Chief, was fatally wounded, Admiral Nomura, the naval Commander-in-Chief, lost an eye, Shigemitsu, the Minister, received severe injuries necessitating the amputation of a leg, while Murai, the Consul-General, General Uyeda, and Kawabata, President of the Japanese Residents' Association, were amongst a number of others wounded by the explosion.

The news of the outrage caused a world-wide sensation and aroused grave anxiety, lest it should result in further bitterness between Japan and China and postpone indefinitely the conclusion of the truce agreement, just as it was about to be signed. These fears, however, were quickly dispelled by the Japanese decision to treat the truce negotiations and the bombing incident as two entirely separate matters and to go ahead with the signing of the agreement. Six days later, therefore, it was signed, under conditions probably without precedent for the conclusion of an important international undertaking. Not only were the two principal Japanese signatories, Shigemitsu and General Uyeda, in hospital suffering from wounds, but so too was Quo Tai-chi, one of the Chinese signatories. Unlike the two Japanese, Quo had been the victim of an assault by some of his own countrymen who, by way of expressing their opposition to the truce terms, had attacked him with bricks and stones two days before. A final dramatic touch to these unusual circumstances was added when Shigemitsu, having appended his signature to the document, was wheeled off to the operating theatre to have his leg amputated. The Japanese Press was understandably full of praise for the moral and physical courage of all three of these signatories, and it was a welcome change to find the Japanese papers eulogizing Sir Miles Lampson, the British Minister to Nanking, for the part played by him as mediator in the truce negotiations.

So ended the Shanghai operations launched in February, and by the end of May the last Japanese troops had left; but with the resultant easing of tension went the unfortunate readiness of foreign military observers to down-grade the Japanese Army as a competent fighting machine. As already noted, false conclusions had been drawn from the initial wariness and consequent slowness of the Japanese in driving back the Chinese; but now, in addition, there was a misinterpretation of the reasons for the Japanese withdrawal. This was brought home to me a month or so later by a conversation I had with General Sir Neill Malcolm during a visit he paid to Japan. As former commander of the British Army on the Rhine and, far earlier in his career, as editor of a brilliant collection of essays and lectures entitled *The Science of War*[1]—a text-book I had studied as a cadet at Sandhurst in pre-1914 days— Sir Neill was clearly one whose opinions on military matters were deserving of the highest respect. It was with some amazement, therefore, that I listened to the deductions he had drawn from the Japanese handling of the Shanghai operations. Expressing his surprise at the calmness with which the Japanese had taken the withdrawal from Shanghai, he said he could not understand how unconcerned they seemed about the defeat they had suffered. On my asking him what defeat he had in mind, he replied that the Japanese withdrawal from Shanghai was generally regarded by competent observers in China as an acknowledgement of defeat; he himself agreed with this verdict. What was even more surprising was that he then went on to draw a parallel between the Japanese withdrawal from Shanghai and the British evacuation of Gallipoli in 1915. As the Japanese withdrew in accordance with the undertaking given at the outset of the operations—and only after carrying out their declared aim of driving the Chinese back to the 20-kilometre line and obtaining international guarantees

[1] These essays and lectures were by Colonel G. F. R. Henderson, the British biographer of Stonewall Jackson.

P

that they would remain there—it seemed incredible that anyone, least of all a soldier of such distinction, could see any
similarity between the Shanghai withdrawal and the evacuation of
Gallipoli.

General Malcolm, however, was by no means the only distinguished soldier to misjudge Japanese fighting ability and to
misinterpret the withdrawal. From then on, until the myth of
Japanese inferiority gave way for a time to the myth of Japanese
invincibility, the complacency born of these false deductions was
reflected time and again in the comments of officers of high
standing.

On the same day, 29 February, that the Japanese reinforcements had landed at Liuho, the Commission appointed by the
League of Nations to carry out an on-the-spot enquiry into the
Manchurian dispute arrived in Tokyo. The time of its arrival was
perhaps unpropitious; not only was the Shanghai situation at a
critical stage, but the particular situation into which the Commission was to enquire underwent a fundamental change on the
very next day, when Manchuria was formally inaugurated as an
independent State under Pu Yi. Nor was the assassination of
Inouye Junnosuke, the former Japanese Finance Minister, a week
later, a happy omen. Lord Lytton, who headed the Commission,
was nevertheless warmly welcomed and made a most favourable
impression on the Japanese, who were genuinely convinced that
the outcome of his enquiries would be entirely in their favour.
This was reflected in a private talk I had, some days later, with
Iwanaga, who expressed his delight that at last the foreign
criticism levelled at Japan would be quietened, now that a
statesman of Lord Lytton's calibre was about to see for himself
just what the facts were. The trouble, he said, was that so much of
the criticism, especially in the early stages, had been of an un-
informed nature, dictated more by the heart than by the head; as
a result, the Japanese no longer bothered to take proper heed of
such bits of sound, constructive criticism as might be interspersed
with it. He felt, however, that the visit of the League Commission
had already done some good, as Lord Lytton, by his calm,
dignified bearing and by his open-minded, impartial attitude had
greatly impressed those who had met him. The Japanese, it
seemed, had been prepared to find the Commission with views,
critical of Japan, already firmly fixed. Instead, they had found its
members both tactful and patient, and ready to hear and consider

the Japanese viewpoint. Confidence in the Commission's fair and impartial investigation of the whole problem had therefore replaced the scepticism which had formerly prevailed. Iwanaga's final comment, patently sincere, was a tribute to British statesmanship. Laying his hand on my shoulder he remarked with a slightly rueful smile, 'You English people! We envy you. You have so many of these broad-minded, impartial, dignified statesmen like Lord Lytton. That is what Japan needs too, but what we lack so badly.'

Although this initial attitude towards the Commission was to undergo a sad change later, the favourable impression given at the outset was enhanced by Lord Lytton's outspoken rebukes to his Chinese audiences when visiting China, prior to going on to Manchuria. The Chinese were correspondingly upset when he warned them, 'While a nation is fomenting hatred and hostile feelings against another country, she cannot expect the League to interfere and save her from the consequences'; nor did they like it when, at a dinner in his honour, he took them to task for failing to observe their treaty obligations. When finally, however, the report of the Commission on its findings was published on 2 October, the position was reversed and the Japanese people as a whole were genuinely amazed at the criticisms of some of their actions contained in it. To an outside observer, the report in general seemed reasonably objective and impartial, delivering praise and blame to Japan and China alike. It found many of Japan's grievances justified, but condemned her method of redressing them; but the general feeling amongst the Japanese was probably summed up fairly accurately in an interview with foreign correspondents given by Shiratori, who asserted that the report contained 'much that is unfair to Japan and nothing unfair to China'. He complained, too, that it was unduly confined to Manchuria and paid too little attention to conditions in China and the Far East in general. To isolate the Manchurian question from these other considerations, he contended, was like tearing a sentence from its context. His main criticism, however, was levelled against the report's assertion that Manchoukuo was the creation of the Japanese General Staff and did not represent the wishes of the people as a whole.

The comment of a Japanese friend, to whom I mentioned this criticism later in the day, was revealing. Freely admitting that he himself had always been extremely dubious of the genuineness of the independence movement and had hoped that it would not be encouraged, he maintained that there was a large body of Japanese opinion that considered the policy of setting up an independent state of Manchuria had been a mistake. The general feeling amongst both opponents and proponents of that policy, however, was that, as it had now been implemented, there was no other course than to back up the Government and show a united front to the world. It was simply a case of sink or swim; there could be no turning back.

This bowing to circumstances, this readiness to accept and support *faits accomplis* by excusing them, even when disapproving of them—my country right or wrong—was a Japanese character-istic which was to become increasingly noticeable in the years ahead and was both a strength and a weakness. It was interesting, however, to hear Sir Francis Lindley's private comments on the report a day or so later. While agreeing that it was a fine piece of work in many respects and that its animadversions on the way in which Manchurian independence had been brought about were justified, he considered that, like so much else since the 1914–18 war, it was too much based on what he called 'nobility of purpose' and too little on the hard facts of the situation. In saying this he recalled a discussion he had had on this very point with Lord Cecil, shortly before coming out to Japan as Ambassador. He had pointed out to him that the reason why other countries tended to regard the British as hypocritical was, that we were so fond of trying to make out that all our own actions were based on this 'nobility of purpose'. When the Japanese or any other nations claimed a similar basis for their actions, however, we just did not believe them.

Before dealing with developments subsequent to the publica-tion of the Lytton Report in October, something more must be said of events during the earlier months of the year. In the realm of international affairs, in addition to the charges and counter-charges levelled by Japan and the League against each other, there was the inevitable Japanese friction with America and Soviet Russia, the two great non-members of the League. The resentment felt at the American attempt to persuade the Japanese to withdraw all their warships from the vicinity of the Shanghai waterfront has already been mentioned, but it was the implied criticism and accusations levelled against Japan by the American Secretary of State in a letter of 23 February to Senator

Borah that caused the main ill-feeling. As Stimson himself admitted later, this letter was intended, in part, as a message of encouragement to China and as a reminder to Japan that, if she violated the Nine-Power Pact, the other signatories of that instrument might feel themselves released from the other agreements reached at the Washington Conference, as these treaties and the Nine-Power Pact were interdependent. No direct charges were made, but the implications were clear—an accusation that Japan had ignored her obligations under the terms of the Pact and a barely-concealed threat that the United States might therefore feel freed from the restrictions on naval armaments and fortifications in the Western Pacific imposed by the Washington naval agreements. The Japanese reaction was immediate and vitriolic. The accusations were hotly refuted and the threats denounced. Public opinion, already dangerously excited, burst into flame. A leading article in the *Asahi* reflected, in more moderate terms, the general feeling. Declaring that it was not by doubting Japan's motives but by co-operating with her that America would enable China to pull herself together and stand on her own feet, the paper went on to remind the United States that the Washington Conference had entailed sacrifices by all its participants and not by America alone; moreover, it contended, the naval agreements were not dependent on the Nine-Power Pact, as the deliberations on the former had been completed before those on the latter had begun.

The feelings of resentment aroused by this letter were changed to something approaching alarm when, a few days later, Washington ordered the greater part of the United States Navy to concentrate in the Pacific, bringing the total of warships west of the Panama Canal to one hundred and ninety-nine vessels. These included 12 battleships, 17 cruisers, 33 submarines, 81 destroyers and 3 aircraft-carriers. The main purpose of this move, it soon became known, was concerned with naval manœuvres, which had opened recently around Hawaii, but it was unfortunate that it should have coincided with the tension over Shanghai. What was not foreseeable was that the new technique, used with such success on these manœuvres earlier in the month by Admiral Yarnell, the commander of the attacking force, was to be copied rather less than ten years later with devastating effect by the Japanese in their onslaught on Pearl Harbour. Instead of carrying out a naval attack with a great invasion fleet of battleships and cruisers, whose progress across the Pacific towards the Hawaian islands might have been detected, he employed a task-force—a new concept at that time—consisting of two aircraft-carriers escorted by a handful of destroyers. Favoured by poor weather conditions, which made observation by the defenders difficult, he drove full speed ahead, without lights and in radio silence, until sixty miles off Oahu, when he launched his planes in the darkness before dawn and delivered a devastating blow from the air. By this means he was able, in theory, to destroy the enemy's aircraft on the ground, the ships in the harbour, and all the principal military installations on shore.

The lesson taught might have seemed clear enough; but, though appreciated by some American naval officers, it was ignored by Washington. The Japanese, on the other hand, took it to heart, and the plans evolved by Yarnell were to serve as a blue-print for their attack on Pearl Harbour in December 1941. Nor was this all. Yarnell's success was seen to have been due in part to the fact that his attack was launched at dawn on a Sunday, when the defenders were reckoned, quite rightly, to be less on the alert than on a week-day. It was a point of detail noted and acted upon by the Japanese when the time came for them to act.

To return, however, to the opening months of 1932. Japan's strained relations with the United States at that period were paralleled by a similar strain in her relations with Soviet Russia. Charges and counter-charges, alarums and excursions, followed in rapid succession. To a Kremlin complaint late in February that Japan was assisting the White Russians in Manchuria to plot against the Soviet, Tokyo replied with a flat denial. There was friction, too, over Japan's requests to use the Chinese Eastern Railway for the transportation of troops for the suppression of Chinese irregulars and bandits; but the Russians, being anxious to avoid a clash, eventually gave their sanction. Then, at the end of February, came a disquieting consular report from Vladivostok. Approximately two army corps of Soviet troops, it said, had been concentrated in and around that city and a force of some 100,000 had been assembled in the Ussuri district, large reinforcements having arrived there from European Russia since December. Work on fortifications, transportation of food and munitions, and other similar activities were also reported, and the Japanese Consul asserted that local Russians considered a clash with Japan inevitable before very long. As a little bit of light relief he added that the Russians were characterising the Japanese as being 'as detestable as cholera bacteria'.

Friction and mutual distrust there certainly was, but close observers considered rightly that Soviet Russia was far too anxious to complete its Five-Year Plan to engage in war with Japan or with anyone else at the moment; these alleged preparations were thought, therefore, to be purely defensive in nature, aimed primarily at stirring up the people to believe in a menace from without in order to divert their attention from internal affairs. From talks with Japanese officers and others, it seemed nevertheless that a section of the Japanese Army was strongly advocating that matters should be brought to a head with the Russians before they had time to complete their economic and industrial reorganization; but the general impression was that neither Japan nor Russia wanted war at a time when both countries were preoccupied with so many other serious problems. As the next few years were to show, this impression was well justified; but from the spring of 1932 onwards, foreign correspondents in Tokyo were bombarded at frequent intervals, from their head offices in London, New York and elsewhere, with queries or instructions concerning sensational reports of Japanese–Soviet tension and of impending hostilities. Apart, however, from the clashes on the Korean border and at Nomanhan in 1938 and 1939 respectively, there was to be no general flare-up until the last week of the Pacific War in August 1945.

Although the constantly recurring reports of serious Japanese–Soviet tension and of impending hostilities from 1932 onwards were to prove largely illusory, it was perhaps significant that Hirota Koki, the Japanese Ambassador in Moscow when these reports first started, was known to have had close connections with the Black Dragon Society, whose proclaimed aim had always been to drive the Russians out of Manchuria across the Amur, the Black Dragon River from which it derived its name. Some eighteen months later, Hirota was to become Minister of Foreign Affairs for the first time. As such, he was to earn the liking and respect of the leading foreign diplomats in Japan; but this did not save him from the death-sentence meted out on him as a major war criminal in 1947, largely as a result of Soviet pressure.

It was while world attention was concentrated on the negotiations for a truce settlement of the Shanghai trouble, and on the growing tension between Japan and the two great non-members of the League of Nations, that the investigations into the assassination of Inouye Junnosuke on 9 February and of Baron Takuma Dan on 5 March began to reveal the dangerous and extensive ramifications of the plot which had led to their murder. The first indication of the powerful forces of reaction in the background of these two outrages came on 8 March, when the Japanese Press reported that Ono, the Chief of Police, had threatened to resign; the reason given was that 'wholly uncontrolled factors have made and are making it impossible for the police to carry investigations further'. The exact nature of the 'uncontrolled factors' could only be guessed, but to anyone familiar with the background of the ultra-nationalist movement in Japan, there seemed little doubt that this somewhat cryptic statement referred to the leader of the Black Dragon Society, Toyama Mitsuru, and his powerful friends in high places. For close on half a century, this strangely enigmatic figure, who was seldom mentioned by name except in terms of almost awed respect, had cast an insidious spell over many of the leading statesmen and politicians and had exercised a baneful influence over them. Though commonly believed to have been behind most of the 'patriotic murders' in Japan since the 1880s, he had acquired so powerful a sway as the embodiment of patriotic rectitude and fervour, a kind of Great High Priest of the super-patriotic cult, that he was above criticism and virtually sacrosanct—untouchable and immune from the normal processes of law.

When, on the day after the threatened resignation of the Chief of Police, it was announced that two un-named influential reactionaries were believed to have been the instigators of the murders of Inouye and Dan, it was generally assumed that these were Toyama and his powerful henchman, Uchida Ryohei; and when, soon after, it was revealed that one of the wanted men was hiding in the house of 'a certain influential personage' which the police had been 'unable to enter', it seemed reasonably clear that the personage was Toyama. But no paper or individual dared to say this openly. The nearest approach to doing so came on 24 March, when a member of the Upper House took the Government to task for its failure to touch 'certain figures in the background of the Blood Brotherhood'.

Although employing all these euphemisms in order to avoid identifying him by name, Toyama was, of course, known to everyone by repute. As the investigations into the murders proceeded, however, names of other fanatical nationalists, hitherto unknown to the general public, began to appear; but whereas Toyama and his immediate circle had always been concerned primarily with matters of foreign policy, the principal figures now emerging into the limelight were dreamers of revolutionary reforms in the social, political, and economic life of the country, preachers of violence for the purpose of turning the clock back to a distant and largely mythical Utopian past. Two of these fanatical visionaries in particular, Gondo Seikyo and Inouye Nissho, stood out as instigators of the murders; before long they were to be linked up also with the assassination of Inukai, the Premier, on 15 May and with subsequent political murder plots. Both Gondo, a scholar of the ancient classics and a disciple of Kropotkin, and Nissho, a Buddhist priest teaching a fiery blend of nationalism and religion, operated 'schools' at which they expounded their own particular brands of philosophy. Others besides them were shown to have instigated the youthful assassins, but it was largely on their teachings that the initial murder plots were based.

By the end of March, police investigations had revealed the names of close on twenty of the most prominent statesmen, politicians, bankers, and industrialists, who had been marked out for 'removal' by individual members of the *Ketsumeidan* (Blood Brotherhood)—the terrorist body concerned in the plot—and thirteen members of this gang had been indicted for murder or attempted murder. Fortunately, Konuma, the murderer of the Finance Minister, had acted precipitately and upset the plans. With Baron Dan's assassination a month later the police had therefore been able to obtain the necessary clues to nip the rest of the plot in the bud. The real nature of the whole affair was revealed by Hishinuma, the youth who had murdered Dan. Its aim, he declared, was to get rid of the established political parties, but in order to hasten their collapse it was necessary first of all to remove what he called 'the dollar daimyos', who financed them. This was confirmed by other evidence, which showed that the youths had been incited to sign a blood pact in order to bring about the desired reforms by 'removing the corrupt political parties and their capitalist allies'.

From this, and from much else that came out in the course of the investigations, it became increasingly clear that the plot reflected, in violent form, the widespread discontent and growing resentment against the party politicians, who were held to have placed personal and party interests above national interests, and against the long-established policy of helping the growth of commerce and industry at the expense of the heavily burdened farmers. Japanese history is strewn with stories of peasant revolts and insurrections against the hard lot imposed on the farming communities by the central or local authorities. In this latest manifestation of peasant unrest, it was a revolt against party government and the capitalists who financed the parties for their own benefit; but what made it all the more dangerous was, that it was exploited by fanatical nationalists in the name of patriotism and gave rise to a peculiar Japanese blend of fascism and national socialism. This sought to bring the Emperor nearer to the people by ridding the country of the 'evil councillors' around the Throne, doing away with bureaucratic control and capitalism, and, if some extremists had their way, even putting an end to government from the centre.

Apart from the widespread ramifications of the plot, it came as a shock to the authorities to find that those involved in it included members of reactionary student organizations. These bodies were shown to contain elements far more dangerous to the State than the 'reds' and the 'pinks', whom they had always watched so closely. As a Japanese friend remarked to me ruefully, what was wanted in Japan was some sort of safety-valve as in England, both for the 'rights' and the 'lefts'. In England, your diehard Tory eases his feelings by writing to the papers, your 'parlour bolshie' gets his grievances off his chest by holding forth from a soap-box in Hyde Park or elsewhere. If the leading Japanese statesmen, financiers and politicians would also follow the example of their British counterparts by expounding their views in letters to the *Asahi* or some other respectable paper, that, too, might do some good; but they don't.

There was probably much truth in this contention, as the extremists were left free to deliver fiery denunciations and exhortations in pamphlets and paid advertisements in the papers without fear of contradiction, so long as their sentiments were clothed in terms of patriotic indignation. An example of this was seen on 9 March, when several papers published a manifesto from the *Shinso*, a body composed of reactionary politicians, denouncing Shidehara, Yoshizawa, and Inukai for weak-kneed policy towards foreign countries; it also warned the United States not to irritate Japan further. Inflammatory in tone, it was clearly intended to stir up national sentiment against the statesmen mentioned, as well as against the United States; but it remained unanswered.

The *Shimso* was frequently inserting inflammatory advertisements of this kind; although seemingly unconnected with the murder plots, they must have served to incite the plotters. A similar denunciation of Inouye Junnosuke some weeks earlier had been followed by Inouye's assassination. This latest outburst was to be followed by the assassination of Inukai. The accusations against him and Yoshizawa, however, were said to have been due in part to the personal grievance of the industrial magnate Kuhara Fusanosuke, who financed the organization. From what I was told by a well-informed Japanese friend, Kuhara had helped to bring about the fall of the Wakatsuki government three months earlier and bore a grudge against Inukai for having failed to reward him with a Cabinet post for doing so. As Yoshizawa was Inukai's son-in-law, he was selected for denunciation too. Whatever the truth of this assertion may have been, it was certainly true that the dangerous growth of a fascist-like movement in Japan was due, not only to genuine grievances and a distorted sense of patriotism, but also to the unscrupulous machinations of ambitious individuals who, with axes of their own to grind, cloaked their true aims under the guise of patriotism. This, in turn, influenced the Government in its attitude towards criticisms from abroad and forced it to take an ever stronger and more uncompromising stand, lest any readiness to show a more accommodating spirit should precipitate a full-fledged outbreak of fascism in Japan.

That such a danger existed was clear from talks I had at the time with Japanese friends in positions to know. Admitting that he had, until quite recently rather laughed at the idea, Iwanaga said he now regarded the establishment of a fascist régime as a very real possibility before long. Although it did not appear to be properly organized as yet, a movement closely akin to fascism was making considerable headway in the towns and cities, and the people, disgusted with the party politicians, were looking for a strong leader. Then, too, many conservative Japanese, though opposed to violence, were shocked and disgusted by certain aspects of the ultra-modernism and Americanization of Japanese life that had come in so much in recent years;

much of the growing reactionary sentiment was simply a revolt against the introduction of what he called 'this jazz age' and against its deteriorating effect on the moral fibre of the people. Army men like Araki, he said, considered that the operations in Manchuria and Shanghai had done some good, in that they had helped to restore the national spirit; but, Iwanaga admitted, the implications for the future would be serious indeed if warlike measures were to be advocated as the best remedy whenever the national spirit showed signs of flagging.

Opinions on the likelihood of a fascist coup in the near future differed considerably, but it was generally agreed that a strong national government under a strong national leader was urgently required if further deterioration of the internal situation was to be checked. The two names most frequently mentioned as possible candidates for this leadership were Admiral Saito and Baron Hiranuma, but again there were divided opinions as to their suitability. Saito was regarded by some as too old and Hiranuma too conservative. What was feared by some was that, if Hiranuma became Premier, he might merely pave the way for the establishment of a full-blooded fascist régime, much as Kerensky had paved the way for the Bolsheviks in Russia. There was also the fear that, if neither Hiranuma nor Saito was appointed, the Army might step in to prevent the situation from getting out of control. In the event, it was Saito who was chosen, but that was not until another Premier had fallen victim to reactionary assassins; the circumstances of his murder were to show that fanatical young naval and military officers had joined forces with peasant malcontents and ultra-nationalist civilian terrorists in liquidating those whom they considered were acting contrary to national interests. But before dealing with this disturbing development, a brief postscript may be added to this chapter.

Hitler had not yet come to power, but some months earlier a Nazi representative, posing as a Press correspondent, had arrived in Japan. Known as Don Gato, the Cat, he had found himself ignored by the German Embassy and by the German community in general. But he received a more ready welcome from the extreme nationalist fraternity in Tokyo, and in mid-April I learned on good authority that he was paying almost daily visits to Uchida Ryohei, Toyama Mitsuru's right-hand man in the Black Dragon Society. They were birds of the same feather and the information threw a revealing sidelight on the developing situation.

PLATE V.   Admiral Viscount Saito Makoto
He was five times Navy Minister; twice Governor-
General of Korea; Premier in 1932–4; assassinated
in February 1936

贈

ケネデー君

元帥伯爵東郷平八

Admiral Count H. Togo

PLATE VI. Admiral Count Togo Heihachiro
The 'Nelson of Japan', he died in May 1934, three days
after the twenty-ninth anniversary of his great victory
at Tsushima, when he destroyed the Russian Fleet

CHAPTER XVII

Government by Assassination

Sunday 15 May, which was to prove so fateful for Japan, broke warm and sunny. Returning to Tokyo with my wife towards evening after a day in the country, we chanced to pass by the Metropolitan Police Headquarters. Milling around in the open space outside, like a swarm of angry bees, were large numbers of police. We speculated as to the cause of all this activity. A strong force of them had been employed the previous evening in controlling the crowds, which had turned out to welcome Charlie Chaplin on his arrival in the Japanese capital; we decided, therefore, that the police had probably been called out once more in case of need, as the famous comedian had been scheduled to pay a courtesy call on the Prime Minister that afternoon.

It was not until we got back to our house that we learned the real reason. There I found a message awaiting me to say that a series of outrages had been perpetrated an hour or so earlier. Hand grenades had been thrown into the Police Headquarters and other public buildings, attempts had been made to destroy electric power stations and, most serious of all, Inukai Tsuyoshi, the Prime Minister, had been shot and fatally wounded. An unsuccessful attempt had also been made on the life of Count Makino, Lord Keeper of the Privy Seal; although not revealed until some months later, Charlie Chaplin, too, had narrowly escaped being a victim.[1]

As further details came in, it quickly became clear that this was something vastly more portentous than the murders of Hamaguchi, Inouye and Takuma Dan; these had been the work of deluded young fanatics acting singly, but the latest outrages were plainly the outcome of a widespread plot, carried out by

[1] This revelation was made during the trial of those concerned in the outrages. When asked to explain why his assassination had been contemplated, the naïve reply was: 'Chaplin is a popular figure in the United States and the darling of the Capitalist class. We believed that by killing him, we would bring about war with America; thus we would, in effect, kill two birds with one stone.'

organized bands of terrorists. What was particularly disturbing was, that the assailants included young naval officers and military cadets, acting in conjunction with embittered farmers and other civilian extremists. Military hotheads had, of course, been connected with the abortive 'incidents' of March and October the previous year, and investigations into the recent murders of Inouye Junnosuke and Baron Dan had revealed that some young naval officers had played a part in instigating these assassinations; but open participation in outrages of the kind that had just taken place was a new and extremely ominous development, boding ill for the future. A further serious deterioration in naval and military discipline was but one of the disquieting conclusions to be drawn from it.

Some indication of the motives of the assailants was given in handbills scattered around during the attack on the Police Headquarters. On these was printed a fiery manifesto, issued in the name of 'young naval and military officers and peasant sympathizers'. Calling on the nation to rise in arms against the capitalists, the political parties, and the 'tyrannical authorities', it demanded the liquidation of 'the traitors and the privileged classes'. Except that all this was demanded 'in the name of the Emperor', the document might well have been drawn up in Moscow.

During the preliminary examination of the culprits in the months that followed, these same aims were to be repeated *ad nauseam* and revealed a strange amalgam of extreme leftist and rightist philosophy, strongly tinctured with Japanese mysticism and chauvinism. From the evidence given later at the formal trials of those implicated in these and in subsequent murder plots, however, one point in particular emerged with ever-increasing clarity. This was, that although the various acts of terrorism were planned with the definite object of purging the country of real and imaginary evils, and of bringing about a national renaissance, it was the action of the Hamaguchi Government, a government based on a political party, in ratifying the London Naval Treaty in 1930 against the advice of the Chief of the Naval Staff that had sparked off the growing volume of social, political and economic unrest. Fanatically but short-sightedly patriotic, the defendants were incapable of appreciating that financial stability was just as important as armaments when it came to the question of national defence. Consequently, the Government was considered unpatriotic for listening to the advice of the financiers, and the financiers were denounced as traitors for giving such advice. From this it was but a short step to the political parties and 'privileged classes', on account of their financial connections, and to the 'patriotic necessity' of purging the country of all such elements, in order to bring about national reform.

As will be seen later, it was the revelation of the growing intensity of the feelings aroused over the question of naval ratios, as laid down in the London and Washington naval treaties, that led Japan eventually to terminate both these agreements and thereby pave the way towards rapprochement with Germany and to Pearl Harbour. During the days and weeks immediately fol- lowing the outrages of 15 May 1932, however, it was the revela- tion of the dangerous state of the internal situation in Japan that impressed close observers most forcibly. How serious the implica- tions of these happenings were regarded was reflected in the comments made by friends, both Japanese and foreign, with whom I discussed the matter at the time. Amongst these were two Russians, one of them being Nagi, the *Tass* correspondent, who had succeeded Romm in that appointment some ten or twelve months earlier. The other was Dmitri Abrikosov, whom I had known since my army days, when he was Counsellor to the Czarist Embassy in Tokyo; being unable to return to his own country, he had remained on in Japan as a private resident after Japan's recognition of the Soviet régime in 1925.[1] Although in diametrically opposite 'camps' and refusing to have anything to do with one another, their views on the situation were markedly similar; both considered that violent revolution was almost inevitable.

Basing this belief largely on the manifesto issued by the assail- ants, and on the very similar programme of the nationalistic *Seisantō*,[2] Nagi brushed aside my comment that, despite the com- munistic flavour of both these documents, they nevertheless professed loyalty to the Throne. 'Up to 1905,' he retorted, 'we Russians looked to the Czar as "the little Father", and our move- ment was directed against the capitalists and bureaucracy.' The

[1] Under the title, *Revelations of a Russian Diplomat*, his posthumous memoirs, edited by George Alexander Lensen, were published in 1964, by the University of Washington Press.

[2] The *Seisantō* had been formed in November 1931 under the aegis of the Black Dragon Society. Like the national socialists, who had broken away from the social democrats some months later, its members included a number of former left-wing radicals.

people of Japan, he went on to say, regarded Count Makino and other court officials near the Throne as standing between the Emperor and themselves; their removal was therefore demanded— just as was that of Rasputin. If, as was widely expected at the time, the ultra-conservative Vice-President of the Privy Council, Baron Hiranuma, was to replace the murdered Inukai as Premier, Nagi was convinced that he would prove to be a Japanese Kerensky and that his appointment would be the prelude to revolution. This, he considered, would most certainly break out if the situation developed in such a way as to necessitate action by the Army, as the troops would refuse to fire on the people and the present 'monarchical communism', as he called it, would quickly change to anti-monarchical revolution as it did in Russia.

On mentioning these remarks to Abrikosov and asking what he thought of them, he replied without hesitation that Nagi's summing up of the situation was undoubtedly correct; it tallied with his own, he said, and he added another parallel between what was happening in Japan and what had happened in Russia. This was the attempt to stir up the farmers to demand equal distribution of land, nominally in the name of the Emperor. In Russia, revolutionary agents, posing as Czarist officials, used to make their way into the agricultural districts and tell the peasants that, if the existing régime were overthrown, the Czar would have the land held by the landlords handed over to those who tilled the soil.

While the prospect of revolution was clearly welcome to Nagi and feared by Abrikosov, they were at one in believing that Japan was heading in that direction. Nor were they alone in this belief; it was shared, too, by a goodly number of Japanese with whom I discussed the matter and certainly played its part during the week that elapsed between the murder of Inukai and the appointment of a successor to the Premiership. Of the four whose names were most freely mentioned as likely candidates for the post, Dr Suzuki Kisaburo, who succeeded Inukai as President of the *Seiyukai*, was ruled out because the Army refused to support another purely party Cabinet and was demanding the formation of a national government; General Ugaki was passed over because he had aroused the dislike and distrust of a section of the Army for his broad-minded outlook; Hiranuma was rejected because of the fear that he might prove a Kerensky. The fourth mentioned was Admiral Viscount Saito who, being advanced in

years, weakened in health, and living in retirement since resigning
from the Governor-Generalship of Korea the previous summer,
seemed the most unlikely of the quartet to be chosen to assume
the Premiership at a time of such crisis as that now facing the
country. The announcement of his appointment, therefore, came
as a surprise to most, although it was generally agreed that his
selection would have a reassuring effect, both at home and abroad,
provided his age and health did not prove too great a handicap.
His statesmanlike qualities had been shown, both at Geneva in
1927 and subsequently as Governor-General of Korea; moreover,
while liberal-minded, he was recognized as a strict disciplinarian,
a man of courage, and absolutely straight. Although he was to
meet the fate of so many of Japan's finest leaders four years later,
when he died at the hands of fanatical assassins, his appointment
did, in fact, do much to restore the faith and confidence of the
nation, which had been badly shaken by the sordid intrigues,
corruption, and self-interest of the party politicians as a whole.
If he failed to prevent the subsequent fascist-like developments,
he did at least help to hold them in check for the time being and
saved the country from the kind of revolution envisaged by
Nagi, Abrikosov and others.

   While developments in the situation in Japan appeared to have
some striking similarities to those that had led to the revolution
in Russia, they did, in fact, bear even closer resemblance to past
events in Japan's own history. Violent reaction had been an
outstanding feature at various times throughout the centuries;
so, too, had political murders. The 1930s were no exception.
Whether harping back nostalgically, as the extremists were doing,
to the romanticized days of the seventh century, with the slogan,
'Give the land to the people and tighten the bonds between the
Throne and the people as was done at the time of the Taikwa
reforms'; or whether drawing parallels with the overthrow of the
Tokugawa régime and the Restoration of 1868, or with the
Satsuma Rebellion, which had been aimed, not at the Emperor
but against those considered to be usurping his prerogatives;
whether basing their plans and actions on these or on other famous
episodes in their country's history, the reaction was typically
Japanese, not just a pale reflection of the Russian way. It was
significant, therefore, that, as more and more details of the background to the recent outrages were revealed in the course of
the police investigations, it became increasingly clear that the

assailants had been strongly influenced by the social and political philosophies expounded by nationalist thinkers at private 'schools', founded for the purpose of studying and propagating their theories. Similar 'schools' had flourished in the closing years of Tokugawa rule and had been largely responsible for the plans formulated for the overthrow of the Tokugawas, for resistance to the Western 'barbarians' who were trying, at that time, to force Japan to open her gates to intercourse with the outside world, and for obtaining strategic footholds on the neighbouring main-land of Asia. Prince Ito, and others among the subsequent makers of modern Japan, had been 'disciples' of these nineteenth century theoreticians; and now, in the 1930s, similar schools of thought were propounding social and political theories aimed at bringing about a national renaissance by violent means, a revolution to be known as the Shōwa Restoration.

The Kropotkin philosopher Gondo and the Nichiren priest Inouye Nissho, who had already figured in connection with the murder of Baron Dan, were amongst those who operated such schools and were shown to have instigated the outrages of 15 May. A terrorist reformer, who preached the need of drastic reform in politics and economics, Nissho, by his fiery zeal, was shown to have exercised a strong influence on the impressionable minds of the young naval participants and was the actual leader of the *Ketsumeidan*, the Blood Brotherhood. Another 'teacher', whose name now came into prominence, was the Tolstoyan Tachibana Kosaburo. Founder and head of the euphemistically named *Aikyojuku* (Home of Love), he was leader of the Farmers' Death Band, whose members had joined with the young naval officers and military cadets in these latest outrages. Known as a 'philoso-pher of the soil', he was a thinker rather than a doer; but his fiery eloquence, combined with his slogan of 'Soil, Brotherhood, and Toil', stirred his followers into action.

There were others besides these who had played an insidious part. Not least amongst them was Okawa Shumei, a former employee of the South Manchurian Railway. A born intriguer and chauvinist, who urged violence and provided money, arms and ammunition, he was disliked and distrusted even by his fellow plotters; he was to figure later as a major war criminal after the Pacific War, but evaded the punishment due to him by being diagnosed as mad and consigned to a mental institution accord-ingly. Amongst them, too, was Kita Ikki, whose book, *Nihon*

Kaizo Hoan Taiko (National Reconstruction of Japan Outline), advocating extreme reforms, had been banned when first published as far back as 1919, but had later become the Bible of the more extreme nationalist elements among the younger Army officers. Kita, unlike Okawa, was to face a firing squad in 1936 for his part in the Army mutiny of that year.

One other, whose name figured freely in the preliminary investigations and subsequent trials, was Lieutenant-Commander Fujii Hitoshi, whose implication in earlier outrages, and whose death in action during the Shanghai operations, have already been mentioned. Imbued with the idea of uniting all the peoples of Asia under Japanese leadership in order to 'chastise the tyranny of the white races and thus enforce moral principles throughout the world', he had been enraged by the ratification of the London Naval Treaty, which he linked with white oppression. Determined to punish those whom he held responsible for this act of 'treachery' in truckling to the West, he had set about planning how best to purge the country of 'the political leaders, plutocrats and privileged classes', whom he accused of corruption and lack of patriotism, and of leading the country to ruin. He had planned to rid the country of all these 'traitors' before 1936, in order to ensure that, when the London Naval Treaty came up for consideration once more, the task of securing Japan's just demands would not again be in the hands of those who placed party, financial and diplomatic interests above those of the nation. He died, however, before his aims had been attained, but not before he had been able to embue others with his doctrines and to organize them for the series of outrages culminating in those of 15 May. The fact that he had died in action, 'a hero's death', made an emotional appeal, which served to gain sympathy for his views.

Detailed accounts of these and subsequent murder plots can be found in other works, notably in Byas's *Government by Assassination* and Storry's *The Double Patriots*. Such details as have been given above have been taken from the diaries and notes I made at the time and should be sufficient to indicate the dangerous elements behind the situation that was then developing. From what has been said of Commander Fujii's ideas, however, it will be seen how anger over the London Naval Treaty, bitterness against party politicians, capitalists and bureaucratic statesmen, and resentment against the 'arrogance' of the white races, were all combined to create an explosive mixture.

This last constituent, embracing the doctrine of Pan-Asia, was significant. The slogan of 'Asia for the Asiatics' under Japanese leadership had hitherto played but a minor role in stirring up national sentiment and had been regarded by the people at large, and by government circles, as of little more than academic interest; but from now onwards it was to assume a growing importance in the scheme of things. By March 1933, the idea of bringing the countries of Asia together in a league or bloc under the leadership of Japan had taken more concrete form in the creation of the *Dai Azia Kyokai* (Great Asia Association), a body in which a number of prominent naval, military and civilian officials were linked in its membership with civilian extremists. It was significant, too, that although Toyama Mitsuru, for long the High Priest of ultra-nationalism and a strong advocate of Pan-Asian ideals, did not figure directly in the investigations into the outrages of 15 May, his third son, Hidezo, was found to have been implicated; and on 26 June, little more than a month after the perpetration of these outrages, *The Japan Times*, an English-language paper owned and edited by Japanese for foreign consumption, issued a special four-page supplement, devoted entirely to eulogizing Toyama Mitsuru himself. Had the eulogies been contributed by irresponsible reactionary hotheads, such fulsome praise might have been understandable; but they were not. The contributors were, in fact, some of the leading Japanese statesmen and politicians including, posthumously and ironically, the recently murdered Premier, Inukai. Noting this, I recalled the remark of a prominent Japanese, whom I had questioned about Toyama at the time of Baron Dan's murder a bare three months earlier. Toyama, he had assured me, was now a back number and just a figurehead; then, half-jokingly, he had added, 'The present Premier, Inukai, has always been a close friend of his; but of course, if Toyama had ever considered that he was acting contrary to national interests, he would not have hesitated to have him removed.'

Surprising though it was that the contributors were prominent statesmen and politicians, it seemed little short of amazing, and particularly disturbing, that two of them—Hirota, the Ambassador to Moscow, and Nagai Ryutaro, Minister of Overseas Affairs— gave special praise to Toyama for having openly flouted both his own and the British Government in taking Rash Bihari Bose under his protection, when that Indian terrorist sought refuge in

Japan in 1916. The fact that some of the other contributors paid high tribute to Toyama for having instigated the bombing of Count Okuma for his failure to obtain the revision of the 'unequal treaties' in the late 1880s, and for having planned to murder Prince Ito if he had failed to fall in with the wishes of those demanding war with Russia in 1904, served to show how sadly distorted was the idea of what constituted true patriotism, even among some of Japan's leading figures.

When, on the day following the appearance of this special supplement, I questioned a member of the *Japan Times* staff about it and pointed out that it was hardly calculated to enhance Japan's prestige in the eyes of the world, he replied blandly that it had been issued for the express purpose of showing foreigners what a great man and fine patriot Toyama was. While, however, this no doubt reflected the views of others besides himself, it was certainly not the universal sentiment. Several of my Japanese friends expressed disgust and contempt for the publication of such a supplement, and the anglophile Count Soyeshima confessed to me, in what was clearly genuine distress, that not only the recent political murders but also these fulsome eulogies of Toyama, made him ashamed of his own countrymen.

Disturbing as were these eulogies of one who had instigated so many outrages in the past, a disquieting feature of the immediate aftermath of the events of 15 May was the attitude of a section of the Japanese Press; while deploring the excesses, it urged leniency on the perpetrators, on the grounds that their motives were fundamentally patriotic. It reflected a mentality which was to become increasingly marked and pernicious in its effects in the months ahead, when police investigations led to indictments, indictments to preliminary examinations, and preliminary examinations to public trials and sentences.

With Inukai's death in May 1932 and the dangerous state of ferment revealed by his murder, the new Saito Government was, however, faced with two alternatives; either it had to take drastic steps to restore Army discipline abroad and to deal with violence and intimidation at home, or it must adopt a *laissez faire* attitude towards developments in Manchuria and leniency towards the misguided patriots in Japan. The first of these two alternatives seemed likely to precipitate open revolution; the second might ease the internal situation, but would certainly aggravate world opinion. In the event, the Government chose the latter course as the lesser of two evils; Manchoukuo was accorded recognition as an independent state, and finally Japan quit the League. It was a fundamental reorientation of policy, marking a turn to open defiance from the former deference shown to the League and to the West in general. Largely responsible for this change was Count Uchida who, during his tenure of office as President of the South Manchurian Railway since June 1931, had been won over to the views of the Kwantung Army and, in effect, became its mouthpiece when appointed Foreign Minister in the Saito Cabinet twelve months later.

The vital bearing of the Manchurian question on Japan's explosive internal situation was becoming increasingly evident. Strategically, and from the point of view of Japan's economic welfare, Manchuria was not inaptly regarded as her life-line. For both the Army and the Navy, its security was therefore of paramount importance. So far as the Navy was concerned, it was largely because the existing naval ratios were considered inadequate for ensuring Manchuria's safety in the event of a war with the United States that the London Naval Treaty was denounced in such vehement terms. For the Army, the main concern was to see it built up as a bulwark or strategic barrier against Soviet Russia. This tallied with the views of the ultra-nationalist Black Dragon Society, whose primary aim had always been to drive the Russians across the Amur, the Black Dragon River. As the years went by, the members of that entirely civilian body had propagated their views among impressionable Japanese officers who had, in consequence, become strong advocates of a forward policy. To the armed services and extreme nationalists alike, therefore, Manchuria represented the keystone of Japan's very existence and had to be made secure at all costs. But, from the early 1920s, an additional feature had been brought into the picture by the appearance of quasi-socialist bodies, embued with ideas of radical reform. Strongly tinged with anarchist theories, they were as ready to advocate violence to achieve their aims as were the ultra-nationalists who, at the start, had been their bitterest opponents. Capitalism was denounced because it introduced class conflict, party government because it put party interests before those of the nation and led to corrupt practices through its alliance with capitalism, and Western thought because it resulted in what they called, 'a blind imitation of Western materialism' and divided Japan from her fellow Asiatics.

This is perhaps an over-simplification of an extremely complex and constantly shifting situation, riven by conflicting cross-currents and factionalism; but it should serve to indicate how it was that, after the world depression had set in in 1929 and had hit both Japan and Manchuria, these somewhat anarchistic bodies were able to influence politically-minded young officers, who had genuine sympathy with the consequent sorry lot of the hard-hit rural communities and peasantry, from whom their best recruits came. Radical reform, on the lines advocated, seemed to them to offer the best solution to the economic crisis facing the country. Socialism, a conception formerly held in abhorrence on account of its anti-monarchical outlook, therefore took on a new connotation, especially when, in its new guise, it stressed loyalty to the Throne and aimed at bringing the Emperor closer to his people by removing 'the evil counsellors' (Court officials) around him. With this went a merger with patriotic ideals and a form of Pan-Asianism, which depicted Japan as a fellow-sufferer from Western arrogance and oppression and the natural leader of a crusade to liberate her Asiatic brethren from Western domination and servitude.

By equating the socialist ideal of social equality and the more even distribution of wealth, with racial equality and equal division of territory and natural resources, this new brand of socialism made a wide appeal. It fell in line with the aims of ultra-nationalist bodies like the Black Dragon Society, which had for long advocated Pan-Asianism under Japanese leadership; it appealed to the chauvinist predilections of politically-minded officers, who recognized its implications for the future—Japan as leader and master of a united Asia and territorial expansion at the expense of the Western overlords, who had dominated much of Asia for so long; and it made an emotional appeal to the Japanese people at large by making them feel they had a mission to perform. This, they felt, was to stand up at last to the Western nations, who had baulked them at Geneva and had always tended to regard them as inferiors on account of their colour; it encouraged them, too, to lead a crusade to free their Asiatic brothers from Western bondage. This combination of imperialist ambitions and national mission was to have far-reaching effects a few years later and was first made manifest in the creation and recognition of Manchoukuo. Not only did these two actions serve imperialist purposes but, by the principle of racial harmony laid down in the founding of the new State, they provided a pattern for a future united Asia in which, to re-phrase George Orwell, all would be equal, but Japan would be more equal than the others.

It was not until May 1933, just one year after Inukai's assassination, that the long-awaited results of the preliminary examinations were announced, with eleven military cadets and ten naval lieutenants indicted on the charge of mutiny; twenty civilians, including some connected with a separate plot to murder Admiral Saito and Count Makino, were charged with murder and attempted murder. Then came the trial of the civilians and the court martial of the naval and military participants. The preliminary examination had already revealed the names of twenty or more leading Japanese statesmen, politicians, and others who had been marked out for assassination; but the naval court martial showed that, in addition to planning the murder of Admirals Takarabe, Okada and Taniguchi, and of General Ugaki, it had also been planned to murder the American Ambassador and Consul-General. There had been plans, too, to seize some naval aircraft, and to use them for carrying out an air raid on Tokyo. By this means it was hoped to create panic, necessitating the application of martial law. In spite, however, of such startling disclosures and of other evidence produced, both at the naval and at the military courts martial, petitions for leniency came pouring in, and cities as far away as Nagasaki were placarded with demands for clemency.

Deplorable as was this tendency to show more sympathy for the deluded 'patriots' than for the luckless victims, the strong feelings aroused amongst junior naval officers by the death sentences demanded for three of the defendants at the naval court martial indicated a most dangerous undercurrent in the Navy. The intensity of the prevailing sentiment among young naval officers was reflected in the attempt by one of them to commit *harakiri*, by way of protest, and by attempts to hold indignation meetings at Yokosuka and other naval stations. Only a strong personal appeal from one who was revered and respected throughout the Navy could, it was felt, prevent serious trouble and the undermining of naval morale. And so it came about that the ageing Nelson of Japan, Admiral Count Togo—an almost godlike figure in the eyes of the Navy—emerged momentarily from his well-earned retirement. This he did in order to address an appeal to the Fleet on 16 September 1933, through the medium of the Navy Minister, urging the need for calmness, prudence and self-respect.

From this, and from talks I had at the time with our own Naval Attaché and with Japanese naval friends, it was clear that senior officers were seriously concerned over the ill-discipline among junior commissioned ranks, evidenced by the agitation stirred up against the Procurator for demanding such stiff sentences. Most of the more senior officers, it seemed, were in favour of drastic punishment in order to show that the law could not be broken with impunity; but there were indications that they did not all share this view and that there was considerable internal dissension on this matter. Whatever the truth may have been, the Procurator's demands were found to have been whittled down very considerably when finally the sentences were pronounced in November 1933; the death sentences on the three principal offenders had been reduced to long-term imprisonment, and the prison sentences on the remainder had been cut. Owing to the intensity of the emotions aroused by the trial, however, extreme precautions were taken on the day the sentences were promulgated; not only was the courtroom itself surrounded by armed guards, but security measures of the most rigorous nature were adopted in and around the Yokosuka naval base. In view of the fact that the authorities were said to have received over a million letters demanding clemency (more than a thousand of them written in blood and some of them containing the severed fingers of the writers), the precautions were probably merited. The relative leniency of the sentences pronounced seemed to indicate that the judges had feared to pass the sentences of death and life imprisonment lest the defendants be regarded as martyrs and even more serious trouble precipitated.

Although the lightening of the sentences may have helped to stave off a serious explosion, it called forth invidious comparisons with the rejection, three days earlier, of the appeal against the death sentence on Sagoya, who had assassinated Hamaguchi in 1930; and although the sentences on the twenty civilians concerned in the outrages of May 1932 were also considerably less than those originally demanded by the Procurator, the fact that they were heavier than those imposed on either the naval or the military participants, called forth strong censure when finally sentence was delivered on them in February 1934. It was significant of the growing readiness to condone crimes perpetrated in the sacred name of patriotism that when, only a day or two earlier, Nagaoka, the assassin of Premier Hara on the eve of the Washington Conference in 1921, was released from prison, he was treated more like a returning hero than a cold-blooded murderer.

While the naval trials had revealed the intensity of feeling against the London Naval Treaty in naval circles—especially among the more junior officers—the military cadets and their sympathizers had been more concerned with the grievous lot of the farming communities and with those whom they held responsible for it. For reasons already explained, Army officers in general were extremely sympathetic towards the tenant farmers and peasantry. When, however, the outrages of 15 May 1932 revealed how explosive the situation had become, opinion in the highest ranks of the Army as to the best way to deal with it was seen to be divided. As a well-placed Japanese friend explained to me at the time, the Army as a whole was sympathetic towards the motives of the conspirators, but disapproved the violence employed and was fearful lest worse should follow. It was not prepared to risk the outbreak of revolution and would therefore step in and take control of the situation, if it looked like developing too fast or too far. Ironically, although some of the civilian extremists wished to avoid military dictatorship, this was just what the officers concerned in the abortive plots of March and October the previous year had wanted—to create a situation which would force the Army to take control. Where the division of opinion occurred in the Army was over the question of whether to deal leniently with the military cadets in order to avoid making martyrs of them, or to adopt such drastic measures for restoring discipline that others would be deterred from resorting to violence and revolution. Those who urged leniency won their way and the cadets escaped with relatively light sentences, on the grounds that they had been led astray by the naval culprits and had taken no part in the actual murder of the Premier.

Although the Army was showing an increasing tendency to interfere in government affairs outside its legitimate province, it had no wish to take over the governance of the country on its own; to do so would involve shouldering responsibility for whatever happened. This is just what it wished to avoid. Like the 'shadow rulers', who have played so important a part throughout the history of Japan, it preferred to exert pressure from behind the scenes rather than to seize power openly and accept the responsibilities involved. From private talks I had at the time with senior Japanese officers and others, it seemed clear, therefore, that the Army was firmly convinced that, in order to ease the rapidly deteriorating situation, it should have a greater say in the Government's agrarian policy. It would have preferred a national government, but it was prepared to support even a party Cabinet, provided the Government would pledge its support to the Army's economic programme. This included a change in the taxation system, aiming at relief of the farming population, and the application of a moratorium on the huge debts contracted by the farmers and small retailers. While, however, the Army recognized that the removal of abuses connected with the party system, and the betterment of the conditions of the agricultural communities, were essential if worse developments were to be avoided, the politicians were unable to pledge their full support to the Army's proposals, as their own power was largely dependent on the party spoil system, which, in turn, was closely allied to big business. The point at issue was, therefore, one primarily of domestic concern, but of fundamental importance. Being traditionally scornful of wealth and largely recruited from the rural districts, the Army was naturally sympathetic towards the embittered, poverty-stricken farmers, who, besides being severely hit by the collapse of the American market for Japanese silk through the prevailing world depression, were bled by taxation for the purpose of assisting trade and industry. The politicians, on the other hand, recognized that support of commerce and industry was essential for the economic welfare of the country and that this support would have to be seriously curtailed if the Army's demands were accepted. The desperate plight of the farmers was nevertheless appreciated, and the urgent necessity of relief for the agricultural districts—especially in Northern Japan, where many thousands were said to be on the verge of starvation—was occupying the attention of the Diet; and well it might, as delegations of angry peasants and farmers, demanding immediate relief in no uncertain terms, were descending on Tokyo with increasing frequency. To add to the Government's worries, reactionary and radical organizations were exploiting the farmers' grievances for the purpose of launching a country-wide movement for the overthrow of the existing political order. The world depression, which had brought industrial unemployment as well as rural destitution, had, in fact, created an ugly mood, ripe for exploitation.

That the Army's proposals, for a moratorium on the debts contracted by the farmers, were not without justification was shown by figures published at the time and quoted later in the trials of those implicated in the outrages of May 1932. According to these figures, these debts aggregated no less than five thousand million yen, on which interest had to be paid at the exorbitant rate of 10 per cent per year. In addition, tenant farmers were paying out seven hundred and fifty million yen a year in rent. The main reason for these crippling debts was that, proportionately, the burden of taxation was far heavier on the farmer than on any other section of the community; in national, prefectural and town and village taxes he paid double what the merchant paid and more than three times as much as the manufacturer.

It was facts such as these, together with the drastic remedies prescribed in the writings and teachings of Kita Ikki, Suzuki Kyo, Gondo and others, that served to incite so many young officers into a form of perverted idealism; it was a philosophy akin to that expressed by Brutus when explaining his reason for slaying Caesar. His words, 'It was not that I loved Caesar less but that I loved Rome more', were, in fact, quoted by defending counsel in the course of the 1933 trials by way of providing an extenuating parallel. The quotation merely echoed the assertion of one of the defendants, who had declared, 'We had no enmity towards Premier Inukai personally. We respect and honour his memory and only regret that his death was necessary in order to renovate and restore the life of the nation.'

Variations on the theme, 'It is expedient that one man should die', were repeated time and again; so, too, was the proclaimed readiness of the defendants to accept the death sentence, albeit with the proviso that their death should not be in vain. In the constant reiteration of such sentiments there was no question of mock heroics. Behind it all was the fanatical belief that by no other means than by the violence, to which they had resorted, could the nation be regenerated. With this went the readiness to accept gladly the death penalty for what they had done.

To the Japanese people at large, brought up as they were to regard 'purity of motive' as of far greater importance than the crime committed, such sentiments as these made an irresistible emotional appeal. Taken in conjunction with the extraordinary freedom given to the defendants to use the court as a platform from which to expound and disseminate their views, it was perhaps but inevitable, therefore, that such strong feelings of sympathy for the accused, and of indignation against those demanding drastic punishment, should have been aroused. The consequent spread of these tenets, and the emotional upsurge caused by the trials, however, were to play an insidious part in influencing developments in the years ahead. The decision to terminate the Washington and London naval agreements in 1936, the further deterioration of naval and military discipline, the rise of xenophobia, chauvinism, and anti-British and anti-American sentiment, the gradual materialization of Pan-Asian dreams, in which Japan would unite and lead the countries of Asia against their Western masters, and rapprochement with Nazi Germany; all these, and other developments as well, were to be influenced to a greater or less extent by the doctrines expounded at the trials and by the sympathy aroused for the defendants. Rational thinking largely ceased; emotional reaction took its place.

CHAPTER XVIII

Manchoukuo Developments

Dramatic as were the revelations and the emotional outbursts during the eighteen months or so which followed the outrages of 15 May 1932, the Army's determination to go ahead with its plans for strengthening its hold on Manchuria, and converting the new 'independent' state into a bastion against Soviet Russia, was made amply clear during that same period. Threats and fulminations from Geneva, Washington and other world centres had shown that censure and denunciation alone were insufficient to deter the Japanese; they had merely served to irritate and drive the nation at large into the arms of the extremists. Unless moral disapproval was to be backed by force, more harm than good would be done; but it was already reasonably clear that none of the major Powers was prepared to use force. The fiasco of the resolution passed by the League Council on 24 October the previous year, demanding the immediate withdrawal of all Japanese troops to the railway zone, had shown that the League had no intention of implementing its demands; these had merely inflamed public opinion in Japan and encouraged false hopes in China. The League Assembly resolution five months later, supporting the proposals of the American Secretary of State, Henry Stimson, for non-recognition of the newly created Manchoukuo, had likewise proved futile, as Stimson had made it clear that the United States were unable to go beyond moral disapproval of Japan and that sanctions of any kind were out of the question. By the time of Inukai's murder, therefore, Japan had taken the measure of American and League threats, and felt reasonably safe in going ahead with its plans regarding Manchuria.

So far as the question of Japan recognizing the new state was concerned, Shiratori let it be known to myself and other foreign correspondents, early in June 1932, that the Government was unlikely to accord recognition before the League meeting in September. As the Lytton Commission was expected to submit its report on its findings about that time, much, he said, would depend on what it said and how the Powers reacted to it. If the attitude at Geneva proved unfavourable, Japan, he intimated, would probably withdraw from the League and recognize Man-choukuo. When, however, Count Uchida, the newly appointed Foreign Minister, invited the foreign correspondents to an in-formal talk a few days later, he requested them not to ask him anything about the question of recognition, although, just prior to the interview, Shiratori had elaborated on what he himself had told us previously. If and when Japan entered into treaty relations with Manchoukuo, he had said, the Anglo-Iraq Treaty would serve as a useful guide; but, he had added with a sly dig at the American correspondents present, Japan regarded America's re-cognition of Panama in 1903 as a far closer parallel so far as the development of the Manchoukuo question was concerned.

From these and other straws in the wind, it seemed reasonably certain that Japan would probably accord recognition before long, but that nothing definite had yet been decided, either as to the timing or to the exact form it would take. As it was generally believed that the Army was pressing for speedy recognition, it came as something of a surprise, therefore, when General Mazaki, Vice-Chief of the General Staff, on returning from a three-week tour of inspection in Manchuria, put a damper on the hopes of those who were vociferously demanding immediate recognition of the new state. In a Press interview published on 11 July, he upbraided his countrymen for lack of patience and compared Man-choukuo to a newly-hatched chicken, which they were wanting to treat as a full-fledged hen capable of laying eggs.

That Shiratori was stung by these remarks was indicated in a talk I had with him a day or two later. Hitting out at those who were fearful of according recognition, he launched forth into a philosophical disquisition on the advisability of Japan withdraw-ing from the League, not necessarily on account of the Man-churian question, but in order to carry out a re-orientation of her foreign policy. This, he contended, might well come about, as there was a growing feeling that Japan would do better to turn to Asia for support and friendship and to set up some kind of Asiatic Monroe Doctrine—a 'Back-to-Asia' movement, as he put it—as both Europe and America had proved to be broken reeds. Although Shiratori was clearly expressing his own predilections, which were not necessarily those of the Japanese Government, similar views were being increasingly voiced by the more reac-tionary elements in the country. Coming from a man in Shiratori's position, they seemed all the more significant.

If Shiratori had been upset by Mazaki's remarks, he was angered still more by the two meetings, which Lord Lytton and the other members of his Commission had with Count Uchida on their final brief visit to Japan before leaving for Geneva on 15 July. On the grounds that the details of what had transpired had to be kept secret, Shiratori at first confined himself to remarking, with considerable vehemence, that Japan would never agree to Manchuria being returned to an anti-Japanese China. There was, however, no intention, he said, of recognizing Manchoukuo until Japan was satisfied that the new régime was sufficiently stable to warrant her concluding a treaty with it at the same time as she accorded recognition. Once this had been done, Japan would refuse to negotiate regarding Manchuria, either with the League or with China; to do so would be to interfere with Manchoukuo's sovereign rights. His words seemed to imply that, until recognition was actually given, the door was still open for negotiation; but some days later, on 21 July, in strict confidence he showed some of the foreign correspondents, including myself, the stenographic record of the two meetings. From these it was clear that there had been some extremely straight talking on the part of Lord Lytton and his colleagues, and a marked brusqueness and stubbornness in Uchida's replies to their queries. The members of the Commission had not minced their words, but had expressed their conviction quite frankly that Japan was guilty of violating the Nine-Power Pact and other agreements; unless she gave up her present course of action, they had warned, she would incur the moral censure of the whole world. Flatly denying these accusations, Uchida had replied bluntly to the effect that the Western Powers could think what they liked, but it would not deter Japan; furthermore, he had said, the Nine-Power Pact had nothing to do with the League, so it had no right to bring it up. Shiratori's own reaction to the attitude adopted by the Commission was one of barely suppressed indignation.

These being the sentiments of the Lytton Commission, there seemed little doubt that the League itself, on receipt of the final report, would take the same line and condemn Japan accordingly —as, in fact, it did, seven months later. One point in the heated exchange of views, however, was apparently taken to heart. This concerned the type of Japanese employed as officials by the Government of Manchoukuo. To Lord Lytton's criticism of their actions, Uchida had replied that the Japanese Government was in no way responsible, as these men were private individuals and Japan had nothing to do with their appointment. To this, back had come the retort that, in many respects, outright annexation of Manchuria might almost be preferable to mere recognition of Manchoukuo; the officials would then have to be appointed by Japan, and presumably she would be careful to send none but the best. The sarcasm clearly hit its mark; actual annexation never took place, but soon after this exchange of acerbities the Japanese Government, in order to ensure the fruits of annexation without its attendant troubles and responsibilities, took steps to ensure that only officials of the highest quality were sent as representatives and advisers to the Manchoukuo Government.

Significant as were these stenographic records for the future of Japan's relations with the League, the revelation in them that Lord Lytton had put in a good word for Soviet interests in Manchuria, and had criticized the way in which Japan was seemingly ready to ignore them, had a humorous repercussion. Nagi, the *Tass* correspondent, had been present when these records were shown to us and came round to see me about them afterwards. Expressing his surprise at what Lord Lytton had said, he remarked wryly that he had never expected to find a British statesman standing up for Soviet rights!

A talk I had had with Zumoto Motosada the previous day had served to indicate that the threat to these interests was likely to be of a long-drawn nature. Count Uchida, who had been President of the South Manchurian Railway since June 1931 until his recent appointment as Foreign Minister, had been succeeded in his former post by Kajiwara Nakaji, a prominent banker. As the Army had expressed strong objection to the new incumbent, I questioned Zumoto as to the reason for this. On his replying that it was because Kajiwara was not considered to be a man of sufficient calibre for the post, now that it entailed the management and supervision of *all* the railways in Manchuria, including the Chinese Eastern Railway, I suggested that surely this inclusion was but a temporary measure. 'No', came the reply, 'Permanent. From now onwards the Chinese Eastern Railway and all other railways in Manchuria, including those under construction or planned, will be under Japanese control, either directly or indirectly, and the Soviet are resigned to it'. The Soviet invasion of Manchuria thirteen years later, in the last week of the Pacific War, was to show that Moscow was by no means resigned permanently to

R

Japan's control of the C.E.R., but Zumoto's assertion was a clear indication of Japan's determined attempt to take over Russian rights and interests in Northern Manchuria for good and all.

It was during this talk that Zumoto told me of a remark made to him a few days earlier by General McCoy, the American member of the Lytton Commission. On Zumoto asking him why the Commission had decided to cut short its final visit to Tokyo instead of staying on and having talks with Japanese businessmen and others, he had received the curt reply, 'After hearing what Uchida and Araki had to say, we realized that it would be sheer waste of time to interview anyone else.' After seeing the stenographic record of the two interviews with Uchida, McCoy's retort seemed not unreasonable.

Uchida's brusque and cavalier attitude towards Lord Lytton and his fellow members was hardly calculated to further Japan's case when finally it was presented at Geneva a few months later. From the point of view of Anglo-Japanese relations it was deplorable, as the Japanese people at large, indignant at the strictures laid on their country in the Commission's report, tended to blame Britain for them. Lord Lytton was British, the Commission was known as the Lytton Commission and its report as the Lytton Report; Britain, so ran the argument, was therefore at the bottom of it all. In the highly emotional atmosphere prevailing at the time, clear thinking went by the board; the fact that Lord Lytton had been appointed, not by Britain but by the League, and that the other four members of the Commission were American, French, German and Italian respectively, was overlooked. So, too, was the fact that all five had been in total agreement.

Unfortunate though Uchida's handling of the Lytton Commission had been, the straight-speaking of its members at the two meetings had served to jerk the Japanese Government into realizing the necessity of selecting a representative capable of expounding Japan's case with clarity and conviction at the crucial meeting of the League in September. Matsuoka Yosuke, it will be recalled, had made a very favourable impression on Lord Hailsham and other Western delegates by his masterly exposition on Manchuria at the Conference of the Institute of Pacific Relations in Kyoto in 1929; he had played an all-important part, moreover, in the developments that had followed the outbreak of the Manchurian 'Incident' in September 1931. It was no great surprise, therefore, when, within a fortnight of the Commission's departure from Japan, he was appointed to head the Japanese delegation which was to be sent to Geneva. It was with some foreboding, however, that I returned from lunching with him a few days before he left. Although friendly towards me personally, he was aggressively outspoken in his criticisms, not only of the League in general but of Britain and the United States in particular. He had always hitherto, he said, considered that Japan's interests were best served by close and friendly relations with those two Powers; but their attitude in recent months was forcing him to revise his opinion and he was beginning to feel that it would be better to look elsewhere for support and friendship, possibly to Germany or Soviet Russia. If London and Washington ranged themselves against Japan when the Lytton Report was published and brought up for discussion at the coming meeting of the League, he would certainly work for a reversal of Japan's foreign policy.

Eight more years were to pass before Matsuoka himself became Foreign Minister; that was after Admiral Yonai's Cabinet had been forced to resign in July 1940, because it was considered too friendly and deferential to Britain and America and too anti-German. That his remarks to me on that occasion in the summer of 1932 had been said in earnest was then made clear, not only by his vicious denunciations of Britain and the United States, but also by his concluding the Tripartite Pact of Mutual Assistance with the Axis Powers in September 1940 and the Neutrality Pact with Russia seven months later.

Following Matsuoka's appointment to head the Japanese delegation to Geneva, developments aiming at the tightening of Japan's control over Manchuria moved swiftly. Within twenty-four hours of his appointment, a Cabinet decision to appoint a senior general officer as special envoy to Manchoukuo with plenipotentiary powers was announced; a fortnight later General Muto[1] was formally installed as such and also as Commander-in-Chief. With him as his Chief of Staff was to go General Koiso, the Vice-Minister of War. This was followed on 25 August by a speech in the Diet, in which Count Uchida explained Japan's reasons for having decided to recognize Manchoukuo in the immediate future; and a week later Shiratori confided to myself and other foreign

---

[1] Accepting responsibility for the participation of military cadets in the outrages of 15 May, Muto had resigned from the post of Director-General of Military Education a week or so later.

correspondents that a treaty with Manchoukuo was to be signed and put into effect on 15 September. This treaty, he explained, was to be in the nature of a defensive alliance, with mutual respect for each other's territorial sovereignty; Japan was to be given the right to station troops anywhere in Manchuria and, in return, was to undertake both the internal and external defence of Manchoukuo. Although he emphasized that there was no question of establishing a protectorate, it seemed clear that, in effect, this is what it would be. What appeared strange, however, was that not only was the Japanese Press forbidden to publish this information, but that it had been withheld from the diplomatic missions in Tokyo. Acute embarrassment was therefore caused to other departmental heads in the Japanese Foreign Office on learning that Shiratori had divulged it to foreign correspondents, who had, in turn, passed it on to their respective embassies.

Count Uchida's speech the previous week had already brought strong criticism from Geneva, London and Washington; the reaction to the news of the projected defensive alliance, followed as it was on the 15th by the formal recognition of Manchoukuo and the signing of the treaty, merely added to it. It showed clearly that Japan had contrived to provide a *fait accompli* before the League had either received, or been in a position to consider, the published report of the Lytton Commission's findings. While, however, the Japanese Government's handling of the whole matter had been as clumsy and inept as the handling of the Twenty-One Demands had been in 1915, the almost hysterical cries of execration, which came from some quarters abroad, showed that Westerners could be just as moved by emotion to the detriment of clear thinking as could the Japanese themselves. The fact that China, seemingly the victim of oppression, had won so much sympathy ever since Japan's incursion into Manchuria twelve months before, was perhaps understandable; but to dispassionate observers, who recalled the background and had first-hand knowledge of conditions in China, it was nauseating to read the hypocritical mouthings and misleading statements put out by Chinese representatives abroad. It was distressing, too, to note the gullibility of so many Westerners in accepting them at their face value.

A typical example of this was seen in Press despatches describing the reaction to Uchida's announcement of the decision to recognize Manchoukuo. In one of these, Quo Tai-chi, the Chinese

Minister in London, was quoted as talking glibly of China 'standing in Asia today as an exponent of everything that Englishmen and Americans hold dear with regard to enlightened government'. It was a picturesque hyperbole, but hardly in accordance with reality; this was far more bluntly and accurately portrayed by a British journalist long resident in China who, not long before, had censured the Chinese Nationalist Government for its 'unmitigated repression and rapacity'. This was not just the judgment of a disgruntled 'old China hand'; it was largely confirmed by the Lytton Report itself which, though highly critical of some of Japan's actions, indicted China and the actions of the Chinese Government in no unmeasured terms. Chinese propagandists and their sympathizers tended to soft-pedal these indictments, and many of the latter, never having read it, genuinely believed that the Report exonerated China entirely and condemned Japan. Equally false impressions were given by those who spoke of China as a united nation. Even at the height of his power, Chiang Kai-shek had never controlled more than half of the eighteen provinces comprising China Proper and was constantly being faced with rebellious generals. At the very time that Japan was deciding to recognize Manchoukuo, the political situation in China was rendered still more chaotic by the resignation of Wang Ching-wei, second only to Chiang himself in the Nationalist hierarchy, and of Chang Hsueh-liang, who denounced each other in the most vehement terms.

Strongly critical of Japan though the reaction abroad was when she accorded formal recognition to Manchoukuo, foreign diplomats in Tokyo were inclined to express more detached views when speaking in private. Amongst those with whom I discussed the matter at the time was Sir Francis Lindley; he said quite frankly that he saw nothing effective that any of the Powers could do about it and that the best thing would be to recognize the fact straight away and make the best of the existing situation. There was nothing to be gained, he considered, by a mere gesture of disapproval, such as the withdrawal of diplomatic representatives from Japan; nor was there anything to be gained by the other Powers refusing to recognize Manchoukuo, now that Japan had taken steps to ensure that its brain-child would remain in being. He pointed out, however, a significant fact, indicating that the new state seemed likely to extend its borders to include Mongolia as well as Manchuria. The English translation of the Japanese

Government's statement of the 15th mentioned only Manchuria; the original in Japanese referred all the time to Manchuria *and* Mongolia.

Whether the term 'Mongolia' was intended to embrace the Soviet-dominated Outer Mongolia as well as Inner Mongolia was not clear, but I could not help recalling a recent article in the *Kaikosha Kiji* by General Araki, the War Minister. In it he had emphasized the need to clear up the ambiguous situation in Outer Mongolia, in order to find out whether it was really independent, as claimed by Moscow, or under Soviet control. Seen in the context of the Government statement, this reference to Outer Mongolia had a somewhat ominous ring, seeming to indicate that Japan was preparing to risk a head-on clash with the Soviet. As events were to show, however, the Government itself was only envisaging the incorporation of Inner Mongolia into the territorial confines of Manchoukuo. Although overlooked at the time, this should perhaps have been evident from the start, since Manchoukuo, as successor to the Mukden régime, claimed to be the rightful owner of Jehol, the Inner Mongolian province bordering Manchuria on the south-west and sharing the Great Wall as its border with North China. The basis for this contention was that Jehol had been placed under Mukden's administration in December 1928, at the time when Chang Hsueh-liang declared his allegiance to the Nationalist Government in Nanking.

Developments leading towards the eventual inclusion of Jehol within the Manchoukuo fold were, in fact, already under way by the time that Japan announced its formal recognition of the new state; but this was not, at first, generally realized. Starting with the seizure of a Japanese liaison officer by Chinese troops in Jehol in mid-July, accusations and counter-accusations were soon being exchanged between the Japanese and the Chinese. A month later came reports of clashes between Japanese and Jehol troops, and Shiratori let it be known that strong action was likely to be taken before long to put an end to the unsatisfactory situation; Jehol, he intimated, would probably be taken over by Manchoukuo eventually. It was not, however, until the following February, after prolonged attempts to reach a peaceful settlement had failed, that the threatened operations began; but by then the confines of Manchoukuo had been extended in another direction. This was achieved by a series of hard-hitting blows which, in effect, had brought the whole of North Manchuria, including the

full length of the Chinese Eastern Railway, under Japanese control. Preceded in late October 1932 by anti-bandit operations in
the southern regions of Manchuria, for the purpose of completing
the work of pacification in accordance with Japan's obligations
under the new Defensive Alliance with Manchoukuo, by mid-
November there were clear indications that more serious developments were likely in the north; there, 250 Japanese civilians had
been seized by Su Ping-wen, an independent Chinese commander,
who was holding them as hostages in Manchuli, Hailar and other
centres. Negotiations for their release having failed, the Japanese,
disregarding the exposure of their lines of communication to
raiders, launched an offensive on 1 December; within a week the
relatively small force employed had advanced some 600 kilometres
westwards, through the heart of the Khingan mountains under
Arctic conditions, as far as Manchuli. Two months later, with Su
Ping-wen out of the way and all North Manchuria west of Harbin
virtually under Japanese control, Japanese troops were despatched
eastwards to occupy the eastern border town of Pogranitchnaya;
they now, therefore, controlled the whole length of the Chinese
Eastern Railway, from Manchuli on the Soviet border in the west
to Pogranitchnaya on the Soviet border in the east, a distance of
some 1,200 kilometres in a direct line and 1,800 kilometres or so
in actual rail length. And here a brief digression may be excusable.

British officers, who had had the good fortune to be seconded
for attachment to Japanese Army units, had always been impressed
by the emphasis placed by the Japanese on endurance tests under
extremes of heat and cold in their peace-time training and by their
readiness to accept risks when pressing home hard-hitting attacks.
The rapidity and skill with which the operations against Su Ping-
wen had been carried out under the severest climatic conditions
(the Tsitsihar operations in late 1931 and the Jehol operations,
which were to follow in February 1933, provided other good examples) merely went to show how valuable this peace-time training had been and what folly it was to under-rate the Japanese Army
as a fighting machine. The tragedy was, that those who drew the
wrong conclusions from the Shanghai operations completely overlooked the proof of Japanese fighting ability provided by the
operations in North Manchuria and Inner Mongolia and failed to
rectify the mistaken lessons drawn from Shanghai.

Within a month of the successful offensive against Su Ping-wen,
fighting had broken out at Shanhaikwan, the gateway to North

China in the south. On discussing this with Colonel James, who had succeeded Colonel Simson as British Military Attaché some months earlier, he told me he had learned from the Japanese General Staff that instructions were being sent to do everything possible to localize the fighting and prevent its spreading into North China. This seemed reassuring; and when I went round to the War Office after seeing him, I found the place deserted and still closed down for the New Year holidays. This, too, seemed to indicate that the fighting had not been anticipated and that it was not expected to develop into anything serious. The dangerous potentialities, however, were seen when, a week later, a Japanese cavalry detachment was detailed to occupy Chiumenkuo, a pass on the Chinese side of the Great Wall just north of Shanhaikwan. This, it was explained, had been done for the twofold purpose of preventing the encirclement of the Japanese forces at Shanhaikwan and of cutting off four of Chang Hsueh-liang's brigades in south-east Jehol; these were said to be menacing the Japanese line of communication between Chinchow and Shanhaikwan, the main railway line running through the narrow strip separating eastern Jehol from the sea.

When, a month later, I spoke to Colonel Homma, a close friend of Army days who had recently returned from a tour of duty as Japanese Military Attaché in London,[1] he confided to me that hopes of a peaceful settlement were by then practically exhausted and that preparations for probable military action were therefore under way. He was unable to commit himself to any definite statement regarding the possible extension of the operations into the Peking–Tientsin area, because, as he put it, it was necessary to 'keep the Chinese guessing' as to the Army's intentions; but he emphasized that, in drawing up their plans, the need to avoid

---

[1] Homma, who had been attached to the British Army in France during the final stages of the Great War, had later been attached to a British regiment in Aldershot and had subsequently served in India as Japanese Military Representative in Simla, before being appointed Military Attaché in London. Through his close connections with the British Army, he had won the friendship of a wide circle of British officers and was, in consequence, regarded as too pro-British by the more extreme elements in the Japanese Army. During the later stages of the Pacific War, he was to be one of the few officers who supported those who strove quietly in the background to bring about a negotiated peace. Ironically, he was to face a firing squad in Manila in 1947, having been held technically responsible for the Bataan Death March, as he had been C.-in-C. of the invading forces at the time it took place.

endangering foreign lives and interests in North China was being borne in mind. It was no great surprise, therefore, when, on 21 February, reports of a clash at Chaoyanssu, on the Jehol border, were followed quickly by the news that the Manchoukuo Government had decided to issue a 24-hour ultimatum, demanding the immediate withdrawal of all Chang's troops from Jehol; if they failed to do so, they would be driven out by force. By the following day, the initial steps for the coming Japanese offensive had been taken, and rapid thrusts forward into the mountainous country beyond were soon being carried out from a number of points along the eastern border of Jehol in the face of raging snow-storms and temperatures around 30 degrees below freezing point. No attempt was made to seize the passes into North China, these being left open deliberately for the purpose of driving the Chinese through them out of Jehol and then sealing them off. So rapid had been the Japanese advance and so relentless the pursuit of the demoralized Chinese forces that by 4 March, little more than a week after the start of the campaign, the ancient city of Jehol, capital of the province of that name, was in Japanese hands and the main fighting was over. The danger of worse to come, however, was by no means at an end, as the Chinese, having been driven out of Jehol, sought to lure the Japanese into North China in the hope of creating complications between Japan and the foreign Powers, who had their own garrisons there. This was just what the Japanese Government wished to avoid.

Although the Japanese made no attempt to cross into North China in pursuit, the Chinese were reported to be bringing up reinforcements and munitions for the purpose of trying to re-occupy the passes, one of which, the Kupeikou Pass, they still held. Unless, therefore, the Chinese could be persuaded to enter into negotiations for a withdrawal of their troops and for the creation of a neutral zone along their side of the Great Wall,[1] it became increasingly clear that the Japanese might feel compelled to send troops into North China. The difficulty was to find some responsible Chinese with whom to negotiate, as Chang, holding himself responsible for the Jehol debacle, had resigned. The consequent state of tension continued for two months, heightened at one stage by a brief sally over the border by the Japanese; but,

---

[1] The original proposal, made before the start of the Jehol operations, had been for a neutral zone on both sides of the Wall, but the Chinese had rejected it out of hand.

in accordance with a promise made by General Araki, the Japanese troops had been withdrawn as soon as the immediate purpose had been achieved. Unfortunately, this voluntary withdrawal had been depicted by Chinese propagandists as a great Chinese victory. Falling victim to their own propaganda, they imagined they had the Japanese on the run and made preparations for a counterstroke, aiming at the recovery of Jehol. Following a warning issued by the War Office in Tokyo on 2 May, the Japanese therefore launched an offensive across the Wall into North China and matters looked serious for a time, especially when T. V. Soong, the Chinese Minister in Washington, was reported to have urged Nanking not to conclude an armistice, as he hoped to persuade the United States to intervene if the Japanese could be drawn on to Peking.

From talks I had with Colonel Homma and others, however, it seemed clear that the Japanese had no intention of being lured into such a trap, and Homma added a further reason for hoping that it would not be necessary for them to occupy either Peking or Tientsin. If they did so, it would mean keeping them there for some time, but the Army, he said, was anxious to clear up the situation without delay, as the troops were badly needed in North Manchuria. The War Office was therefore understandably indignant when, on 24 May, Shiratori tipped off the foreign correspondents with the news that the Chinese had put forward proposals for a truce agreement. As the Army had promised that the negotiations would be kept secret until completed, the fear was that Shiratori's indiscretion might cause the Chinese to call off the talks. Considerable relief was felt, therefore, when the announcement came that a truce had been finally signed at Tangku on the last day of May and the threat to Peking and Tientsin removed. It was significant of the disunity in the Chinese Nationalist ranks, however, that the trouble-making Feng Yu-hsiang and other dissident elements, seeking to reap benefits for themselves, denounced Nanking for having agreed to the truce.

It only remains to add that Shiratori's indiscretions, the latest of which might well have wrecked the truce negotiations, had by now become notorious; they had caused so much embarrassment to Japanese diplomats abroad, that Arita, the Vice-Minister of Foreign Affairs, had resigned recently in protest, and early in June Shiratori was replaced as the official Foreign Office spokesman. His successor was Amau Eiji, who had just returned from Moscow, where he had been Counsellor to the Japanese Embassy. Both Shigemitsu, who had succeeded Arita, and Amau, the new spokesman, were to figure prominently later on the international scene, the former as Ambassador in London and subsequently as Foreign Minister, the latter as nominal author of the Amau Statement, laying down the policy of 'Hands Off China'.

Although explosive to the point of rudeness at times, Shiratori had got on well with most of the foreign correspondents, who found his outspoken comments and caustic asides both refreshing and stimulating; but in view of his frequent indiscretions, it was always a mystery how he had been able to retain his post so long.[1] On a number of occasions I had discussed this matter with well-placed Japanese friends, but they seemed as genuinely in the dark as I was; all agreed, nevertheless, that he must have had powerful friends in the background. On one occasion, however, shortly before Shiratori's replacement, Count Soyeshima spoke out very strongly to me about him. Asserting that he was disliked and distrusted by the whole Foreign Office with the exception of the Foreign Minister, Count Uchida, he claimed, too, that the Imperial Household officials were also up in arms against him. This, he said, was because of his discourteous attitude when making his weekly reports on the international situation to the Emperor, and because of his alleged failure to interpret correctly when called upon to act as interpreter for foreign diplomats at audiences with His Imperial Majesty. Particularly revealing in its bearing on Anglo-Japanese relations was his assertion that Shiratori was trying to get the able Matsudaira Tsuneo removed from his post as Ambassador in London, as he considered him too friendly to Britain. Although this attempt had so far been without success, Matsudaira, in private correspondence with Soyeshima, had expressed grave concern over the way things were going. Fearing lest the letters should fall into wrong hands, Soyeshima had taken the precaution to destroy them as soon as he had read their contents. It was no doubt a wise precaution, as future developments were to show that those who worked for the maintenance of friendly relations with Britain were to meet with increasing difficulties and hostility.

[1] Fifteen years later, at the War Crime Trials in Tokyo in 1948, Shiratori, who had been Ambassador in Rome at the time when the Tripartite Pact was concluded in 1940 (see p. 337), was sentenced to life imprisonment for his part in working for a military alliance with Germany and Italy.

CHAPTER XIX

Japan, the League and Great Britain

By recognizing Manchoukuo and entering into alliance with it before the Lytton Report had been published, Japan had, in effect, jumped the gun and added to the difficulties of the League by presenting it with a *fait accompli*. This, at least, was the view expressed by Mr de Valera at the meeting of the League Council nine days later when, as President of that body, he deplored the action taken by the Japanese Government and declared that it was 'calculated to prejudice the settlement of the dispute'.

On 25 September 1932, the same day that this statement was made, Japan asked to be allowed six weeks in which to study the Report before it was brought up for consideration. In the very slender hope that this postponement might give her time to re-consider her action and reverse the steps she had already taken, the request was therefore granted. When, however, the Japanese observations on the Report were eventually handed over to the Council (the Report itself having been published in the meantime on 2 October), the whole matter was transferred for action to the League Assembly, which met on 6 December to consider it. It was a procedure which aroused outspoken criticism in Japan, the Japanese Press accusing the Council of trying to evade responsi-bility for the solution of the dispute by passing it on to the Assembly before coming to any decision themselves.

The reason for this transfer, and its consequences, call for a word of explanation. It was the Council, not the Assembly, which had appointed the Lytton Commission; the original idea had there-fore been that the Report should be submitted to the Council for consideration. At the height of the Shanghai operations early in the year, however, the Chinese, knowing that they would have more powerful support in the Assembly than they were ever likely to have in the Council, had had the dispute transferred to the larger body.[1] It was to the Assembly, therefore, that the Council

[1] By invoking Articles X and XV of the League Covenant on 29 January, the Chinese obliged the League to turn from conciliation to adjudication of responsibility and possible sanctions.

handed over the Report for consideration and action after receiving the Japanese observations on it. The Chinese reasoning was
to prove well justified. The handful of major Powers on the
Council urged conciliation and were opposed to judgment, which
would only inflame Japanese feelings and precipitate a dangerous
situation. Having a far larger stake in the outcome of the discussions, and being fully aware that the main burden would fall on
them for any action that had to be taken, the Council very naturally
adopted a more sober outlook than the numerous small nations in
the Assembly. These latter, most of whom were far removed from
the scene of trouble and lacked any material interests in the Far
East that were liable to suffer, could and did show a moral fervour
and determination to carry out the Covenant to the letter, such as
the Great Powers could not afford to emulate.

Bearing all this in mind, it was interesting to note the reactions
of some of the leading foreign diplomats in Tokyo to the discussions in Geneva. Cynicism, pessimism, and annoyance with
their own home governments for ignoring their warnings and
recommendations, seemed common to them all when speaking in
private. As Weillschott, the Italian Chargé d'Affaires, remarked to
me late in November, 'All our governments insist on keeping up
the fiction that China is as well-organized and competent a state
as any in existence and a faithful observer of all her international
obligations and agreements. They know that this is the very
reverse of the truth; they know, too, that it is the rotten condition
of China that is at the bottom of the whole trouble and that, so
long as fiction takes the place of fact, no real solution is possible;
but no one has the courage to get up and say so, lest it damage
their trade interests in China.'

That consideration of national interests should influence the
attitude of the Powers towards the dispute was understandable;
but, this being so, it was perhaps inevitable that professional
diplomats should adopt an air of cynicism when such considerations were so often cloaked under expressions of righteous
indignation and moral censure by speakers at Geneva. Baron de
Bassompière, the Belgian Ambassador, more or less admitted this
when, a few days after my talk with Weillschott, he remarked that
no Belgian government could afford to side with Japan at Geneva,
as Belgium had to consider her trade interests in China; the
Chinese would take it out of them if they did so. It remained
for Abrikosov, the one-time Czarist diplomat, to sum up the

consequences of all this. It was, he said, hardly surprising that Japan felt she could not hope for a fair, disinterested verdict from the Powers, when the effect on their own particular interests carried so much greater weight with them than did the justice or otherwise of Japan's case. In effect, he added, she is being treated like a prisoner at the bar, and by a packed jury at that. Being himself a trained diplomat, but no longer responsible to any government, he could, of course, afford to take a more detached view than his former diplomatic colleagues.

It was while lunching with him and Baron de Bassompière at the Tokyo Club that these remarks were made, and Abrikosov interspersed the conversation with a flow of comments, half-serious, half-bantering, on the difference between the pre-War and post-War school of diplomats. The former, he maintained, gained a reputation for wisdom because of their reticence, though their silence was often due to lack of knowledge. The post-War school, on the other hand, with its cry of 'Open Diplomacy', liked to hold forth loquaciously and, with an air of wisdom, show how simple it was, at least in theory, to settle the affairs of nations. In actual fact, however, the assumed wisdom was largely imaginary and he considered that the pre-War reticence, even though it might have been only a veil for ignorance, did far less harm.

That this view was shared by others, and that it had a close bearing on the discussions at Geneva, was reflected in private talks I had with a number of the senior diplomats in Tokyo. The general consensus of opinion seemed to be that the pre-War methods of secret diplomacy, despite its defects, was on the whole less pernicious in its effects than the new open diplomacy. Instead of producing important international agreements by heart to heart talks between responsible statesmen, who were fully conversant with all the ins and outs of the question under discussion and able to express their opinions freely and frankly in private, 'open diplomacy' required that the public be kept fully informed of all that was going on. The statesmen had to mouth the platitudes expected of them and mob psychology—which was seldom ruled by wisdom, by understanding, or by fairness and impartiality—was promptly brought into play. Important business transactions between commercial concerns or banking institutions could never be brought about by such methods, yet statesmen were expected to work for peace and good-will among nations by such means.

That there was not a little truth in this was shown by the embittered exchange of acerbities which marked the discussions at Geneva itself, and by the polemics in which the public Press indulged, in Japan and in the other countries mainly concerned. This dog-fight continued, almost without intermission, from November 1932 onwards until March the following year, when Japan finally walked out of the League, with Matsuoka flinging back at the assembled delegates the cutting taunt, 'Let him who is guiltless cast the first stone.' The feelings aroused by the controversy were plainly reflected in a comment made to me by Sir Francis Lindley, who remarked wryly, 'If it has done nothing else, this Manchurian business has proved more clearly than ever before that it is impossible for Britain to serve the interests of the League whole-heartedly without damaging her own'.

This conflict of national and League interests, together with the problem of how to resolve it, was constantly in the minds of foreign diplomats in Japan at this time; but from discussions I had with a number of them; it was clear that they did not always see eye to eye with their home governments as to how their own national interests could best be served. Some of them, in private conversation, were extremely frank about this and critical of their own governments for ignoring their advice. Typical of those who spoke in this vein was General Pabst, the Dutch Minister, who had formerly been the Netherlands Military Attaché in Japan and had no delusions about the situation. Like so many other foreign diplomats in Tokyo, he said, he had been advising his government all along to urge the League to stand clear of driving Japan into a corner by denouncing her as an aggressor and threatening to apply sanctions against her. Any such threat, he considered, would prove useless and would only make matters worse, as he felt certain that none of the Great Powers would be prepared to carry the threat into effect. The only result would therefore be, that the League's prestige would be severely damaged and Japan shown that she could flout world opinion with impunity. Wait and give Manchoukuo time to prove or disprove its stability, was his advice, which appeared to be that of most of the other foreign diplomats in Tokyo. It seemed, however, to have fallen on deaf ears, and Geneva appeared to think that Japan was only bluffing and would climb down if the necessary moral pressure was applied.

General Pabst's fears were to prove well-founded. The threat to apply sanctions did not materialize, but Japan was denounced as an aggressor and thereupon withdrew from the League. As the denunciation was not followed by any punitive action, the only result was to anger Japan and undermine the prestige of the League. The writing on the wall was clear; the League was unprepared to protect a fellow-member and collective security was shown to be a delusion.

These remarks by General Pabst were made to me towards the end of November 1932, a week or so before the main discussions in the League Assembly were opened; but in a subsequent talk in February, by which time tempers, both in Geneva and in Tokyo, were rising rapidly, he drew me aside after a dinner at his Legation for a quiet talk on the situation. Highly critical of the League, he spoke in scathing terms of those members of it who, though in the forefront in demanding drastic measures against Japan, knew well that they themselves would not be called upon to share the burden of any such action. Picking on Switzerland as one of the most bellicose, he recalled that she had made a reservation, at the time of entering the League, that she would never be called upon to do anything if ever sanctions were applied against an erring member. No wonder she feels safe in demanding stern measures, he added caustically, when she herself will have no responsibility if action is taken—and the same is true of the others amongst the most vociferous.

Bellicose as were the members of the League with the least responsibility, Japanese stubbornness made the task of those who sought to ease the growing tension all the harder. By early January 1933 it seemed clear that, unless Japan was prepared to compromise to some extent, it would be difficult to avert the application of paragraph 4 of Article XV of the League Covenant, empowering the Council to make recommendations if attempts to effect a settlement of the dispute had failed. If this should happen and the recommendations proved unacceptable by Japan, a head-on collision between her and the League appeared inevitable. Whitehall accordingly instructed Sir Francis Lindley to see Count Uchida, with a view to impressing on him the need for Japan to adopt a more conciliatory attitude at Geneva if such a danger was to be avoided. From what Sir Francis told me about this visit when I saw him next day, it was clear that Shiratori had been fully justified when, six months earlier, he had asserted that Japan, once she had recognized Manchoukuo, would refuse to negotiate either with the League or with China concerning Manchuria. This was, in effect, confirmed by Uchida when, in reply to Lindley's urgings, he made it clear that there were two points on which Japan was inflexible—refusal to withdraw her recognition of Manchoukuo and refusal to consider any third-party interference in the settlement of the Manchurian question.

As February followed January, national sentiment in Japan became increasingly inflamed against the League in general, but particularly against Dr Beneš and Czecho-Slovakia, who were amongst the foremost in demanding dire punishment of the Japanese. The bitterness felt was reflected in the bitter reproach voiced to me by Shiratori, who charged the Czechs with gross ingratitude after the help given them some fourteen or fifteen years earlier in Siberia. They would be sorry for it one day, he declared, as Japan would never forget. Japan's alliance with Nazi Germany seven years later, after Hitler had over-run Czecho-Slovakia, perhaps proved him right in part. Shiratori, however, was not alone in feeling resentful against the Czechs and others of the smaller nations, who were clamouring for stern measures against Japan. In London, the *Evening Standard* was only echoing what some of the other British papers were saying when, a few weeks earlier, it had declared that, if sanctions were imposed, the main task of enforcing them would fall on the Royal Navy. This, it declared, would mean that Britain would become the instrument for carrying out 'a policy dictated by Czecho-Slovakia for the vindication of interests which are mainly American'.

Accusing Geneva of disturbing the peace of the Far East by justifying and legalizing the Chinese boycott, and by denying the independence of Manchoukuo and Japan's rights of self-defence, mass meetings were held in Tokyo, urging immediate withdrawal from the League; and by mid-February Shiratori was expressing his belief to foreign correspondents that withdrawal was now a foregone conclusion. The Japanese Press, however, seemed divided in opinion as to the wisdom of quitting; but when finally the decision to withdraw was announced, the Press, the political parties, and the country in general closed ranks and expressed their support—a characteristic Japanese reaction when their country is faced with danger from without as the result of a vital decision.

It was only after studying and considering the details of the Assembly's projected recommendations that the Government had decided that they were unacceptable and had reached its decision to withdraw from the League, irrespective of whether rejection was followed by the application of sanctions or not. The potential dangers of the situation resulting from rejection were therefore fully recognized by the Japanese people at large. More than a month was to pass, however, before the decision was put into effect and Japan withdrew from the League on 27 March. In the intervening period, feelings ran high and the League was denounced in no unmeasured terms for encouraging the Chinese to refuse to negotiate with Japan direct and for precipitating the consequent dangerous situation. The extremists, whose influence was once more to the fore, availed themselves of the opportunity to exploit national sentiment by harping on the colour question. The white races, they declared, were purposely stirring up the Asiatics against each other—notably the Chinese against the Japanese— lest they combine against the West in order to achieve freedom from Western domination, and a section of the Press suggested that national unity, resulting from the decision to quit the League, was the first step towards the establishment of an Asiatic Monroe Doctrine. It was considered significant therefore when, on the League voting its approval of the Lytton Report and of its own recommendations by 41 votes to one on 24 February, it was noted that 'all the nations which abstained from voting were coloured peoples'. Among these was Siam, who was picked out for special praise during a debate in the Diet, when a member declared, 'At a time when Japan is faced by the unfriendly nations of the West, it is doubly gratifying to find a fellow-Asiatic friend.' For this reason, he called on the Government to 'pay special attention to this when drawing up its future Far Eastern policy'. The expression of such sentiments served to foreshadow the coming change in policy and the move towards Pan-Asianism under Japanese leadership, although Siam could hardly have foreseen the part that she herself was to be forced into playing in it some eight or nine years later.

What was perhaps difficult for the majority of people outside Japan to appreciate was, that the Japanese were genuinely baffled and enraged that the Western countries had not supported them against the Chinese. This was particularly so in the matter of Chinese boycotts, which the Japanese maintained were just as much a form of warfare as were military operations. The League Covenant gave protection to countries suffering from military action, but gave none to those against whom boycotts were directed. This the Japanese considered illogical and discriminatory, and they were particularly incensed with Britain who, having herself been the victim of Chinese boycotts and violation of agreements only a few years before, had been expected to sympathize with Japan in her predicament and support her contention. With the entire population emotionally overwrought, and all clear thinking vitiated by Press reports representing Britain and the United States as 'instigators' of Chinese intransigence, the Government took the line that it had no option but to fall in with popular sentiment.

Significant though this sentiment was for the future, it was significant, too, that on 22 February, three days before the League passed the recommendations which finally led to Japan's withdrawal, the Navy Office in Tokyo issued a semi-official statement declaring, 'The Mandate Islands are Japan's life-line on sea as Manchuria is on land. Japan will never surrender them.' It was a clear forewarning.

As no imposition of sanctions followed Japan's withdrawal from the League on 27 March, tension began to ease, although Matsuoka, in a broadcast speech made on his return from Geneva a month later, called on his countrymen to realize the seriousness of the national emergency facing Japan and urged them to act and think accordingly. At this point, therefore, it may be as well to turn back to the period immediately following the publication of the Lytton Report on 2 October the previous year, in order to see how Japan's relations with the principal Western Powers were being affected.

In view of the criticism to which Lord Lytton himself was subjected when the details of the Report were made known, I was much interested to learn from Count Soyeshima, when I met him at a dinner party a few days later, that he had just received a letter from him—posted in Colombo on his way back to Geneva—and also one from Sir Austen Chamberlain. Both of them, he said, had stressed their friendship for Japan, but Sir Austen had warned him of the embarrassment which some of Japan's recent actions had caused to her friends in England and of the severe strain which these actions had placed on their continued friendship. Though clearly distressed by these remarks, Soyeshima held Count Uchida mainly to blame for the harm done to Anglo-Japanese relations and even more so for the strictures contained in the Lytton Report. Lord Lytton, he said, had wanted to stay longer in Japan on his visit in July, as he had planned to have more talks with the leading statesmen, politicians and business-men with a view to obtaining their views and clearing up certain points; but Uchida had made it very clear to the Commission that he would prefer their departure to their continued presence. The talks, which might have proved helpful to the Japanese cause, had therefore to be omitted and the Commission had left Japan with a feeling of frustration and resentment, which was reflected, to Japan's disadvantage, in the Report when published.

That the strictures in the Report aroused strong feelings in Japan was understandable; but, bearing in mind what Soyeshima had said, it was with particular interest that I listened to what Colonel Homma had to say, when I saw him a day or two later. Admitting that, for internal consumption, he had, in his official capacity, to appear somewhat critical of the Report, he went on to remark quite frankly that he personally considered it a very good report on the whole, even though it contained some un-palatable statements. While Japan, he added, cared little about what the smaller nations might say, she was anxious to win British support. He had been much upset to find on his return from England, however, that many Japanese seemed to think that Britain was bound to take an anti-Japanese stand, on account of trade competition in China. When I told Sir Francis Lindley of these remarks about Japan hoping for British support at Geneva, he replied wryly that Britain, unfortunately, was not a free agent, as she had to keep in with America on account of the War Debt question. I recalled this comment when, four months later, stres-sing his disgust with British policy at Geneva, he gave it as his opinion that it was dictated in no small part by a desire to court American favour and expressed a fear lest the United States should drag us into trouble with Japan. He was particularly outspoken on that occasion, however, about what he called 'our slavish adherence to impractical League principles', and he showed me a despatch he was drafting on what he dubbed 'the crass stupidity' of some of the League's recommendations. In particular he castig-ated the first of these, which insisted on the withdrawal of all Japanese troops to the railway zone; it was a demand which had been flatly rejected sixteen months earlier and was now manifestly more impossible of acceptance by Japan than ever. By supporting such recommendations, he said, the Government was shown to be living in a world of make-believe, similar to that conjured up by Lord Cecil in a recent letter to *The Times*. In it Lord Cecil had blandly contended that Japan would come to heel if the League brought sufficient pressure to bear on her. Remarking acidly that such treatment would have just the opposite effect, Sir Francis declared that nothing would be more calculated to unite the whole country together and play into the hands of the Army and the extremists.

Angry though he was with Lord Cecil's 'fatuous assertions' and with the British Government and the League being swayed by such pipe-dreams, he was glad to see that Winston Churchill was reported as having hit out at the way in which the United States had induced Britain to give up the Anglo-Japanese Alliance and cut down our Navy, and now wanted us to clear up the consequent mess in the Far East. The harm, however, had been done, and Sir Francis was deeply disturbed by the growing anti-British sentiment in Japan.

That there were prominent Japanese in the armed services who shared this view was soon to become evident from unofficial probings. These had started a week or two earlier, when I was approached by a go-between of General Araki's to sound me out about the possibility of arranging for unofficial discussions between the General and Sir Francis. The original approach had been made towards the end of January by Metzger, a Hungarian correspondent, who had said that a Japanese friend of his, a former Army officer named Yamada Kozo, was anxious to meet me. Yamada, he explained, was working for Admiral Arima, General Oshima, (War Minister at the time of Prince Arthur's visit in 1918), and others, who wanted to bring about closer relations with Britain and, if possible, a virtual resumption of the former alliance. No mention was made at that time of Araki's connection with this group and it was not until 1 November, more than nine months later, that Araki's name was mentioned for the first time. I had met Yamada on two or three occasions in the meantime, and he now sent me a message to say that Araki had asked him to find out if I would be prepared to let Snow, the British Chargé d'Affaires,[1] know that he, Araki, would greatly appreciate an informal talk with him for the purpose of having a frank discussion on Anglo-Japanese relations and on the possibilities of a return to the old alliance or something like it. It was an interesting proposal, though it seemed doubtful if diplomatic

[1] Sir Francis Lindley was by then on leave in England.

etiquette would permit even informal talks of this kind between the War Minister and the acting head of a diplomatic mission. However, I sounded out Snow about it and recalled to him how Colonel Homma had confided to me, some months previously, that Araki had become an advocate of a return to the Alliance. Homma had admitted at the time that this sudden change from his former somewhat anti-British attitude was rather surprising; but this message from Yamada seemed to indicate that Araki was in earnest.

Snow's initial reaction implied that he could not take the proposal seriously; but by the end of November, after I had passed on the gist of further talks with Yamada, he became more interested and told me he was cabling the main details to London. What was of particular importance and significance, if true, was Yamada's assertion that Araki's wish to work for closer relations with Britain was due to the Emperor having intimated to him, through Prince Fushimi, the Chief of the Naval Staff, that it was his earnest desire that he should do so.[1] The Emperor, according to Yamada, had been strongly influenced by his mother, the Dowager Empress, who was much worried about the anti-British trend and was anxious for a return to closer friendship. This was because Britain was the sole remaining monarchical nation among the Great Powers other than Japan, and also because of the admiration and respect she herself felt for the British Royal Family, which she regarded as a model for the Japanese Imperial Family. The Dowager Empress, he had added, had always been a firm advocate of Anglo-Japanese friendship and had been largely instrumental in influencing Count Okuma, who was Premier at the time, to enter the war against Germany in 1914 in support of Britain.

Apart from this expression of the Emperor's personal wishes, Yamada had explained other reasons for Araki's advocacy of closer friendship and co-operation between Britain and Japan. Firm and friendly bonds between them were essential for the peace of the Far East. Without them, he said, China would be left free to continue playing off the one against the other to the disadvantage of each, while Soviet Russia would remain a constant menace to both. It was, he maintained, because Japan had

---

[1] As mentioned on p. 97, the message to Araki appeared to have come from the Dowager Empress, acting on behalf of her son, the Emperor, rather than from the Emperor himself.

no assurance of help from Britain, or from any other country, that she had sought to strengthen her position in Manchuria against the threat of Soviet encroachment.

On my asking if Araki would have the Army behind him in this policy of closer relations with Britain, Yamada had asserted that he would. There was, he admitted, a certain amount of anti-British sentiment among Japanese officers, but it was confined mainly to regimental officers, who had nothing to do with foreign relations or national policy. Even if Araki was replaced as War Minister, his successor would most certainly work with the same object in view, as the Emperor had willed it and no responsible senior officer would disobey his will.

Following Snow's cable to London in November 1933 reporting the gist of Yamada's remarks, there had been further probings and an informal meeting between him and General Araki; but it was not until after Sir Francis Lindley's return from leave towards the end of the year that any serious talks took place. Sir Francis himself had been a bit dubious at the start about the prospects of any useful purpose being served by such discussions, as he felt that Araki was too much of a mystic and a visionary in his outlook. He certainly tended that way and, unlike the great majority of Japanese officers, he was extremely verbose at times and liable to be carried away in a torrent of words when expounding his views on the philosophy of Kōdō, the Imperial Way; but, being an idealist by nature and a soldier by profession, he always gave one the impression of being honest and upright, a man of simple tastes, and kindly and courteous towards others, no matter how senior or how junior they might be.

Whatever his initial doubts may have been, Sir Francis finally decided that no harm would be done by informal talks and that they might do some good. Having ascertained, therefore, that neither the British Foreign Office nor the Japanese Foreign Minister had any objections, a meeting was arranged in February 1934 and took place in the seclusion of a quiet country inn in Atami, a well-known hot-spring resort some seventy or eighty miles south-west of Tokyo. As Araki had impressed on me that no word of the talks should leak out to the Press, there was a slightly humorous air of conspiracy about this first meeting. Sir Francis set off with me, ostensibly for a round of golf, and Araki, on welcoming us at the inn in which he was staying, started off by inviting us to join him in a bathe in his private bath-house as a preliminary to the discussions. This was, of course, in keeping with Japanese practice at hot-spring resorts; but Sir Francis quickly made it clear that he had come for a friendly talk; he could therefore dispense with the bathe.

Of this and subsequent meetings between him and General Araki no more need be said. No doubt they helped, at least for the time being, to ensure that the Higher Command of the Japanese Army would show itself favourably disposed towards assisting a return to more friendly relations with Britain; but for reasons beyond their control, the co-operation between the two countries, at which Araki aimed, failed to materialize. Before turning to consider some of these reasons, however, one more reference to Araki's effort in this direction may be noted. This concerned the arrival of Lord Newton in Tokyo on a short visit towards the end of March. Learning that he was the biographer and an ardent admirer of Lord Landsdowne, the negotiator of the original Anglo-Japanese Alliance, Araki invited him to an informal luncheon party in the hope of enlisting his aid in the cause of closer relations between Britain and Japan. Sir Francis was unable to attend, as he was laid up with a bout of influenza; but the party, consisting of Araki, Lord Newton, Colonel James, Yamada and myself, took place in a most friendly atmosphere, enlivened by extremely pungent comments on Soviet Russia and the United States by Lord Newton, a remarkably outspoken old gentleman of seventy-seven, with very decided views and not given to mincing his words. Araki's hopes of bringing about a revival of the Alliance, or something akin to it, were never to be realized, but he clearly found an ally in the person of Lord Landsdowne's biographer.

While Araki was trying his hand at diplomacy in this somewhat visionary way, developments in other fields of endeavour were serving to worsen, rather than improve, Anglo-Japanese relations. Sections of the Press, both in Japan and in England, seemed bent on causing the maximum of mischief by accusations and counter-accusations, misrepresentation and sensational revelations with little or no foundation. The sudden announcement in April 1933, that Britain had given notice of the Indian Government's intention to abrogate the Indo-Japanese Commercial Convention of 1904, added further to Japanese resentment over the way in which both tariff and immigration barriers were being raised against Japan in various parts of the world, to the detriment of Japanese

trade and of the pressing question of Japan's surplus population.

Responsible officials took the announcement calmly, even
though they felt that prior warning should have been given, so
that Japan might have been afforded a chance to carry out some
kind of export or price control as an alternative to annulment of
the Convention; but the people at large were convinced that the
abrogation was intended, at least in part, to bring economic pressure to bear on Japan on behalf of the League, and that Lanca-
shire's cotton interests were also to blame. Feeling therefore ran
high and was exploited to the full by Pan-Asiatic enthusiasts, who
plastered walls and hoardings in Tokyo with placards, calling on
the peoples of Japan, China and India to rise together and
'emancipate India from British bondage'. A bare six weeks earlier,
Britain had called forth considerable criticism by placing an
embargo on the supply of arms; but as it applied to China as well
as to Japan and hit the former harder than the latter, Japanese
reaction had not been as great as it was over the Indo-Japanese
Convention. As, however, no other country had followed the
British lead, the arms embargo had been called off in mid-March;
the only result had therefore been to leave a feeling of irritation,
for what Sir Francis Lindley described with some heat as 'one of
those noble but futile gestures to which we seem so prone.'

A broadcast by Matsuoka early in May did nothing to allay the
growth of anti-British sentiment, for he asserted that 'Britain's
sudden change of front against Japan' was due to her fear of an
anti-British boycott in South China; and there were the inevitable
Press criticisms that British policy, both at Geneva and since
Japan's withdrawal from the League, was dictated more by a
desire to keep in with the United States, on account of the War
Debts question, than by a purely disinterested judgment. From
Sir Francis Lindley's comments to me earlier, there seemed to be
some justification for this last criticism; but, true or not, it did
nothing to stop the vilification of Britain by Albin Johnson, an
American journalist who, while visiting Japan in the summer of
1933, joined in the chorus of anti-British diatribes and sought to
lay the blame on Britain for the failure to reach an amicable
settlement of the Sino-Japanese dispute at Geneva.

Galling and disturbing as was the campaign of falsehood and
abuse carried out by a large section of the Japanese Press, it was
equally distressing to the handful of British correspondents in

Tokyo to find how often their own cables to London had, when published, been either compressed or re-worded in such a way as to alter their whole meaning and, not infrequently, give them an anti-Japanese slant. Time and again, too, their messages, bearing on matters of international importance, were ignored or relegated to an inconspicuous corner, and correspondents received cabled instructions from their London offices to cut down their despatches to the barest minimum. Sometimes these instructions were understandable, but in one instance the reason given was that all interest was absorbed in the Irish Sweepstake and the Derby, and in another because it was absorbed in the Test Match! Such explanations called to mind the rueful comment of Sir Reginald Craddock, in his *Dilemma in India*, that the British public was far too absorbed in cricket and sports in general to spare time to trouble about the vital problems of India. This criticism applied with equal force to the vital problems of the Far East and was well summed up by a prominent British correspondent in Shanghai, who complained that the British Press was becoming increasingly provincial in its requirements. There was perhaps no small grain of truth, too, in the remark made to me by Glenn Babb, one of the soundest and most objective of the American correspondents in Tokyo. The British Press, he observed with particular reference to its love of sensationalism, appeared to be going through much the same phase as the American Press (thanks to Hearst) some twenty years earlier. It seemed to him, in fact, to be 'out-Americaning America, in much the same way as modern British novels are out-Frenching the French.'

The British Press, of course, was not alone in sensationalizing the news and, from time to time, admonishing its correspondents in Japan to confine their reports to 'head-line news'. The American humorist, Will Rogers, probably got nearer to the truth than he realized when, during a visit to Japan about this time, he remarked in his inimitable way to a group of foreign correspondents in Tokyo, 'Trouble with you boys is that you all want to write headlines instead of news'. What he probably failed to realize was that they were often forced to do so by the instructions received from their head offices. It was perhaps hardly surprising, therefore, that newspaper readers, all too many of whom take their news of foreign affairs from sensational, and often misleading, headlines, tended to be led astray by what they had read.[1]

[1] Some instances of the faking, wangling, and twisting of news during the

There was little doubt that the lack of a sense of proportion in the priority given to sporting events and 'human interest' stories over matters of vital importance, combined with sensationalism and the slanting of news, had much to answer for, both in Britain and Japan, at a time when clear understanding of developments in the Far East was so essential. These developments included the beginnings of a rapprochement between Japan and Germany, a revival of the naval armaments question, and a growing tension between Japan and Soviet Russia. More will be said about them in the following chapter.

period under review are given in an article by the present author in the August 1937 issue of *The Nineteenth Century*, under the title, *This Freedom of the Press*.

CHAPTER XX

The Changing Face of External Relations

As mentioned in a previous chapter, a Nazi agent calling himself Don Gato (his real name was Zahnder) had arrived in Japan about the beginning of 1932. Of no importance in himself, he was, nevertheless, a symptom. Ignored at the start by the German Embassy and by the German community in general, he was soon on close terms with some of the more extreme Japanese elements in Tokyo. With Hitler's rise to power a year later, the attitude of German diplomatic officials towards this Nazi representative started to change; even Japanese officialdom began to tread warily in regard to the new régime. This was evidenced in a private talk I had, early in March 1933, with a Polish diplomat. He confided to me that Nagai Matsuzo, the newly-appointed Japanese Ambassador to Germany, who was to have stopped off in Warsaw for a week on his way to Berlin, had cancelled his visit; this, he said, was for fear of causing offence to the new rulers of Germany. It was not without significance, therefore, that a 'congratulatory meeting', in honour of Hitler's success at the polls, had been held on 5 March under the auspices of two extremist organizations, the *Seisantō* and the *Jimmukai*, and that Don Gato was among the principal speakers.

Giving me details of this meeting, the Hungarian correspondent Metzger, who had attended it, said that Don Gato had harped on 'the Jewish peril' and had warned his hearers that Jews were the greatest danger to nationalism, as they were by nature international. Their influence, he had asserted, was being brought to bear against Japan, both at Geneva and in the realm of international finance, and he cautioned the Japanese concerning the danger of having so many Jews among the instructors at the Ueno Academy of Music and at the Foreign Languages School. As there were, in fact, very few Jews in Japan, it seemed almost incredible that the Japanese would take any notice of such vapourings; yet the fact remained that the Jewish question had actually been brought up in the course of a debate in the Diet only a week or two previously, and among the ultra-nationalist societies was one, the *Kokkyo Semmei Dan*, which boasted of a publication devoted entirely to 'the prevention of a Jewish invasion'. The lunatic fringe, admittedly, but nonetheless symptomatic.

While Hitler's rise to power naturally had its effect on the German Embassy in Tokyo, a meeting held by the German community in June that year, to discuss what attitude to adopt towards Hitlerism, showed that Don Gato himself was by no means popular. From one who had attended the gathering, I learned that he had been taken sternly to task for assuming a foreign name and for using foreign terms when addressing such a meeting and telling those present that it was their duty to uphold German nationalism. He was also strongly criticized for his derogatory remarks about the German Consul-General in Yokohama.

With Germans in Japan still undecided as to the attitude they should adopt towards the new Nazi régime, indications of a closer relationship between Japan and Germany were beginning to appear. Travelling back to Tokyo late in July after a week-end in the hills, I got into conversation with two Germans. One of them, von Etzdorf of the German Embassy, I knew. He introduced me to his companion, who proved to be a gunner colonel named Ott, attached to an artillery regiment in Nagoya. He told me he was hoping later to do a course at the Staff College in Tokyo and von Etzdorf mentioned that a Military Attaché and a Naval Attaché were to be sent out from Berlin shortly. The fact that no such representatives of the German armed services had been appointed since 1914, and that Ott was the first German officer to be attached to the Japanese Army since then, seemed to indicate that relations between the two countries were becoming more intimate than for a long time past. A Military Attaché was, in fact, appointed some months later and it was Ott himself who was given this appointment.[1]

With Germany's withdrawal from the League in October 1933, a fellow-feeling began to develop between the two recalcitrant former members of that body, and fears that Germany's action would increase the tendency towards a Japanese-German rapprochement were expressed in London. Press reports to that effect, however, were ridiculed by Amau, who had by then replaced Shiratori as Foreign Office Spokesman. The fundamentals

[1] In 1938, after promotion to Major-General, Ott succeeded von Dirksen as German Ambassador in Tokyo.

of Japan's foreign policy, he emphasized, had been laid down in the Imperial Rescript issued on the occasion of Japan's with-drawal from the League on 27 March; these would not be affected by any change in the European situation.

With the advent of 1934 came reports of an agreement reached between Japan and Germany for the exchange of radio broadcasts; but when lunching at the Tokyo Club with Amau and Iwanaga, I was assured there was nothing political about this; it was purely a 'cultural rapprochement', on the same lines as the broadcasts exchanged between Japan and the United States. If Britain would like to carry out a similar exchange, Amau said, Japan would be delighted. From talks I had had earlier with Sir Francis Lindley, however, it was clear that he was worried about the growing signs of a rapprochement and he stressed the importance of keeping an eye on German propaganda. He seemed particularly apprehensive lest a rapprochement would be followed by German recognition of Manchoukuo, as this would only serve to complicate matters. His apprehensions on this score had been aroused by a visit paid to Manchoukuo by the German Embassy Counsellor, Dr Kolb, a visit which the Japanese Press interpreted as a preliminary step towards recognition. But when I sounded out Kolb about this report at a dinner party a few days later, he dismissed it with a laugh and contended that, in actual fact, Germany would prob-ably be one of the last countries to recognize the new state. To do so, he said, would lay her open to Chinese retaliation in such a way as to damage her important trade interests in China. As Germany had been deprived of her former extrality rights in that country, this would place her in a particularly unfavourable position.

While the question of a Japanese-German rapprochement was exercising the minds of interested observers, it was with some surprise that I learned through Yamada, towards the end of February, that von Dirksen, who had recently arrived in Japan as the new German Ambassador, had been down to Atami to see General Araki. Von Dirksen, it seemed, had exchanged views with him on the subject of national socialism in Germany, and Araki had stressed a wish to strengthen the relations between the two countries. I was assured, however, that Araki's aim was to link this up with an Anglo-Japanese rapprochement, as he re-membered that the original idea, at the turn of the century, had been for an alliance between Britain, Japan and Germany and not just an Anglo-Japanese Alliance. He was said to be delighted, therefore, at the news that satisfactory talks were taking place in Berlin between Mr Eden and Herr Hitler. At the same time, it was stressed to me that, whereas Araki himself was taking the initiative in seeking to restore closer relations with Britain, the initiative in the matter of strengthening the ties between Japan and Germany had come from Dirksen. Araki's dreams of an Anglo-German-Japanese combination were, of course, to remain unfulfilled, and nearly three more years were to pass before the first concrete manifestation of a Japanese-German rapprochement was to be brought about in the form of the Anti-Comintern Pact of November 1936. At this point, however, it is necessary to turn back to see how Japan's relations with the United States had been faring in the meantime.

From the early summer of 1932 onwards, the state of Japanese–American relations was mainly conditioned by the question of naval armaments. This had been brought to the fore once more in June that year, when President Hoover had put forward proposals for an all-round cut in armaments. Presented to the Disarmament Conference, whose opening at Geneva in February had coincided with the start of the Shanghai operations, the Hoover plan came as a veritable bombshell; it served to galvanize the assembled delegates into action by proposing that every country should reduce its land, sea, and air armaments by about one-third. The initial reaction in Japan was neither enthusiastic nor wholly hostile, though considerable scepticism was expressed about the practicability of what, at first sight, seemed a somewhat idealistic gesture. When, however, closer study of the detailed naval proposals revealed that the one-third reduction applied to warships still in the blue-print stage as well as to those already constructed, it quickly became evident that Japan would be expected to scrap far more actual tonnage than America. Britain, it was true, would be even worse off in this respect than Japan, but this fact was conveniently overlooked by Japanese ultra-nationalists, who claimed that the proposals were a put-up job on the part of the other four big naval Powers to isolate Japan internationally and, in the case of America, to weaken Japan's defences against the United States. Recalling the fate of Hamaguchi and Inouye Junnosuke as a result of the indignation aroused by the ratification of the London Naval Treaty in 1930, these extremists gave clear warning to the present government of what might happen if it agreed to the Hoover proposals. The Government was, of course, only too well aware of the dangers facing its members to take any such risks; it was a recognition that was to tie the hands both of it, and of subsequent Japanese governments, at the naval talks in the years ahead. It was not that Cabinet ministers were fearful for their own lives. What they feared was the revival of unrest and distrust among those whose confidence and support were essential.

By the end of June, Admiral Nagano, Japan's chief naval representative at Geneva, had been notified that the Navy was strongly opposed to the greater part of the proposed naval reductions. It was considered that they would weaken national defence to a dangerous extent; they would also entail a complete cessation of shipbuilding for four years, with a consequent increase of unemployment. This notification was followed a few days later by instructions from the Japanese Foreign Office to Matsudaira to reject the Hoover proposals. It seemed evident, therefore, that the American President had made a tactical error and had hindered rather than helped towards a settlement of the disarmament problem. Intentionally or not, his proposal for an all-round reduction of one-third amounted to suggesting that America, by a short cut, should attain the goal of actual parity with Britain as against the existing theoretical parity, and an actual 10-10-6 ratio in heavy cruisers instead of a theoretical one. This was to be done by the simple process of getting Britain and Japan to make real reductions and sacrifices, while much of the American reduction would be confined to the scrapping of blue prints and of ships which they did not require. These latter included no less than 165,000 tons of destroyers— twice as many as Britain would have to scrap and four times as many as Japan; but as it was well known that the United States had far more destroyers than she wanted, the sacrifice would be more apparent than real. It was the question of cruisers, however, which aroused some of the greatest indignation. To both Britain and Japan, so dependent on their sea communications, large numbers of light cruisers were essential; yet Britain was called upon to reduce her over-all cruiser tonnage by 120,000 tons and Japan by 77,000; America was actually to increase hers by 33,000 and was mainly interested in heavy cruisers, capable of offensive action. It was perhaps hardly surprising, therefore, that a British naval officer, who had been working at the Admiralty when the

Hoover plan was announced, told me some time later that the comments of his brother officers on learning its details had been quite unrepeatable. His own belief was, that the whole Board of Admiralty would have resigned if the proposals had been accepted.

In view of the all-important part that aircraft were to play in the Pacific War some ten years later, it may be noted that the Hoover plan called for the reduction of aircraft-carriers by 14,000 tons for Britain and 8,000 tons for Japan, whilst the United States would be allowed an additional 9,500 tons. Six months later, when Japan put forward new proposals of her own, she proposed the total abolition of aircraft-carriers and the prohibition of platforms and landing decks on warships for naval planes. This was on the grounds that they were essentially for offensive purposes, whereas the principle on which she proposed to base reduction was a decrease in the power of attack and an increase in defensive power. With this same object in view, she also proposed the reduction in size of all types of warships, especially capital ships and heavy cruisers. When, a day or two later, I discussed these proposals with Captain Legge, the British Naval Attaché, he spoke enthusiastically about them, especially the Japanese attempt to tackle the question of aerial warfare. 'A damn clever move! Damn clever!' he commented. 'They are the first nation to have the courage to get up and make a real effort to curb it. It proves them to be a great nation, by God it does!'

The Hoover proposals had, by this time, gone by the board and Hoover himself had been defeated in the Presidential elections, to be replaced by Roosevelt. With him had gone Stimson, although he continued to play his part until the actual inauguration of the new President, shortly before Japan's withdrawal from the League in the following March. In August 1932, however, while still in office, he had aroused strong indignation in Tokyo by a speech, in which he virtually accused Japan of aggression. The question of recognizing Manchoukuo was then still in the balance; but the speech, according to Shiratori, had aggravated matters and was more likely to hasten than impede recognition, especially if, as the Government had reason to believe, the Lytton Report would refuse to recommend direct negotiations between Japan and China.

With Stimson's replacement by Cordell Hull as Secretary of State, Japanese-American relations, which had been under con-

T

siderable strain, began to show improvement. The new Administration continued to uphold the doctrine of non-recognition and to adhere to the policy of active collaboration with the League, but it also set about easing the tension left by Stimson and abating the contentious note-writing, which had caused so much irritation in Japan. No protest was lodged when Japan, after adding Jehol to the territory of her Manchoukuo protégé, rounded off her operations in North China by forcing the Chinese to sign the Tangku Truce Agreement in May 1933. Six months later, in November the same year, Washington, it is true, recognized the Soviet régime and restored diplomatic relations with Russia after a lapse of sixteen years; but although this was by no means to the liking of Japan, it was set off by the withdrawal of the American Fleet from the Pacific as a gesture of goodwill towards her.

Further signs of improved relations were to follow, but with the question of naval armaments forever in the background, the underlying mutual suspicions continued to come to the surface from time to time. The declaration of policy issued in Washington on 29 June that year was a case in point. In it, Swanson, the new Secretary of the Navy, stressed four points which were calculated to revive Japan's worst fears. It was essential, Swanson said, to 'maintain the Navy in sufficient strength to guard the continental and overseas possessions of the United States'; to 'create, maintain, and operate a navy second to none'; to 'provide great radius of action in all classes of fighting ships', and to 'develop national aviation primarily for operations with the Fleet'. It was perhaps inevitable that the enunciation of these four principles caused serious apprehensions in Japan; it led her, too, to carry out her second replenishment programme which, though drawn up some time previously, had apparently been only tentative at the outset, although allowance for a first instalment had been made in the Budget submitted earlier in the year. That, at least, was the view expressed to me at the time by Captain Vivian, who had recently succeeded Monty Legge as British Naval Attaché. The four aims enunciated by Swanson did indeed appear to strike at the fundamental principle on which the Washington Treaty had been based—the fixation of naval power in such proportions as to make each of the three principal signatories invulnerable in its own waters, but insufficiently powerful to cross the seas to attack one of the others.

The reductions put forward in the Japanese proposals of

December 1932 had, in fact, been based on much the same principle—a decrease in the power of attack, an increase in defensive power. On the other hand, it was significant that, in these proposals, any suggestion for the apportionment of definite ratios, like those laid down in the Washington and London treaties, had been studiously avoided. The reason for this was made clear by a Japanese friend, who impressed on me that the objection to these two treaties, especially the latter, was largely due to the implications conveyed by the ratios. They were based on prestige rather than defensive requirements, and implied that Japan was regarded as an inferior. Not only did this, in Japanese eyes, add insult to injury and wound the lively susceptibilities of Japanese nationalists; it also lowered Japan in the eyes of the Chinese, who were therefore all the readier to resort to provocative action against her. That this seemingly invidious comparison rankled sorely was not open to doubt, but the Japanese were apt to overlook the fact that all three countries had made sacrifices. Apart from the wound it had caused to her *amour propre*, Japan had made no greater sacrifice than the other two. On the other hand, Japan had a more legitimate grievance over the Nine-Power Pact, with its 'self-denying ordinance' *vis à vis* China, which the Americans were forever charging her with violating. Being far more vitally and immediately concerned with her difficult and lawless neighbour than were the other signatories, she had been called upon to sacrifice far more than they had.

The tragedy was that Admiral Kato Tomosaburo, who had shown such statesmanlike qualities at the Washington Conference in 1921, had died less than two years after it had ended, before he had had time to eliminate the influence of the anti-naval ratio faction. After the murder of Inukai in March 1932, this faction had started to gain control. It was significant of this that, in late September 1933, revised naval regulations were promulgated, enlarging the powers of the Chief of the Naval Staff and giving him the final say as to the naval strength required for national defence. As Captain Vivian remarked to me at the time, this settled the knotty question of the Supreme Command once and for all. Even if a civilian were to act once more as Navy Minister *pro tem*—as had happened in the case of Hamaguchi at the time of the London Naval Treaty—he would never again be in a position to over-rule the Chief of the Naval Staff. It was significant, too, that two months later there was a big shake-up in the

Higher Command of the Navy, calculated to place the Big Navy advocates in key positions—apparently in order to quieten the unrest which had been aroused among the younger naval officers by the sentences recently imposed on those concerned in the outrages of May the previous year.

With both Japan and the United States launching out on new building programmes, and with acrimonious remarks being bandied around by hot-heads in both countries, Roosevelt's attempts to improve relations seemed likely to be hampered; but they were by no means fruitless, for the Japanese Government seemed anxious to respond. This was indicated in a talk I had with Amau at the end of September, when he described, as 'a *ballon d'essai* to see how Washington would respond', a report that Hirota, who had just succeeded Uchida as Foreign Minister, had decided to make a special bid for American friendship. This was to be done by arranging for an interchange of unofficial 'envoys' to explain and study the situation in their respective countries. Some indication of the favourable response was given a week or two later, when Glenn Babb, the Associated Press Correspondent, told me of a dinner, given the previous evening by Mr Grew, the American Ambassador, to Hirota and the four principal American Press correspondents. The dinner had been arranged for the express purpose of a frank discussion on Japanese-American relations and on how to improve them. He himself had been one of the four correspondents invited to it and he had come away convinced that Hirota was genuinely doing his best to restore more friendly relations. With that object in view, he was said to have had a heart-to-heart talk with Toyama Mitsuru and other ultra-nationalist leaders, for the purpose of explaining the situation and seeking their support in achieving his aim. Confirmation of this was impossible to obtain; but as Hirota was a protégé of Toyama, who had paid for his education in his student days, it seemed perfectly credible and in accordance with traditional practice in Japan.

In making a bid for American friendship, it seemed clear that the Government had been influenced to no small extent by anxiety over Russian intentions and over the development of the Soviet Union as a great military power. The Japanese were, in fact, becoming painfully aware that they could not afford to antagonize both Russia and the United States at the same time; nor could they afford to enter into armament races with both, the one on land, the other on sea. They had been perturbed when, in the previous December, Sino-Soviet relations had been restored, as they feared it might portend a fresh attempt by Moscow to sovietize China; but they professed unconcern at the reported imminence of the establishment of American-Soviet diplomatic relations. There were, nevertheless, indications that this prospect worried them considerably. A Press despatch from Peking served to increase these apprehensions. It quoted Bourgmalov, the Soviet Ambassador, as declaring that his country would never go to war with Japan so long as the United States withheld recognition from the Soviet Union; if it did, Japan would be in a position to flood America with anti-Soviet propaganda, while the Soviet would be debarred from counteracting it effectively. Once recognition had been accorded, however, Moscow and Tokyo would be on equal terms in this respect. Although he stressed that recognition would not, in itself, lead the Russians to plunge into war with Japan, the inference seemed clear; a Japanese-Soviet armed conflict would become more likely.

With the announcement on 17 November 1933 that the United States had at last recognized the Soviet régime and had resumed diplomatic relations with the Russians, the situation began to develop in such a way as to make Japanese fears seem justified. Seven months earlier, a new Soviet Ambassador had arrived in Tokyo. This was Constantin Yurenev, who was to suffer the fate of so many other Soviet officials in the purges of 1937; but at the time of his appointment this was still unforeseen. During his first few months in Japan, Japanese-Soviet relations remained relatively friendly and revolved mainly around negotiations for the sale of the Chinese Eastern Railway, now renamed the North Manchurian Railway. A few weeks after his arrival came reports that Karakhan had intimated to Ota, the Japanese Ambassador in Moscow, that the Soviet would be prepared to consider its sale, 'if the Chinese wanted to purchase it'. This was taken to mean Manchoukuo rather than China. It was followed early in May by an exchange of asperities between Moscow and Tokyo regarding a frontier incident near Pogranitchnaya, the eastern terminus of the railway, and the disclosure that Arita, the Japanese Vice-Minister of Foreign Affairs, had proposed to Yurenev that a conference should be held in Tokyo between Japan, the Soviet, and Manchoukuo. Its purpose would be to seek a solution of outstanding differences arising from Soviet interests in Manchuria, revolving around the Chinese Eastern Railway question, the Pogranitchnaya incident, and rights of navigation on the Sungari River. Next day came the news that Litvinov had made a definite offer to sell the railway. Confirming the report, Shiratori explained to foreign correspondents that Litvinov had intimated to Ota that the offer was open either to Japan or Manchoukuo. On Ota remarking that this would be tantamount to Soviet recognition of Manchoukuo, Litvinov had replied that he was well aware of this, but it did not matter, as the Soviet had not been a signatory of the League resolution against recognition.

The Moscow offer appeared to indicate Russian anxiety to clear up the situation and to liquidate Soviet interests in Manchuria, in order to remove the main source of friction. It seemed possible, too, that it was a bid for Japanese friendship, based on the hope that Japan, who was seemingly hovering between a desire for friendship with Britain or with Russia (as had been the case in 1901), might be induced to fall in with the policy of friendship with the latter as advocated unsuccessfully by Prince Ito at the turn of the century.

Litvinov's comments on Manchoukuo recognition were carried a step further a few days later, when Yurenev informed the Japanese Foreign Minister that the Soviet was prepared to recognize Manchoukuo if it would purchase the railway. Negotiations were accordingly opened in Tokyo towards the end of June, with Japanese Government representatives attending as 'observers', ready to assist and mediate if required. From an early stage, however, differences of opinion arose concerning the price to be paid and whether the Soviet's uncontested right of control over the railway entitled her to claim actual ownership. The wrangle went on interminably and by the end of August it was clear that no progress had been made. It was with considerable interest, therefore, that I learned from Yurenev himself that, unless Manchoukuo showed some spirit of compromise within the next two months, the Soviet would probably break off negotiations. If, he added, Manchoukuo thereupon proceeded to take over the railway by force, the Soviet would make no attempt to stop them, but would make a strong protest and reserve all rights, with a view to taking whatever action might be necessary later.

This seemed to indicate that the Soviet had no intention of seeking a war just then, but I was struck by the rather contemptuous comments made by members of Yurenev's staff concerning the Japanese Army and Air Force. They seemed to have drawn much the same mistaken conclusions as some British observers had formed, when they maintained that the Shanghai operations of early 1932 had proved the Japanese to be of a far lower military standard than previously reckoned. If the Russians discounted Japanese military ability and efficiency as much as they appeared to do, it seemed possible that they might suffer for their error, as they had in 1904, if ever they came to blows once more.

These remarks by Yurenev and members of his staff were made at a dinner given at the Soviet Embassy to the principal foreign correspondents, for the purpose of introducing them to the Soviet delegates negotiating the sale of the Chinese Eastern Railway. And here a word must be said, in this connection, about a significant change that had taken place since Yurenev's arrival in Japan nearly six months earlier. Prior to his coming, little encouragement had been given for close contact between the British and American correspondents in Tokyo and Soviet Embassy officials; now the position had been reversed. I myself was frequently being invited, not only to formal dinner parties at the Embassy, but also to informal tête-à-tête meals with Yurenev and Golkovitch. The latter was an entertaining and friendly young Soviet diplomat, commonly reputed to be the representative of the notorious O.G.P.U. We were generally joined by Nagi, the *Tass* correspondent.

This attempt to cultivate the friendship of British and American correspondents was all part and parcel of a change in Soviet foreign policy. The anxiety caused by Japan's incursion into North Manchuria, and by Hitler's rise to power, had led the Russians to ingratiate themselves with others who looked askance at Japanese militancy and German Nazi-ism. Having obtained America's long-deferred recognition of the Soviet régime, they began to put out feelers for more friendly relations with the League, which hitherto they had criticized unsparingly. In an interview with the American correspondent Duranty in Moscow on Christmas Day 1933, little more than a month after the resumption of diplomatic relations with the United States, Stalin expressed the view that the League of Nations might act as a brake to war, now that both Japan and Germany had withdrawn from that body. Nine months later, the U.S.S.R. entered that much maligned organization and, by her advocacy of disarmament and collective security, set to work to build up a picture of herself as the champion of peace and goodwill.

How seriously concerned the Russians had been over developments in North Manchuria was indicated in a talk I had with Nagi, the *Tass* correspondent, early in September 1933. A few days earlier, Golkovitch had admitted to me quite frankly that the Soviet troops in Eastern Siberia had been strongly reinforced of late. His assertion that this was a purely precautionary measure seemed to be shared by the Japanese War Office, which announced soon after that Imperial sanction had been obtained for the reduction of Japanese military strength in Manchuria from four and a half divisions to three and a half. The Army would hardly have agreed to this if it had felt seriously worried about the Soviet concentrations on the Manchurian borders. When I asked Nagi if it was true, as reported in the Japanese Press, that the Soviet Far Eastern Army was now equal in strength to more than half that of the whole Japanese Army he professed ignorance, but expressed himself satisfied that the Russians now had sufficient strength in Siberia to overcome any Japanese threat. Eighteen months before, he said, the Soviet would have been placed in a very serious position if the Japanese had struck out at them, but the intervening period had enabled them to strengthen themselves and make preparations to such an extent that all cause for anxiety had been removed. He seemed convinced, however, that a clash was likely in the very near future, as the Japanese, according to him, recognized that it was now or never; time was in favour of the Soviet, as every year from now on would see the Soviet position strengthened and the Japanese weakened.

The War Office in Tokyo may not have been unduly perturbed about the Soviet reinforcements, but at the end of September it issued a statement, apparently by way of obtaining support for the Army replenishment programme, asserting that the Soviet now possessed a peace-time army of 1,290,000, complete with the most powerful and up-to-date arms and equipment. Russian military preparations in the Far East had been increased to such an extent, the statement went on to say, that large appropriations were urgently required for mechanizing the Japanese Army, in order to protect the Japanese Empire and its ally, Manchoukuo, from this serious threat. The ten divisions and 300 tanks which the Russians were estimated to have in the Far East did not appear to worry the War Office so much as the Soviet air strength concentrated there. This was said to comprise several hundred aircraft, including scores of bombers 'with power to attack the Japanese capital as soon as war breaks out between the two countries'. Recognition of the dangers of air attack was as implicit in this as it had been when, nine months earlier, Japan had put forward her proposals to the naval Powers for the abolition of aircraft-carriers and the prohibition of landing decks and platforms on warships for naval planes.

When I questioned Amau about this statement the following day and expressed my belief that the Army, as a whole, was not particularly anxious for a war with Russia, at least for the present, he replied somewhat cryptically, 'Yes. But that depends on what you mean by the Army.' It seemed a pertinent remark, as there were, in fact, two opposing schools of thought in the Japanese Army, just as there had been in the years immediately preceding the Russo-Japanese War of 1904-5. One urged the necessity of completing the Army's preparations before risking a war, on which the very existence of Japan might depend; the other took the view, 'Now or Never', as delay favoured the Soviet side. In 1904, it was the fear of Russia gaining possession of Korea, 'the arrow pointed at Japan's heart', that had urged Japan forward; now it was the fear that, so long as Russia held Vladivostok and the Maritime Provinces of Eastern Siberia, Japan would be within striking range by air and by submarine. The fact was that, owing to the development of aviation, Japan's strategic frontiers now extended beyond the Maritime Provinces, several hundred miles inland. The Soviet, on the other hand, had a growing economic interest in these provinces and an increasing need for an outlet into the Pacific.

From early November 1933, when Molotov gave vent to a diatribe against Japan on the occasion of the Moscow celebrations for the sixteenth anniversary of the Bolshevik Revolution, until the end of the following February, when tension eased for the time being, Litvinov, Kaganovitch, Voroshilov, Budenyi, Blucher and other Soviet leaders took it in turn to thunder imprecations against Japan, accompanied by allegations that she was about to launch war on the U.S.S.R. The Japanese Government, in contrast, remained outwardly calm, Araki, as War Minister, declaring that Japan had no intention of fighting, Hirota, the Foreign Minister, stressing his desire to settle differences with the Russians by peaceful means and expressing his regret at the series of provocative speeches by the Soviet leaders, while Saito, the Premier, and Admiral Osumi, the Minister of Navy, issued statements deprecating the constant talk of 'the coming clash'. A comment by Amau to foreign correspondents seemed to reflect the view held in government circles. It was a Russian characteristic, he remarked, to shout and bluster when feeling unsure of themselves. Japan, he maintained, would have far more cause for anxiety if Moscow remained quiet and composed. It was an assertion which called to mind Kipling's poem, 'The Truce of the Bear'. He nevertheless took the Soviet leaders to task for fomenting trouble by means of irresponsible statements, charging Japan with preparing to invade Russian territory.

The Soviet fulminations and accusations, however, were not without effect in some quarters. Sir Francis Lindley was inclined to share Amau's views; but Colonel James, who agreed with him, nevertheless considered the rapidity with which the Japanese were going ahead with the construction of three new railways in North Manchuria was rather significant. From him I learned that Colonel Mast, the French Military Attaché, was convinced that Japan and Russia would be at war before long. Colonel Baron, whom Mast had succeeded a short time before, had been of the same opinion. There were many Japanese and others, too, who considered that war was imminent, and the widespread feeling of tension was reflected in urgent enquiries, received by foreign correspondents from their head offices on New Year's Day 1934, concerning rumours that Japan had declared war on Russia. The rumours were groundless, but they were indicative of the tense atmosphere produced by the succession of allegations launched by the Soviet leaders. The effect of these accusations were seen again a month later, when Rainey, the Speaker of the American House of Representatives, was quoted as holding forth on the inevitability of war between Japan and the Soviet in the near future. By then, however, there were already signs that the tension was easing; and Dr Kolb, Counsellor to the German Embassy, told me one reason for believing that this was so. For some months past, he said, Yurenev had been persistently telling Voretsch, the German Ambassador in Tokyo until the end of 1933, that war with Japan was a virtual certainty by the Spring of 1934. Of late, however, he had apparently altered his opinion and now seemed to think that the danger of war had been averted, at least for the time being. A possible explanation, Kolb suggested jokingly, was that the Russians felt it was quite safe to fulminate against the Japanese while the spring was still far off and the winter lay between; but now, with spring drawing near, they considered it inadvisable to goad Japan on, lest it precipitate her into action. 'The influence of the seasons on Soviet policy', he observed with a twinkle in his eye.

CHAPTER XXI

The Internal Scene

The eighteen months following Japan's recognition of Manchou-kuo in September 1932, had, as has been seen, witnessed a series of crises revolving around her relations with the West. The storm leading to strained relations with the United States, and to her withdrawal from the League of Nations, had been followed by deterioration of her relations with Britain and serious tension with Soviet Russia. By the spring of 1934, however, the situation had eased for the moment. Relations with Britain and America were showing signs of improvement, an easing of tension with the U.S.S.R. seemed evident, and there were the beginnings of a rapprochement with Germany. But before going on to recount the developments which followed, a glance at the internal situation in Japan during this period is necessary for a proper understanding of the background to these and subsequent developments.

Following, as they did, the abortive plots of March and October the previous year, the outrages of 15 May 1932 had revealed with startling clarity the extent to which the widespread anxieties and discontent, aroused by economic, political, and ideological considerations, had combined to foster a radical fanaticism among junior officers in Army and Navy alike. Both military and civilian leadership were being challenged, and radical reform in both foreign and internal policies was being demanded. It was a challenge which neither the Government nor the leaders of the armed services could ignore with impunity, if worse troubles were to be avoided. The Army and Navy, while disapproving the resort to violence, were at heart sympathetic towards the aims of the junior and middle-grade officers and sought to ease the situation by appeasement. The Government, for fear of precipitating an internal revolution, adopted an attitude of more uncompromising opposition to the exhortations of Geneva and the Western Powers. The more extreme elements in the country, however, remained unmollified and showed their dissatisfaction in a further series of assassination plots, aimed at removing all those in high positions who stood in their way.

In August 1932 came the news that four extremists had been arrested for plotting the murder of Admiral Saito, the Premier, Viscount Takahashi, the Finance Minister, and other leading personalities. Two months later, another assassination plot was unearthed in the course of police investigations into the distribution of inflammatory circulars among young officers. The intended victims in this instance were Count Makino, Lord Keeper of the Privy Seal, and General Ugaki, both of whom were advocates of moderation and were denounced accordingly as 'evil counsellors'. A more serious conspiracy, by a body calling itself *Shimpeitai* (Soldiers of the Gods), was nipped in the bud in July the following year, when police rounded up a group of some fifty conspirators assembled at the Meiji Shrine in Tokyo. They protested that they were gathered there to pray for aid to overcome the national crisis and for divine assistance to strengthen national defence, which they considered had been seriously impaired by the London Naval Treaty of 1930; but it soon became clear that the aid they sought was for the success of a full-scale assassination plot on 11 July. While the Cabinet was in session that day, the Premier's official residence was to have been attacked and the whole Cabinet murdered. Simultaneously, Makino's house was to have been set on fire and Makino himself put to death. Six men were formally indicted on the charge of attempted murder and incendiarism in this connection at the end of September and several others were arrested and indicted during the next few months; but as more details came to light, it became increasingly evident that there were plots within plots. The first indication of this came at the time of the indictment in September, when it was reported that the plot had been financed by a group of men, who hoped to rig the market and reap large profits as a result of the panic created by the murders. A month later, a Japanese friend told me in strict confidence that pressure was being exerted from behind the scenes to curb the police investigations, as they had already exposed unexpected connections and were likely to reveal 'things which ought not to be made known' relating to developments in Manchuria.

To what extent, if any, the pressure was effective I never learned, but a few weeks later, on the night of 13 November, police raided a building in which a number of plotters had assembled, preparatory to putting the initial stage of their plans into action the following day by shooting Dr Suzuki, President of the *Seiyukai*, at a party meeting in Kawagoe. He was to have been the first of a number of victims, who were to include the aged *Genro*, Prince Saionji, Baron Wakatsuki, General Ugaki, Admiral Takarabe and several other prominent personalities. A ban was placed on the news until March the following year, 1934, when the full details were announced and showed that the plot was connected with the Blood Brotherhood, the May 1932 outrages, and the *Shimpeitai* affair. As in the case of earlier plots, the Metropolitan Police Headquarters had been marked out once more for attack, and a final dramatic touch was to be given by the sixteen members of the Saitama Death Defying Band—as the plotters called themselves—assembling on the plaza fronting the Nijubashi, which led to the Imperial Palace, and solemnly disembowelling themselves. This was by way of signifying their sincerity in striving for national reconstruction and was to have been carried out after shouting three banzais for the Emperor.

Of less consequence than these murder plots, but reflecting the same highly-charged emotional atmosphere, was the sudden and unexpected appearance, in August 1932, of an aged relic of feudal days, whose views had clearly not moved with the times. This was the nonagenarian Count Tanaka Mitsuaki, who demanded that Count Makino and Dr Ikki, the Imperial Household Minister, should assume responsibility for certain unspecified but allegedly 'grave occurrences' by resigning; failure to do so, he asserted, was likely to have serious consequences. Four years previously, the leading Tokyo daily, the *Asahi*, had been raided by ultra-nationalists for refusing to publish a manifesto demanding the resignation of these same two liberal-minded statesmen, who had since figured as targets for would-be assassins. It seemed likely, therefore, that Tanaka, who had fought on the Imperial side in the Restoration War of 1868 and again, on the same side, in the Satsuma Rebellion, had been instigated to take this step by reactionary groups; these had worked on his old clan prejudices (Makino being a Satsuma man, while Tanaka was of the rival Tosa clan) and on his keen sense of devotion to the Throne. From subsequent inside information, however, it seemed that Tanaka's appearance on the scene was due primarily to his concern over the absence of an heir to the Throne. The Emperor had daughters, but no son and, under the Salic Law adopted by Japan in 1889, women were debarred from the succession. Being of the 'old school', Tanaka considered it was Makino's duty to ensure male issue for the Emperor by providing him with an imperial concubine. It was Makino's failure to adopt this procedure that led to Tanaka demanding his resignation, the unspecified 'grave occurrences' being, in fact, his refusal to countenance any such measure. The main opposition to the introduction of a concubine, however, was said to have come from Sekiya, Vice-Minister of the Imperial Household, who, being a Christian, was naturally averse to the suggestion. Tanaka, therefore, indicated that the demand for Makino's removal might be withdrawn if Sekiya resigned; but the only result of all this manœuvring was that six months later, in February 1933, Ikki resigned and was succeeded by Yuasa Kurahei, formerly Chief Civil Administrator in Korea. Early on the morning of 23 December that year, however, Tokyo residents were awakened by two long-drawn siren blasts, announcing the glad tidings that the Empress had given birth to the long-awaited son and heir. The threat of a serious dynastic crisis was over, and six days later, amidst nation-wide rejoicings and celebrations, elaborate ritual dating from remotest times marked the ceremony of naming the infant Crown Prince, Akihito.

While the mentality revealed by the Tanaka affair, like that of those behind the assassination plots, was a clear manifestation of the strong influence still exerted by the philosophy of feudal times, other developments since the autumn of 1932 showed that the extreme Leftists were still as active as the ultra-nationalist Right-wingers. Although the news was banned for several months, a countrywide round-up of Communists was carried out by the police on 30 October that year, some 2,200 alleged Communists being arrested in the course of the swoop. In addition, according to the official announcement, no less than 6,900 radicals had been taken into custody since the advent of that year within the jurisdictions of the Metropolitan Police Board alone. The great majority of those arrested were in their early twenties, but it was significant that two university professors, a judge of the Tokyo District Court, and Shibata Toshio, son of the Chief Secretary of the Cabinet, were also among those detained.

The October round-up had resulted from important clues obtained during the examination of men connected with a bank raid earlier in the month, the object of the raid having been to secure funds for Communist activities. The nature of these activities was said to have been revealed in evidence procured during the police action that followed. This showed that, on the supposition that Japan would be plunged into war over the Manchurian question, the Communists were planning to avail themselves of the opportunity to launch a revolutionary uprising. Whether this evidence was well-founded or not, fear of a Communist uprising was to haunt the mind of at least one Japanese Premier, Prince Konoye, during the concluding stages of the Pacific War a decade or more later. The year 1932, however, was to be the peak year for the number of Communist suspects arrested; but although another large-scale round-up took place at the end of February 1933, some indication of the flimsiness of the evidence leading to these and similar arrests was reflected in figures published late that year. These showed that, out of over 20,000 alleged Communists arrested since the start of 1931, only 701 had been indicted; the remainder had been released for lack of hard evidence. Communism was undoubtedly a potential threat, but the right-wing extremists were, in fact, a far greater immediate menace. Their respective doctrines may have been equally insidious, but the Communists seldom resorted to violent measures, whereas intimidation and violence were the hall-mark of the ultra-nationalists who, moreover, since 1931, had sought and obtained the mass support which previously they had lacked.

Hag-ridden by the spectre of Communism though the authorities may have been, it was the more immediate threat from the extreme right that exerted the main influence on Government actions and policy. Saito's Coalition Government, which had replaced the *Seiyukai* Administration of the murdered Inukai in May 1932, had, from the start, been subjected to considerable strain through the jealousies of its *Seiyukai* and *Minseito* components. It was to Saito's credit, however, that he contrived to keep these rival elements under control. This he did by means of a policy which a Japanese friend of mine described as 'acting like a blind man ensuring safety in a crowded thoroughfare by standing still instead of trying to force his way through'.

General Araki, who had been War Minister in the previous Cabinet, had wished to resign, holding himself responsible for the participation of military cadets in the outrages of 15 May; but he had been persuaded that it was his duty to accept the same post in the new Government, as he was considered to be the best man to handle the critical situation that had arisen in the Army. For a man of his temperament and upbringing, it must have been far harder for him to stay on than to resign. That this was so was made clear in an address he made to the Diet soon after. Expressing his condemnation of, and regrets for, the action taken by the cadets, he went on to explain that he himself had pondered deeply on whether to resign or not by way of atonement, but had finally decided that he could serve the Throne better by remaining in office than by resigning. His decision was undoubtedly right, but it brought on him the criticism of those who considered he should have resigned, while his outspoken condemnation of the cadets lost him the popularity of the younger officer elements in the Army, who had previously idolized him. So far as the new Government itself was concerned, the view held by the ultra-nationalists was revealing and was reflected in an interview given by Uchida Ryohei, Toyama Mitsuru's right-hand man, to Alsot, the Havas correspondent, who gave me the details of it at the time. Uchida predicted that the Saito Government would last not more than six months and would then be succeeded by a right-wing government under Baron Hiranuma. This, he forecast, would remain in office about a year and would pave the way for the Shōwa Restoration, which would be brought about in 1934 by nationalist extremists. The prediction was to prove incorrect, but it served to indicate the lines on which the extreme right-wing was thinking and seemed to show that there was some justification for the fears of those who felt that Hiranuma, if ever he came to power, would prove a Japanese Kerensky.

While the growing pressure from right-wing extremists was an ever-present anxiety for the Government, its more immediate concern was with the financial situation. By the autumn of 1932, a tendency was already noticeable in some of the papers to criticize the fighting services for their exorbitant demands at a time when funds were so hard to raise. The total budget estimates for 1933, drawn up late the previous year, showed a deficit of over 900,000,000 yen, which would have to be met by bond issues. A growing volume of criticism and apprehension was therefore being voiced in the Press and elsewhere concerning the situation that would arise if the Cabinet persisted in its policy of unlimited borrowing and filling the huge deficit by issuing bonds. Even so, the general feeling was that nothing should be done to overturn the Saito Government, as it would be difficult to find one more competent to steer the country through the existing crisis. Owing, however, to Japan's commitments under the Manchoukuo

U

Protocol, which necessitated the retention of large numbers of troops in Manchuria, it was widely feared that the financial situation would become increasingly critical. It was with this fear in mind that Dr Ashida, at that time a Lower House deputy but destined to become Premier some fifteen years later, created something of a sensation in January 1933 by unusually blunt questioning in the Diet. Virtually accusing the Army of dictating the country's foreign policy, he went on to ask why it was that both the armed services were demanding such large appropriations and thereby unbalancing the Budget to so serious an extent. Indignant members demanded that he retract his remarks, but he refused to do so. I myself was inadvertently brought into the picture and censured, both in the Diet and in the Japanese Press, as a cabled despatch of mine, reporting what he had said, was published in Geneva in a distorted form. This made it appear that the Japanese delegation there, headed by Matsuoka, had also come under Ashida's fire and that Ashida had been acting as the *Seiyukai* spokesman. In consequence, Matsuoka, himself a member of that party, cabled indignantly to the *Seiyukai* President, threatening to resign from the party if the report was true. On his being assured that the report was without foundation, I myself was attacked for sending false information. I was able to clear myself of the charge, but when speaking to Ashida about it a few days later, I was met with the smiling remark, 'Even though the distorted version that was cabled back to Japan quoted me incorrectly, it expressed my real sentiments more accurately than my actual words did.'

Ashida was not alone in his criticism of the armed forces. The papers, it is true, continued to indulge in chauvinistic outbursts, but in talks with some of the leading Japanese journalists in the autumn of 1933, I listened to extremely outspoken criticisms of the Army for its financial demands and for some of the 'foolish and high-handed actions' taken by it in Manchuria and elsewhere. If the views expressed were as genuine as they appeared to be, it seemed clear that a strong anti-military sentiment was developing beneath the surface. That this was so was largely confirmed by a Japanese friend who, a month or two later, confided to me that the people were getting tired of the way in which the Army was working in the background and pulling strings all the time. There was a widespread feeling, therefore, that the military leaders should either come out into the open and accept full responsibility, or else leave the Government free to act, without interference from behind the scenes. The military authorities, he said, would probably be only too glad to assume power openly if they felt sure of popular support, but they lacked confidence in their ability to obtain it if they did so and feared that national unity would be seriously undermined if support was not forthcoming. What he said was probably true. Another eight years were, however, to pass before circumstances forced the Army to assume responsibility openly for the government of the country and for its policies. This was when General Tojo became Premier in October 1941 and, for a time, combined the Premiership with the posts of War Minister and Chief of the General Staff. In the meantime, however, criticism of the Army continued and in January 1934 became so strong in the newly opened Diet session that the *Meirinkai*, a reactionary organization of retired officers, issued a fiery statement threatening the party politicians with 'very grave consequences indeed' if they continued to attack the military so vehemently in the Diet and thereby helped to alienate the civil population from the Army.

With the Army demanding ever-increasing appropriations, the Government was hard put to it to curb their insistence and to find the necessary money to cover the growing deficit between revenue and expenditure. The prolonged and heated wrangles which took place in drawing up the estimates for 1934 threatened, for a time, to wreck the Cabinet; but the Budget figures for presentation to the Diet were finally fixed early in December 1933. They showed that the percentage of the total Budget allotted to the fighting services had risen from 27.1 per cent for the year which saw the outbreak of the Manchurian trouble, to 44.3 per cent three years later. While, however, the Government's attempt to curb expenditure was understandable, Colonel James, the British Military Attaché, with whom I discussed the matter at the time, considered that the re-arming and mechanization of the Army, which largely accounted for the increasing appropriations, could be interpreted, not as preparation for war as some were apt to think, but as a long-delayed need for modernizing the Army and bringing it up to date. He was, of course, right. Sanction for the creation of Japan's first two tank regiments had been announced in October, new types of infantry guns and bridging equipment had been noted on the autumn manœuvres, the Army Air Force was being strengthened, and divisional artillery was being re-equipped. In all these directions the Army had been lagging behind the land and air forces of the Soviet, and it was the potential threat of the Russians that Japan's military leaders had mainly in mind when insisting on adequate appropriations for modernization in arms, equipment and training. From a strictly military point of view, therefore, the Army's demands were understandable; but the Government had financial and other difficulties to consider as well as the purely military aspect. There was, in fact, a constant struggle between the Premier, the Foreign Minister, and the Finance Minister on the one hand and the two Service Ministers on the other. It was a struggle which was finally resolved, at least temporarily, at the last of five meetings of the Five-Ministers' Conference held on 20 October 1933. According to the official announcement made at that time, a full and frank exchange of views had resulted in an agreement on the funda-mental principle of co-ordinating foreign policy, finance and national defence. 'Pacific Diplomacy with Military Preparedness' was the term used in defining this principle, which concerned the relative values of finance, diplomacy, and armaments in the con-text of national defence. It was perhaps indicative, therefore, of the desire to implement this 'Pacific Diplomacy' that the veteran statesman Viscount Ishii, speaking at a dinner given in his honour by the Japan Economic League a few days earlier, had stressed the necessity for Japan to control her exports and standardize the prices of her manufactured goods. He urged this because, during a recent visit he had made to Europe and America, he had been forced to the conclusion that Japan's trade was a far greater worry and annoyance to foreign countries than were her actions in Manchuria.

While the Government was striving to find some way in which to compose the conflicting claims of foreign policy, finance and national defence, developments which augured ill for the future of parliamentary democracy in Japan were taking place in the field of party politics. As far back as the spring of 1931, Mori Kaku, Secretary-General of the *Seiyukai*, had caused something of a sensation by advocating reform on national-socialist lines and had come out in favour of creating a dictatorial form of government through the alliance of his party with the Army. The 1920s, it is true, had already seen moves in the direction of national socialism, but these had come from small left-wing and right-wing groups outside the main sphere of party politics.

Mori Kaku's action was in a different category and marked the start of the gradual break-up of parliamentary democracy, which was to end ten years later with the dissolution of political parties in September 1941. The defection of Adachi Kenzo and Nakano Seigo, two outstanding right-wing members of the *Minseitō*, in December 1931, the formation of a State Socialist Party at the end of May 1932, and the increasing desertion of members from the Social-Democratic Party to the ranks of the *Seisantō* and other reactionary organizations, were further indications of the way in which things were moving. They were followed late in 1933 by a development which was, in some respects, even more significant than these. This was nothing less than a call for the abolition of all political parties, on the grounds that they stood in the way of national unity at a time of extreme national crisis. The demand was made, not by an irresponsible right-wing fanatic, but by Matsuoka Yosuke who, earlier in the year, had been Japan's chief delegate at Geneva. Having issued a manifesto urging an end to the existing parliamentary system, he announced his secession from the *Seiyukai* and resigned his seat in the Diet. Two months later a further nail was driven into the coffin of party politics by the disgraceful scenes in the Diet, which followed the charges of graft hurled at leading politicians. The charges appeared to have been trumped up, with little or no foundation, but the fact that they were being bandied about and given so much publicity merely added to the growing contempt for party politicians and for the capitalists and wealthy landowners to whom they looked for financial support. With this contempt went a readiness to look for new leadership and for an end to the existing political system. Dr Ashida, who had witnessed the riotous scenes in the Diet, reflected the feelings of many responsible Japanese when he told me later that the behaviour of the Diet members taking part in them had made him feel thoroughly ashamed of his own people. Another well-balanced Japanese friend, Count Kabayama, however, expressed a more optimistic and unusual view. Referring to the recently re-published *Creevey Papers*, he remarked that Britain had been at her greatest in courage and tenacity, energy and enterprise, literature, painting and architecture, at the very time when she was at her lowest depth in political morality, with sordid scandals, bribery and corruption widespread. Perhaps, he suggested hopefully, Japan was going through a similar phase and Japanese politics might not therefore warrant the pessimism that they appeared to call for.

Political morality was certainly at a low ebb, but the irony of the situation was, that the best elements in Japanese political life were just those for whose blood the right-wing extremists were calling so loudly. Saito, the Premier, the octogenarian Finance Minister Takahashi, and the Foreign Minister, Hirota, were amongst those most constantly denounced by the ultra-nationalists. Commenting on this one day, Iwanaga, who was on close terms with all three of them, told me sorrowfully that Takahashi's age was beginning to tell on him and he tired very easily. It would be a bad day for the Government, he considered, if the old man had to resign, as it was his prestige, even more than Saito's, that kept the Cabinet together. Apart from his prestige, he was immensely popular, both in the Cabinet and with responsible Japanese everywhere, even though some of his Government colleagues, especially General Araki, felt irked at times. This was because, on account of his age and far longer experience of ministerial work, he was apt to treat them as inexperienced youngsters. It was not, however, Takahashi who resigned a few days after this talk in January 1934, but Araki. The reason given for his resignation was ill-health, but rumour had it that, owing to his recent tendency towards moderation, his influence among the younger officer group had been on the wane; the Army had therefore decided to replace him.

In the meantime, with the prospect of a new naval conference in view, the question of naval agreements and their value was coming to the fore once more. The trial and sentence of the naval participants in the outrages of May 1932 had aroused widespread sympathy for them, and their bitter denunciation of those responsible for the London Naval Treaty had won much support. It was significant, therefore, that the first authoritative reply to these denunciations came in the autumn of 1933 from Baron Wakatsuki, who had led the Japanese delegation at the London talks in 1930. Speaking at a *Minseitō* rally on 10 October, he made a vigorous defence of the treaty and, while admitting its imperfections, expressed his conviction that acceptance of it had served Japan's best interests and had saved her from crippling expenditure on armaments. This said, he then went on to warn his hearers that failure to reach agreement at the naval conference projected for 1935 would precipitate a new Japanese-American armament race disastrous to Japan, as she lacked the economic and financial resources possessed by the United States. Wakatsuki's statement was headline news in Japan and, in view of the interest being shown abroad in the Disarmament Conference taking place in Geneva and in Germany's current intransigence in the matter of armaments, it seemed to be of timely international importance; but, rather surprisingly, after cabling it to London, I received a reprimand for sending news which not a single paper had thought worth while publishing. It seemed a strange commentary on the question of what constitutes news. In Japan itself the speech received a mixed welcome, the leading papers applauding it, while the *Yoyokai*, an association of retired naval officers, denounced it strongly. Some five or six weeks later, Wakatsuki, for his courageous defence of the hated treaty, was rewarded by an attempt made on his life by two indignant self-styled patriots.

What troubled many responsible Japanese about the forthcoming conference to which Wakatsuki had referred, was that, whether or not a satisfactory agreement was reached, Japan was likely to suffer. If, as a result of failure, a new race in armaments was the outcome, Japan would be crippled financially; if, as a result of agreement, further naval reduction or a naval holiday was brought about, the armament industries would receive a serious blow and would be left with a quantity of idle and useless plant on their hands. In the consequent slump and rise in unemployment, social unrest and discontent would increase to a dangerous extent.

With these and other considerations in view, the question of the naval conference due in 1935 came in for considerable comment. Some months prior to Wakatsuki's speech, the well-known writer on naval topics, Hector Bywater, had contended that naval limitation conferences were apt to promote more ill-will than good-will and that the pre-War method of each country fixing its armaments in accordance with its own requirements was far less harmful in the long run. The trouble with the post-War system of conferences for reduction or limitation of armaments, he had said, was that, in effect, each nation tried to impose its own will on the others and aroused ill-feelings accordingly. These views met with a ready response in Japan and by early 1934 were being reflected in articles in the Press and by comments in the Diet. Speaking in the Diet towards the end of January that year, Yasumi Saburo, a retired admiral, stressed 'the vicious circle' of armament reduction, economy, and feelings of insecurity arising from agreements reached at such conferences. Reduction of armaments saved expenses for the time being, but reduced the feeling of security which, in turn, led to demands for still higher appropriations. It was a view that was to be repeated, in effect, a year or two later in England by Admiral Richmond. Economy at the expense of security, he declared, was apt to prove false economy; it served to create exaggerated fears regarding the safety of the nation and led eventually to excited demands for an increase of armaments in order to ensure security.

Admiral Yasumi's comments were followed a day or two later by Admiral Osumi, the Navy Minister, confirming that Japan intended to demand a higher ratio at the next naval conference. This was no great surprise, but it served to increase the likelihood that the conference would end in failure and in a consequent race in armaments. The fears aroused by such a prospect were reflected in the warning voiced in the Upper House by Yoshizawa Ken-kichi, Foreign Minister in the murdered Inukai's Cabinet, that it would be better to call off the naval conference than to risk its failure. Sir Francis Lindley, with whom I discussed this suggestion, inclined to agree with it and expressed his opinion that the conference would probably never be held. Failure to reach agreement, he said, seemed almost certain and would inevitably result in mutual recriminations and exacerbated feelings, followed by a more deadly race in armaments than if no conference had been held. Events were to prove him wrong on the first assumption, but all too right on the second.

The official Japanese naval attitude towards the projected conference was expressed on 3 February by Admiral Osumi, who declared, in a somewhat Delphic utterance, that 'with the immediate situation extremely delicate, it is best to maintain the utmost silence. If Japan says she is not afraid to risk a naval construction race, she will be accused of adopting a challenging attitude; if she indicates that she is anxious for an agreement, she will be considered timid and treated accordingly.'

While this was the official view, there was a growing feeling in Japan that, far from contributing to peace, the retention of naval ratios merely served to stimulate each country to carry out construction up to treaty limits, irrespective of actual requirements. This feeling was strengthened by reports from Washington, that American Congressmen and others were backing up the Big Navy advocates in the United States by asserting that 'Japan would never have invaded Manchuria or occupied Shanghai if our navy had been up to treaty strength'. In saying this, they were, in effect, admitting that the so-called 'treaty navy', which they advocated, would be capable of offensive action 5,000 miles away from American home waters. As one leading Japanese paper, the *Mainichi* remarked, 'We do not object to parity in mid-Pacific, but we must insist on a margin of superiority for ourselves in our home waters. That is the only way to enjoy security.' The *Mainichi's* comment reflected the views of the general public; but with hot-heads on both sides of the Pacific exchanging challenging statements, the prospects of a satisfactory agreement seemed extremely poor. It was hardly surprising, therefore, that the advisability of calling off the projected conference was finding many supporters. It seemed significant, however, that Admiral Suetsugu, who had recently been appointed Commander-in-Chief of the Combined Fleet, had raised a storm in the United States by the outspoken and somewhat indiscreet comments on America attributed to him in a Japanese magazine, remarks which he refused either to con-firm or refute. Perhaps equally significant was the unexpected resignation of Admiral Baron Abo, a member of the Supreme Military Council, who had been closely connected with Admiral Takarabe and others identified with the signing of the London Naval Treaty. Abo resigned in January, ostensibly on the grounds of ill health, but it was widely reported that the real reason was his objection to Admiral Suetsugu, a strong opponent of the treaty, being appointed to the key post of the Combined Fleet.

CHAPTER XXII

Manchuria, the Keystone

Of vital importance though the question of naval armaments was, Manchuria was the central factor in the rise of military influence, in the reorientation of Japanese foreign policy, in the gradual trend towards anti-Westernism and Pan-Asianism and, to no small extent, in the growth of the radical reform movement with its anarchistic philosophy of violence. In 1920 I had been to Manchuria as a military observer, and in 1924 I had gone there in connection with the oil business. It was with a view, therefore, to studying the situation in the two-year old Manchoukuo that I paid yet another visit there in April 1934.

I had been urged to do this by General Araki, who wanted me to judge for myself what progress had been made in transforming it into the 'earthly paradise' which, in his visionary way, he envisaged for its future. By way of showing his appreciation for such assistance as I had been able to give in paving the way for his private talks at the British Embassy in Tokyo, he armed me with letters of introduction to the leading military and civilian personalities in the new State. This he did in order to ensure facilities to travel wherever I wished to go, to meet whomever I wished to question, and to see whatever I wished to see.

Before leaving, I had a talk with Colonel James, who had paid a similar visit a few months earlier and had been much impressed by what he had seen and heard. He was a bit worried, however, by reports that Japan was about to increase the number of her troops out there by two divisions and that a clash with the Russians was imminent. Previous reports of the same kind had proved groundless and he himself was inclined to believe that the two divisions were replacements, not reinforcements; but both the General Staff and the War Office in Tokyo had been evasive when he questioned them. He asked me, therefore, to keep my eyes and ears open for any indications tending either to confirm or refute these reports. In the event I was fortunate and was soon in a position to disprove them.

Landing at Yuki, on the north-east coast of Korea, after

crossing from Niigata in a small Japanese ship, I had my first introduction to the developments taking place in the matter of improved communications between Korea and Manchuria. Ten years previously, when I had visited Yuki for the first time, it had been little more than a fishing village, with very indifferent road communications and no railway; now it was a town with a population of some 20,000; and in place of the former small stone jetty, there were several large wharves and other facilities for loading, unloading, and storage. The construction of a railway line southward, to link at Seishin with the line to Seoul, was nearing completion, while northward it was connected by rail with Nanyo, on the Korean border, where it joined the Kainei-Kirin railway, planned in 1909, but only constructed since the outbreak of the Manchurian trouble in September 1931. Even more impressive was the development work in progress nine or ten miles south, at the small fishing village of Rashin. There, a large area of marshy ground was being reclaimed and filled in with material obtained from the neighbouring cliffs. These were being blasted and torn down to provide a further wide expanse of level ground. On this was to be built a port city of 300,000 people, with facilities for handling 3,000,000 tons of cargo a year. It was planned to make it the main port of ingress and egress for Manchuria in the years to come.

Having inspected the work at both Yuki and Rashin, I left Yuki that evening by train for Kirin, a journey of some nineteen hours. The greater part was through a section of Manchuria which was clearly still far from pacified, as we were accompanied by armed guards, and at every station a detachment of troops with bayonets fixed was drawn up on the platform. It was, however, at a small hostel in Kirin, where I stopped off for a night, that I received confirmation that the two divisions recently sent to Manchuria were replacements, not reinforcements. The only other guests at the inn were some Japanese officers who, on finding that I spoke their language and had formerly been attached to their Army, invited me to join them in one of their rooms for drinks and a talk. From them I learned that they were returning to Japan shortly with the rest of their division, which was being relieved by another sent out from home. They spoke freely, too, about the progress being made in the construction of road and railway communications in Manchuria, the work of bandit suppression, the land settlement scheme under which it was hoped to attract a million Japanese immigrants a year and thereby ease the growing pressure of population in Japan, and sundry other matters of interest. These included their views on the reliability of their Manchoukuo allies. With the loyalty of the Manchoukuo troops and with their co-operation in the work of bandit suppression and pacification in general they appeared well satisfied. On the other hand, owing to the language difficulty, there was little direct intercourse between them and the Japanese soldiery: but relations were friendly and there was little friction. It was an assessment largely borne out by what I saw and heard later in other parts of Manchuria.

Whether the native inhabitants of Manchoukuo were as satisfied with the Japanese as the Japanese professed to be with them was difficult to tell. On the surface they appeared friendly and co-operative, and the few Manchoukuo officials to whom I spoke, most but not all through the medium of an interpreter, showed no outward signs of hostility or grievance. From British and American residents in Mukden and Harbin I heard both praise and criticism of the Japanese and the new régime. On the whole, they appeared favourable to the Japanese and, though inclined to be cynical, gave them full credit for the reforms carried out in regard to currency and other matters and in the improvement of communications. Of the native inhabitants, it was considered that 90 per cent were wholly indifferent as to who governed them, so long as they were left in peace to enjoy the fruits of their labour; and although most of the intelligentzia had either fled or were reluctant to co-operate with the new régime at the outset, they were beginning to accept the inevitable.

Like in the case of Korea, however, it seemed clear that, although the Japanese were bringing great material benefits to the people and improvements in communications and administration, docility and co-operation were required in return. Apart from irrigation works, hydro-electric schemes, and other projects planned or in progress for the purpose of transforming Manchoukuo into 'an earthly paradise', material improvements were evident in all the principal towns and cities visited. Perhaps nowhere was this more in evidence than in the capital city of Hsinking, the former Changchun. When last I had been there fourteen years before, it had been no more than a small, rather squalid little provincial town, the junction between the South Manchurian Railway and the southern branch of the Chinese

Eastern Railway; it was also the boundary between the Japanese and Russian spheres of interest. By the Spring of 1934, grandiloquent plans to transform it into a city worthy of its new status were already in operation and left one impressed by the extraordinary vigour and enterprise displayed in their conception and execution.

It was while in Hsinking that I received the final proof that the two divisions recently sent to Manchuria were there purely as replacements. An opportunity was also provided for disproving reports that war with Russia was imminent and that all Japanese military units in Manchoukuo had therefore been brought up to full war strength. At Kirin, as already mentioned, I had learned that at least one of the two divisions was relieving another, but at Hsinking I had the unexpected experience of being invited by General Hishikari, the Japanese Commander-in-Chief, to a farewell banquet given by him to the commanders and senior officers of the two divisions leaving for home. The report that Japanese military formations had been brought up to war strength in anticipation of hostilities with the Russians was shown, a day or two later, to be as devoid of foundation as the reported reinforcements. Having been invited to attend a military review in honour of the Japanese Emperor's birthday, I was able to see for myself that the troops parading were still on a peace footing, infantry with only three companies to the battalion instead of the wartime four, and artillery, cavalry, and transport on a similar scale.

Apart from these visual and oral proofs, it seemed clear also, from talks with General Hishikari and other senior officers, that there was no expectation of an imminent clash with the Russians. It was with some surprise, therefore, that on mentioning this to a member of the small British community in Harbin a few days later, I met at first with incredulity and had some difficulty in convincing him that this was so. Even more astonishing and revealing was the greeting I received from his wife, when I went to dine at his house. A very charming 'White' Russian, she displayed evident distress in both voice and gesture as she greeted me with the words, 'I am terribly upset to hear from my husband that you do not consider war with the Soviet is likely in the immediate future. I have been praying and hoping for it week after week, month after month, and always in vain, but I really did think that it was coming at last.' It was a sentiment that I found prevalent among the large community of 'White' Russian refugees who had settled in Manchuria and no doubt accounted, to some extent, for the frequent reports of an imminent clash. The wish was father to the thought.

In spite, however, of this lady's bitter hatred of the Soviet, at whose hands she and her sister had suffered severely in the early days of the Revolution, she frankly admitted that in 1929 she would have welcomed the Soviet or anyone else who could have put a stop to Chinese arrogance and aggressiveness after Manchuria had come under Nationalist administration. The Chinese at that time, she said, used to spit at her and others in the streets. Much as she detested the Soviet, she had been heartily glad therefore when, in the summer of that year, they took military action and 'put the Chinese in their proper place'.

Both she and her husband, on the other hand, spoke highly of the general behaviour and quiet efficiency of the Japanese troops in Harbin, and of the way in which they had tackled the disastrous floods in the summer of 1932 and prevented the spread of disease. The Chinese had laughed when the Japanese started damming the water; but if dams and dykes had not been built, most of the city would have been destroyed when the severe frost set in, as the ice would have crumbled the foundations of the lime-stone buildings and brought them crashing down. The Chinese were equally scornful of inoculation, which the Japanese, to check the spread of disease, made compulsory. One result of this was, that a regular trade in the sale of certificates was set up by those who had been inoculated to those who had not. Those who bought these certificates were able to evade inoculation, while those who sold them had to undergo a second inoculation; many died in consequence.

In the talks at Harbin, as in those at Hsinking and elsewhere, there was much of political, military, and general interest. In so far as military matters were concerned, I was constantly struck by the fact that there was a far greater frankness and readiness to impart information than, generally speaking, there was in Tokyo. No doubt Araki's letters of introduction did much to smooth the way, but in part this was due to the fact that, amongst senior officers holding important staff appointments, there were several old friends with whom I had served in 1919 in the Shizuoka Regiment or who had been instructors or fellow-students during my attachment to the Infantry School at Chiba in 1920. At Hsinking, Mukden, Anganchi, Taonan, Jehol, and at almost all the other places visited, I found one or more old friends of Army days, who treated me, not as a peregrinating foreign journalist, but as a former brother officer. In Harbin itself I came across the 34th Infantry Regiment, to which I had once been attached, and there, too, was another old friend, serving as Staff Officer to General Wakayama, Commander of the 3rd Division. The General himself was a genial, kindly soul, very short of stature, but a keen, capable officer of extraordinary frankness. His Chief of Staff, Colonel Sato, was equally frank and friendly, and devoted the best part of a morning to explaining in detail, with the aid of a large-scale map, the disposition of the troops in the wide area under his control. He had served in England shortly after the War and spoke with genuine feelings of affection for the Sherwood Foresters, to whom he had been attached.

From the talks at Harbin I learned much about the conditions on the Manchurian-Soviet border. The much-talked-of tension was, I found, greatly exaggerated, and neither forts nor Japanese troops were maintained in the immediate vicinity. The Soviet side, however, was now strongly defended, with 'pill-boxes' strung along almost the whole length, at intervals of a few hundred yards and, as a rule, wire entanglements in between. I had hoped to inspect these conditions for myself and my Japanese friends promised me an air-lift and full facilities for doing so if I went; but, much to my regret, I was unable to spare the time. Instead, I had to content myself with visits to Tsitsihar and Peianchen, the latter being, at that time, the nearest railhead to the Soviet border along the Amur some 200 miles northward.

One point of interest mentioned in connection with Japanese-Soviet relations was that, although Communists were active, both in propaganda and in perpetrating outrages in Manchuria, the Japanese authorities seemed satisfied that those responsible for the outrages carried them out on their own initiative and not at Soviet instigation. On the other hand, propaganda frequently took the form of distributing pamphlets to Japanese soldiers in cafés and restaurants, where the waitresses would ask them why they, as proletarians, were fighting fellow-proletarians in Manchuria on the orders of bourgeois officers. Colonel Shimamoto, Chief of Gendarmerie in Harbin, who told me of this, laughed as he did so and added, 'The fact is, that Japanese officers are often more proletarian in origin and outlook than the conscript soldiers they command.'

These personal observations on the Manchurian situation in the spring of 1934 are but some of many recorded at the time. They are already over-long, but three more items may be mentioned. The first of these concerned a talk I had with Tani Masayuki, Counsellor to the Japanese Embassy in Hsinking, whom I had known well when he was in Tokyo and who was later to become Foreign Minister. Referring to Lord Lloyd's *Egypt Since Cromer* as his 'Bible', he spoke enthusiastically of it as a guide for himself and other Japanese officials engaged in drawing up policy plans for Manchoukuo. By noting where British policy and administration in Egypt had succeeded and where it had failed, it was hoped to avoid the British mistakes and apply to Manchoukuo those measures which had brought success. Quoting Lord Lloyd's judgment, that the real danger to those countries which had come under British control arose when the claims of good administration were subordinated to the claims of political theory, and that the main duty of government was to provide good administration, not to force constitutional development, he emphasized that these were the guiding rules to be applied to Manchoukuo. Another lesson derived from Lord Lloyd's book, he said, was that emphasis on higher education tended to create half-baked students and disgruntled intellectuals; what was required for a backward agrarian people was a sound, practical education to assist in raising the standard of agriculture and the general physical and moral development of the people. To my query as to whether Lyautey's work in Morocco was not also serving as a model, he replied with an emphatic negative, but remarked that British policy in Iraq was being studied closely with a view to putting Manchoukuo firmly on its feet. Then, with a twinkle in his eye, he added, 'But we do not propose to urge Manchoukuo to enter the League of Nations.'

It was a day or two after this talk that, wholly unexpectedly, I was received in private audience by the former Chief Executive, Pu Yi, who, a month previously, had been proclaimed Emperor of Manchoukuo under the name of Kwangteh. Of slight build, he wore thick, smoked glasses and had the hands of a sculptor's model. Throughout our talk, which ranged over a variety of subjects, I was struck by his easy unassuming manner and extreme courtesy. When I commented on this later to the Manchoukuo official who had acted as interpreter, he replied in a confidential tone, 'Our Emperor is a good man and has great ideas if only he can carry them out.' On my asking him if he saw any reason why he should not be able to do so, he replied somewhat cryptically. 'It is doubtful if he can, as the future is uncertain.' I tried to press him to explain just what he meant by this, but his only reply was, 'I cannot say more, but you can guess what I mean.' It was an unsatisfactory answer, but from what I heard later it seemed evident that it bore on Japanese opposition to the Emperor's dream of restoring the monarchy in China, with himself as the ruler of a united Chinese Empire.

Twelve years later the Emperor Kwangteh, demoted once more to plain Pu Yi, was to be produced by the Russians as a witness at the War Crime Trials in Tokyo. He proved to be a very unreliable witness, as he himself has since admitted in his autobiography and as is clear from the transcript of his evidence at the trial; but it is of interest to recall that, both at my audience with him in 1934 and again at the trials in 1946, he spoke bitterly of his old British tutor, Sir Reginald Johnston, and made wholly unfounded accusations against him. It was, in fact, with considerable surprise that I listened to him denouncing Sir Reginald for having written his recently-published work, *Twilight in the Forbidden City*. I myself had just read the book and had been struck by the very favourable and sympathetic portrayal of the young emperor given in its pages. The Emperor admitted that he had contributed the Foreword, but he said he had not read the book and had no intention of doing so. He had, he said, been dissuaded from reading it by friends, who had told him that it was slanderous of himself and scurrilous about his companions in the old Forbidden City. It was true, of course, that the author had denounced in scathing terms the terrible atmosphere of sordid intrigue and scandal which, in conjunction with the eunuch system, had flourished in those strange, make-believe surroundings, but nothing derogatory was written about Pu Yi himself. Though listening attentively to my rebuttal of the charge that he himself had been slandered and held up to ridicule, the Emperor was clearly not prepared to accept my assurances that he had been misinformed. Brushing them aside, he remarked sorrowfully that the respect and affection he used to feel for his old tutor had been shattered for all time.

It was not until my return to England some months later that the explanation of all this became evident. Sir Reginald, who was then in London, listened with interest to my account of what had

x

transpired, for it served to confirm what he had already heard from the Emperor's brother, who was staying with him at the time. This was to the effect that officials of the old régime in the Forbidden City, whose rottenness and corruption had been exposed in his book, had been making their way to Hsinking and trying to restore the old corrupt system. Furious with Sir Reginald for having exposed them, and fearful lest the Emperor should learn of their own misdeeds, they had dissuaded him from reading the book by giving him a totally misleading account of it. Sir Reginald died a few years later, but it is pleasant to recall that, through the assistance of Japanese friends in Manchuria, he was able, shortly before his death, to prove to the Emperor the falsity of the information given to him. The breach was seemingly healed and he paid a visit to Hsinking at the personal invitation of his former pupil.

Less agreeable was the fact that, in August 1946, Pu Yi renewed his attack on his old tutor at the War Crime Trials in Tokyo, slandering and vilifying him, though he was now dead and no longer able to defend himself. In the years that followed, however, he apparently came to realize that he had been unfair to him. In his autobiography, *From Emperor to Citizen*, a translation of which was published in London by Collet's in 1965, he depicts Sir Reginald as a kindly, honest character, a man with obvious limitations but fully deserving the affection and respect of his former pupil. Somewhat ironically, it may be added, Pu Yi, at the time of his death in October 1967, was living in Peking once more, a convert to Communism after prolonged indoctrination in prison and, apparently, a junior official in a government department—a strange end for the last of a line of monarchs, who had ruled over China from 1644 to 1911.

As a postscript of minor historical interest it may be added that, following the Vatican's decision to accord diplomatic recognition to Manchoukuo, a French bishop, who was to act as Chargé d'Affaires in Hsinking, was received in private audience by the Emperor Kwangteh on the same day that I was. Accompanied by a French priest from Kirin and a Japanese priest from Tokyo, he was to have been the first foreigner to be accorded this privilege since Pu Yi ascended the Throne. Much to my embarrassment, however, he was asked to let me go before him, as I had to catch a plane leaving for Harbin at noon that day. Inadvertently, therefore, official versions to the contrary, I was the first western foreigner to be received in audience by the newly-created Emperor!

It was a week or so after this audience that I received the first clue to the riddle presented by the cryptic utterance of the interpreter mentioned earlier in this account. Being by then in Mukden, I had occasion to meet Colonel (later General) Doihara, whose behind-the-scenes activities had earned for him the soubriquet of 'the Lawrence of Manchuria'. Thirteen years later, he was to be one of six senior Japanese officials sentenced to death and hanged as a major war criminal. Thick-set, heavily-built, with clipped moustache, he had the appearance of a jovial country merchant rather than that of a scheming military officer; but there was a quiet tone of assurance in his voice when he spoke, betokening that there was very much more in him than appeared on the surface.

In view of subsequent developments, Doihara's comments on North China and Inner Mongolia were not without significance. Despite official pronouncements to the contrary, it was widely believed at the time that the recent enthronement of the Emperor Kwangteh was but the prelude to an attempt to restore him to the throne in Peking. North China and, later perhaps, the whole of China would then be linked with Manchuria as in the days of the old monarchy. This being the current belief, I felt that Doihara, who had played so important a part in assisting the flight of Pu Yi from Tientsin to Manchuria, late in 1931, was probably well-placed to know what truth there was in it. I therefore questioned him on the matter and he replied most emphatically that the belief was wholly unfounded. From what he and others told me subsequently, the impression I received was that, although there were many among the members of the former imperial court in Peking who hoped to see this brought about, the Japanese themselves were utterly opposed to any such development and wished to keep Manchoukuo entirely separate from China.[1] North China, he admitted, might perhaps break away from the Nationalist Government in Nanking and declare its independence as Manchoukuo had done, but he thought it unlikely that it would ever join up with Manchoukuo. In saying this, it seems probable that he was already contemplating, if not actually planning, some such development, as a so-called independence movement was launched in North China only a few months later.

[1] This has now been confirmed by Pu Yi himself in his autobiography.

CHAPTER XXIII

National Policies and National Defence

On the evening of 17 April 1934, a few days before I set off for Manchuria, the Foreign Office in Tokyo issued a statement which took everyone by surprise. Although described as 'unofficial', it was a clear warning that Japan was no longer prepared to tolerate any interference prejudicial to her own interests in Chinese affairs. Issued by Amau, the Foreign Office Spokesman, it became known as the Amau Statement and proclaimed a policy summed up in the words 'Hands Off China'. It went even further than the so-called Far Eastern Monroe Doctrine and, to a large extent, was a re-hash of the famous Twenty-One Demands. In effect, it laid down that China's foreign policy should be under Japanese guidance and that Japan should be the final arbiter as to what outside assistance China might or might not receive.

When I questioned him about it the following day, Amau asserted that it was merely intended to clarify the policy of 'peace and harmony' with Britain, America, Russia and China, enunciated by Hirota in his speech to the Diet in January. It seemed, however, to cut right across the Open Door and Equal Opportunity principle and other international undertakings. This was, in fact, the view widely expressed abroad, despite Amau's contention that it implied no such deviation. Its aim, he maintained, was merely to show that Japan was prepared to oppose any action by other Powers that might lead to the disturbance of peace in East Asia.

Although he did not say so, it seemed probable that, in making this assertion, Amau had in mind the anxiety felt in recent months concerning the potential threat to Formosa posed by the construction of airfields in Amoy and Foochow; the cost of their construction was being met, reputedly, by the proceeds of an American wheat and cotton loan to China. Taken in conjunction with an alleged secret agreement between the United States and China connected with the construction of these aerodromes, this was regarded as a violation of the Sino-Japanese agreement concerning the province of Fukien and had been the subject of questioning in the Diet. Apprehensions on this score had been increased by reports from Washington of a speech in February by General William Mitchell, former head of the American Army Air Force. After declaring that the outcome of the next war would be decided by bombing attacks on vital centres of the enemy's country, he had added bluntly, 'Our most dangerous enemy is Japan.'

To what extent the Amau Statement was the outcome of Japan's anxiety about the Fukien airfields and America's alleged assistance in their construction was never made clear at the time, although Shigemitsu, who was then Vice-Minister for Foreign Affairs, asserted to me some months later that it had been intended primarily 'for home consumption and internal effect'. It was hardly surprising, however, that the Statement called forth some very strong criticism abroad. The general impression seemed nevertheless to be, that it was another instance of clumsy handling on the part of Japanese officialdom and that it was inopportune at a time when Hirota was endeavouring to improve relations with the United States and others. Some observers were inclined, on the other hand, to think that its real intention was to bring matters to a head, so that everyone would know exactly what Japan's position was, instead of just leaving things alone and letting the situation simmer indefinitely. From private talks I had with Japanese friends, the former of these two views seemed fairly widespread in Japan itself, including among Japanese Army officers, one of whom conveyed a message to me from General Araki. This was to the effect that he and other Army leaders were much upset by the way in which the Statement had been put out, but were greatly impressed by the calm attitude adopted by the British Government.

In spite of the criticisms from abroad, foreign diplomats in Japan seemed, on the whole, not to be unduly perturbed. One, in fact, expressed his views to me in forthright terms. This was Baron de Bassompière, the Belgian Ambassador, who said he considered that any country in Japan's position would be perfectly justified in seeking to prevent the arming and training of China's military forces by foreign nations. If the League and the Powers in general disliked the Hands-Off-China policy, he said, they had only themselves to blame. It was they who were preventing Japan and China from composing their differences and it was they who, in consequence, were responsible for the continuance of the existing unstable state of affairs in China, an instability which was the cause of the policy enunciated in the Amau Statement. Instead of continuing their present attitude towards Japan and China, the Powers should, in his opinion, reverse their policy and do everything possible to facilitate a settlement of the differences between the two.

Fundamentally, he contended, the error in the attitude of the Powers arose from their policy being based on a fiction contained in the Nine-Power Pact. The Pact revolved in great part around 'the maintenance of the peace and administrative and territorial integrity of China'. But, as he put it, how can any Power solemnly bind itself to maintain two things which have never existed in China in modern times. Though spoken in confidence at the time, it was a surprisingly outspoken commentary by a leading foreign diplomat.

In this talk, which took place shortly after my return from Manchuria, he expressed deep concern over the attitude of the Western Powers towards the Far East in general and towards Japan in particular. The various governments of the West, he considered, were likely to bring about a very dangerous situation if they continued their present line of policy and refused to heed the warnings of their own diplomatic representatives in Japan. His views were, in many respects, similar to those expressed to me on various occasions by Sir Francis Lindley and he repeated a remark which he said had been made to him by Sir Francis, just prior to leaving for home a short time before. 'I am leaving Japan and resigning,' he quoted him as saying, 'because it is perfectly useless for me to stay on here when none of my recommendations are heeded by my government.' This alleged remark brought to mind the action of an earlier British Ambassador, Sir Charles Eliot, who had wished to resign in 1922 when, contrary to his advice and warnings, the Anglo-Japanese Alliance had been abrogated.

Turning to the question of Manchoukuo, Baron de Bassompière said he had strongly urged the Belgian Government to take the initiative in recognizing the new State on the occasion of Pu Yi's enthronement in March. It had afforded a golden opportunity, he felt, for Belgium and all the other Powers to rectify the folly of the non-recognition resolution at Geneva without losing face. The Vatican, he remarked, had wisely ignored the resolution and had recognized the new régime, although he admitted that, not being a member of the League, it had not been bound by this undertaking. His own government, however, had turned down his recommendation in the same way as, a year previously, it had refused to heed his warnings that Japan would quit the League and thereby deal it a serious blow, if its members insisted on approving the Lytton Report.

By continuing to withhold recognition, he contended, the Powers were more guilty than Japan in creating a dangerous state of tension and instability in the Far East. Their attitude merely served to provoke Japan and play into the hands of the hot-heads; it also led China to think, quite wrongly, that she could depend on the armed support of the Powers if necessary and could therefore continue safely to flout Japan and refuse to enter into direct negotiations with her; and it gave Soviet Russia reason to believe that she could depend on the moral support of the Powers against Japan in the event of a clash and that she could therefore adopt a more aggressive and provocative attitude towards Japan. As a result of these Chinese and Russian reactions to the Powers' attitude towards her, Japan was compelled to strengthen her own position still further, thus adding to the tension. The outcome of this attitude was perfectly logical; what was illogical was the attitude adopted by the Powers, who were even indulging in what he termed 'the criminal folly' of encouraging the Soviet to enter the League and to use it as an instrument of its own policy towards Japan, 'the one country in Asia which is able and prepared to fight the Soviet system'.

One aspect of the non-recognition principle on which he touched had been impressed on me during my recent visit to Manchuria. This was the difficulty it created for foreign consular officials stationed there. Our own Consul-General in Mukden, Paul Butler, with whom I had stayed for a day or two, was much worried at the time about the murder of a Canadian missionary at Chengchiatun in suspicious circumstances; but he could not communicate with the Manchoukuo authorities about it as, in principle, there were no such people. How on earth, he said, can one negotiate in a case like this, or on matters of trade or anything else, when the authorities concerned are regarded as non-existent? Non-recognition, with the Alice-in-Wonderland atmosphere it created, clearly had its difficulties.

Butler's reference to trade matters had recalled to mind the remark made to me a year or so previously by Komai Tokuzo, the political adventurer mentioned in a previous chapter. The promise to observe the principle of the Open Door and Equal Opportunity contained in the Manchoukuo declaration of independence in February 1932, he said, presupposed reciprocity; the promise held good, therefore, only in the case of countries formally recognizing Manchoukuo. While, however, he maintained that Manchoukuo was fully justified in taking this stand, he asserted that, in practice, they were quite prepared to accord equal opportunity to individuals and firms friendly to Manchoukuo, even though they came from countries withholding recognition.

His remarks, which had caused something of a stir when cabled abroad, arose out of a question I put to him concerning the projected formation of a Japanese-Manchoukuo economic bloc, with favoured tariff treatment for Japan. Though hardly in accordance with the promise of equal opportunity, there was a widespread feeling among close observers that, after all the risks and responsibilities taken by Japan, she could hardly be expected to content herself with getting no more advantage than nations which had taken none. As the Western nations were raising both immigration and tariff barriers against Japan, it seemed essential to let her have a favourable outlet somewhere, and where better than in Manchoukuo? To keep both her people and her goods bottled up seemed asking for trouble in the years to come; the sooner the world came to realize this the better. It was a truism summed up in the warning given by the liberal-minded Dr Nitobe at the Banff Conference of the Institute of Pacific Relations in August 1933, when he declared, 'Nations in danger of economic strangulation will eventually resort to force in order to improve their positions'.

The view, that Japan must be given breathing space and that Manchuria was the natural outlet, was shared by at least one member of the Goodwill Mission under the Australian Foreign Minister, Mr Latham, which came out to Japan in May 1934. Expressing this belief to me, he went on to say that Australia had always regretted the termination of the Anglo-Japanese Alliance, as it had been her greatest safeguard. Now that this safeguard had been removed, the fear was, that Japan's relations with the British Empire and the United States would become so embittered over the Manchurian issue that war might eventually become inevitable. The justification of this assessment was to be proved all too forcibly by subsequent developments.

Apart from the economic aspects of Manchuria as a breathing space for Japan if the raising of immigration bars and tariff barriers against her in other countries was to be continued, there was also the consideration, voiced by the Belgian Ambassador, that Japan was the only country in Asia able and prepared to stand up to the Soviet. A memorandum sent to me some weeks earlier by General Araki's henchman, Yamada, served to emphasize this. It was a paper, seemingly drawn up by Araki himself, dealing with the Soviet threat to Manchuria and its bearing on other developments on the neighbouring mainland. Though smacking of propaganda in parts, it described Manchuria as 'the only strategic dam to resist a Soviet inundation of the Far East', and contended that Japan's actions had been the outcome of her realization that she had no choice but to secure a firm foothold, in order to prevent 'the western extremity of [her] Empire' from suffering this fate. From what was said in this memorandum, and from what I myself had been told by Japanese officers and others during my Manchurian trip, it seemed clear that the Japanese were genuinely fearful of Soviet penetration into Inner Mongolia and viewed with apprehension the progress being made in the sovietization of Sinkiang. This impression was to be strengthened in January the following year, when Japanese troops sought to obtain a foothold in the Inner Mongolian province of Chahar, and Manchoukuo troops clashed with Outer Mongolian forces near Boir Nor, in the Barga region. They were but minor incidents in the field of Japanese-Soviet rivalry, but were to prove the prelude to more serious incidents of the same kind a few years later. It was perhaps significant that, only a few days prior to these two clashes, the Japanese Foreign Minister, Hirota, speaking in the Diet on 22 January 1935, had expressed relief that the Chinese Nationalists had at last forced the main Chinese Communist forces out of Kiangsi and Fukien. At the same time he had voiced his apprehension that the Communists were 'said to be establishing contact with their allies in Kweichow and Szechuan and moving westward into remoter regions'. In view of later developments, his concern was to prove well merited. The withdrawal of the Chinese Communists, to which he referred, heralded the start of the famous Long March, which was to end with the establishment of the Chinese Soviet Government in the remote region of Yenan. There, they were to prove a thorn in the Japanese flesh a few years later; from there, too, after Japan's defeat in 1945, they were to rally the country under their banner, overthrow the Nationalist régime, and seize control of the whole of China.

It was in this same speech in January 1935 that Hirota, referring to the withdrawal of the Chinese Communists 'westward into remoter regions', added the warning, 'In view of this fact, coupled with reports of the sovietization of Sinkiang, the Japanese Government will be obliged to continue to watch with concern the activities of the Communist Party and its armies in China.' It was this constant fear of 'the Soviet inundation of the Far East', through the instrumentality of Communism, that accounted so much for Japanese actions in that area. The tragedy was that, by these actions, Japan played into the hands of the Soviet and its Communist allies. Ironically, she ended by diverting her own attention from the traditional Russian enemy and turning against Britain and the United States, the two main bulwarks against Soviet imperialism and Communist subversion.

In connection with Japanese-Soviet relations, it may be noted in passing that, towards the end of 1933, there was an addition to the group of foreign correspondents in Japan. This was Dr Richard Sorge, who arrived in Tokyo as correspondent for the *Frankfurter Zeitung* and other German papers. Quiet, unassuming and intelligent, he seemed a likeable character. Little did anyone imagine that, some eight years later, he would be exposed as Moscow's master-spy in the Far East and pay the penalty for his activities. His exposure brought about the dismissal of the German Ambassador, Major-General Ott, who, believing him to be a loyal fellow countryman, had taken him completely into his confidence.

Although, in 1934, the Japanese people as a whole were still thinking largely in terms of landward precautions, with Russia as the chief potential enemy, there were increasing signs of Japan's anxiety to strengthen her position in Far Eastern waters. In March the previous year, the ebullient Matsuoka had annoyed the Japanese Foreign Office by his outspoken advocacy of a non-aggression pact with Holland in respect of the Dutch East Indies, a matter on which he had no authority to speak. Some weeks later, however, negotiations for an arbitration treaty with the Netherlands were said to be nearing agreement, although some difficulties had yet to be overcome. Holland wanted a proviso that issues arising between the two countries should be submitted to the World Court, but Japan declined to commit herself to this, as she was thinking of withdrawing from that body on account of its being an organ of the League. Then, in the summer of that year, the French occupied a small group of islands lying between Indo-China and the Philippines. Japan disputed their right to do so and claimed the sovereign rights and interests for herself. Further indications of growing concern with her position in the Western Pacific were reflected in the alarm expressed when, in January 1934, it was reported from London that Britain and France might sell their mandated islands in the Pacific to the United States as part-payment of their war debts. The report was apparently groundless, but was typical of the mischief-making rumours circulating so freely at the time and adding to the feeling of insecurity and unrest. Had it proved true, it would have provided the 'stepping-stones' across the Pacific which the Americans then lacked and would have given Japan real cause for anxiety. There were, it is true, reports at that time that the Japanese, contrary to their pledges, were fortifying their own mandate islands; but Hirota flatly denied this when the Australian Goodwill Mission visited Japan a few months later, and I was assured by a member of the mission that Mr Latham was fully satisfied with this denial, as he knew from other sources that what Hirota had told him was correct. The member of Mr Latham's staff who told me this also contended that the Australians were in full sympathy with the Japanese over their contention that their mandate was received from the High Allied Council, not from the League; the League, therefore, had no right to demand the return of the islands now that Japan had left that body. The Australians, he said, held the same view regarding their own mandate.

It was a few days after this talk towards the end of May 1934 that Britain put forward proposals to Japan, the United States, France and Italy for preliminary discussions in London on the naval conference projected for the following year. The Japanese Press showed great interest, but was worried lest Britain and America should formulate a new Rapidan Agreement and attempt to force Japan to accept it, as they had in 1930. It was emphasized, too, that although Japan would demand the abolition of the existing ratios, she merely wanted parity conceded in principle, in accordance with the sovereign rights of national defence. Apart from the implication of inferiority, ratios, it was claimed, compelled Japan and the other signatories to build up categories which were not needed and to leave themselves deficient in categories essential for national defence. On my questioning Admiral Sakano[1] about this, he frankly admitted the difficulties of coming to an agreement and the impossibility of Japanese delegates agreeing to less than their own countrymen demanded. 'We cannot', he said, 'afford to ignore the aftermath of the London Naval Treaty or what happened on 15 May two years ago.'

Sakano's remark was shown to have had some justification when, a week later, he was forced to resign, owing to the outcry caused by a statement of his favourable to General Ugaki, who was expected to succeed Admiral Viscount Saito as Premier shortly. A section of the Navy was bitterly opposed to his being given the Premiership at this juncture, as they feared that his broad-minded outlook would be fatal to Japan at the coming naval conference. From what I learned from Japanese friends at the time, there would almost certainly have been a fresh outbreak of terrorism if he had been appointed to this post and strict precautions were already being taken against possible attempts on his life.

Ugaki was only one of several regarded as possible candidates for the Premiership in succession to Saito. One of the others was Prince Konoye, who was then president of the House of Peers and was about to leave for the United States, ostensibly to see his son, but partly on a kind of good-will mission. I had met him on a number of occasions and had been struck by his appearance—a fine-looking patrician, unusually tall for a Japanese, swarthy, ruddy complexion, a clipped moustache and fine aquiline features, though a slightly drooping lower lip detracted from an otherwise strikingly handsome face. Still in his early forties, he was reputed to have the confidence of the Army—a most valuable asset—and was widely regarded as a coming man. Knowing him to be a close friend of his, I asked Iwanaga what he thought of him as a possible Premier and received an unexpected reply. Konoye, he agreed, was a close personal friend of his, but he felt bound to admit that he was not the man to handle a serious crisis; he was too weak-willed. It was because of this that his friends had persuaded him to go to America, as they feared that,

[1] Sakano, whom I had known well since 1925, when I was first introduced to him by Admiral Funakoshi, had been liaison officer in Malta during the last year or so of the 1914–18 War. Like Funakoshi, who had been Naval Attaché in London during that war and was present at the Battle of Jutland, he was very well disposed towards Britain and the Royal Navy.

on account of this weakness, he would only harm his future if he was offered the Premiership and accepted it. They were fearful, too, that he might pledge himself to the Army to carry out their ideas in return for their support in the event of his becoming the Emperor's First Minister.

Konoye had many estimable qualities, but his friends had diagnosed his failings correctly. Admiral Okada succeeded Saito a month or so later and Konoye was dropped for the time being; but he was to become Premier three times between 1937 and 1941, and during his terms of office Japan, largely due to his weakness of character and failure to stand up to his army friends, slid steadily towards the war which was to end in her defeat. That he had personal courage and was undeterred by extremist attempts to assassinate him is beyond dispute, but in December 1945 he was to take his own life rather than suffer the humiliation of imprisonment and trial as a major war-criminal.

It was at the time that Konoye was being freely canvassed as a possible successor to Saito that, in a private discussion with Shigemitsu on Anglo-Japanese relations, the Japanese Vice-Minister of Foreign Affairs, as he was then, put forward a suggestion for Anglo-Japanese commercial and industrial co-operation in China, which he considered would be mutually beneficial. Britain and Japan, he suggested, should agree together that North China be regarded as Japan's special field for commercial and industrial exploitation; South China would be Britain's preserve for similar activities. In between, in the Yangtse Valley, there should be joint undertakings, with Jardine Matheson, for example, co-operating with Mitsui—and so on. The mutual benefits, he felt, would be three-fold:—cut-throat competition would be eliminated; British and Japanese interests would be interlocked in such a way that each would support the other in China; and with their interests so closely related, the Japanese would be able to rest assured of British support against Soviet encroachment in China, while the British would be equally assured that the Japanese would defend their mutual interests. Britain, he added, could supply the capital where needed and be assured of safe investment, while Japan, in the case of railways and the like, might be left to administer and operate them.

There were some obvious snags to this, but it seemed to offer a basis for consideration. The only other person present at the talk was Christopher (now Sir Christopher) Chancellor, at that time Managing-Director of Reuters in Shanghai. It seemed likely, therefore, that Shigemitsu was putting forward the suggestion as a *balon d'essai* for him to fly, for the benefit of the great business tycoons in Shanghai, when he got back there. Whether the industrialists of the two countries would be prepared to work together in this way was, of course, a moot point. The difficulty of bringing about the desired co-operation was admitted; but it was known that the British industrialist, Sir Harry McGowan, since visiting Japan the previous year, had been strongly advocating Anglo-Japanese industrial co-operation, in spite of his former disbelief in its feasibility.

With the question of Anglo-Japanese relations constantly recurring, the month of May 1934 ended with the death of one who had been a foremost upholder of the Alliance in its heyday. On the 29th anniversary of his great victory over the Russian Fleet at the battle of Tsushima, news came that Admiral Togo, the Nelson of Japan, was seriously ill and had fallen into a critical condition. Three days later, on 30 May, he died. There was mourning throughout the land and eulogistic messages of condolence poured in from all over the world. Among them was one from Admiral Dreyer, Commander-in-Chief of the British China Squadron, who hastened to Japan in H.M.S. *Suffolk* to attend the funeral.

Those in Japan who remembered with pride the days when Britain had become their ally, were growing fewer and the sentimental attachment to their former ally was no longer shared by the younger generation of naval officers. All they recalled was that Britain had, in their view, jilted Japan in order to win favour with America, Japan's most dangerous naval rival. This view received all too much encouragement in the autumn of 1934 from reports that an agreement between Britain and the United States, for an Anglo-American naval defence line connecting Alaska with Australia, was likely if the coming naval conference reached a deadlock; the joint strategic scheme envisaged the construction of a new naval base in Australia, which would harbour American warships if necessary. Similar reports, urging the necessity of Britain and the United States working out a joint plan for the protection of their interests in the Pacific in case the naval talks ended in failure, also began to circulate; and General Mitchell was quoted in a Press despatch from Washington as pressing for the construction of a fleet of powerful dirigibles with a cruising range of from 6,000 to 8,000 miles, capable of attacking Japan and laying it waste. Britain was in no way responsible for these reports, but they played into the hands of those in Japan who were demanding an increase in land, sea and air armaments to off-set those of the United States and Russia; they were hardly calculated to bring about a reasonable agreement at the coming talks.

So far as Japan was concerned, the preliminary discussions opened in London in late October, when Rear-Admiral Yamamoto Isoroku arrived in England to take part in them. He proved to be a tough negotiator in pressing the Japanese point of view, but he was no fire-brand. When, later, he became Vice-Minister of the Navy, he vigorously opposed those demanding the strengthening of Japan's ties with Germany and Italy and was strongly averse to making enemies of Britain and America. By taking this stand, he aroused the enmity of the extremists. Fearing, it was said, that he would be assassinated if he remained in Tokyo, the Supreme War Council sent him to sea as Commander-in-Chief of the Combined Fleet, a post he still held at the outbreak of the Pacific War and until April 1943, when he was shot down while flying to Bourgainville for a personal reconnaissance of the situation there. A strategist of a high order, his was the brain which, when the war he had opposed became inevitable, worked out the plan so successfully executed at Pearl Harbour.

I myself was back in England by the time he arrived in London in October 1934 and had a long talk with him. Though careful to reveal nothing that was not already known, he replied to my questions at considerable length and spoke in friendly vein. Stressing that Japan wished to retain the agreement about non-fortification in the Pacific, he said she was prepared to forgo this rather than agree to retention of the ratio system. Referring to a report that he had indicated readiness to abolish submarines in return for the abolition of aircraft-carriers, he explained that this was due to a misapprehension. It had arisen from the fact that he had spoken to the Press in English without an interpreter; his English was poor and he had apparently made himself misunderstood. Japan, he recalled, had pledged herself not to abuse the use of submarines against merchantmen in wartime, but she could not agree to the abolition of underwater craft. The submarine, he maintained, was the cheapest and most effective weapon for defence in Japanese waters and would be essential in the event of a war with the Soviet who, he believed, had about twenty at Vladivostok, capable of attacks on troop-ships crossing the Japan Sea.

It was this possibility of a clash with Russia, rather than with either Britain or America, on which he spoke mainly, but he was adamant that the ratio system must go. The implication was, however, that this insistence was aimed primarily at establishing the principle of equality rather than at leaving Japan free to build up to the maximum limit. It only went to confirm the impression I had received from a talk with Captain Oka, the Japanese Naval Attaché, a few weeks earlier. Expressing his personal belief that the preliminary talks were doomed to failure and that the conference projected for the following year would never materialize, Oka had stressed his reasons for this gloomy forecast. The American Government, he said, had already made it clear that the United States would never agree to abolition of the ratios. Japan, however, could not afford to give way on this point; national sentiment was so intense that a violent internal explosion was inevitable if the Government did so.

During the weeks that followed, it became increasingly evident that these two opposing views were irreconcilable. By the latter part of November, the Americans were wanting to break off the talks, as Japan had definitely rejected the ratios; but the British were opposed to throwing up the sponge and were at variance with the United States on the subject of a separate Anglo-American agreement. Washington seemed to think that such an agreement would make Japan more amenable to reason, but Britain considered it would have the reverse effect. Japan, for her part, remained firm on the question of ratios, but stressed that she had no objection to Britain having greater armaments than herself, as her widespread commitments required them. With America, on the other hand, she claimed she must have at least global equality, as the United States were in a position to transfer their whole fleet to the Pacific through the Panama Canal. The Americans, however, as Admiral Richmond was to point out a few weeks later,[1] were determined, for prestige sake, to have equality with Britain and to be able, if necessary, to carry out

---

[1] At a week-end course on international affairs at the Bonar Law College on 2 March 1935. I myself had spoken on similar lines in a talk I gave at this course earlier in the day and had been taken to task by some of those present for expressing such heretical views.

operations in the Western Pacific, whereas Japan wished to ensure that the United States would never be in a position to take offensive action in those waters. She therefore proposed a new agreement based on the twin principles of (a) non-aggression and non-menace, and (b) equality of national security and provision for the drastic reduction or abolition of such specifically offensive weapons as capital ships, aircraft-carriers, and heavy cruisers.

This was, to some extent, in line with the British plea to restrict the types and size of ships, as it would limit the cost and prevent a rival from designing new types, which would render existing vessels obsolete. Germany had already posed this possibility with her 'pocket battleships'. Had the British proposal been accepted, and a new agreement concluded, Japan would not have been free, as she was after the breakdown of the subsequent conference in January 1936, to spring on the world three 70,000-ton *Yamato* class battleships, which she hoped would provide her with bargaining power in some future negotiations with Britain and the United States.

With the preliminary talks at a deadlock, Japan, on 29 December, announced her intention of terminating the Washington Naval Treaty as from 31 December 1936. This was in accordance with the statutory obligation of giving two years' notice, but the date chosen for ending the agreement was significant; it coincided with the date on which the London Naval Treaty was due to expire if no agreement for its renewal had been reached in the meantime.

Foreseeing the disastrous consequences if that treaty were not renewed, the septuagenarian Admiral Viscount Saito, who had handed over the premiership to Admiral Okada four months earlier, wrote an article for the *Christian Science Monitor*, appealing to reason and moderation and discussing, with courageous frankness, the great issues then under discussion at the preliminary talks in London. The gist of it was published in *The Times* of 21 November 1934. Stressing the necessity, if the Washington Treaty was abrogated, of starting anew at the conference scheduled for the following year, he gave warning that 'a devastating naval building race' would be inevitable if the projected conference failed and he castigated both Japanese and foreign writers alike, as well as propagandists, politicians, and nationalist extremists, for beclouding fact with fiction. Rhetoric, he said, was taking the place of reason, while propaganda in all countries was complicating the problem even more. 'The great welter of half-information and misinformation and the backlog of propaganda', he feared, might well 'foredoom the conference to failure.'

Urging that naval forces should be limited by mutual agreement to 'fleets just large enough to provide protection to our commerce and our coast-lines', he deplored the terrible waste of money on inflated armaments at the expense of the poverty-stricken people and wrote with feeling of the dreadful burden of depression in Japan, which would become immeasurably heavier 'if an unbridled naval race is the result of an unsuccessful conference in London in 1935.' With considerable courage he wrote of the 'great pressure [that] has been brought to bear on the Premier (Admiral Okada) to force cancellation of Japan's allegiance to the terms of the 10–10–6 ratio' and roundly denounced the *Seiyukai* for 'taking advantage of an international crisis to further its own ends' and for 'seeking to ride the wave of propaganda so that it can gain control of the politics of Japan.' Even more courageous were his direct allusions to the Emperor who, he declared, 'will not allow the Navy to proceed uncontrolled' and 'will not tolerate an unbridled programme for the future.'

Although trouncing foreign as well as Japanese writers and propagandists for their share in the responsibility for the existing crisis, he was clearly laying up trouble for himself and taking his life in his hands by writing so forcefully—and in an American paper at that. Little more than a year later he was to pay the penalty, assassination at the hands of extremist young officers. That Admiral Okada, whom he had revealed was under such pressure to abrogate the Washington Treaty, did not share his fate was due to accident, not design; the assailants murdered his brother-in-law in mistake for him.

CHAPTER XXIV

Epilogue

For reasons explained in the introductory chapter, it is not intended to deal in any detail with events following the breakdown
of the preliminary naval talks in London at the end of 1934. It
only remains, therefore, to round off the picture by providing
some sidelights and observations on the main developments leading from that point onwards to Japan's fateful plunge into war
in December 1941.

What is perhaps of importance to note is that the period from
September 1931, when the Manchurian 'Incident' started, down
to the attack on Pearl Harbour ten years later, fell into three
fairly well-defined stages. The first, which ended with the outbreak of the North China 'Incident' in July 1937, centred largely
around Japan's attempt to strengthen her position in Manchuria
and, in the words of the memorandum sent to me by General
Araki shortly before my return to England, to transform it into
'a strategic dam to resist a Soviet inundation of the Far East'.
The second phase, which continued until the Spring of 1940, saw
a switch-over to China as the main object of her endeavours; it
was marked by her unsuccessful attempt to negotiate a settlement
(which would include co-operation with Japan in preventing the
bolshevization of East Asia) and by the consequent rapid escalation of her 'undeclared war'. Finally came the eighteen months
or so preceding the start of the Pacific War; with pronouncements
on the newly-defined Co-prosperity Sphere and Greater East
Asia, it saw the war clouds spreading ominously over South-East
Asia, in Japan's effort to block supplies to China and to secure
control of natural resources required for herself.

This is perhaps an over-simplified assessment of an extremely
complex series of developments in which geographical, economic,
and strategic considerations, internal pressures, and the interplay
of international relations and rivalries played an all-important
part; but in broad outline it may be said to represent the main
features of what took place.

With Russia's relinquishment of her last tangible asset in her former sphere of influence by the sale of the North Manchurian Railway (the former Chinese Eastern Railway) in March 1935, Japan's aims in Manchuria had been advanced very considerably. By then, too, the deterioration in Anglo-Japanese relations, which had been so marked in the early days of Japan's attempt to strengthen her position in that area, had seen a welcome easing. The naval conference convened in December that year, it is true, had ended in failure and put an end to the Washington and London naval agreements of 1922 and 1930; but it was clear from private talks I had with Admiral Nagano and other members of his delegation that the Japanese, while insisting on the abolition of the ratio system, had a sympathetic understanding of British requirements. Japan, it was stressed, fully recognized that Britain, on account of her scattered possessions, required a larger navy than herself; but so long as the United States insisted on parity with Britain, Japan must insist on parity with both Britain and America. Failure to achieve this equality would mean that America, with a preponderance of heavy cruisers, would be capable of offensive action across the Pacific and be a threat to Japan's national defence.

The underlying feelings of friendship towards Britain held by the Japanese as a whole were reflected at a farewell dinner to the Japanese delegation in January 1936. It was a friendly, informal gathering, which ended abruptly on a sadly dramatic note. As we sat talking, a news bulletin was brought in and quietly circulated. It was brief but ominous. 'The King's life is moving peacefully towards its close' was all it said, but the meaning was all too clear. With barely concealed emotion, the Japanese guests rose from their seats and solemnly left the building, followed by their British hosts. Barely two hours later, King George V had passed away.

This feeling of friendship and sympathy was shown again a few days later, when the Japanese Army chiefs, on learning that a memorial service was to be held at the English church in Tokyo, expressed their wish to pay their respects to the late British monarch and offered to provide a Guard of Honour of 1,000 officers and men from the Guards Division. For some inexplicable reason, however, this friendly gesture was declined. From talks with members of the Japanese Embassy in London at the time, it was clear that they felt deeply hurt by this response. The Army nevertheless swallowed its pride; except for General Minami, who was away at the time, and General Watanabe who was ill, every full general in the Japanese Army attended the service.

Britain, for her part, was in an invidious position, both before and after that time. As Sir Robert (later Lord) Vansittart defined it in a lecture at the Imperial Defence College some months before the naval conference, her aim was to strive for both Japanese and American friendship and to avoid any attempt to court the one at the expense of the other. The difficulties of this balancing feat were obvious and were put to a hard test at the conference; for, though sympathetic towards Japan's stand, Britain was, in effect, faced with the alternatives of agreeing to naval parity with the United States, who were not prepared to concede parity to Japan, or of being outbuilt by the American Navy as had been threatened in 1921 if the Anglo-Japanese Alliance had not been scrapped. The balancing feat to which Vansittart had alluded was, incidentally, made all the harder at times by the obligations which Britain owed as a member of the League of Nations.

There were, however, occasions when British statesmen, through indifference or lack of tact, gave deep offence to their Japanese opposite numbers. An instance of this was brought to my attention by Mr Nagai, Japan's chief delegate to the naval conference. I had known him well since the days when he was Counsellor to the Japanese Embassy in London in 1921 and I myself was at the War Office; but I was surprised when he confided to me that what had upset him, just as much as the breakdown of the conference a few days earlier, was his reception by Mr Eden. As head of the Japanese delegation he had expected that he would have been given an opportunity to meet the British Foreign Secretary for private talks; but although he had been in London for nearly two months, all his requests for an interview had been turned down on one pretext or another.[1] He had met him on one occasion only, at a dinner party, but Mr Eden had studiously avoided discussing politics and had quickly turned the conversation to more trivial matters. This, Mr Nagai remarked ruefully, had been in strong contrast to the reception given him by Ribbentrop, whom he had visited in Berlin shortly before.

Nagai had met neither of these two young statesmen previously

[1] Yoshizawa Kenkichi, while on a visit to London in the autumn of 1936, told me sorrowfully of a similar rebuff he himself had had. As a former Foreign Minister, he had hoped his visit would afford him an opportunity for informal talks with Sir John Simon or some other high official in the Foreign Office, but his attempts to arrange for an interview were met with bland regrets that they were all too busy to see him.

and he had looked forward to making their personal acquaintance while he was in Europe; he had heard such conflicting opinions of both that he had wanted to judge for himself. Both of them, he had found, seemed to have little real understanding of Far Eastern affairs; but whereas Eden had virtually snubbed him, Ribbentrop had been extremely friendly and forthcoming. He had shown readiness to listen to what he had to say and had put a number of searching questions to him. Eden may have had good reasons for his seeming indifference, but the impression left on Nagai by these two contrasting attitudes was unfortunate. As he no doubt reported his impressions to the Japanese Foreign Office on his return to Tokyo, it may well have helped to turn the scales in favour of Germany. Certain it is that a bare eight months later, in September 1936, the first concrete evidence of a rapprochement had materialized in the form of the Anti-Comintern Pact between Japan and Germany. A year later, Italy was to add her weight to it.

The conclusion of the pact with Germany more or less coincided with the arrival, in England, of Yoshida Shigeru as Japan's new Ambassador. That he was genuinely anxious to strengthen the ties between Britain and Japan was generally recognized; but, rightly or wrongly, there was a widespread feeling in British official circles that his was a lone voice and that, in his attempts to bring about a friendly agreement, he was acting largely on his own initiative, without the full backing of his government. That he was hampered both by anti-British sentiment in Japan and by anti-Japanese elements in England, however, was beyond dispute. When I asked him about this and as to whether he found much change in London since he was last there fifteen years before, he replied smilingly, 'Yes! I find the friends of Japan more friendly and the hostile critics more hostile.'

Although Yoshida set himself to work for an improvement in Anglo-Japanese relations, an event which occurred at the end of 1936 was to have repercussions which rendered his efforts abortive. This was the kidnapping of Chiang Kai-shek at Sian, where the Generalissimo was cajoled into agreeing to end his attempts to exterminate the Chinese Communists and to join with them in preventing any further Japanese encroachments in China. The outcome of this agreement was to be seen in the fateful developments touched off by the clash at the Marco Polo Bridge barely six months later.

For some months prior to this last incident, Yoshida had been engaged in private talks with the Foreign Office in London about the possibilities of settling Anglo-Japanese differences and mis-understandings. The fact that such discussions were in progress was purposely kept quiet, lest they be hampered by premature disclosure; but with the outbreak of the North China 'Incident' in July 1937 and the rapid spread of the fighting to Shanghai—despite the efforts of the Japanese Government to localize the trouble—the talks were brought to an abrupt halt and a serious deterioration of Anglo-Japanese relations set in as one develop-ment followed another.

The deep concern felt by Yoshida and his family at this un-expected turn of events was made evident in a talk I had with his wife at a dinner party early in 1938. It had been her husband's great ambition on being appointed Ambassador, she said, to bring about a return to the old friendly relations between the two countries. He had had great hopes of the negotiations he had initiated a year or so earlier; but the outbreak of the China trouble had dashed his hopes to the ground and for some time past he had been so upset by what was happening that he had been unable to eat or sleep properly. Speaking in a voice charged with emotion, she had expressed her own and her husband's feelings in her concluding words, 'It is like some terrible nightmare to us both'.

The grave developments arising from the outbreak of hostilities in the summer of 1937 are now a matter of history. The wounding of the British Ambassador to China, the bombing of open towns and cities, the sinking of the American *Panay* and the British *Ladybird*, the sack of Nanking, and the increasing threats to British interests in the Yangtse Valley, to Hong Kong, and to the whole question of foreign rights and interests revolving around the principle of the Open Door and Equal Opportunity; all these, and other developments as well, aroused growing criticism of Japan as her efforts to force the Chinese to capitulate and nego-tiate on her terms led her to extend the area of operations ever further southwards. As in 1932, so again in 1937, there was talk of imposing economic boycotts and sanctions, and in November that year a draft resolution was passed at the Brussels Conference, threatening action which its movers were in no position to take. The only effect, therefore, was to increase Japan's intransigence and confirm her in the belief that she could safely ignore any further threats.

That the more moderate elements in Japan were deeply concerned and anxious to see the fighting brought to an end is beyond
question; but, like the Americans in Vietnam some thirty years
later, miscalculations about the enemy's staying powers and will
to resist had led to an escalation never anticipated at the outset.
In addition, the explosive situation in Japan, indicated by the
series of political assassinations and attempted coups—not least,
the Army mutiny of February 1936—forced successive governments, in their fear of full-scale revolution at home, to adopt
measures which, in more normal times, they would never have
contemplated. There was, too, the inevitable reaction to foreign
criticism in the form of an ever-increasing upsurge of national
sentiment; but, for the great majority of Japanese, Soviet Russia
and the Communist creed still loomed as the principal danger.
Time and again, in the feelers put out for a peaceful settlement
with China, Sino-Japanese co-operation against Soviet and Communist machinations was stressed as one of the outstanding aims.
By the close of 1937, with this aim in view, it was being intimated
therefore that, if China would acknowledge defeat, Japan would
be lenient; she would seek to make her an ally, or at least a good
friend, rather than treat her with severity and leave her with a
grudge. Bismarck's policy after Sadowa would be followed, not
his policy after Sedan.

But it was particularly unfortunate that, at the start of the
upheaval in China, Japan had Prince Konoye as her Prime
Minister. The forebodings, which Iwanaga had expressed to me
about him shortly before I left Japan, proved all too well-founded;
both on this, his first time in that high office, and on the two
subsequent occasions during the next four years when he held
that important post, he failed lamentably. Some time before he
assumed the Premiership for the first time, another prominent
personality, General Ugaki, had been ordered by the Emperor to
form a government. Had he succeeded in doing so, the prediction
made when his horoscope was cast in 1929 would have proved
correct and Konoye might never have become Prime Minister.
But the Army, still bitter with him for having cut its strength in
1925, had refused to nominate a War Minister to serve under him.
His attempt to carry out his sovereign's command had therefore
failed. He served for some months as Foreign Minister under
Prince Konoye in 1938, and during his term of office he strove
hard to bring about an improvement in his country's relations

with Britain, but he did so in the face of increasingly serious opposition.

With Ugaki's resignation in the autumn of that year the situation worsened, although a statement by his successor, Arita Hachiro, in March the following year, showed that the Government was not prepared to barter away the friendship of Japan's former ally in the interests of her ideological partners, Germany and Italy, who wanted to convert the Anti-Comintern Pact into a military alliance. Subsequent Japanese governments continued to aim at retaining friendship with both Britain and the United States; but Konoye, in spite of his personal opposition to the attempts being made to strengthen Japan's ties with the two Axis partners, finally gave way to pressure from the Army and from his Foreign Minister, Matsuoka Yosuke, who by then had become obsessed with hostility towards both Britain and America and convinced that Germany would win the war which, by then, had been launched in Europe. As a result Japan, in September 1940, joined Germany and Italy in a Mutual Aid Treaty. Although aimed primarily at deterring the United States from entering the war in the west or from resorting to military action against Japan in the Far East, it showed how well-founded had been the warning given nineteen years earlier, that abrogation of the Anglo-Japanese Alliance would leave Japan isolated and resentful and might lead her eventually to turn to Germany as an ally. What no one could have foreseen in 1921 was that this development would come about at a time when Britain was locked in mortal combat with Germany once more and, under an all-out bombing offensive from the air, was faced with the imminent danger of invasion by victory-drunk Nazi hordes.

The growing fear of isolation, the steady build-up of a war mentality, and a feeling of exasperation with Britain who, along with the Soviet Union, was being held responsible for the prolongation of the war in China, thereby causing heavy loss of Japanese lives: these were among the main contributory causes of the mounting anti-British sentiment in Japan, where Britain was being used as a convenient scape-goat to explain away the continued failure of the Army to bring the Chinese Nationalists to heel. As such, they played no small part in bringing about the Government's decision to enter into alliance with the two Axis Powers. While, however, Matsuoka was largely responsible for this latest development, it was not without significance that the

Japanese ambassadors in Berlin and Rome at that time were the strongly pro-German General Oshima and the reactionary Shiratori, whose frequent indiscretions had led to his removal from the post of Foreign Office Spokesman in Tokyo in 1933.

It was clear, nonetheless, that thoughtful Japanese were far from happy about their country's relations with the Nazis. Talks with Japanese friends in London had shown that even the Anti-Comintern Pact had given them cause for concern. By withdrawing from the League of Nations in 1933, they had hoped that Japan would at least be quit of any further European entanglements; but by concluding that pact with Germany and Italy, they feared that their country might be dragged back into them. This fear was increased when the Mutual Aid Treaty was signed. At a luncheon party given by Viscount Kano in May 1941, eight months after its conclusion, I was struck by the outspoken criticisms made by some of those present. These included Shigemitsu Mamoru, who had succeeded Yoshida as Ambassador, and Colonel Tatsumi, his Military Attaché, both of whom were highly critical of Matsuoka and his pro-German policy. The feeling of apprehension, and even of repugnance, expressed by them was voiced also by some of the other Japanese guests to whom I spoke; the general gist of their comments was that they dreaded the prospect of being dragged into the War on Germany's side and made to fight for the Nazis.

The deep concern expressed by Shigemitsu was reflected in the fact that, a bare month after this luncheon, having obtained the necessary sanction he returned to Japan. This he did in order to 'open up my mind to the Foreign Minister' as he put it in his subsequent memoirs, and to register his conviction that the ultimate defeat of Germany was inevitable.[1] It was through no fault of his own that he failed to disabuse the ebullient Matsuoka.

While, however, this feeling was shared by many Japanese, developments since the outbreak of the 'undeclared war' in China in 1937 had become increasingly ominous. The Japanese General Staff, which had supported whole-heartedly the seizure of Manchuria in 1931, had been strongly opposed to the Government's decision in January 1938 to fight on until Chiang Kai-shek had been utterly defeated. Foreseeing the dangers if the war was allowed to spread any further, they had urged that hostilities be ended by diplomatic negotiations; but they had been over-ruled.[2]

[1] *Japan and Her Destiny*, p. 215.   [2] Crowley, *Japan's Quest for Autonomy*, p. 351.

By the close of that year, therefore, Japanese forces were already in South China, where they had landed in Bias Bay and occupied Canton for the purpose of cutting off supplies to the Chinese from Hong Kong, and statements were circulating about the New Order in East Asia. A final attempt was also being made to induce Chiang to seek a settlement with Japan, which would include a break with the Communists and a united front with her against Soviet encroachments.

From this last attempt to obtain Chiang's acquiescence came at least one important result. This was that Wang Ching-wei, second only to Chiang Kai-shek in the Chinese Nationalist hierarchy, fell foul of the other Chinese leaders for urging acceptance of the Japanese terms—albeit with reservations—as a basis for negotiations; soon after, he established a government of his own in Nanking. Rather less than two years later, in November 1940, he concluded a treaty, which gave Japan the right to maintain armed forces in China, to use China for strategic purposes, and to have access to China's natural sources. Like the Manchurian agreement of 1932, which had given her similar extensive rights in Manchoukuo, this treaty with Wang accorded a superficially legal right to virtual control over China.

The irony of the situation by the advent of 1939, when Chiang Kai-shek rejected the final peace offer, was that the Japanese, in their anxiety to obtain Chinese co-operation against the spread of Soviet influence and Communism in East Asia, had acted in such a way as to drive the Chinese into seeking Soviet aid. Fundamentally, the fact was that both Japan and Soviet Russia were striving for the mastery of East Asia. Owing to the lack of cohesion among the Chinese people, China therefore seemed destined to fall under the domination of one or the other of her two powerful neighbours. Japan, for her part, was convinced that the only way to prevent the bolshevization of China was to compel the Chinese to accept Japanese aid in stemming the Soviet flood. The Russians, on the other hand, welcomed the Sino-Japanese conflict and considered that the longer it lasted the better. The longer it lasted, the more would the two contestants be weakened; Moscow's chance of exploiting the resulting chaos and dissatisfaction in both countries would therefore be increased.

The tension between Japan and the Soviet had, in fact, been marked by the first serious armed clash between the two a few months before Japan's final attempt to persuade Chiang to come to terms with her. This was in the summer of 1938, at Chang-kufeng on the Korean–Siberian border, and was followed in May the next year by the even more dangerous conflict in the Nomon-han area of the ill-defined border-line between Manchoukuo and Outer Mongolia. Nominally the clash was between those two states; but with Japan allied to the former and Russia to the latter, the main participants in the prolonged and bitter fighting that followed were the Japanese and the Russians.

While, however, the Japanese Army as a whole still regarded the Soviet as the main menace to Japan's security, the escalation of the operations in China and the proclamation of the New Order in East Asia which, in effect, put an end to the principle of the Open Door and Equal Opportunity, aroused increasing re-sentment and apprehension among the Western Powers. Along with this went a mounting of extreme nationalism in Japan itself and a growing inability of senior officers in the Japanese armed forces to control the actions of their subordinates, many of whom held key posts in the War Office and General Staff.

With the situation becoming increasingly tense, a private talk I had towards the end of 1939 with Mr Shigemitsu was revealing. Expressing his concern about the adverse effect on Anglo-Japan-ese relations, he remarked that the whole situation in the Far East had undergone such drastic changes in the past year or two that the old conceptions no longer held good; the best way for Britain to protect her interests, therefore, was to recognize the new situa-tion and to co-operate with Japan. While appreciating that the British stand at the outset had been dictated in large part by her obligations to the League of Nations, he maintained that, as the League was now virtually dead in so far as its original form was concerned—Germany, Italy and Japan out of it and Russia in—the time had come for Britain to recognize and acknowledge that fact; she should start afresh, therefore, unburdened by the League findings and resolutions, which had been such a drag on her freedom of action in the past. Without specifying the particular findings and resolutions he had in mind, it seemed clear, from previous remarks, that he was referring mainly to the continued ban on recognizing Manchoukuo; this, in Japanese eyes, con-trasted strongly with the rescinding of the resolution on non-recognition of Italy's annexation of Abyssinia. To the Japanese it appeared clear proof of their contention that different standards were applied to East and West.

With the seizure of Hainan in February 1939 and of the strategically placed Spratly islands in the following month, Washington, which had hitherto done its best to avoid any action likely to upset American relations with Japan to any serious extent, decided that the time had come to show that she could not stand aside indefinitely. She had, it is true, given a jolt to Japan a few months earlier by granting a credit of £5,000,000 to China, but now came orders for the United States Fleet to return to the Pacific. This was followed up a few months later by the announcement of her intention to abrogate the Treaty of Friendship and Commerce, which had been in operation since 1911. As the Japanese were given six months' notice of the ending of the treaty, the implication was clear; unless they mended their ways during the intervening period, they would have to suffer the economic consequences.

Commercial and industrial circles in Japan, fully alive to what these would be, pressed strongly for the negotiation of a new treaty based on greater consideration for American interests; but the Army and civilian extremists, who had for long preached the doctrine of economic self-sufficiency, regarded the American action as a heaven-sent opportunity for breaking free from economic dependence on the Anglo-Saxon Powers. Apart from this, the Army was not prepared to modify its policy to suit the United States. When, therefore, the six months ended in January the following year, the two countries were left without a treaty, a dangerous condition of affairs which continued until the attack on Pearl Harbour nearly two years later.

Welcome as were the more direct steps that the United States were taking to curb Japan, the British Government had, since the start of the upheaval in July 1937, been hampered, not only by its pre-occupation with developments in Europe, but also by failure to obtain American co-operation and to know just how much it could rely on American assistance if the worst came to the worst. As is now known, both Churchill and Eden were to be seriously handicapped in this way, right down to the time of Pearl Harbour. For this, the strong isolationist sentiment in the United States was largely to blame; but the difficulties of keeping in step with Washington had been summed up, as far back as February 1932, by Sir Robert Lindsay who, in one of his despatches, had remarked ruefully that the United States Government 'is never able to take firm engagements and that their support in any given contingency can never be relied on without question'.[1] Apart from this, American policy in the Far East was apt to change with every change of Administration and, as Griswold has shown, Cordell Hull's actions in 1937 had been much less ostentatious and provocative than Stimson's in 1932. Moreover, after Stimson's departure from office, United States policy underwent the change of aiming at the preservation of the Open Door in China and at naval predominance in the Pacific rather than at the preservation of Chinese territorial integrity.[2]

By the time the Japanese-American Treaty was brought to an end in January 1940, the Second World War was already four months old. The announcement of the Nazi-Soviet Pact in August 1939 had come as a shock to Japan and had brought angry criticism from the Japanese public in general. As a Japanese friend remarked to me at the time, 'That makes the Anti-Comintern Pact a scrap of paper and should put an end to any further talk of an alliance with Germany'. He was, of course, wrong about the latter part of his comment; but the fact that Britain and France had eventually stood up to Hitler made a favourable impression, which lasted until the 'phoney war' period ended abruptly in May 1940.

With the fall of France and the British withdrawal from Dunkirk, the situation in the Far East deteriorated rapidly. The Co-prosperity slogan had been coined a month or two earlier; now came the extension of the New Order in East Asia to cover Greater East Asia, a term which was to include the South Seas. Taking advantage of British and French troubles, further steps were taken to close supply routes to China. Nanning had already been occupied in October 1939 for the purpose of stopping supplies from Indo-China, and in September 1940, after adopting measures to put an end to the passage of supplies by the Haiphong–Kumming railway and by the Burma road, Japan forced Vichy France to conclude an agreement giving her virtual control of northern Indo-China. Following the collapse of Holland, she had also indicated the possibility of action in the Dutch East Indies to ensure her own supplies of oil. American reaction to the move into Indo-China was marked by the imposition of an embargo on any further supplies of iron and steel.

Japan's action, a month or two later, in withdrawing 100,000

---

[1] *Documents on British Foreign Policy 1919–1939*, 2nd Series, vol. IX, p. 649.
[2] Griswold, op. cit., pp. 462 and 466.

officers and men from China and moving them to Hainan and Formosa, caused considerable speculation as to the purpose of the transfer; it was not until later that it became known that they had been sent there for the training in jungle warfare, in which they were to prove themselves so adept little more than a year later.

In spite of all the Japanese efforts to force China into acquiescence with their demands, the Chinese continued to fight on and there was a growing tendency among foreign observers to talk of the Japanese being 'bogged down in China' and therefore incapable of any action against the Western Powers. In Singapore, an obvious target for attack, there was an increasing and dangerous air of complacency; catch-phrases about its being an 'impregnable fortress' with 'impenetrable jungles' to guard it from the rear, and also about Japanese inefficiency, were being freely bandied around. Alarmed by this readiness to under-rate the dangers, the British Embassy in Tokyo despatched its Military Attaché, Colonel Wards, to this vital naval base, to warn the officers of the garrison that complacency was unwarranted. Having had long first-hand experience of the Japanese Army, both in Japan and in China, he stressed the danger of under-rating Japanese military ability, but his words went unheeded. Of the way in which he was rebuffed and ridiculed, not only by some of the 200 or so officers present at his talk, but also by the Army Commander, who acted as chairman, Colonel Wards, an old friend from Japan days, told me some years later; but his account of what happened need not be given here. A mordaunt comment by Compton Mackenzie must suffice as a telling footnote. After saying how sadly Japanese fighting efficiency was underestimated by the military authorities, both in Singapore and Hong Kong, he ends with the remark, 'People shook their heads over what they considered the "defeatism" of Wards's opinion, and his expert knowledge was not invited again.'[1]

In meeting with this incredulity, Wards was in good company. Some six years earlier, in February 1935, General Sir Richard O'Connor, a former brother officer of mine and at that time still only a major, told me he was to act the following day as spokesman for one of the syndicates into which those attending the course at the Imperial Defence College were divided. From a careful study of the situation, he had, he said, been forced to the conclusion

[1] *Eastern Epic*, vol. I, p. 227.

that it would be possible for Japan to seize possession of Singapore by means of a sudden rapid thrust; he was going to expound this belief in his talk next day. Many years later, in a letter replying to a query I had put to him, he recalled what he had said on that occasion about his reasons for believing that the Japanese were quite capable of taking Singapore and about how they could do it. In a somewhat laconic remark at the end of this letter he added, 'I do recall, however, that my solution for capturing Singapore successfully was rather discounted at the time, and I and my syndicate were considered a bit alarmist.'

Of Japan's advance southwards, subsequent to her entry into northern Indo-China in September 1940, all that need be said is that she extended her influence over Thailand by acting as mediator in that country's dispute with Indo-China; then four months later, in July 1941, she secured bases for herself in southern Indo-China. Both of these actions posed an increasing threat to the whole of South-East Asia; the second one led to Britain, America and Holland imposing an oil embargo on Japan. The Japanese were therefore left with only two alternatives, either to climb down or go to war in order to avoid the economic strangulation which the run-down of her oil reserves would have entailed. Almost to the end, however, the Army continued to regard Russia as the main threat to her national defence, although the fear had been eased to some extent by the conclusion of a Neutrality Pact with that traditional enemy of Japan in April that year. The likelihood of an attack on her exposed flank if the southward advance was continued had therefore been reduced.

Hitler's invasion of Russia without pre-warning to his Japanese partner, only a few weeks after this pact had been signed, had caused a temporary cooling of Japanese–German relations; but, following as it did the disillusionment caused by Germany's entry into virtual alliance with the Soviet close on two years earlier, the general feeling was reflected in a statement by the Japanese Minister for Overseas Affairs, 'We have been taught how unreliable are international treaties; the only thing we can depend upon is our nation.'

It was, however, the imposition of the embargo placed on oil, steel, scrap iron and other materials, first by the Americans and, immediately after, by the British and Dutch, that proved the decisive factor. The Navy, which had hitherto been opposed to war with Britain and America, was forced to the conclusion that

Japan would have to fight if a diplomatic settlement was un-
obtainable in the very near future and had already adopted
measures to provide against such a contingency. Of the talks
which followed in Washington there is no need to tell. With their
failure to reach a satisfactory settlement within the time limit set
by her naval and military leaders, Japan launched the offensive
which, after staggering victories at the start, led her to defeat and
surrender rather less than four years later. Within a week of its
commencement, the Mutual Aid Treaty with Germany and Italy
had been converted into a Triple Military Alliance; and so, almost
twenty years to the day since the announcement at Washington
that the Anglo-Japanese Alliance was to end, the worst fears of
those who had argued against its abrogation had been realized.
What is so strangely ironical today is that the United States, once
the bitter opponents of that alliance, are now themselves allied to
Japan. The one difference is that the binding link between them
is called, not an alliance but a security pact.

z

Bibliographical Notes

Apart from the Saionji-Harada Memoirs and the voluminous material produced at the War Crimes' Trial in Tokyo, six of the volumes included in the three series of *Documents on British Foreign Policy 1919–1939*, published by H.M. Stationery Office, deal with the period under review and are valuable sources of information. These are:

> First Series, vol. VI (June 1919 to April 1920), pp. 562–1074, on Far East.
> vol. XIV (April 1920 to February 1922), Far Eastern Affairs.
> Second Series, vol. VIII (1929–31), Anglo-Chinese Relations and Japanese Actions in Manchuria.
> vol. IX (1931–2), The Far Eastern Crisis.
> Third Series, vols. VIII and IX (August 1938 to September 1939), British Policy in the Far East.

Among other primary sources are the *Report of the Lytton Commission*, published in 1932 by the League of Nations, and *Japan's Observations on the Lytton Report*. The following memoirs, written by prominent actors in the events recorded in these pages, are also of value:

> *Japan and Her Destiny*, by Shigemitsu Mamoru, Japanese Ambassador in London 1938–41, after three years as Vice-Minister of Foreign Affairs and two years as Ambassador in Moscow (Hutchinson, 1958).
> *Ten Years in Japan*, by Joseph Grew, U.S. Ambassador in Tokyo 1932–41 (Hammond, Hammond, 1946).
> *Behind the Japanese Mask*, by Sir Robert Craigie, British Ambassador in Tokyo 1937–41 (Hutchinson, 1946).
> *The Far Eastern Crisis*, by Henry Stimson, U.S. Secretary of State 1929–33 (Harper, 1936).
> *Broken Thread*, by Major-General F. S. G. Piggott, British Military Attaché in Tokyo 1922–6 and 1936–9 (Gale & Polden, 1950).

While these books deal primarily with Far Eastern developments during parts of the period in question, much first-hand information on these developments is to be found also in the Churchill volumes on *The Second World War*, in *The Eden Memoirs*, and in *The White House Papers of Harry L. Hopkins*.

On specific subjects and developments, the following call for mention:

Foreign Policy:

Griswold, *The Far Eastern Policy of the United States* (Yale University

Press, 1962); Viscount Ishii, *Diplomatic Commentaries* (Oxford University Press, 1936); Takeuchi, *War and Diplomacy in the Japanese Empire* (Allen & Unwin, 1936); F. C. Jones, *Japan's New Order in East Asia 1937–45* (Oxford University Press, 1954); and Ian Nish, *The Anglo-Japanese Alliance* (University of London, Athlone Press, 1966).

The Manchurian Outbreak:

Yoshihashi, *Conspiracy at Mukden* (Yale University Press, 1963); Ogata, *Defiance in Manchuria* (University of California, 1964); Cutlack, *The Manchurian Arena* (Angus & Robertson, Sydney, 1934); and Penlington, *The Mukden Mandate* (Maruzen, Tokyo, 1932).

The Siberian Intervention:

Ullman, *Intervention and the War* (Oxford University Press, 1961).

The Sorge Spy Case:

Deakin and Storry, *The Case of Richard Sorge* (Chatto & Windus, 1966); Chalmers Johnson, *An Instance of Treason* (Heinemann, 1965); and Major-General Willoughby, *Sorge: Soviet Master Spy* (William Kimber, 1952).

Assassination Plots:

Storry, *The Double Patriots* (Chatto & Windus, 1957); and Byas, *Government by Assassination* (Allen & Unwin, 1943).

Pu Yi and Manchoukuo:

Sir Reginald Johnston, *Twilight in the Forbidden City* (Gollancz, 1934); and Pu Yi, two-volume autobiography, *From Emperor to Citizen* (Collet's, 1964 and 1965).

Naval:

Hector Bywater, *Sea-Power in the Pacific* (Constable, 1921) and *Navies and Nations* (Constable, 1927); and Ito, *The End of the Imperial Japanese Navy* (Weidenfeld & Nicolson, 1962).

Military:

Kennedy, *The Military side of Japanese Life* (Constable, 1924) and *Some Aspects of Japan and Her Defence Forces* (Kegan Paul, 1928).

The 1920s:

Morgan Young, *Japan Under Taisho Tenno* (Allen & Unwin, 1928); and Kennedy, *The Changing Fabric of Japan* (Constable, 1930).

Biographies:

Butow, *Tojo and the Coming of the War* (Princeton University Press, 1961). Although journalistic in style, John Dean Potter's studies of Admiral Yamamoto, *Admiral of the Pacific* (Heinemann, 1965) and of General Yamashita, *A Soldier Must Hang* (Four-Square paperback, 1964) should also be noted.

Other books to which reference has been made:

Abrikosov, Dmitri, *Revelations of a Russian Diplomat* (University of Washington Press, 1964).

Chatfield, Admiral Lord, *It Might Happen Again* (William Heinemann, 1947).

Craddock, Sir Reginald, *The Dilemma in India* (Constable, 1929).

Crowley, James, *Japan's Quest for Autonomy* (Princeton University Press, 1966).

Esthus, Raymond, *Theodore Roosevelt and Japan* (University of Washington Press, 1966).

Grey of Falloden, Lord, *Twenty-Five Years* (Hodder & Stoughton, 1929).

Henderson, Colonel G. F. R., *The Science of War* (Longman's, 1912).

Horne, Alistair, *The Price of Glory* (Macmillan, 1962).

Kirby, Major-General, *The War Against Japan*, vol. I (H.M Stationery Office, 1957).

Lloyd, Lord, *Egypt Since Cromer*, vols. I and II (Macmillan, 1933-4).

Mackenzie, Sir Compton, *Eastern Epic*, vol. I (Chatto & Windus, 1951).

Maxwell, Sir Herbert, *The Creevey Papers* (John Murray, 1905).

Maruyama Masao, *Thought and Behaviour in Modern Japanese Politics* (Oxford University Press, 1963).

Montgomery, Field-Marshal Lord, *The Path to Leadership* (Collins, 1961).

Moore, Frederick, *With Japan's Leaders* (Chapman & Hall, 1943).

Nitobe Inazo, *Bushidō* (Teibi Publishing Co., Tokyo, 1909).

Sato Kojiro, *If Japan and America Fight* (Meguro Bunten, Tokyo, 1920).

Sunderland, J. T., *India in Bondage* (New York, 1929).

Tanin and Yohan, *Militarism and Fascism in Japan* (Martin Laurence, 1934).

Vansittart, Sir Robert, *Roots of the Trouble* (Hutchinson, 1941).

Youssoupoff, Prince, *Rasputin, His Malignant Influence and Assassination* (Jonathan Cape, 1927).

Index of Persons

Subject Index